Race or Ethnicity?

RACE
OR ETHNICITY?

On Black and Latino Identity

EDITED BY JORGE J. E. GRACIA

CORNELL UNIVERSITY PRESS

ITHACA AND LONDON

First published 2007 by Cornell University Press
First printing, Cornell Paperbacks, 2007

Printed in the United States of America

Library of Congress Cataloging-in-Publication Data

Race or ethnicity? : on Black and Latino identity / edited by Jorge J. E. Gracia.
    p. cm.
  Includes bibliographical references and index.
  ISBN 978-0-8014-4544-6 (cloth : alk. paper) — ISBN 978-0-8014-7359-3 (pbk. : alk. paper)
   1. African Americans—Race identity.   2. Hispanic Americans—Ethnic identity.   3. Race—Philosophy.   4. Ethnicity—Philosophy.   I. Gracia, Jorge J. E.

  E185.625.R32 2007
  305.868′073—dc22

2006039785

Cornell University Press strives to use environmentally responsible suppliers and materials to the fullest extent possible in the publishing of its books. Such materials include vegetable-based, low-VOC inks and acid-free papers that are recycled, totally chlorine-free, or partly composed of nonwood fibers. For further information, visit our website at www.cornellpress.cornell.edu.

Cloth printing   10 9 8 7 6 5 4 3 2 1
Paperback printing   10 9 8 7 6 5 4 3 2 1

Contents

Contributors

LINDA MARTÍN ALCOFF is professor of philosophy, women's studies, and political science at Syracuse University. She is currently the director of Women's Studies. Her books and anthologies include *Feminist Epistemologies* (with Elizabeth Potter) (1993), *Real Knowing: New Versions of the Coherence Theory* (1996), *Epistemology: The Big Questions* (1998), *Thinking from the Underside of History* (with Eduardo Mendieta) (2000), *Singing in the Fire: Tales of Women in Philosophy* (2003), and *Visible Identities: Race, Gender, and the Self* (2006).

KWAME ANTHONY APPIAH is Laurance S. Rockefeller University Professor of Philosophy at the University Center for Human Values at Princeton University. Among his books are *In My Father's House: Africa in the Philosophy of Culture* (1992), *Color Conscious: The Political Morality of Race* (with Amy Gutmann) (1996), *Thinking It Through* (2003), and *The Ethics of Identity* (2005). His most recent book is titled *Cosmopolitanism: Ethics in a World of Strangers* (2006); he is now finishing *Experiments in Ethics,* which will be published by Harvard University Press.

ROBERT BERNASCONI is Moss Professor of Philosophy at the University of Memphis. He is the author of two books on Heidegger and has written numerous articles. He is the editor of *Race* (2001), *The Idea of Race* (with Tommy Lott) (2000), and *Race and Racism in Continental Philosophy* (with Sybol Cook) (2003). He has also edited three sets of reprints documenting the history of the scientific concept of race in the eighteenth and nineteenth centuries for Thoemmes Press.

J. ANGELO CORLETT is professor of philosophy and ethics at San Diego State University. He is the author of numerous articles and of the following books: *Justice and Rights* (forthcoming); *Interpreting Plato's Dialogues* (2005); *Race, Racism, and Reparations* (2003); *Terrorism: A Philosophical Analysis* (2003); *Responsibility and Punishment* (3rd ed., 2006); and *Analyzing Social Knowledge* (1996). He is editor-in-chief of *The Journal of Ethics: An International Philosophical Review* (1997–present). He is also editor of and contributor to *Equality and Liberty: Analyzing Rawls and Nozick* (1991).

J. L. A. GARCÍA is professor of philosophy at Boston College. His published articles include "Identity Confusions," *Philosophy and Social Criticism* 30, no. 7 (2006): 839–62; "Revisiting African-American Perspectives and Medical Ethics," in *African American Bioethics: Culture, Race, and Identity,* edited by Lawrence Prograis and Edmund Pellegrino (forthcoming); "Three Sites of Racism: Social Structures, Value Judgments, and Vice," in *Racism in Mind,* edited by Michael Levine and Tamas Pataki (2004); "Three Scalarities: Racialization, Racism, and Race," *Theory and Research in Education* 1, no. 3 (2003); "The Racial Contract Hypothesis," *Philosophia Africana* 4, no. 1 (2001); "Racism and Racial Discourse," *Philosophical Forum* 32, no. 2 (2001); and "Is Being Hispanic an Identity?" *Philosophy and Social Criticism* 27, no. 2 (2001).

JORGE J. E. GRACIA holds the Samuel P. Capen Chair in Philosophy and is State University of New York Distinguished Professor at the University at Buffalo. Among his recent books are *Surviving Race, Ethnicity, and Nationality: A Challenge for the Twenty-First Century* (2005), *Old Wine in New Skins: The Role of Tradition in Communication, Knowledge, and Group Identity* (67th Marquette Aquinas Lecture 2003), *Hispanic/Latino Identity: A Philosophical Perspective* (2000), *How Can We Know What God Means? The Interpretation of Revelation* (2000), and he has recently edited *Hispanics/Latinos in the United States* (2000).

HOWARD McGARY is Professor II (Distinguished Professor) of Philosophy at Rutgers University. He has published numerous articles and the following books: *Race and Social Justice* (1999); *Social Justice and Local Development Policy* (with others) (1993); *Between Slavery and Freedom: Philosophy and American Slavery* (with Bill E. Lawson) (1992).

EDUARDO MENDIETA is associate professor of philosophy at Stony Brook University. He is the author of numerous articles and of *Adventures of Transcendental Philosophy* (2002) and *Global Fragments: Latin Americanism, Globalizations, and Critical Theory* (forthcoming). He has edited a dozen books, the most recent being *Take Care of Freedom and Truth Will Take Care of Itself: Interviews with Richard Rorty* (2006); a book of interviews with Angela Davis, *Abolition Democracy: Beyond Prisons, Torture, and Empire* (2005); and *The Frankfurt School on Religion* (2005).

SUSANA NUCCETELLI is associate professor of philosophy at the University of Texas–Pan American. Some of her recent articles have appeared in *Analysis, The Southern Journal of Philosophy, Philosophical Forum, Metaphilosophy,* and *The Journal of Law, Medicine, and Ethics.* She is the editor of *New Essays on Semantic Externalism and Self-Knowledge* (2003) and coeditor of *Themes from G. E. Moore: New Essays in Epistemology and Ethics* (forthcoming) and *Latin American Philosophy* (2004). She is author of *Latin American Thought: Philosophical Problems and Arguments* (2002) and chaired the American Philosophical Association's Committee on Hispanics.

KENNETH SHOCKLEY is assistant professor of philosophy at the University at Buffalo. Among his publications are "Centering Value Pluralism," *Southwestern Philosophical Review* 21, no. 1 (2005); "The Conundrum of Collective Commitment," *Social Theory and Practice* 30, no. 4 (2004); "Thinking through Collectives," *Social Theory and Practice* 30, no. 1 (2004); and "Quine's Ethical Dilemma," *Dialectica* 54, no. 4 (1998).

DIEGO A. VON VACANO is assistant professor of political science at Texas A&M University. He is the author of *The Art of Power: Machiavelli, Nietzsche, and the Making of Aesthetic Political Theory* (2007) and "Football and Philosophy," in *Philosophy Today* (newsletter of the British Society for Applied Philosophy) 17, no. 45 (2004). He is working on a book on the problem of racial identity in Latin American political theory and is planning to coedit a collection of articles on that topic with Jorge Gracia.

NAOMI ZACK is professor of philosophy at the University of Oregon. She is the author of numerous articles and of the following books: *Race and Mixed Race* (1993), *Bachelors of Science* (1996), *Philosophy of Science and Race* (2002), *Inclusive Feminism* (2005), and *Thinking about Race* (2nd ed., 2005). She is also the editor of *American Mixed Race* (1995), *Race / Sex* (1997), and *Women of Color in Philosophy* (2002).

Preface

What is race? What is ethnicity? Should we think of them as identities? Can they be effectively individuated? How are they related? How do the relations between them influence pressing issues concerned with social identity, gender, racism, assimilation, exploitation, justice, the law, and public policy? And how are the answers to these questions affected by the Black and Latino experiences in the United States?

The primary aim of this collection of essays is to pose and answer some of these questions from a variety of perspectives. Although much work has been done on the philosophy of race in the past century in the United States, the concept of ethnicity has only recently awakened the interest of American philosophers, and the relations between race and ethnicity remain largely unexplored. Moreover, no collective effort has been undertaken so far to put African Americans and Latinos side by side in order to see commonalities and differences in their experiences and the social challenges they face.

The discussion is divided into two parts, dealing, on the one hand, with the nature and relation between race and ethnicity and, on the other, with the social consequences of the complex relations between them. Part I explores in particular the debated topic of racial and ethnic identities: Does it make sense to speak of racial and ethnic identities, and especially of Black and Latino identities? And if it does make sense, how should these identities be conceptualized, and how are they related to gender? Part II moves in a more applied direction. It examines how race and ethnicity have influenced the lot of some social groups in significant ways. How do racially defined institutions deal with racial assimilation? How do different conceptions of race and ethnicity influence public policy and various forms of racism? How can exploited racial and ethnic groups be effectively recognized? And what is the role of affect in social justice as dispensed by the courts?

A note on the text: Just as the views of the authors about race and ethnicity differ, so do their preferences in hyphenating and capitalizing terms; we have honored the preferences of the authors rather than impose an unwanted consistency.

The publication of this volume was made possible by the cooperation of many persons. Above all, I am grateful to the contributors who took the time to write their essays and to revise them in various ways to make them fit thematically into the volume. Their good-natured cooperation and sense of humor in light of my pesterings made the process a pleasure rather than a chore. I am also grateful to those who provided support at various stages of the project. In particular, financial support from the Samuel P. Capen Chair in Philosophy at the University at Buffalo was essential, and logistics support by the staff of the Department of Philosophy was most welcome. I also acknowledge the useful suggestions and interest of Roger Haydon, at Cornell University Press and the expert assistance in the production process of Teresa Jesionowski. Finally, I am also grateful to Susan Smith for preparing the index to the volume.

JORGE J. E. GRACIA

Buffalo, New York

Race or Ethnicity?

Race or Ethnicity? An Introduction

JORGE J. E. GRACIA

The common folk view of race and ethnicity in the United States appears to be that the first has to do with biology and genetics and the second with culture. If this conception were scientifically and morally acceptable, it would not be difficult to draw an exact distinction between race and ethnicity and to work out the details of their relations and their ethical and political implications. However, this view has been challenged in the past twenty years, with the result that neither the biological/genetic conception of race nor the cultural conception of ethnicity have survived unscathed. Indeed, most scientists and philosophers working on these topics reject their viability.

1. The Challenges to Race and Ethnicity

The challenges to these views about race and ethnicity have come from many sides, but two in particular have had the greatest impact. One is factual, the other epistemic.

A. The Factual Challenge

The factual challenge argues that the concepts of race and ethnicity do not correspond to anything real outside the mind and therefore need to be abandoned.[1] The factual part of this claim against race has been supported by recent

---

1. See, for example, K. Anthony Appiah, "Race, Culture, Identity: Misunderstood Connections," in *Color Conscious: The Political Morality of Race,* ed. Appiah and Amy Gutmann (Princeton: Princeton Uni-

genetic research and used by philosophers in various ways.[2] Among the facts frequently cited are the following three:

First, genetic differences between races are minuscule if compared with what the races have in common. The bases used to establish racial distinctions are insignificant insofar as there can be greater genetic difference between two individual human beings who presumably belong to the same race than between two races.[3]

Second, scientific studies have demonstrated that either single genes, or the various forms they can take, are present in all populations. Therefore "no single gene is sufficient for classifying human populations into systematic categories," let alone racial ones.[4]

Third, no strict correlation exists between the directly observable traits of a person, such *phenotypes* as skin color and hair texture, and genetic inherited factors, known as *genotypes*.[5] The reason is that some phenotypes are the result of complex genetic relationships, often involving the environment.[6]

Factual challenges are also directed against ethnicity. One of these argues, for example, that those who use ethnic labels often assume that ethnic groups are homogeneous, forgetting obvious differences among the members of the groups and sometimes of subgroups within the groups.[7] The case of Hispanics or Latinos is frequently cited in this context. These terms are used to refer to a very large group of persons that includes Puerto Ricans, Cubans, Mexicans, and Argentinians, among many others, as well as such individual persons as Jorge Gracia and Linda Alcoff. But neither these subgroups nor their members are homogenous. The differences between Puerto Ricans and Argentinians, or Mexicans and Cubans are substantial, for they trace their ancestry to peoples that differed widely in such important factors as language, religion, and even ge-

---

versity Press, 1996), 30–105; and Naomi Zack's chapter in this volume and her *Philosophy of Science and Race* (New York: Routledge, 2002).

2. For a short history of the science of race, see L. Luca Cavalli-Sforza et al., *The History and Geography of Human Genes* (Princeton: Princeton University Press, 1994), 16–20.

3. Masatoshi Nei and A. K. Roychoudhury, "Genetic Relationship and Evolution of Human Races," *Evolutionary Biology* 14 (1982): 1–59; "Genetic Variation within and between the Three Major Races of Man, Caucasoids, Negroids, and Mongoloids," *American Journal of Human Genetics* 26 (1974): 421–43; and "Gene Differences between Caucasian, Negro, and Japanese Populations," *Science* 177 (1972): 434–35.

4. Cavalli-Sforza et al., *History and Geography of Human Genes,* 19; and Pierre L. van den Berghe, "Does Race Matter?" in *Race and Racism,* ed. Bernard Boxill (Oxford: Oxford University Press, 2001), 103.

5. Cavalli-Sforza et al., *History and Geography of Human Genes,* 6–7; R. C. Lewontin, "Race," in *Encyclopedia Americana* (Danbury, CN: Grolier, 1989), 23:116–22.

6. James C. King, *The Biology of Race* (Berkeley: University of California Press, 1981), 20–21, 28–29, and 33–34.

7. C. Lentz, "'Tribalism' and 'Ethnicity' in Africa: A Review of Four Decades of Anglophone Research," *Cahiers des Sciences Humaines* 31 (1995): 305.

netic makeup.[8] So what do they have in common other than a name? Yet, a common ethnic label tends to make us think of them as the same.

Indeed, supporters of this challenge frequently note that thinking in ethnic terms is generally founded on stereotypes that lack proper bases in fact. Stereotypes are *hasty* generalizations that paint an erroneous picture of people and should be avoided.

In short, racial and ethnic characterizations do not entail much that is generally associated with them, failing to represent accurately the reality of the persons they purport to describe. For this reason they should be abandoned. In this volume the main advocate for this position is Naomi Zack. She attacks some recent articles that try to find some justification for the notion of race, and proposes not only abandoning it, but turning the discussion toward gender instead.

B. The Epistemic Challenge

The epistemic challenge to race and ethnicity argues that we have no effective criteria to establish membership in races or ethne. Consider race. It is common to think that race can be easily ascertained, but in fact the criteria used to determine it changes from person to person, group to group, context to context, place to place, country to country, and time to time. In Cuba, Black (i.e., *negro*) entails no appearance of mixture with "White" (i.e., *blanco*). A person who appears mixed is not Black or White, but *mulato* (a mixture of Black and White). But in the United States, Black requires only that one have some Black ancestry. According to the One-Drop Rule, one drop of Black blood makes a person Black. Clearly the criteria for belonging to the Black race in Cuba and the United States are different. A person could be Black in this country and not Black in Cuba. So who is right? Epistemically, we have a significant conflict, for differing racial criteria preclude agreement as to who qualifies as a member of a race.

The epistemic difficulties surrounding the notion of race are not limited to variability. The accessibility of the evidence used to satisfy the criteria also poses problems. How can one tell whether a person is Black or White? It seems to be a matter of simple inspection, for no one goes around subjecting people to any kind of rigorous tests. Someone is judged Black because he or she "looks" Black. And the same applies to Whites. But, of course, visual inspection is quite unreliable, because what might appear to be dark skin to someone might appear as lighter skin to another, and factors such as lighting and context surely affect

---

8. See Jorge J. E. Gracia, *Hispanic / Latino Identity: A Philosophical Perspective* (Oxford: Blackwell, 2000), 97–100.

judgment. The literature provides many examples of the problems posed by the evidence given for racial classification in various places, including the United States. Indeed, the phenomenon of "passing" attests to the unreliability of the evidence used to establish racial membership.

Clearly, so the argument goes, serious epistemic questions concerning racial belonging remain unresolved. We think and act as if we could be certain who is and who is not Black, but we cannot be sure that the means we use to back up our thoughts and actions are justified.[9] The criteria of races we use appear ineffective, whether they have to do with color, lineage, or culture.

The epistemic criteria for ethnicity pose even more serious problems than do those of race. Indeed, their generally contextual character and variability is one of the major objections raised against Affirmative Action for ethnic groups. That criteria of membership in ethnic groups is imprecise and changes makes them unreliable. What criteria do we use to identify Latinos, for example?[10] Fluency in Spanish? Clearly not, for many persons considered Latinos do not speak Spanish at all or speak Spanish only as a second language. Food? Again no, for there is no food that is common to all Latinos. Music? Religion? Race? None of these work. So which criteria do we, or can we, use? These difficulties apply, mutatis mutandis, to other ethnic groups as well.

2. Responses to the Challenge

These and other arguments against common conceptions of race and ethnicity have prompted a number of philosophers to develop alternative ways of thinking about race and ethnicity. Of the many strategies that have been proposed, four stand out. The first proposes to replace race with ethnicity. The second replaces race with the concept of racial identity. A third alternative combines race and ethnicity either in the concept of ethnic race or the concept of racial ethnicity. And a fourth keeps race and ethnicity separate, but develops new ways of conceiving them.

---

9. W. E. B. Du Bois made the argument that mixing of "Blacks" with other races is so widespread that it is impossible to discern a Negro race, in *The Health and Physique of the Negro American. Report of a Social Study Made under the Direction of Atlanta University; Together with the Proceedings of the Eleventh Conference for the Study of the Negro Problems, Held at Atlanta University, on May the 29th, 1906*, repr. in *Atlanta University Publications (Numbers 7–11—1902–1906)* (New York: Octagon, 1968), 2:16.

10. Leonardo Zaibert and Elizabeth Millán-Zaibert, "Universalism, Particularism, and Group Rights: The Case of Hispanics," in *Hispanics/Latinos in the United States: Ethnicity, Race, and Rights,* ed. Jorge J. E. Gracia and Pablo De Greiff (New York: Routledge, 2000), 167–79.

A. Race Is Replaced by Ethnicity

In *Race, Racism, and Reparations*, J. Angelo Corlett proposes to replace race with ethnicity, a position restated, clarified, and further elaborated in a chapter in this volume. Accepting the force of the arguments developed by Appiah and others against race, Corlett concludes that the concept of race must be abandoned and should be replaced instead with the concept of ethnicity. But he tells us that ethnicity can be approached in two different ways: in terms of "public-policy" or "metaphysically." The primary aim of a public-policy analysis of ethnicity is "to accurately classify people into categories of ethnicity for purposes of justice under the law."[11] The purpose of a metaphysical analysis is to determine what it is to be, say, Latino.

The public policy analysis yields a criterion of ethnicity based on genealogy: "for public policy considerations, genealogy ought to be construed as both a necessary and sufficient condition of award or benefit." Genealogy, according to Corlett, "serves more than any other philosophical conception of who and what we are" for purposes of reparations and other social policies, such as affirmative action.[12] But, of course, there is more to belonging to an ethnic group than genealogy. To be a Latino, for example, is more than just having Latino ancestry. Here is where the metaphysical analysis comes in. The result is a graded conception of ethnicity, as Corlett illustrates with the case of Latinos:

> *Aside from public policy consideration*, however, factors that would go toward making one more or less a Latino may include the degree to which one knows and respects a Latino language or dialect thereof; possesses and respects a traditional Latino name; engages in and respects Latino culture or parts thereof; accepts and respects himself or herself as a Latino; is accepted and respected as a Latino by other Latinos; and is construed as a Latino by outgroup members. . . . each of these conditions admits of degrees. . . [but] neither [*sic*] . . . is either necessary or sufficient to make one a Latino.[13]

In short, the metaphysical view of ethnicity involves a list of conditions each of which is subject to degree. The public policy view also is subject to degree, insofar as descent ties vary in number and proximity, but unlike the metaphysical view of ethnicity, it is presented as a necessary and sufficient condition for the implementation of public policy. According to Corlett, these two conceptions provide what we need without having to use the inaccurate conception

11. J. Angelo Corlett, *Race, Racism, and Reparations* (Ithaca: Cornell University Press, 2003), 51, 46.
12. Ibid., 51, 60.
13. Ibid., 51.

of race. This position has not gone without challenge. Jorge García argues forcefully against it in a chapter of this volume.

B. Race Is Replaced by Racial Identity

K. Anthony Appiah defends the view that the notion of race should be replaced by the notion of racial identity in "Race, Culture, and Identity," further elaborating some aspects of this view in a chapter in this collection. The concept of racial identity, according to him, reflects more accurately our discourse about races, racial phenomena, and racial groups. But what is racial identity? As Appiah puts it, in a racial identity

> a label R [is] associated with [1] *ascriptions* by most people (where ascription involves descriptive criteria for applying the label); and [2] *identifications* by those who fall under it (where identification implies a shaping role for the label in the intentional acts of the possessor, so that they sometimes act *as an R*), where there is a history of associating possessors of the label with an inherited racial essence (even if some who use the label no longer believe in racial essences).[14]

The conditions of racial identity are three: ascription by others, self-identification by the labeled, and a set of descriptions that has a historical association to a label involving a racial essence. These descriptions are used for ascriptions and as norms for action. It does not signify for racial identity, then, whether race is real or not, or even whether there is a consistent concept of race. What matters is that people label some other people and themselves and that the labels include a notion of inherited racial essence. A racial essence consists of a set of conditions regarded as necessary and sufficient for a particular race, whether in fact such a set exists or not.

For Appiah, then, labeling is crucial, for the label comes first, and it is only later that such features as cultural traits are linked to it. In short, "collective identities . . . provide what we might call scripts: narratives that people can use in shaping their life plans and in telling their life stories."[15]

Appiah does away with the confusing, and both biologically and culturally unfounded, notion of race. But he keeps what he takes to be important in it, namely, a sense of identity that informs our behavior and how we think of ourselves and others.

---

14. Appiah, "Race, Culture, and Identity," 81–82.
15. Ibid., 89, 97.

C. Race and Ethnicity Are Replaced by Ethnic Race or Racial Ethnicity

The attempts to undermine the separation between race and ethnicity seem to go back historically at least to Alain Locke, as Robert Bernasconi argues in a chapter in this volume. They arise from two concerns: (1) race appears to have an ethnic dimension[16] and (2) ethnicity seems generally to be racialized.[17] The first concern prompts an attempt to substitute the single notion of ethnic race for the separate notions of race and ethnicity, as we see in the case of Alain Locke. The second concern yields the view that substitutes the single notion of racial ethnicity for the other two, as suggested by Linda Alcoff in general, and as applied to Latinos/Hispanics in particular by Eduardo Mendieta, in their chapters included here.

At least three significant reasons are given for (1). The first appeals to history. Historical discussions of race always include ethnic elements, and racial divisions have always involved cultural differences. Blacks have generally been characterized as being different from Whites not just in terms of descent and physical phenotypes, but also in terms of customs, attitudes, and achievements, indicating that the notion of race always involves ethnic factors.[18]

The second reason appeals to scientific facts. The concept of race cannot be distinguished clearly from the concept of ethnicity, because the physical phenotypes on which it is based are not easily distinguishable from cultural ones. Most phenotypes result from both physical and environmental forces, and racial phenotypes are no exception.[19]

The third reason is pragmatic. Attempts to separate the concept of race from the concept of ethnicity are always unsuccessful, so it is useless to keep trying. Consider the change of the label 'Black' to 'African American,' for example. In spite of the efforts to develop a conception of Blacks as an identity based on ethnicity, by changing the name to "African Americans," the supposedly ethnic label has become racial.[20]

---

16. This approach goes back to Du Bois in *The Conservation of Races,* The American Negro Academy Occasional Papers, no. 2 (Washington, DC: American Negro Academy, 1897), and to Alain Locke (see Robert Bernasconi's chapter in this volume). See also Paul Gilroy, *The Black Atlantic: Modernity and Double Consciousness* (Cambridge: Harvard University Press, 1993).

17. Milton Gordon, *The Scope of Sociology* (New York: Oxford University Press, 1988), 119, 130–31; Linda M. Alcoff, "Is Latina/o Identity a Racial Identity?" in *Hispanics/Latinos in the United States,* ed. Gracia and De Greiff, 23–44.

18. See, for example, Leopold Senghor, "What Is Negritude?" *West Africa* (November 4, 1961): 1211; Jean-Paul Sartre, "Black Orpheus," in *Race,* ed. Robert Bernasconi (Malden, MA: Blackwell, 2001), 125.

19. King, *Biology of Race,* 20–21, 28–9, 33–34; Cavalli-Sforza et al., *History and Geography of Human Genes,* 4–5, 7, 17–18.

20. Alcoff, "Is Latina/o Identity a Racial Identity?" 36 ff., and Robert Gooding-Williams, "Race, Multiculturalism, and Democracy," in *Race,* ed. Bernasconi, 244.

The three most common reasons given for replacing the concepts of race and ethnicity with the concept of a racial ethnicity are similar to the ones we have seen. The first argues that historical conceptions of ethnicity always involve racial elements, such as reference to physical phenotypes and descent.[21]

The second reasons that the concept of ethnicity cannot be separated from the concept of race because this is the way humans think. We are hardwired to think of our ethnicity as an essence based on descent.[22]

And third, attempts to separate ethnicity from race usually fail, so there is no point in continuing the effort. Consider for example the case of Latinos, who are generally regarded as a racial group in spite of efforts to the contrary by both Latinos and many non-Latinos.[23]

In short, the concepts of race and ethnicity appear to be hopelessly entangled with each other and thus incapable of separation. The phenomenon of the oreo, in which one speaks of the same person being Black on the outside (i.e., racially) and White in the inside (i.e., ethnically), indicates the difficulties of keeping these two concepts separate. Indeed, in this case the terms *Black* and *White* appear to be used racially and ethnically. Race and ethnicity appear to be indistinguishable.

D. Old Conceptions of Race and Ethnicity Are Replaced by New Ones

Not everyone agrees that the best strategy to meet the factual and epistemic challenges to race and ethnicity consists in substituting the concept of ethnicity for the concept of race, replacing the concept of race with the concept of racial identity, or combining the concepts of race and ethnicity into the concepts of racial ethnicity or ethnic race. Some authors attempt to develop new ways of conceiving race and ethnicity that can still be used to understand these phenomena. For example, in a chapter in this book, Diego von Vacano argues that the synthetic way of conceiving race in Latin America is a good model for the rest of the world, including the United States, insofar as it undermines the Black/White dichotomy current in most places. And Susana Nuccetelli, also in a chapter here, attacks functionalist interpretations of ethnicity that require awareness for membership. Other recent attempts to develop new conceptions of race and ethnicity are inspired by Du Bois's notion

21. Alcoff, "Is Latina/o Identity a Racial Identity?"

22. Francisco J. Gil-White, "Sorting Is Not Categorization: A Critique of the Claim That Brazilians Have Fuzzy Racial Categories," *Cognition and Culture* 1 (2001): 1–23; and "How Thick Is Blood? The Plot Thickens . . . : If Ethnic Actors Are Primordialists, What Remains of the Circumstantialist/Primordialist Controversy?" *Ethnic and Racial Studies* 22 (1999): 789–820.

23. Alcoff, "Is Latina/o Identity a Racial Identity?"

of the family.[24] Let me present the version I defend in the chapter included in this volume.

I name my position concerning ethnicity the "Familial-Historical View" and my position concerning race the "Genetic Common-Bundle View."[25] My contention is that these views explain various phenomena associated with race and ethnicity that are hard to explain otherwise and thus help clarify their relations and eliminate some of the confusions that surround them. Here is a formulation of the Familial-Historical View of an ethnos that serves to distinguish it from a race:

> An ethnos is a subgroup of individual humans who satisfy the following conditions: they (1) belong to many generations; (2) are organized as a family and break down into extended families; and (3) are united through historical relations that produce features which, in context, serve (i) to identify the members of the group and (ii) to distinguish them from members of other groups.

The main tenet of this position is that the unity of an ethnos is similar to that of a family, and as such there is no necessarily identifiable feature, or set of features, that is shared by all members of an ethnic group throughout the history of the group. This accounts for the lack of agreement concerning any particular conditions, or even kinds of conditions, that are necessary and sufficient for ethnicity. Members of an ethnos are tied by the same kind of thing that ties the members of a family, as Wittgenstein would say.[26] They belong to the same group because they are historically related, as a father is to a daughter, an aunt to a nephew, and grandparents to grandchildren. Wittgenstein's metaphor of family resemblance is particularly appropriate in this case, for one does not need to be tied genetically to other members of a family to be a member of the family.

This conception of ethnicity contrasts with the Genetic Common-Bundle View of race. Here is a formulation that serves to distinguish a race from an ethnos:

24. See W. E. B. Du Bois, "The Conservation of Races," in *W. E. B. Du Bois Speaks: Speeches and Addresses 1890–1919,* ed. Philip S. Foner (New York: Pathfinders, 1970), 74, and *Dusk of Dawn: An Essay toward an Autobiography of a Race Concept* (New York: Harcourt, Brace, 1940), 117.

25. For a more detailed defense, see Jorge J. E. Gracia, *Surviving Race, Ethnicity, and Nationality: A Challenge for the Twenty-First Century* (Lanham, MD: Rowman and Littlefield, 2005), chapters 3 and 4 in particular. Anna Stubblefield argues for a familial view of race in *Ethics along the Color Line* (Ithaca: Cornell University Press, 2005), particularly chapter 5.

26. Ludwig Wittgenstein, *Philosophical Investigations,* trans. G. E. M. Anscombe (New York: Macmillan, 1981), 32, §67.

> A race is a subgroup of individual human beings who satisfy the following two conditions: (1) each member of the group is linked by descent to another member of the group who is in turn also linked by descent to at least some third member of the group; and (2) each member of the group has one or more physical features that are (i) genetically transmittable, (ii) generally associated with the group, and (iii) perceptually perspicuous.

In order for a group of people to constitute a race, the members of the group have to be linked by descent and have one or more physical features that are genetically transmittable, generally associated with the group, and perceptually perspicuous. As Boxill argues, inherited traits are essential to the notion of race, even when race is understood to be constructed.[27] Moreover, these conditions can also function epistemically: knowing that a person satisfies them with respect to a race entails the identification of the person as a member of that race.

Neither one of these conditions, taken by itself, is sufficient for racial membership. Being related by descent to a member of some race, who is in turn related by descent to at least some third member of that race, is not sufficient for someone to be a member of the pertinent race, insofar as the person in question may not share in any of the features generally associated with members of it. And having features associated with a certain race does not automatically make a person a member of the race or serve effectively to identify the person as such. Spaniards from southern Spain are frequently as dark as people regarded as member of the Black race. Yet, because they do not satisfy the descent condition, no one thinks of them as Black.

This view of race does not have to contend with the factual or epistemic objections voiced earlier. As I argue in a chapter contained in this volume, races can be individuated both metaphysically and epistemically without having to resort to uniform criteria. However, there are dissenting voices to this position, as in clear in the chapters by Zack and García included in this volume.

3. Moral and Political Dimensions

Apart from the questions concerned with the reality or unreality of races and ethne, of their relations, and of the proper way to conceive them, race and ethnicity have been, from the very beginning, the locus of moral and political reflection. This reflection falls into various categories, but there are at least four that deserve mention in this context. First, philosophers have frequently used

---

27. Bernard Boxill, introduction to *Race and Racism* (Oxford: Oxford University Press, 2001), 1–42.

moral or political reasons to argue for and against the use of racial and ethnic categories; second, they have discussed the moral and ethical roles that race and ethnicity may play; third, they have drawn out the moral and political implications of particular views of race and ethnicity; and fourth, they have tried to show how the conceptions of race and ethnicity, and their social implications, are rooted in other social phenomena. Here I cannot consider all, indeed not even most, of the important reflections in these categories. But several of the chapters in part II of this book discuss in particular the last three categories. For example, Corlett addresses the conditions under which racial, ethnic, and gender classifications justify social policies intended to rectify past injustices; Alcoff addresses the complex consequences of ethnic and racial labeling for the treatment of groups; Shockley investigates the implications of the recognition of exploited of racial and ethnic groups; and Mendieta explores the role of affect in the development of the laws that govern social policy. In order to avoid redundance, the examples provided below will consist primarily of moral and political arguments used to undermine or support the use of racial and ethnic categories, that is, I will provide only a discussion of the first category mentioned above.

A. Moral Arguments

Moral arguments are used both to support and undermine the use of racial and ethnic categories. Those used to undermine them aim to show that this use is harmful to some persons within or without the groups that the categories pick out and are, therefore, immoral; those offered in support try to do just the opposite. Among the many moral reasons given against the use of racial and ethnic categories, three are most frequently found in pertinent discussions. Their thrust is to argue for some kind of racial or ethnic eliminativism. This view, which is discussed by Howard McGary in a chapter in this volume, seeks to eliminate racial and ethnic categories.

One argument notes that racial and ethnic labels generally have negative connotations. For example, 'Latino/a' connotes laziness, drug abuse and dealing, poor linguistic skills, unreliability, and so on. So the use of labels such as this tends to promote an adverse context for those to whom they are applied, often leading to discrimination and even abuse. For this reason, the use of racial and ethnic labels should be eliminated from discourse.[28]

Another reason given why racial and ethnic classifications should be abandoned is that they tend to support the status quo of inferiority in which racial

28. For arguments of this sort, see Gracia, *Hispanic/Latino Identity*, 21–6.

and ethnic groups find themselves.[29] The use of terms like *Black* or *Hispanic* in a country like the United States, where the powerful elite belongs to the group of "Whites" and Anglos, places members of the subordinate groups at a social disadvantage. And this disadvantage tends to continue unless extraordinary efforts are made to change it.

A third argument claims that the history of racial and ethnic naming indicates that these labels are usually imposed on dominated groups by dominant groups and do not reflect the views of the dominated. This is an arbitrary exercise of power that is usually motivated by perverse goals and often has dire consequences for the dominated.[30] Who invented the label `Black,' for example? Surely not Blacks; it seems to have been invented by slave owners. And what was it invented for but to control and oppress a population? It is immoral, then, to continue to use labels such as "Black."[31]

These arguments could easily lead one to conclude that it is a serious mistake to continue to talk about race and ethnicity. There are moral reasons that militate against the use of these categories and the concepts and terms that accompany them. Indeed, even mentioning them might be counterproductive. Yet, the case for their use has also been forcefully made. Here are three moral reasons often given as support.

First, race and ethnicity have influenced, and still influence, the course of human history in significant ways and have substantially affected the lives of individual persons.[32] Can we deny the presence of oppression based on them? Can we brush aside that these categories have been, and still are, the cause of wars and genocide? Because we cannot, it becomes very difficult to argue that we should do away with racial and ethnicity categories.[33] If these categories have had such a significant impact on human history as a whole, and on the lives of individual persons, how can we dispense with them? How can we talk about the abuses associated with them if the language of race and ethnicity is eliminated?

Second, the understanding of past, and even present, human history makes no sense without reference to race and ethnicity.[34] How can we understand the causes of racial and ethnic discrimination without referring to race and

29. David B. Wilkins, "Two Paths to the Mountaintop? The Role of Legal Education in Shaping the Values of Black Corporate Lawyers," *Stanford Law Review* 45 (July 1993): 1981–2026.

30. Frantz Fanon, "The Lived Experience of the Black," in *Race,* ed. Bernasconi, 184–202.

31. Michael Omi and Howard Winant, *Racial Formation in the United States: From the 1960s to the 1990s,* 2nd ed. (New York: Routledge, 1994), 56.

32. Charles Mills, "But What Are You Really?" in *Blackness Visible: Essays on Philosophy and Race* (Ithaca: Cornell University Press, 1998), 41–66.

33. Linda M. Alcoff, "Toward a Phenomenology of Racial Embodiment," and Robert Gooding-Williams, "Race, Multiculturalism, and Democracy," both in *Race,* ed. Bernasconi, 237–59.

34. Du Bois, *The Conservation of Races,* 7.

ethnicity? How can we understand the nature of racism and ethnicism without them?

Third, the future is built on the past and charting a course for the future that is different from the past requires understanding the past. So, if we wish to prevent in the future the ills resulting from racism and ethnicism, we need to use the language and concepts of race and ethnicity. Refusing to accept the role of race in our experience in particular, and even to talk about it, only serves to exacerbate racism. It also misses the point that the notions of race and ethnicity can be used to correct social ills, provide meaning, and develop a beneficial sense of identity in people.[35]

B. Political Arguments

The political arguments against the use of racial and ethnic categories try to establish that such use is harmful to the body politic, and arguments given in favor of that use try to establish just the reverse. One argument for each position should suffice as illustration.

One articulation of the political case for the use of the categories of race and ethnicity is often framed in terms of a larger agenda that is often called "the politics of difference."[36] This term refers to political attempts at making room in American society for groups who do not fit the prevailing Anglo-American view of the nation. David Miller describes the case made by those who support the politics of difference as follows:

> Group identity, whether sexual, cultural, or ethnic, should not merely be expressed in private settings, but should be carried into the arena of politics—that is, one should participate politically *as* a gay, a religious fundamentalist, or a black—and political institutions should operate in such a way as to respect these group differences. On the one hand, they must validate group identities by ensuring that the various groups are represented in politics *as* groups; on the other hand, they must ensure that the policies that emerge show equal respect for the values and cultural demands of each group—there should, if necessary, be subsidies for the activities that each group regards as central to its identity; educational materials must avoid discriminatory judgments which imply that one cultural norm might be superior to another; and so forth.[37]

35. Iris Marion Young, "Social Movements and the Politics of Difference," in *Race and Racism,* ed. Boxill, 383–421.

36. For the politics of difference, see Iris Marion Young, "Together in Difference: Transforming the Logic of Group Political Conflict," in *The Rights of Minority Cultures,* ed. Will Kymlicka (Oxford: Oxford University Press, 1995), 155–76.

37. David Miller, *On Nationality* (Oxford: Clarendon Press, 1995), 132.

According to supporters of the politics of difference, the body politic should be conceived as made up of different groups, each with its own identity, whether racial, ethnic, religious, or sexual, and not as composed of individual persons. From this follows that politics should take into account group differences, and be guided by them, so that no group is given any advantages over others. This kind of reasoning is frequently used to support programs such as affirmative action, which are intended to address inequities not between individuals, but between groups.

The use of political reasons against the use of racial and ethnic categories can be illustrated with the case made by opponents of the politics of difference. According to them, this view and the political strategy it endorses pose especial dangers to the body politic. Consider Jean Bethke Elshtain's formulation:

> To the extent that citizens begin to retribalize into ethnic or other "fixed identity" groups, democracy falters. Any possibility for human dialogue, for democratic communication and commonality, vanishes as so much froth on the polluted sea of phony equality. Difference becomes more and more exclusivist. If you are black and I am white, by definition I do not and cannot, in principle, "get it." There is no way that we can negotiate the space between our given differences. We are just stuck with them, stuck in what political thinkers used to call "ascriptive characteristics"—things we cannot change about ourselves. Mired in the cement of our own identities, we need never deal with one another. Not really. One of us will win and one of us will lose the cultural war or the political struggle. That's what it's all about: power of the most reductive, impositional sort.[38]

The argument against the politics of difference, then, is that the assertion of group identities, including racial and ethnic identities, taken together with the political strategy that it implies, undermines democracy and leads to a system in which power ultimately determines justice. Democracy is based on individuals coming together in a decision-making process for the good of all. But the recognition and encouragement of group identities within a nation undermines this foundation, insofar as it transfers power from the individual to the group, retribalizes the nation, and determines policy on the basis of how much power particular groups have. The political well-being of a nation, then, requires the promotion of racial and ethnic identity.

38. Jean Bethke Elshtain, *Democracy on Trial* (New York: Basic Books, 1995), 74.

4. Race or Ethnicity?

From the preceding discussion, it should be clear that the philosophical issues surrounding race, ethnicity, and the relations between the two are both varied and complex. Four of these stand out and are particularly addressed in the chapters of this book. Perhaps the most basic has to do with the reality of race and ethnicity. Do these exist independently of the mind or are they mere conceptions created by individuals or societies in response to various challenges and motivations? Both views are common. Some authors argue that race is a biological reality while others think of it as a social construction. And some authors think ethnic groups exist while others regard them as imaginary.

The conclusions one reaches concerning the reality of race and ethnicity affect the way one resolves another issue: whether the concepts of race and ethnos should continue to inform our discourse or whether they should be abandoned. Again, there is strong disagreement on this. Some authors argue that, regardless of whether race and ethnicity are real or not, we need concepts of race and ethnicity for ethical, political, and historical reasons. But others counter argue that no solution to the many social abuses and problems these concepts have caused is possible until they are permanently banished from our thinking and discourse.

The discussion of the reality of race and ethnicity and whether these concepts should continue to be used raises a question about their appropriate understanding. And here there is also substantial disagreement. Some authors still consider race to be a biological reality in some sense, others argue that it is a mere cultural phenomenon, and still others conceive it in familial terms. Something similar applies to ethnicity: for some authors, ethnicity is a matter of descent, whereas others favor cultural or familial conceptions of it.

Different understandings of race and ethnicity generate different ways of looking at their relations. The strategies most commonly used break down into three main groups. The first argues for substituting one for the other—sometimes it is race for ethnicity and sometimes it is ethnicity for race. A second strategy argues that they are inseparable. This breaks down into those who propose to combine them into the notion of an ethnic race, and those who propose instead the notion of a racial ethnicity. Finally, there are those who still wish to keep race and ethnicity separate in theory, even if in reality they are often mixed in various ways. Their strategy consists in proposing new conceptions of race and ethnicity that can be kept separate but at the same time explain why, and under what conditions, race and ethnicity combine.

Finally, race and ethnicity are the locus of significant issues concerned with morality and politics. These break down into at least three: first, the moral or political reasons why racial and ethnic categories should or should not be used; second, the role that race and ethnicity may play in morality and politics; and third, the moral and political implications of particular views of race and ethnicity.

In this brief introduction, I have raised some of these issues for readers. The purpose is to help them better understand the philosophical concerns addressed by the various chapters contained in the volume.

RACIAL AND ETHNIC IDENTITY

CHAPTER I

Does Truth Matter to Identity?

KWAME ANTHONY APPIAH

1. Overture

The words *Latino* and *Hispanic* are in wide circulation in contemporary American talk. So, of course, are "Black," "White," "African-American," "Caucasian," "Anglo," "Asian," "Asian-American," "Indian," "Native American," "Arab," and a whole host of other terms for ethno-racial groups.[1] If you asked for an explanation of these terms—pretending to be (or, for that matter, actually being) an ignorant foreigner, trying to make your way into our society—you would get a whole range of incompatible responses. It is easy to imagine a conversation that would go something like this.

A: They're all races: Latino, Black, White, Asian, Indian, and Arab.

B: No they're not. Race is a social construct. They're just names for ethnic groups that some people think are biologically distinguishable. Arabs, like Latinos, can be of any color: look at Sudan.

C: Wait a minute. Most people don't think Latinos are a race.

D: I don't know about most people, but more than two-fifths of Latinos *do* think Latinos are a race; or at least that's what they say if you ask them.

A: But that's ridiculous. Everybody knows that Latinos are of mixed European, Native American, and African ancestry.

D: What do you mean African? Are you telling me that Mexicans are Black?

B: Well, obviously most Mexicans don't *think* they're Black. But some do. That's why I said they're ethnic groups, which are social constructs.

---

1. In this paper, I shall follow the convention of capitalizing all ethno-racial terms.

A: I bet you can't explain to me what your so-called ethnic groups are constructed out of without talking about biological differences.

B: All I need to talk about is beliefs about biological differences: since the beliefs don't need to be true, I don't need to talk about actual differences. And, by the way, you left out some of the mess in Latino *mestizaje:* there are South Asian and East Asian ancestors of Latinos too. They get to be members of the Latino ethnic group because they arrived in the United States from Latin America speaking Spanish.

C: Are you saying if some Mexican Indian who doesn't speak Spanish shows up for work in Iowa, he won't be a Hispanic . . . ?

Well, let me stop this interesting dialogue there, because my concern is not in which of these positions, if any, is correct, but in a different issue that suggests itself as one listens to such conversations.

People clearly use lots of ethno-racial terms to identify people. They also agree over a wide range of cases on the application of those terms: the extension, in our philosopher's jargon, of the relevant predicates. A, B, C, and D are likely to agree that Jesse Jackson is Black; that, whatever he thinks about it, Michael Jackson is, too. They'll agree that a lot of great baseball players are Hispanic, especially Dominicans, right? They'll think it obvious that Yo-Yo Ma is Asian-American. And they may agree that that golf player, what's his name, Tiger something, is confused if he thinks he isn't Black. (Oh, and by the way, most members of Congress: they're White.)

What they're much less likely to agree about is what using these classificatory terms entails. At the beginning of modern philosophy of language, Gottlob Frege proposed an account of the words we use to ascribe properties ("predicates," that is) according to which people who understood them associated each such word with a sense, which he said was a "mode of determining" the class of things that had that property. (I'll follow custom in calling that class of things the "extension" of the predicate.) It's an elementary fact, which makes trouble for Fregean accounts of meaning, that many of our ethno-racial predicates (actually, many of our predicates, *tout court*) simply don't have public senses: they don't, that is, have shared, public modes of determining the class of things they pick out. Worse, people actually ascribe these predicates to people on the basis of ideas that are not only different but, at least superficially, inconsistent with one another. Recall the imaginary conversation we just listened in on. It's part of A's theory of things that there are races and part of B's theory that there aren't. C thinks Latinos aren't a race; A thinks they are. D thinks Mexicans can't be Black. B thinks they can.

Of course it could be that A, B, C, and D just mean different things by the word *race*. But in at least one of the many senses of that semantically wanton word *mean* they could certainly all be said to know what the English word *race* means; because, in that sense, to know what the word means is just to have sufficient knowledge to use the word properly. And there is not much, so far as I can see, to be said for the view that to know what the word *race* means you must think either that there are or that there aren't any; or that you must think that Latinos are or are not a race; or that you must or must not think Mexicans can be Black.

These difficulties in the semantics of ethno-racial terms and the ontology of their supposed referents have rightly attracted a good deal of philosophical attention in the last couple of decades. But it is a striking fact that while we theorists can hardly be said to agree on what account to give—we have eliminativists, realists, antirealists, constructivists, et cetera—the words themselves seem to work perfectly well in most circumstances for all that.

So the question that suggests itself, the one I would like to introduce in this chapter, is this: How much does it matter to the way these terms work in our social and ethical lives whether the beliefs in which they are embedded are true? And, in fact, I want to consider the question not just for ethno-racial terms but for social-identity terms more broadly, not least because I think the answer for ethno-racial terms is illuminated, as race-theorists have often suggested, by making comparisons with other forms of identity. At the end I'll suggest some lessons for the Latino case.

2. Social Identities

Let me begin by sketching the account of social identity that I use in my own thinking about these questions. This is not a *philosophical analysis of the concept* of a social identity, if by that is meant an account of the term's standard connotation. Nor am I proposing a semantics for identity labels. Rather, what's on offer is a philosophical *explication:* an account of social identity that aims to illuminate important features of the way social identities work. As a result, I feel free to draw on entirely contingent matters of fact in building the account, provided those contingent matters of fact play a central role in the way these social identities work. What makes a feature important or a role central depends, of course, on what your interest in social identities is. The interest that guides this philosophical theory is ethical: it reflects the role social identities play in shaping our lives and projects and in our treatment of one another. This interest distinguishes my project from that of a sociologist or a political scientist, which is likely to be interested in causal stories about the relation between social identity and such things as stratification or political behavior. I find such theories interesting and helpful. But they are in a different line of business.

This explication of social identities derives from an account of them once offered by Ian Hacking, which he called "dynamic nominalism." It is nominalist because you explain how the identities work by talking about the labels for them. So, take a representative label, X, for some identity.

> *There will be criteria of ascription for the term "X";*
> *some people will identify as X's;*
> *some people will treat others as X's; and*
> *there will be norms of identification.*

Each of these notions—*ascription, identification, treatment,* and *norms of identification*—requires commentary.

A. Ascription

A person's criteria of ascription for "X" are properties on the basis of which she sorts people into those to whom she does and those to whom she doesn't apply the label "X." The criteria of ascription need not be the same for every user of the term; indeed, there will rarely be a socially shared set of properties individually necessary and jointly sufficient for being an X. (This is connected with the anti-Fregean point I just made.)

If you cannot give a Fregean account of criteria of ascription, which makes them shared necessary and sufficient conditions for being an X, you might think that you could at least say, for each person, what conditions are necessary and sufficient for her to ascribe the term "X." That is, rather than supposing that the term "X" has a shared extension, you might suppose that it has an extension for each competent user of the term; and that competence consists in there being some relationship between your extension and a normative extension or the extensions used by others or by experts or some such.[2] This is what I once thought; but I now think even this much Fregeanism is too much. I now prefer the following sort of story.

---

2. For those who want to go this way, I suggest the best chance you have is to suppose that someone is competent if their conception picks out most of the Xs in their social environment; where what it is to be an X is explicated in terms of the best scientific account of what it is most users are talking about. One reason I don't favor this approach is that I think that for some social identities the best scientific account is that they're not referring to anything; but then that would make no users competent, if they thought there were any Xs at all.

Here is what characterizes competence with the term "X." There will be certain kinds of people—we can call them "prototypical X's"—such that your criteria of ascription must pick them out as X's. There will be other kinds—"antitypes," let us call them—that your criteria of ascription must exclude. A prototype is not an actual person: it is an abstract entity, a specification of conditions sufficient for being an X; just so, an antitype specifies conditions sufficient for not-being one. But something may be neither a prototype not an antitype of an X. A Cuban-American, most of whose ancestors came to Cuba before the eighteenth century, and who arrived in Florida in 1950 is a prototype of a Latino. A normal European or African who does not speak Spanish or Portuguese and does not come from the Iberian Peninsula is an antitype. List all the prototypes and antitypes and you may find that they do not divide logical space into two classes.

Because prototypes and antitypes don't divide logical space in two, criteria of ascription need not divide actual people into X's and not-X's, either. Rather, they must divide all actual people roughly into three classes, which we can call (modeling ourselves on Max Black's account of metaphor) the positive, negative, and neutral classes. That is, they must make some people, in the positive class, X's; some people, in the negative class, not-X's; and they may leave some people, in the neutral class, as neither determinately X's nor determinately not-X's.[3] (Let me underline that, whereas prototypes are abstract, these classes are classes of actual people. I am not trying to get at the way the predicate works across possibilia.)

This is what competence consists in; but people do not need to know that their criteria of ascription have these features to be competent. And, in general, they won't know what the relationship is between their criteria of ascription and the total human population. So they may well think, for example, that they can divide the world precisely into X's and not-X's, even though there do in fact exist people (people they have not met) who would be in the neutral class for them, if they did know about them. I shall say that someone who has criteria of ascription for an identity-term "X" that meet the conditions for competence has a *conception* of an X.

This is, no doubt, too abstract; so let me just exemplify. Take the term *Asian* as used by Joe Kansas, who has met very few people from anywhere in Asia and very few Asian-Americans either. Joe says "Asians are a race" and ascribes the term "Asian" to everyone who looks a certain way; in fact the sort of way most movie stars in Hong Kong movies look to him. (I'll call this "looking Asian to"

---

3. I said "roughly," just now to acknowledge a complication that I will ignore from now on: these classes will usually each be fuzzy.

Joe.) He also thinks that the label is properly applied to anyone whose ancestors for many generations have come from China or Japan, because he supposes
that everybody in those countries would look Asian to him. Here are some facts
about the North American English term *Asian* that our Kansan need not know:

> Not everyone from the Asian continent is a prototypical Asian.
> Most South Asians are not prototypical Asians.
> Most Han Chinese are.
> The antitypes for "Asian" include most people who "look African" and most who "look
>   European" to Joe.

Now our Kansan will get all the prototypes and antitypes right. Give him a Han
Chinese? "Asian." Give him most Finns or Congolese? "Not Asian." So he's
competent. But, presented with a Kirghiz or a Kazakh or even a Finnish Sámi
(people, let us suppose, of whose existence he is currently unaware) he might
not know what to say. So his conception has a neutral class, even though he
doesn't know this. He may also have false beliefs—such as that almost everyone
in Asia looks roughly the way Chinese people look—even though most people
in Asia do not: more than 2 billion Indians, Pakistanis, Sri Lankans, Burmese,
Vietnamese, Cambodians, Thais, and Laos, for example; let alone many of
China's own minority ethnicities.

It's worth noting two facts that explain why our Kansan can proceed with
the criteria of ascription he currently uses, even though there is a large neutral
class for his conception; and even though his conception is different from yours
or mine.

First, his social world contains very few people in the neutral class for his conception. If they came along often he might feel he had to modify his conception. Or he might engage in semantic deference and say that he needs to ask an
expert whether or not they're Asian, though he might have no idea who the relevant expert was. A doctor, perhaps? An anthropologist? A lexicographer?

A second reason is this: not only do different people have different conceptions of most social identities, their conceptions will often be statistically correlated with (and sociologically explicable in terms of) the social identities they
themselves bear. That's another reason why our Kansan need not notice that he
has a different conception of what it is to be Asian from many other Americans;
he only uses the term in a social circle in which people all have roughly the
same conception.

Over time conceptions of X's can change. But if a term comes to be associated with significantly different prototypes and antitypes, then what we have is
not a new conception of an identity but a new identity. If Brazilians were to

move from using *negro* to refer to people with black skin to using it, as we use Black, to refer to people whose recent ancestors had black skin, that would be a change in that social identity.

What was formerly just a category of persons can also be replaced by a social identity. So, for example, if Foucault was right, once there was a conception of male sexual behavior according to which some men engage in same-sex sex out of lust but most just want sexual intercourse, preferably with someone attractive. The sodomite was just a man who chose to have sex with a boy or another man. This wasn't a social identity, however, since people didn't identify as sodomites.[4] Then, by the late nineteenth century there was a conception of the male homosexual as a kind of person, whose prototypes are men who have an exclusive inclination toward intercourse with other men and whose antitypes are men who have an inclination toward sex only with women. Since plenty of men (in prison, for example) are sodomites but not prototypical homosexuals, and plenty of men (many celibate priests, for example) are not sodomites but are prototypes of the homosexual, these are different things; they are different also because, as I said, only "homosexual" is a social identity. The fact that certain words survived this transition—like the word *sodomite* itself—doesn't mean that they continued to express the same social identity. Indeed, the positive and negative classes for the term *homosexual* as used by most contemporary Americans are very different from the extensions and antiextensions of "sodomite" in American English in 1850.

B. A Brief Excursus: Why Semantic Deference Won't Help

A final set of issues about ascription has to do with the relationship between vernacular and technical uses of identity terms. Because different people have different criteria of ascription, and because many users will have significant neutral classes, there is, in general, not much point in insisting that someone who is neither a prototypical nor an antitypical X is really an X or really not an X. When there is such a point, it is because the identity-term is also to be used in a scientific or technical discourse—physical anthropology, medicine, evolutionary biology, paleontology, sociology—and, within that discourse, there is some reason to maintain consistency of usage. The reason will usually be either explanatory—capturing biological capacities, say—or practical—applying antidiscrimination law, for example. And when there is such a reason, it will often be just as sensible to propose replacing a dichotomous vocabulary—man, woman—with a richer system of classification—male, female, various intersexes—or to

---

4. Not least because the concept lacked what I will call "norms of identification" below.

use a different distinction, not "Latino / Non-Latino" but "treated as Latino / not-treated as Latino."

Take all the people in the United States who you think are clearly socially White and all the ones you think are clearly socially Black. An evolutionary biologist is likely to think that that classification is not much use to her, because both classes contain people with mitochondrial DNA from Europe and both contain people with mitochondrial DNA from Africa; and the males in both groups contain European Y chromosomes and African Y chromosomes. (Where by "European" I mean descended from people whose ancestors for thousands of years before the fifteenth century lived mostly in Europe or the Southern or Eastern Mediterranean littoral and by "African" I mean descended from people whose ancestors lived in sub-Saharan Africa for thousands of years before the fifteenth century.) If she is going to use the terms *Black* and *White* as racial terms, she will probably construct a concept with criteria that are public and determinate; and she will rightly ignore the fact that certain people are prototypically White for the existing social identity, if the concept she needs requires them to be Black. She is also extremely unlikely, for similar reasons, to have much use for the concept "Latino," since it is, from the point of view of filiation, extremely heterogeneous.

I suggested just now that many people use racial terms within a practice of what philosophers of language call "semantic deference."[5] Faced with a case that they can't settle using their everyday standards of ascription, they assume there is some scientific procedure that will do the job; settling the proper racial identity of each person, counting some, perhaps, as mixtures of the basic types. Since, however, there is in fact no science that can assign all Americans (let alone all human beings) clearly to some small set of racial categories that corresponds roughly to Black, White, Latino, Asian, South Asian, Native American (plus the class of those whose ancestors are a mixture of that small set) this route will not in fact get us a definite answer in every case either.

So much for my brief sketch of ascription.

C. Identification

By itself a way of classifying people that works as I have suggested ascription works would not produce what I mean by a social identity. What makes it a social identity of the relevant kind is not just that people identify themselves or

---

5. The basic idea is introduced in Tyler Burge, "Individualism and the Mental," *Midwest Studies in Philosophy* 4 (1979): 73–122. The related idea of *linguistic division of labor* is found in Hilary Putnam, "The Meaning of 'Meaning,'" in *Mind, Language, and Reality:* Philosophical Papers (Cambridge: Cambridge University Press, 1975), 2:215–72.

others as X's but that being-an-X figures in a certain typical way in their thoughts, feelings, and acts. When a person thinks of herself as an X in the relevant way, she *identifies as an X*. What this means is that she sometimes *feels like an X* or *acts as an X*.

An agent *acts as an X* when the thought "because I am an X" figures in her reasons for acting. Here are a couple of examples: Joe Kansas is in Rome (finally). He sees a couple looking lost and hears one of them say, with an American accent, "Gee, honey, I wish I knew which way the Capitol was." Since Joe's just come from there, he goes up to them and explains how to get there. Why? Because he's an American and so are they. (Of course, Giuseppe Romano, not being American, can also help them out. But it can't be for this reason.) Second example: I'm in a class. Someone tells a homophobic joke. I tell them I don't think it's funny. Why do I feel I must tell them? Because I'm gay. (Of course, you, not being gay, can also berate them. Please do. But it can't be for this reason.)

It is not sufficient to identify as an X that you act "because A thinks I am an X." In Zandeland, I know from reading my Evans-Pritchard, if someone shows you a chicken wing in a certain context, it will be because they have consulted a poison oracle that has declared you to be a witch. The right thing to do, to show that you do not in fact feel hostile to the person, is to spray water from your mouth over the chicken wing.[6] You do this because your accuser thinks you are a witch, not because you are one. So you don't identify as a witch. To identify as a witch, you'd have to say to yourself: Let me do this because I am a witch.

Nor is it enough for you to act "because I am a P" where P is a property that you take to be sufficient for ascribing the identity X. If you stay out of the sun because you have white skin and take having skin of your sort to be sufficient for being White, it doesn't follow that you're staying out of the sun because you're White. You may just think that exposing skin like that substantially increases your risk of skin cancer. It has to be "being White" itself that figures in your reasoning. (If, on the other hand, you're worried that you'll tan and be confused with a non-White person, then your being White does figure in your reason for acting.)

And, for completeness, let me add that you can show your identification by abstaining from doing something as an X. Because I am a Democrat (or a Republican), I don't applaud when the president (or a Democratic leader) makes a partisan speech. Here abstaining is a sign of identification, too.

---

6. E. E. Evans-Pritchard, *Witchcraft, Oracles, and Magic among the Azande* (Oxford: Clarendon Press, 1937).

Perhaps you never act or abstain as an American. But, as I said, feelings can constitute identification, too. You discover that hundreds of thousands of Americans responded to the Asian tsunami by sending money. You feel proud to be an American. To *feel like an X* is to respond emotionally in a way that depends on your identity as an X; where your being an X figures in the intentional content of the feeling. The intentional content of the feeling doesn't have to be precisely *that you're an X*, though: you may feel proud of Mary, a fellow American, say. Here your being an American figures in the intentional content of the feeling, because part of the intentional structure of the feeling is that Mary is *an X like me*, even though what you're proud of is not *that you're an X*. (So you can't feel like an X without believing that you are an X.)[7] Never feel pride? How about shame? If you claim you never act, abstain, or feel like an American, I'll suppose you aren't an American; though I recognize that it is a logical possibility that some Americans never identify as such.

How people identify varies across people and across time. So no particular ways of acting or abstaining as an X or feeling as an X are constitutive of the social identity. What's required is only that there should be such expressions of identification.

D. Treatment

Finally, and briefly, to *treat A as an X* is to do something to A where "because A is an X" figures in your reason for doing it to A. So, when Joe tells those fellow Americans the way to the Capitol he's treating them as Americans. He's helping them, in part, "because they're Americans." Supererogatory kindness of this sort is a common form of treatment-as directed toward fellow in-group members. Morally opprobrious unkindness is, alas, an equally frequent form of treatment—as directed toward out-group members. On my account X's have to be differentially treated for "X" to be a social identity. But the patterns of differential treatment can change without the identity changing.

It takes ascription, identification, and treatment for a label to be functioning as the label for a social identity of the sort that I am explicating.

---

7. Strictly speaking it can be belief or making believe: you can respond, in the theater, with pride, say, to Brutus or Mark Anthony's speech over Caesar's body, but only if you are making believe that you are a Roman. Whether or not you want to call the feelings we have in the theater real emotions, their intentional contents depend on our making believe certain things are true which would have to be true for our emotions to make sense outside the theater. Here, of course, I borrow from Kendal Walton's *Mimesis as Make-Believe* (Cambridge: Harvard University Press, 1990).

E. Norms of Identification

One reason that these identities are useful in social life is that once we ascribe an identity to someone we can often make predictions on that basis about what they will and won't do. This is not just because the existence of criteria of ascription entails that members of the group have or tend to have certain properties, though that is true. It is because social identities are associated with norms of behavior for X's. That is the final element of my philosophical explication of the notion.

It's not just that people do and abstain from doing things because they're X's; there are things that, as X's, they ought and ought not to do. The "ought" here is the general practical ought not the special moral one, which, as Bernard Williams taught me, is the "ought" of a peculiar modern institution.[8] What I mean can be exemplified this way. Negatively: Men ought not to wear dresses; Gay men ought not to fall in love with women; Blacks ought not to embarrass the race. Positively: Men ought to open doors for women; Gay people ought to come out; Blacks ought to support affirmative action. To say that these norms exist is evidently not to endorse them. I don't myself endorse any of the norms I just listed. The existence of a norm that X's ought to A amounts only to its being widely thought—and widely known to be thought—that many people believe that X's ought to A. (I put it this way because I think that sometimes it turns out that hardly anybody really believes in the norm; still it exists if people mostly think most people endorse it.) Norms such as these can change, without the associated identity's changing. So an identity isn't constituted, even in part, by its norms. What is constitutive of a social identity is that there are norms of identification associated with it. And, since the existence of the norm entails that it be widely believed that people think that X's ought to A, that is, as I say, one reason such social identities are useful. An X who believes X's ought to A is quite likely to A, after all; this being a measure of his or her sincerity.

You might wonder whether a social identity must also be associated with norms of treatment. Must it be the case that there are norms of the form: One ought/ought not to do A to X's? I am inclined, at the moment, to think that the only norms of treatment there must be are those entailed by norms of identification: so if it is a norm of identification that X's should be nice to X's, then it will follow that there is a way in which X's ought to be treated, at least by other X's. And if it is a norm of identification that men should open doors for women, then it will be a norm of treatment that women should have doors opened for them by men. These norms of treatment are relational: whether you

8. Bernard Williams, *Morality: An Introduction to Ethics* (Cambridge: Cambridge University Press, 1976).

ought to treat X's a certain way depends on what your own identity is. But there doesn't seem to me to need to be, otherwise, a class of norms of treatment that are general: that say that you ought or ought not to do A for X's, whether or not you're an X. (Obviously there are also general moral norms that apply to X's, just because X's are moral subjects. But these aren't connected to the identity specifically.)

3. Identity

In case you haven't noticed, perhaps I should point out how wide a range of predicates of persons fit the general rubric I have laid out. I started with racial names and ethnonyms; and I mentioned sexes: man, woman, intersex; a nationality: American; and a more local identity: Kansan. But I could also have mentioned professional identities: lawyer, doctor, journalist, philosopher; vocations: artist, composer, novelist, philosopher, again; affiliations, formal and informal: Red Sox fan, jazz aficionado, Republican, Catholic, Mason; and other more airy labels: dandy, conservative, cosmopolitan. There are also relations as well as monadic predicates that fit the general rubric: you can be X's father, identify as such, treat someone as X's Dad. There are norms for fatherhood; things Dads ought to do. (If you doubt that what I said about ascription applies here, think again. Two gay men adopt a child. Suppose one of them donated the sperm. Some people will say that she has two fathers, some one, and some won't know what to say. So you have different conceptions and, for some of them, a neutral class. There are prototypical fathers—the genitor who lives with the genetrix and their biological offspring; and there is the antitype, which includes all those who are uncontroversially women and any other person who has no biological descendants and has adopted no one. But plenty of people are neither of these.) There are also relational terms that have a contextually variable range: "is kin to" is an equivalence relation that defines, for each specification of a degree of relatedness, families of that specific degree of remoteness.

I am pointing to this range not just because, like a well-bred philosopher, I am interested in generality, but because this range invites an obvious question. *Why* do we have such a diverse range of social identities and relations? One answer, an etiological one, will talk about our evolution as a social species and the fact that we are designed evolutionarily for the social game of coalition-building in search of food, mates, and protection. This is, I think, a good explanation for our having the sort of psychology of in-group and out-group solidarities and antagonisms that social psychologists have been exploring for the last half century.

But the psychologies that evolution has given us mean that there is a way the world looks from the inside, from the point of view of a creature with that psychology. And from that point of view, I think there is another, equally persuasive answer. We use identities to make our human lives.

For we make our lives *as* men and *as* women; *as* Americans and *as* Canadians, *as* Catholics and Jews; we make them *as* philosophers and novelists; we make them *as* fathers and daughters. The ethical task each of us has, in virtue of our existence as a rational agent, is to construct a life and to try to make it go well. Morality—by which I mean what we owe to one another—is part of the scaffolding on which we make that construction. So are various projects that we voluntarily undertake: Voltaire's garden—the one to whose cultivation he consigned his picaro Candide—was a project that shaped the last part of his life. But identities are another central resource for making our lives.

Because I am a philosopher, there are things that I need to get done in the course of my life if it's to go well. I need to develop a deeper understanding of some central or important questions about human ethical or intellectual life. This is an obligation, fundamentally, to my self, as a philosopher. I entered into this identity gradually, so that there was a time before I was a philosopher; a later time when I couldn't have said; and a time, now, when I am sure that is what I am. It doesn't seem to me exactly that I chose it, though, because I feel, as Socrates did (if you will excuse me for a moment if I sound pretentious, but this is just what I feel) that philosophy chose me.

Identities are diverse and extensive, I think, because people need an enormous diversity of tools for making their lives. Each person needs many options. And, because people are various, the range of options that would be sufficient for each of us won't be sufficient for us all. Indeed, people are making up new identities all the time: "Gay" is basically three decades old, "Goth" is younger. As Mill said, in one of my favorite passages from chapter 3 of *On Liberty*:

> If it were only that people have diversities of taste, that is reason enough for not attempting to shape them all after one model. But different persons also require different conditions for their spiritual development; and can no more exist healthily in the same moral, than all the variety of plants can exist in the same physical atmosphere and climate. The same things which are helps to one person towards the cultivation of his higher nature, are hindrances to another. . . . Unless there is a corresponding diversity in their modes of life, they neither obtain their fair share of happiness, nor grow up to the mental, moral, and aesthetic statures of which their nature is capable.[9]

9. John Stuart Mill, *On Liberty*, in *The Collected Works of John Stuart Mill*, ed. John M. Robson (Toronto: University of Toronto Press, 1963–1991), 18:270.

4. Truth

So much then for what social identities are and why they matter ethically. It should be a good test of this account if it can help us answer the question that I said I wanted to address: How much does it matter to the way these terms work in our social and ethical lives whether the beliefs in which they are embedded are true?

I spoke vaguely of a term's being embedded in a set of beliefs. To explore different ways of interpreting this thought, I shall have to make explicit something about criteria of ascription that I have so far left deliberately obscure. Of course, people apply identity labels on some basis or other. That is all I have assumed. But to say that doesn't yet tell us very much.

A. What Does Having Criteria of Ascription Amount To?
Part One: Simple Internalism

One way to take A's having such and such criteria of ascription for being an X is to suppose that there are properties A uses and knows that A uses in deciding whether someone is an X. Here it is a particular conception of an X that is embedded in a particular person's beliefs. Such an account is, as I shall say, "internalist" because, in asking which beliefs A's use of a term is embedded in, it considers only A's own beliefs. For an internalist, A's use of a term can only be embedded in a belief that p, if A believes that p; and the use of a term is embedded in a belief that p in a community only if it is embedded in the beliefs of (most of) its members. There are social identities for which such an account works pretty well. Most adults assign the label "male" to people they think have penises and "female" to people they think have vaginas. Of course, in our society, most people we meet keep their sexual organs hidden, so we make assignments on the basis of features of appearance that correlate, we believe, with this anatomical fact. If someone has neither kind of external genitalia (or has something in between) most people don't know what to say. If you tell them that there are people whose indifferent gonad differentiated in embryogenesis to produce something that has features of both penis and vagina, they may say they've heard of hermaphrodites. Or they may suggest tentatively, nowadays, that in difficult cases you should go with the sex chromosomes. If you tell them that there are XX people with penises and XY people with vaginas, they are usually very surprised. And once you start talking about Turner's syndrome and Kleinfelter's, people with only one sex chromosome or with three, they'll probably tell you to shut up.

Still, their normal way of going about it will work in most cases they come across. (As Anne Fausto-Sterling has pointed out, a lot of work goes into keeping things this way.)[10] And when anomalies present themselves, people can make their beliefs coherent with each other and with the relevant facts by giving up the idea that everyone is either male or female. Here, notice, a rather central belief about sex—that everybody is either a man or a woman—is pretty easily given up. So the truth of the belief that sex is binary is not, I suspect, very important to the practice of sex-ascription for most people.

Of course, it may matter a great deal in a particular case. If you think of yourself as a heterosexual man and discover that your lover, though anatomically a woman, is chromosomally a man, I suppose that might matter to you; and not just because that makes it unlikely you'll have natural children. On the other hand, it may not matter to you. Love, as they say, may find a way. Still, this sort of case does show that even very central beliefs about a social identity of our own, can be given up without much shift in our lives.

A first conclusion about identity and truth then:

> I: The importance of an identity in social life is not automatically reduced by the discovery that one has importantly false beliefs about it.

More than this, and as a corollary second conclusion:

> II: Beliefs that are conceptually central to an identity concept need not be ethically central.

None of the norms of identification for sex need change much for someone who is clearly male or clearly female when they discover the nonbinarity of biological sex.

B. What Does Having Criteria of Ascription Amount To?
Part Two: More Complicated Internalism

Unfortunately for the simple life people don't always know how their own criteria of ascription work. Consider someone—my countryman, Joe Kansas again—who would apply the term "Black" to every very dark-skinned person in the world (because he was unaware of the remoteness of the most recent common ancestor of most Dravidians, Australasian Aborigines, and Africans) it would not follow that he knew this about himself. He might think he was using some complex amalgam of color, hair, and facial shape. If we are trying to describe the

---

10. Anne Fausto-Sterling, *Sexing the Body: Gender Politics and the Construction of Sexuality* (New York: Basic Books, 2000).

counterfactual contours of someone's use of a social identity term—what properties would make them ascribe it to someone—we cannot assume that they know those contours themselves. We cannot even assume that their application of the term will be unvarying across contexts: they may not be responding to context-independent properties at all.

If Joe Kansas meets Julian Bond, chairman of the NAACP, in Kansas, he may think he looks Black; in Zaire he could perfectly well strike him as White. If "looking Black (to me)" is a property that he uses to ascribe the identity "Black," he is likely to assume that whether or not someone looks Black (to him) is independent of who else is around. It may not be. But again, if this is a fact about Joe, he isn't likely to know it to be a fact about himself. As a result, we cannot assume that the properties Joseph sincerely says he uses in applying a social-identity term are the ones that in fact determine his use of it.

Here is a hypothesis. Most ethno-racial terms in current use today in this country have criteria of ascription for most people that work as follows:

1. In assigning people to these categories, they are responding to properties that they cannot articulate clearly—*looks kind of Mexican, doesn't look White*; and
2. the properties they rely on are sufficient to assign most people they meet to a racial category or to the status "mixed-race"; *but,*
3. in many other places outside their normal social world, the properties they normally respond to would lead them to have very great difficulty in deciding how to assign very many people. (In my jargon, the neutral class outside their normal social context is very large.) Furthermore:
4. The explicit account most people give of the criteria of ascription they use would require them to apply some racial terms to many people they would not in fact apply them to.

Take "Latino" as a label. Many light-brown people (silent Brahmin gas attendants, for example) will be classified as Latino by Anglos in East Texas. Many Spanish-speaking very-dark-skinned people probably won't. And if someone has Dominican parents, is dark-skinned, but does not speak Spanish, a lot of people in the United States will think her Hispanic and a lot won't. Nothing in their individual current practice determines what they should say about these cases.

Or take "Black" and remember these two facts:

Fact 1: All North Americans have African ancestry, if you go sufficiently far back.
Fact 2: Racial passing has been so extensive that it's possible a majority of those North

Americans who are descended from slaves brought to the Americas from Africa are now classified as White.[11]

Some people will tell you that they use the word *Black* to apply to people of African descent; others that they use it to refer to people descended from American slaves. If you tell them Fact 1—that everybody has an African ancestor—they will no doubt revise their view, without reassigning anybody they know to a new category. If you tell them Fact 2—that there's been a huge amount of passing—they may revise it again, without reassignment; or they may start thinking that there are many more light-skinned Negroes than they realized. But, once more, their existing practice doesn't require them to go in any particular direction when they learn either of these new facts. (The closest common ancestor of almost all Africans and Europeans is at least 100,000 years ago. We have many fellow citizens who apparently don't believe that the Earth is that old. Who knows how *they* should react?)

Given all this, I don't think it is helpful to say that people's use of ethno-racial terms is committed to whatever explicit account they sincerely give of it. Any account they offer is a minitheory about themselves, a theory that may be mistaken. It is like the theories undergraduates offer in epistemology classes as to how "we use the word *know*." They use that word correctly. But they cannot give a correct account of their usage. (And unfortunately, so far as I'm aware, for the moment nobody else can either. That's one reason epistemology isn't over.) It will not do, then, to say that people's use of ethno-racial terms is embedded in the beliefs that they express when they try to explain what makes someone Latino, White, or Arab. And this is true even if the identity in question is one with which they identify.

So here is my third claim about truth and identity:

> III: *The fact that someone can't give a true account of how they ascribe an identity doesn't mean that it can't be important to them.*

---

11. This was drawn to my attention by Brent Staples in a Du Bois lecture in early April 2001, and will no doubt be discussed in the book that will be based on this, which I understand will be called *Excavating Race in Mongrel America*. Staples was kind enough to refer me to Robert P. Stuckert, "African Ancestry of the White American Population," *Ohio Journal of Science* 58, no. 3 (1958): 155. The article describes its statistical model and the sorts of data against which it was tested and concludes: "The data presented in this study indicate that the popular belief in the non African background of white persons is invalid. Over twenty-eight million white persons are descendants of persons of African origin." And that was half a century ago.

C. What Does Having Criteria of Ascription Amount To?
Part Two: Externalist Accounts

So far, I have explored the possibility that A's conception of an identity is embedded in a class of beliefs, where the beliefs are A's beliefs. I called such accounts "internalist." But we could take an alternative (what I will call) *externalist* line. There is a positive class and a negative class and a neutral class for each person's criteria of ascription: that is, there is a way she would assign everybody on the planet roughly to one of these three classes, if that person showed up in her environment and answered truthfully questions about him- or herself. The prototypes and antitypes define the permissible limits of individual positive and negative classes. Looking at the matter from the point of view of an individual's conception of the social identity X, we can ask whether there is any property that those in the positive class for her have in common, that is not shared with those in the negative class. But social identities are, in fact, social. So it is a more interesting question, I think, whether there is a property shared by most of those in most of the positive classes of most people that is not shared by most of those in most of the negative classes of most people.

There are many cases where this question is not hard to answer. Suppose, as is often the case, that in a certain local environment, most people are in the positive or negative classes for an identity X according to the criteria of ascription of almost everybody. Then, locally at least, it will appear to everyone that the term "X" has a clear extension. We could say that the term "X" is "roughly determinate" in that social context. In such a case, it does little harm to say, that, in that context, those are the X's. We may then be able to give a biological, psychological, or sociological account, perhaps relativized to that context, of what X's mostly have in common that not-X's don't, an account that ideally also explains why it is that people in that community distinguish between X's and not-X's. Such an account will be externalist: it may refer to facts unknown to some or all members of that community. For the gender "masculine," being sex-chromosomally XY gets most cases right; and biologists will say that sex is important for biological reproduction, and so it's not surprising that we've evolved to notice it. For "queer man" in 1950s America, a sociologist might tell us, it was the disjunction of "is sexually attracted to men," "is not sexually attracted to women," and "has effeminate mannerisms." They can explain the significance of the category because such men breach central gender norms of identification of the period. For the category "witch" in Puritan Massachusetts, a historian might conclude, it was something like being a socially marginal or unpopular woman, and the explanation of its salience takes a long story.

Now the less easily the biological, psychological, sociological, or historical account maps X's into a category that has epistemic interest as an explanatory category of ours, the more likely we are to say not that X is a social construct—which all social identities are—but that it is *only* a social construct. One reason that a concept can seem biologically uninteresting is that it has to be relativized to social contexts. That's why *witch* doesn't seem like a good candidate for a biological category. There is some dispute as to whether the expression "queer man" needs to be relativized to societies: some people think there is a biological fact about brains that explains being sexually attracted to men and not to women and effeminate behavior. I myself think the facts here are not yet at all clear.

Nevertheless, the mere fact that something is only a social construct doesn't mean it isn't real. Money is only a social construct. There's nothing that it corresponds to at some deeper ontological level, so far as I know. But there, for better or for worse, it is. The reason that witches aren't real isn't that *witch* is a social construct: it's that the criteria of ascription for most users of the term *witch* were such that nobody actually satisfied them. They ascribed the word to people because they thought they had a power to harm others whom they disliked by casting spells. Indeed, someone who muttered spells at night, rode around on a broomstick, had a cat that was in fact a devil, and caused people to fall ill would have been a prototypical witch. But no one in fact has such powers, we now know. So, applying their own criteria, there were no witches: to think someone was a witch, you had to have false beliefs about them.

There's an interesting question for my account posed by this case. As it happens, some people, weirdly, did, apparently, identify as witches. But suppose they hadn't? I said that for a category to be a social identity for me, someone had to identify with it. I'm inclined to bite the bullet here. If there hadn't been anyone who identified as a witch, it wouldn't have been a social identity: but it would still have been falsely believed that it met the conditions for being one. You could go the other way, though, and revise the account to say not that anyone actually has to identify but just that there must be norms of identification that would govern a person who did identify. This is a philosophical explication: there's no correct way to go here, unless going one way or the other is clearly more illuminating. I think the way I put it has the advantage that it includes identification, because this is an ethically crucial feature of the standard cases. You might think it a *dis*advantage that *witch* wouldn't have been a social identity if no one had identified as a witch. But actually, as I read the ethnographic literature, there probably are people who identify as witches in most of the many places something like witchcraft has been identified. So *witch* actually is a social identity, in my sense, in most places.

5. Abandoning Identities

I proposed that every social identity has norms of identification and is associated with differential patterns of treatment for those who are and are not X's. Unless a particular social identity is inalterable, we can thus always ask two questions about it: Should we reform it, by changing how we treat people, and by adjusting the expectations expressed in norms of identification? Or, should we abandon it, because its contribution to human lives in our world is, on balance, negative, and reform seems unlikely to make it much better?

I doubt that any social-identity concepts are in fact inalterable. History and anthropology suggest otherwise. In this matter, as Plato and Herodotus both quoted Pindar as saying, "Custom is king of all." It is possible, for each social identity, to imagine a form of human life without it and I know of no argument that more than that is required for us to be able to achieve its elimination. Whatever forms of ascription we use, there is nothing forcing us to identify ourselves or treat others in ways that depend on it. *Brave New World* requires no fathers or mothers.[12] Science fiction and some feminist theory have proposed lives beyond gender, where there are sexual organs and acts but no social identities associated with them. Utopian cosmopolitans have imagined worlds without nationality. Atheists have dreamed of a world without religions. Foucault argued that, until the late nineteenth century, no one was homosexual.

Psychologists or sociologists may think these are impossibilities. But, so far as I can see, all their evidence shows only that we must have some social identities, not that we must have anything like the ones we have. Yes, most people will have sexual desires organized differentially around some features of other people: but though older Greek men famously had sex with male adolescents, they don't appear to have had the social-identity homosexual, without which the social-identity heterosexual makes no sense. Many societies appear to have made a different distinction, based not on the gender of the objects of your sexual desire but on what you wanted to do with them or them to do with you.

I have already mentioned one reason for abandoning an identity-concept that has to do most specifically with epistemic norms: seventeenth-century beliefs about witches were so wildly mistaken that it seems better to abandon the concept than to try to tidy it up. But there are people who have taken a different view. They have reclaimed the term *witch* for a feminist practice, Wicca. I don't think it would serve much purpose to discuss how much connection this usage

12. That depends on a certain technical possibility: in vitro embryogenesis to term. But even if we supposed that wombs were—as I doubt—technologically essential for child making, we could do it all with artificial insemination and take infants from their biological mothers and raise them collectively. Of course, I'm not recommending this and neither was Aldous Huxley.

has with the seventeenth-century usage. I want only to insist that the criteria for ascribing the term *witch* in most contemporary Wicca covens are far different from those that were used in Puritan New England. Still, the response of many of us—give up the concept "witch"—is grounded more, I think, in a sense of its epistemic inadequacies than in the truth that it is a concept with a deeply sexist past.

Discovering an externalist story about an identity you care about can be deeply disturbing. A standard modern externalist account of racial identities, like the account of racial formations offered by Michael Omi and Howard Winant, would provide, if correct, an argument not for reform but for abandonment of racial identities, because it looks as though they keep reconfiguring themselves somehow as mechanisms of oppression, now on a global scale. But I am enough of a Pollyanna to think that it is not yet clear that this is what they must be; and even if they are right, it is not clear to me that their abandonment wouldn't simply lead to oppression's being structured through other concepts.

Since, on the account I gave, the norms of identification aren't constitutive of the social identity, reforming them doesn't require abandoning the identity. But moving to significantly different prototypes and antitypes does entail abandoning the identity. Furthermore, if no one ever identifies as an X or is treated as one, then the predicate may continue, but it ceases to express a social identity. In her well-known book *Ethnic Options* Mary Waters described a process in which white ethnicity became progressively thinner: the norms of identification became few and undemanding and treatment as a Polish-American or an Irish-American became rarer and less significant. At a certain point, for many people, the norms have reached degree zero. If this came to be true of everybody, these social identities would have ceased to exist, even though we could resurrect the criteria of ascription.

6. Justifying Identities

In taking a social identity seriously enough to use it for identification or treatment, a person is usually committed to there being something significant in common to the people to whom she assigns a common identity, though she is not thereby committed to any particular account of what that significant feature is. If someone identifies as Black and lesbian, she's committed to race and sexual orientation, the superordinate categories, being significant enough to warrant the importance she ascribes to them. There is, then, at least one set of truths presupposed by her practice of ascription and her identifications and treatment of people as lesbian, gay, bisexual, transgendered, or straight: truths required for her practice to make sense. But those truths need not be (indeed, normally will not be) known to her in any precise way; and, of course, if there is no such set of truths, then her practice doesn't, in fact, make sense.

Hence we may say that there are beliefs, not in the sense of individual psychological states but in the sense of propositions, presupposed by each person's practice of ascription: namely, those propositions that explain why the relevant social identity deserves the place it has in that person's life. So here is a case where truth does matter, for social identities presuppose certain truths, namely, those that justify the place they have in people's lives. Let me call these truths the "normative grounding" of an identity. Many identities have stories associated with them that are supposed to establish their normative grounding. Religious identities, for example, are usually associated with narratives that entail that that taking up that identity and conforming to its norms of identification offers eternal rewards and acknowledges deep metaphysical truths about the universe.

My fourth claim about truth and identity is this:

> IV: It's important whether a social identity has a normative grounding. This is a claim about truth and identity because the answer to that question will depend on facts; often, but not always, facts of social life.

Notice that a normative grounding has to justify the way the social identity is: not just the fact that there is a social identity with those criteria of ascription, but the fact that there is one with those habits and norms of identification and treatment as well. It's not interesting to know that a social identity with norms of a certain sort would be normatively grounded if it was a response to racism, if there is no racism. And a social identity's normative grounding can fail because its norms need reform in the light of the facts. If a social group has as one of its norms of identification a norm of endogamy and a few more generations of endogamy would produce large numbers of people with severe genetic disorders, then that fact may undermine whatever normative grounding it might once have had for its members.

Now many identities in fact have more than one normative grounding. There are, that is, various stories whose truth is sufficient to justify my sustaining them. For the identity Latino, today, there are (as the other essays in this book attest) competing accounts of why it is worth holding onto; and some accounts that argue that it isn't. In deciding how to respond to these arguments, I think it is important to go carefully in interpreting the assumption that I made a moment ago that, for an identity to be normatively grounded, its members must have something significant in common.

To begin with, it is natural, at least for a philosopher, to suppose, that a significant property must be an intrinsic property—like a biological or cultural trait—a property whose significance has nothing to do with how one acquired it. Showing that racial groups, for example, don't share distinctive biological properties has often been supposed to show that they can't be normatively grounded identities. Justice Scalia appears to think something like this. But this seems to me just plain wrong.

To see why, let's begin with an artificially simple case. Imagine two women, Mary and Jane, with exactly the same biological intrinsic properties. Both of them have skin the color of Bill Clinton. Mary is the daughter of a light-skinned African-American father and a Norwegian immigrant mother; Jane is also the daughter of a Norwegian immigrant but her light-skinned father is White. His closest African-American ancestor, the one who passed, was a woman who lived a century ago. In fact, it is theoretically biologically possible that Jane and Mary should have essentially the same genotype and Jane not have a recent African ancestor at all. Does it follow that Mary's African-American identity, not being correlated with any intrinsic property, is therefore impugned?

"No," you might say, "because they will have different cultural backgrounds, different experiences." But that doesn't have to be so. So suppose that Mary and Jane were swapped at birth in the maternity hospital. (Hey, given their biological similarity this is a natural enough mistake.) Suppose that Mary's White family, being as they say liberal, raised her in a Black neighborhood with Black adoptive brothers? Suppose that the exchange is now revealed: a nurse admits to having swapped the cots. Can't Mary, raised within a Black culture by a White family, just say that she is glad she can now live as a Black person?

The reason why "Yes," seems like the right answer here has, I think, something to do with the fact that American ethno-racial groups membership is characteristically transmitted through families. Almost all our ethno-racial identities conform to a rule like this: If your parents are both X's, you are presumptively an X, too. (This is not a rule about descent, since it applies very often to adopted children; and it is not a rule about biology, since, in part because inheritance is particulate and roughly Mendelian, the biological relatedness of even first cousins is not much higher than that of people without any known kinship relations in the same community.) People related by this sort of family tie—even when conceived as transmitted only by natural descent—need not have any interesting distinctive properties in common. There need be nothing biologically distinctive about my great-grandmother's descendants, specially if both men and women had children in each generation.

Nevertheless, if a property is transmitted within families, it is likely to have a human significance, whether it goes hand in hand with any intrinsic properties or not. Mary is taking up an identity that has traveled for centuries down through her ancestors. Jane could try to take up that identity, too; but she lacks this humanly significant connection.

One way this matters to the case of Latino identity is this: speaking Spanish is an intrinsic property. But speaking your family's language is not. I wish I had learned Spanish in high school. (But it was that or German and I was already interested in philosophy.) Even if I had learned Spanish, though, it wouldn't have one kind of significance to me that it would have for someone who could think of it—as I think of Twi—as a language spoken by my ancestors and my kin. Having a relation of that sort to a language, a practice, or an identity just is the sort of thing that makes human sense: it makes human sense, I think, because we grow up in families; and the experience of sharing languages and cuisines and other practices is part of what gives family life its life in the memory.

A fifth claim about truth and identity, then:

> V: Normative grounding, even for ethnic groups, can rely on historical connections. It does not need to depend on intrinsic properties distinctive of the group.

7. Latino Lessons

Even though people can think an identity is significant enough to bear weight in the way they make their lives without having a story as to why, it will surely occur to most reflective people to wonder what facts underlie the significance of their identities. We may take it on trust, as we take so much on trust in our lives, of course: we are raised to think that our sex, our citizenship, our family relations, and so on, are important. Individuals in our societies have prospered, we may think, on these assumptions; proceeding with them makes it easier for others to deal with and makes our own planning more straightforward, too. It would be risky to abandon these given identities.

But we also know that many forms of identity—ethno-racial ones, nationalities, gender as constructed in most places and times, sexual orientation, religious identities—have been the source of great suffering in human lives. Not only have people done terrible things to out-groups on the basis of these sorts of social identities, the social identities have been burdensome for in-group members. The norms of identification associated with the identity *woman* have often been burdensome independently of the evil that has been done to women by other people, not always men, in the name of ideas about how women ought to behave. *Gay* may have finally come to be a positive identification for many people; but *queer* wasn't much fun. In these circumstances, it strikes me as, at a minimum, desirable to reflect about the identities that most matter to one and about those that matter most in one's society as to whether the claims they presuppose are true. One of the reasons Mill believed in liberty, was that he thought it would permit people to make what he called "experiments of living," trying out options for human life. People could thus find out whether certain options enriched or diminished human possibility; and we could all learn from each other's experiments. He didn't put it this way, but we could say that trying on new identities and reforming the norms of old ones is one important kind of experiment of living.

Latino identities—it is reasonable, I think, to pluralize—are, for the United States, an exploding set of experiments of living. I want, in closing, to draw a consequence for Latino identities from each of my five claims; taking them (for those who keep track of such things) slightly out of order.

I: *The importance of an identity in social life is not automatically reduced by the discovery that one has importantly false beliefs about it.*

People often question Latino identities by saying that most non-Latinos think that Latinos have more in common than they do; or that most people mistakenly think that all Latinos speak Spanish; or some such. But you can't show that an identity is unimportant just by showing that people have importantly false beliefs about it.

II: *Beliefs that are conceptually central to an identity concept need not be ethically central.*

Spanish language is conceptually central to Latino identities, even as more and more Hispanics don't speak Spanish. But even though this conceptual connection is central, the fact that some Hispanics aren't Hispanophone doesn't mean that their being Hispanic can't be ethically central for them.

III: *The fact that someone can't give a true account of how they ascribe an identity doesn't mean that it can't be important to them.*

'Nuff said.

V: *Normative grounding, even for ethnic groups, can rely on historical connections. It does not need to depend on intrinsic properties distinctive of the group.*

So we don't need to define Latino essences to ground Latino identities.

IV: It's important whether a social identity has a normative grounding. This is a claim about truth and identity because the answer to that question will depend on facts; often, but not always, facts of social life.

This claim sets the challenge I think for Latino identities in the United States today. My view—the standard liberal view—is that a social identity, X, is grounded, roughly, by true stories that substantiate affirmative answers to these three questions:

Does identifying as an X enable things of value in the lives of the individuals who take them up through identification?

Are those who don't identify as X's unharmed by the existence of X's?

Are people in general better off with being-X around as a social identity available to some than they would be without it?

An identity that fails one of these tests is in need of abandonment or reform. The task for all of us, but especially for Latinos, is to answer these questions; and, if, in particular, people who identify as Latinos answer the first of these questions in the affirmative, all of us must together try to make a country in which we can say "Yes," to the final two.

CHAPTER 2

Racial and Ethnic Identity?

J. L. A. GARCÍA

Emotion—and, with it, sentiment, affection, desire, preference, choice, and intention—meets race most saliently in two phenomena. The first is racism, wherein individuals invest racial classifications, especially of others, with such affective responses as hatred, disregard, contempt, and callousness, often letting those attitudes infect their personal conduct and poison that of their institutions. The second is what some call "racial identity" and identification, where people invest racial classifications, especially of themselves, with more positive and appealing feelings of pride, affection, loyalty, trust, and commitment. Having developed a somewhat distinctive position on racism over a series of articles during the last ten years, I here wish to turn in a somewhat preliminary way to reflection on racial and ethnic identity.[1]

My discussion, first, raises some problems about the claim that such direction of feelings, projects, loyalties are properly seen as constituting identities. Second, it explores some difficulties that arise in two of the more promising philosophical elaborations of such group identities—those of Jorge J. E. Gracia and J. A. Corlett—accounts that focus on ethnicity rather than on race, and on being Latina/o, more specifically. I find both accounts wanting, especially in Corlett's suggestion that someone's ethnic identity might properly be conceived as comparative and scalar (that is, that it can admit of degrees). Third, I critically examine Linda Alcoff's well-informed, reflective, and spirited defenses of ethnic identities and what she calls "identity politics." My conclusion offers and

---

1. I elaborate the content and implications of a virtues-based account of racism, which focuses on mental states, in García, "Current Conceptions of Racism," *Journal of Social Philosophy* 28 (1997): 5–42; and "Racism as a Model for Understanding Sexism," in *Race/Sex: Their Sameness, Difference, and Interplay,* edited by Naomi Zack (New York: Routledge, 1997), 45–59.

sketches a few proposals—that we strive for a kind of diffidence about claims of racial and ethnic affiliation, recognizing that we are unsure of their content and scope, and on that basis, that we adopt a more deflationary approach to such claims, minimizing consideration of such matters in our deeper self-conceptions and in our emotional and moral lives, therein repudiating the very idea of ethnic and racial identities.

1. Identity and Identification-With

Kwame Anthony Appiah divides his seminal essay in *Color Conscious* into two parts: the first is titled "Against Races," and the second "For Racial Identities." In the former, Appiah argues that there are error and mischief in the racialist thesis that there exist human races, each with a distinctive "essence." The position of the essay's second part is more complicated. Appiah writes, "Racial identity . . . I shall roughly define as a label, *R,* associated with [widespread] . . . descriptive criteria for applying the label, and . . . a shaping role for the label in the intentional acts of the possessors, so that they sometimes act as an *R,* where there is a history of associating possessors of the label with an inherited racial essence."[2] So far, this says only what racial identities would be, not why Appiah is "for" them. In his essay's conclusion, he describes it as having "defended an analytical notion of racial identity."[3] Again, this "defend[s]" the concept only as having application, not as desirable. I once heard Richard Bernstein, questioning Appiah from the audience at a New York City conference several years ago, suggest that Appiah's position on racial identities, and on their associated racial loyalty, solidarity, trust, and pride, amounts to a qualified affirmation, a 'Yes, but . . .' Bernstein then pointedly added that Appiah's discussion so focused on his reservations about racial and some other forms of collective identity—that is, on the 'but' clause—that the grounds for Appiah's affirmation, his 'Yes,' were left obscure.

Appiah now sees group identities as important to many people's values, projects, purposes, sense of community, even the meaning they find in life.[4] By itself, however, that leaves it unclear what if any good is done by specifically *racial*

---

2. Anthony Appiah, "Race, Culture, and Identity: Misunderstood Connections," in *Color Conscious: The Political Morality of Race,* ed. Appiah and Amy Gutmann (Princeton: Princeton University Press, 1996), 80–81. Sally Haslanger has pointed out to me how counterintuitive it is to think an identity of someone could consist in a mere "label."

3. Appiah, "Race, Culture, and Identity," 104.

4. Appiah, *Ethics of Identity* (Princeton: Princeton University Press, 2005), esp. 24–26. Also see chaps. 1, 3 passim.

identities. He does allow that "racial identity can be the basis of resistance to racism." Appiah describes himself, not so convincingly, as "looking forward" to a time when he "tak[es] up, along with others, the fruitful imaginative work of constructing collective identities for a democratic nation in a world of democratic nations."[5] However, that racial identity *could,* or even *can,* be the ground or motive for antiracist struggle does not show it *is* the best such foundation, in either its effectiveness or its moral or epistemic justification. Paul Gilroy suggests that "action against racial hierarchies can proceed more effectively when it has been purged of any lingering respect for the idea of 'race.'" While recognizing that "for many racialized populations, 'race' and the hard-won, oppositional [racial] identities it supports" will not die easily, he calls for its "demise" and deems "liberation from 'race' . . . an especially urgent matter for . . . [such] people as modern blacks in the period after transatlantic slavery."[6] We do not need to pursue the merits of Gilroy's case here. It is enough to observe that the possibility and even availability of what Gilroy calls a "postracial . . . version of what it means to be human" make plain what should be obvious anyway: that Appiah's tepid acknowledgment of some use for racial identity is not much of a "defense" of it normatively.[7]

Naomi Zack allows that "the term 'identity' is ambiguous . . . because it is used to mean both subjective experience and shared group membership that includes history and group self-image."[8] For her, "Identity is that about an individual that he or she reflects on, accepts, and develops, in the self." In contrast, "Identification is what others . . . use to distinguish that individual from others." This latter use seems to me somewhat idiosyncratic. At least, it omits the close connection often asserted between someone's identity on the one hand and that with which and as which she identifies (herself) on the other.[9] Appiah is closer to the norm, I think, in calling "identification: the process through which an individual intentionally shapes her projects—including her plans for

---

5. Appiah, "Race, Culture, and Identity," 105.

6. Paul Gilroy, *Against Race* (Cambridge: Harvard University Press, 2000), 12, 13, 15.

7. Bryant has pointed out that prior to Du Bois's famous call, at the beginning of the twentieth century, for the "conservation of race," there was rather a long history of African American reform activists repudiating the very idea of racial classification as artificial, un-Christian, and un-American in what they saw as its implicit denial of universal human fraternity. For a differing, but underdocumented, view, see Paul Taylor, "Appiah's Uncompleted Argument: W. E. B. Du Bois and the Reality of Race," *Social Theory and Practice* 26 (2000): 103–28.

8. All quotations here are from Naomi Zack, *Thinking about Race* (Belmont, CA: Wadsworth, 1998), 67.

9. Zack concedes that, despite the way she understands the distinction between someone's (or some group's) identity and some process of identification, "the sense of identity that is relevant to race and identity is not entirely free of identification." Ibid., 67.

her own life and her conception of the good—by reference to available labels, available identities."[10]

Someone's "plans for her life and . . . conception of the good" are rather grand, inclusive matters. Even at a more mundane level, some people think that someone's race or ethnicity should matter crucially in determining what she cares about, prefers, likes, wants, and strives for in a variety of areas from music and literature to politics, as well as shaping her feelings of special loyalty, affection, pride, solidarity, and so on. As they see it, someone's race and ethnicity are, or ought to be, parts of her "identity." At least, they hold this for members of some racial or ethnic groups, those who have been systematically oppressed, exploited, and disadvantaged. Such people, they think, ought to be personally—that is, affectively and normatively—*invested in* their race and ethnicity; they ought to *identify with* being Black or Latina/o, for example.

Adrian Piper offers these helpful accounts of the crucial concepts: "Agent A is personally invested in some state of affairs t if the existence of t is a source of personal pleasure, satisfaction, or security to A . . . A identifies with t if A is disposed to identify t as personally meaningful or valuable to A."[11] Plainly, what Piper speaks of in terms of satisfaction, meaningfulness, and value involves a range of affective phenomena including feelings of pride, loyalty, special affections, as well as projects and commitments that touch us emotionally. It is this depth that makes some want to say that race and ethnicity are by their nature, or ought to be by her design, matters of someone's very identity (or "identities").

2. Racial and Ethnic Identity

Though our ethnic classifications are not the same as our racial ones, the concepts themselves are not clearly distinguished. Many of the considerations that motivate racial identity also motivate ethnic identity, and many of the same difficulties that afflict racial identity also afflict ethnic identity. Hereafter, I will seldom attend to the differences.[12] Appiah, recall, offered a "rough" definition of a

---

10. Appiah, "Race, Culture, and Identity," 78.

11. Adrian Piper, "Higher-Order Discrimination," in *Identity, Character, and Morality,* edited by Owen Flanagan and Amélie Rorty (Cambridge: MIT Press, 1990), 296.

12. J. Angelo Corlett, *Race, Racism, and Reparations* (Ithaca: Cornell University Press, 2003), 9, suggests replacing the concept of race with that of ethnicity, David Theo Goldberg combines them into "ethno-race," and Alcoff appears to think the two notions are insufficiently different even in principle to make sense of either replacement or combination. "The differences between race, ethnicity, and culture . . . begin to recede once we look at how the terms are actually used." Linda Alcoff, *Visible Identities: Race, Gender, and the Self* (Oxford: Oxford University Press, 2006), 242.

racial identity as "a label, R, associated with [widespread] . . . descriptive criteria for applying the label, and . . . a shaping role for the label in the intentional acts of the possessors, so that they sometimes act as an R, where there is a history of associating possessors of the label with an inherited racial essence." Appiah allows that, so understood, a person can have a racial identity even if races are illusory and seems to think that someone who, like Appiah himself, does not believe in races may nonetheless coherently and even sensibly strive for such an identity.[13]

This is plainly problematic. Insofar as racial identity involves identifying with one's race and (presumed) racially characteristic features, and involves specifically *racial* solidarity, affection, pride, and loyalty, it cannot be intellectually legitimate in a world without races.[14] If Appiah, Zack, and others are correct in thinking there are no races, then neither ought there to be anything that can count as racial identities. For that matter, even ethnicity is a more problematic notion than generally acknowledged. Ethnic groups seem to be defined by their cultural distinction, but the cultures are themselves sometimes individuated by their connection to the groups. Similarly, like race, ethnic classification involves an uneasy collection of factors—biological, ancestral, religious, linguistic, and cultural—leaving it very unclear just how some are to be classified and what is being said in assigning anyone to this or that ethnic grouping. My focus here, however, will not be on the difficulty that the problems inherent in our ideas of race and ethnicity causes for the concepts of racial and ethnic identity. Rather, I wish to present the enthusiast for racial and ethnic identity with difficulties from another direction, that is, from the concept of identity itself and from complications that afflict efforts to extend it to such supposed 'collective identities' without stretching it past the breaking point.

3. Identity and Group Identity

Our term *identity* derives from the Latin word *idem* (same), and philosophers have chiefly engaged identity-talk when asking whether something is the same

13. "In fact, we might argue that racial identities could persist even if nobody believed in racial essences, provided both ascription [of racial membership by others] and identification [with the race's presumed characteristics by those assigned to it] continue." (Appiah, "Race, Culture, and Identity," 82) Later, Appiah talks approvingly of "identities [as women, Blacks, homosexuals] toward which so many have struggled in dealing with the obstacles created by sexism, racism, homophobia," and even of his own joining their project of "constructing" such "identities." (Ibid., 104)

14. Zack, "Philosophical Racial Essentialism," paper read to Boston University's Institute on Race and Social Division workshop, February 2001. We should also note, contra Appiah, that even if people do have group or collective identities, which I will here dispute, it is implausible to think them mere words ("label[s]").

as what exists in some real or imagined different situation. This is a long way—too long, in my view—from today's talk of ethnic or racial identity and other so-called "group" or "collective" or "social identities."

The social psychologist Erik Erikson seems to have been particularly influential in this shift. One commentator maintains that one "Eriksonian concern is the centrality in human life of a 'sense of identity'—the *construction* of a self that makes sense for the particular individual as well as for *the* community in which that individual lives."[15] I agree with those who argue that efforts to understand someone's ethnicity as consisting in roles or scripts, as the social construction of ethnicity would require, are both implausible and manipulative. We should note that Erikson's view, as summarized, in addition to presupposing the false thesis that each individual lives in only one community, holds both the implausible claim that identities are invented and the dangerous one that someone's identity is constructed in part by others to enable them better to "make sense" of her.[16] The idea seems to have been that everyone needs an image of herself, beginning with a notion of her boundaries, and that the process of developing one is identity-formation. From there it can seem a small step to the claim that a group similarly develops a self-conception, which forms its identity, raising the question of what role, if any, this group self-conception does and ought to play in an individual's own self-concept. At that point, we have entered the territory of collective identity, including ethnic and racial identity.

Appiah suggests that "each person's individual identity is seen as having two dimensions. There is a collective dimension, the intersection of her collective identities; and there is what I will call a personal dimension, consisting of other socially or morally important features of a person . . . that are not themselves the basis of forms of collective identity." He pertinently adds that "only the collective identities count as social categories, kinds of person."[17] This view is multiply problematic. In holding that someone's individual identity includes some subset of her collective identities, it supposes that her identity is both individual and plural, begging an important question. It reduces the person herself simply to her features, the notorious "bundle" view found in Hume, with its egregious inability to account for change, for persistence through time, or for identity across possible situations. It appears also to assume and entail that the only social kinds that exist, the only "kinds of person," are those socially recog-

15. Howard Gardner, "The Enigma of Erik Erikson," *New York Review of Books* (June 24, 1999): 53, emphases added.

16. Though Erikson campaigned against racial hatred, his view opens the door to *our* defining *your* identity in such a way that it fits comfortably into our prejudices about what we regard as different types of people, thereby helping us to "make sense" of you.

17. Appiah, "Race, Culture, and Identity," 93.

nized. Moreover, it is unclear how this could account for the fact that most within a given society may not only misclassify some individuals but mistakenly think some empty classes to have members, as in Appiah's own illuminating example of witch-free societies (some of) whose members falsely believe others (or themselves) to be witches.

How shall we think of identity in connection with ethnic, racial, and other so-called "social identities"? Here is one illuminating suggestion, from Virginia Domínguez:

> Whereas material objects have a concrete existence whether or not people recognize their existence, social identities do not. *An identity is a conception of the self* [emphasis added], a selection of physical, psychological, emotional, or social attributes. . . . It is not an individual as a concrete thing. It is only in the act of naming an identity, defining an identity, or stereotyping an identity that identity emerges as a concrete reality. Not only does that identity have no social relevance when it is not named, it simply does not exist when it has not been conceived and elevated to public consciousness.[18]

Yet there are manifest difficulties in making anyone's identity something imposed on her rather than inherent, something she need not have at all, a matter consisting in how she (or others) think of her rather than in what she unavoidably is. Even if it made sense to think that your being Black or Latina/o was just your being so classified, which I doubt, it seems to be a long way from simply fitting into a recognized category to having an identity.

There are many statements of the form 'S is P,' where P does not give the subject's identity. Why think that being a Hispanic or a Black person is having a special identity—a Hispanic or Black one—especially when the discourse of any such ethnic or racial identity differs so radically from central cases of identity-talk, as in discussion of identity over time or across possible worlds?[19] After all, logically perspicuous identity-talk makes sense only when it naturally finds (or, at least, permits) two-term expression, as in talk of A's being identical with

18. Virginia Domínguez, *White by Definition: Social Classification in Creole Louisiana* (New Brunswick, NJ: Rutgers University Press, 1986), 286, as quoted in Mary C. Waters, *Black Identities: West Indian Immigrant Dreams and American Realities* (Cambridge: Harvard University Press, 1999), 44.

19. Gracia notes that some do or might prefer such terms as *Latina/o*, or *Latin American*, or *Ibero-American* to pick out a larger or smaller subset of the ethnic group(s) he has in mind, and, despite his book's title, carefully argues for the superiority of the term *Hispanic*. Jorge J. E. Gracia, *Hispanic/Latino Identity: A Philosophical Perspective* (Oxford: Blackwell, 2000), chaps. 1, 3. I find his reasoning appealing, but will move freely between talk of things and people Hispanic and those Latina/o, without troubling over the distinction. I will also use the more gender neutral 'Latina/o,' except in quotations, whenever the context leaves gender unspecified.

B (through qualitative changes, across times, in different possible situations).[20] Any inherently nonrelational identity-talk, which the discourse of "ethnic identity" seems to be, is therefore inherently suspect.[21] As the anthropologist Adam Kuper remarks, "The concept 'identity' is an oxymoron used in relation to an individual, since how [sic] can an individual not correspond to himself or herself? . . . The notion of Identity is connected rather to the idea that the self has certain essential properties and some contingent ones. There is a real me."[22] Kuper's last remark, of course, opens the door to construing identity as personal essence, what philosophers have called *haecceitas*. Unfortunately, any such move runs counter to the antiessentialist approach to identity[23] and to the claim that individuals have multiple identities.[24] For there is something odd in suggesting a person could have a plurality of personal essences. Yet claims about individuals having plural identities are staples of recent treatments of ethnic and racial identity.[25]

Ethnic identity is radically dissimilar to identity in its central and clear cases (as in the diachronic or "transworld" identity that philosophers discuss). Racial and ethnic identity does not easily permit formulation in relational form, nor derive from issues of sameness. Where such identities are seen as socially conferred or "constructed," as in Domínguez's account and most others today, they cannot involve the self in her deepest features or personal essence. I suspect talk of "identity" here trades on illicit and misleading hypostatization (reification) in several ways. It disallows the necessary question 'Identical *with* whom/with what?' It loses the necessary connection between identity and sameness. It obscures the question *in respect of* what this and that may be identical, treating identity as if it were not relativized to fields and features. Moreover, when, as in familiar accounts, my ethnic identity hinges on that as which I identify myself (or what others identify me as being), or on that with which I identify (in my

20. One difference is that some people do *talk* of identity in these contexts (e.g., "identity politics"). However, some of us think they should not, and one thing a philosopher should do here is query this sort of naive practice and explore ways of justifying its presuppositions.

21. I hasten to add that I am aware that Frege, Strawson, and Geach, among others, have denied that identity itself is a relation. See Thomas Morris, *Understanding Identity Statements* (New York: Humanities, 1984), esp. chaps. 2 and 5. I do not beg, or even engage, that question. My claim here is only that meaningful identity-*talk* must naturally lend itself to (or, minimally, must allow) formulation in two-term language. It is this test that, whatever the nature (if any) of identity itself, talk of identity across time and across possible worlds passes, and talk of ethnic identity fails.

22. Adam Kuper, *Culture: The Anthropologists' Account* (Cambridge: Harvard University Press, 1999), 234ff.

23. See, especially, Gracia, *Hispanic/Latino Identity*, 48ff.

24. "This [i.e., Gracia's] conception of who we are is open and pluralistic, allowing the coexistence of other, multiple, and variegated identities." Gracia, *Hispanic/Latino Identity*, 69.

25. Ibid., 60; Corlett, "Latino Identity," *Public Affairs Quarterly* 13 (1999): 273–95.

feelings, preferences, etc.), or when I am seen as having multiple identities, then such identity becomes so contingent logically, changing temporally, that it relinquishes that aspect of identity-talk in which whatever warrants the designation as someone's "identity" must be something logically necessary, metaphysically essential, temporally fixed, deep, and comprehensive (exhausting her self).

Gracia's treatment is, to my knowledge, the most metaphysically informed, sensitive, and meticulous elaboration of any such ethno-racial identity.[26] His discussion focuses specifically on the "panethnic" (better, multiethnic) category that he calls "Hispanic identity," but he means it to have more general application. Gracia initially spells out his membership conditions for someone's being Hispanic, with which he seems to identify her having a Hispanic identity, by concentrating on the person's ancestors, especially their history and geography.[27] Comparing his account to Wittgenstein's famous treatment of games in terms of "family resemblance," he insists "there are no common characteristics to all those people whom we wish to call Hispanics," only a network of similarities linking one Hispanic person to another.[28] This creates obvious tension with his claim that all Hispanics share "a common identity of a familial, historical sort."[29] For a shared ethnic identity appears to be a shared quality, insofar as an identity seems to be a quality. Even if having an identity is not having a quality, having an identity *is* a quality.[30]

Gracia's claims pull in opposite directions: one has to go. Gracia must abandon either his antiessentialist claim that Hispanics share no features, or his claim that we share Hispanic identity.[31] Given the difficulty of identifying such a qual-

26. These paragraphs treating Gracia's book are excerpted and adapted from García, "Is Being Hispanic an Identity?" *Philosophy and Social Criticism* 27 (2001): 27–43.

27. "My proposal is to adopt the term 'Hispanic' to refer to us: the people of Iberia, Latin America, and some segments of the population in the United States, after 1492, and to the descendants of these people anywhere in the world as long as they preserve close ties to them. . . . the use of this term does not imply that there are any properties common to all of us throughout history. Its use is justified rather by a web of concrete historical relations that ties us together, and simultaneously separate us from other peoples." Gracia, *Hispanic/Latino Identity*, 52; also see 48.

28. Ibid., 48.

29. Ibid., 44.

30. In *Surviving Race, Ethnicity, and Nationality: A Challenge for the Twenty-First Century* (Lanham, MD: Rowman and Littlefield, 2005), Gracia now clarifies that a group (including ethnic) identity is a kind of quality (or "property"), but only of a second-order type. I cannot here pursue this new wrinkle in Gracia's position, nor do I see whether or how it can turn the trick of enabling him consistently to retain both his antiessentialism about ethnic identities and his claim that they are something in which people share.

31. Strictly speaking, a shared quality is necessary but not sufficient for an essence. So, someone could deny a Hispanic essence while still affirming that some features are universal among Hispanics. As Gracia denies all Hispanics as such share either an essence or even any features, however, we need not attend to the difference.

ity shared by all and only Hispanics, and the fact that any shared Hispanic identity in the absence of shared characteristics could only be an empty one, which is not worth having, I think Gracia (and the rest of us) should abandon the claim that Hispanics as such share an ethnic (or multiethnic) identity.

Gracia adds an important qualification to what he call his Familial-Historical (ancestor-focused) View of Hispanic identity: a Hispanic is someone who belongs to certain geographically defined groups, or has ancestral links to them, *only* if she *also* "preserve[s] some link to those people" or, as he puts it a bit later, "preserve[s] close ties to them."[32] This qualifier adds new problems, some stemming from its vagueness. We want to ask what *sort(s)* of ties are required, and how close they must be. More important, we want to know *why* these ties are needed. If *H,* a descendant of the Iberians, now loses all contact with them and their other descendants, does she at that point cease being Hispanic? (If so, does she lose all ethnicity or just the broad 'panethnic' Hispanic identity, while retaining a narrower ethnic identity, such as Cuban or Puerto Rican?) To affirm that is to reintroduce a cultural element to an ethnic (or pan-, or multiethnic) category shaped by geography and ancestry. We might say that *H* is not culturally Hispanic, in the sense that she diverges from certain ways of thinking and behaving that arose among the Iberians and their descendants and that are thought to characterize the life of some Hispanic groups. However, she still seems to be of their lineage. Should we say, then, that someone's cultural features determine not *whether* she is Hispanic but *how* Hispanic she is? That suggestion is initially appealing. However, I think closer examination of Corlett's careful attempt to develop just such a position reveals insurmountable shortcomings.[33]

4. Scalar and Comparative Ethnoracial Identity

Often nowadays a person's racial or ethnic membership is understood as her ethnic or racial identity, and her ethno-racial identity, or her having such a "group identity" is regarded as a desideratum. As we observed earlier, this identity of hers is taken to involve her "identifying with" her ethnicity or race. The latter project must stress cultural features, taking pride in or striving to acquire preference for what are thought to be some of the group's characteristic musi-

32. Gracia, *Hispanic/Latino Identity,* 48, 52.

33. Most of the following discussion is adapted with minor changes from García, "How Latina? More Latina?" *American Philosophical Association Newsletter on Hispanic/Latino Issues in Philosophy* 1 (2001): 93–97.

cal or literary forms, cultivating or affecting various tongues or distinctive linguistic styles or phrasings, making a point of certain styles of clothing, and so on. These are the marks of having an ethnic identity, it is sometimes thought, at least, of being authentic in it. Appiah notes that "ethnic identities characteristically have cultural distinctions as one of their primary marks. . . . Distinct practices, ideas, norms go with each ethnicity in part because people want to be ethnically distinct, want the sense of solidarity that comes from being unlike others."[34]

Yet immediately a problem arises. For we intuitively think that whether you are, say, a Black person or a Puerto Rican is more a matter of your ancestors' geographic origin and culture than it is of yours. Any talk of degrees or comparatives in regard to something's identity seems patently unacceptable.[35] How can I have my identity, be what I am, *more or less* or *to a certain extent*? Of course, there may be something plausible in the idea that ethnicity itself admits of degrees and comparatives. It may make sense to say some people are more Latina/o than others are, and perhaps, too, we can sometimes legitimately talk of how Latina/o someone is.

Lawrence Blum is a good example of someone who seems to allow for more or less intensive ethnicity. He distinguishes what he calls "thick ethnicity" from "thin ethnicity." The latter is said to be what Herbert Gans calls "symbolic ethnicity" and Waters "voluntary ethnicity." Where "thick," ethnics live "daily li[ves] immersed in and permeated by [their] ethnoracial identity," for "thin ethnics" their "ethnicity is not very salient in their daily existence." Blum also distinguishes "identity ethnicity" from "anti-discrimination ethnicity." In this use, and somewhat surprisingly, "identity ethnicity" (which, confusingly, is itself only one type of ethnic identity) possesses "no cultural content" and is a matter simply of someone's seeing herself as belonging to a certain ethnic group—or of merely realizing that others do, contrary to her own preference and self-classification. Such an individual "take[s] on an ethnic *social* identity without having the *cultural* substance often assumed to accompany it."

Blum's notion of "anti-discrimination" ethnicity seems a poor contrast, since this is a matter of the limits of and reasons for a person's "identification with her group." Someone with such an ethnicity identifies with the group when, "because and insofar as" the group faces discrimination. I think it confused to consider these four types of ethnicity, and worse still to conceive them, as Blum does, as "four forms of ethno-racial identity." His "thick" and "thin" represent a real distinction, but it is a distinction among different extents to which ethnic

---

34. Appiah, "Race, Culture, and Identity," 89.
35. Geach to the contrary, if he is, notwithstanding.

culture pervades daily life, not among depths of *being* Latina/o, etc., nor of having any kind of identity.[36]

This talk can arise and seem reasonable especially in cases of ethnically mixed ancestry. What is problematic is the claim, however initially appealing, that one's ethnic *identity* can admit of comparatives and degrees, that someone's cultural participation and emotional commitments make her ethnic identity greater or less. To see what motivates such a position and how it goes awry, we should return to Corlett's discussion.

Corlett presents his exploration as "a philosophical analysis of the nature of a specific ethnic group," an effort to "analyze the notion of Latino identity," a search for "the nature of a Latino person," an inquiry into "the necessary and sufficient conditions that define membership in a Latino group, ethnically speaking," into "who qualifies as a Latino" and "the nature [or 'properties'] of Latina/ohood."[37] Presumably, the author does not really mean that a Latina/o person has a different "nature" from, say, an Anglo or an Aryan person as that talk suggests. (If he did mean that, then the first thing for him to do would be to show us that we should think there exists such a nature for him or anyone to find.) The issue instead seems to be what it is for a person to be a Latina/o. Note that nothing in this description makes the project into "an analysis of Latino identity," as Corlett also puts it. I see no good reason to speak of "identity" in this discussion at all. Let us begin by treating it as an inquiry into what it is to be a Latina/o, deferring for now the narrower business of her having Latina/o identity.[38]

36. Lawrence Blum, "Ethnicity, Identity, and Community," in *Justice and Caring: The Search for Common Ground in Education*, ed. Michael S. Katz, Nel Noddings, and Kenneth A. Strike (New York: Teachers College Press, 1999), 129–33; 131, emphasis retained; 129; 132. Several of the problems, discussed below, that appear in Corlett's cultural intensive conception of Latina ethnicity and ethnic identity will, I suspect, also be found in Blum's view, though I will not try to make that case here. So-called "identity ethnics" need not identify with their ethnic group at all, need not even identify themselves *as* belonging to it. It is odd to think they reveal *any* type of ethnic identity. For someone to resent discrimination against Ls on the grounds that she is herself (a) L presupposes her ethnic self-classification. This is not a type or form of ethnicity, let alone of ethnic identity.

37. Corlett, "Latino Identity," 274ff., 278, 294, passim.

38. There is a complication here, because in ibid., 35, at note 19, Corlett asserts that being a Latina/o is different things in different places: "Latino identity is contextually contingent. . . . being Latino in East L.A., for instance, is different than [in U.S. usage, I think this should read "from"] one's being Latino in, say, Brazil or Cuba." However, he seems not to think that variation extends to necessary and sufficient conditions. I am not sure how that variation-claim avoids introducing inconsistencies into his account, but I mention the complication for construing his project as specifying what it is to be a Latino. If what it is to be a Latina/o at place P_1 is something different from what it is to be a Latina/o at P_2, then should not Corlett's inquiry be into "what is it to-be-a-Latino-AT-(some-)place-P? (Rather than into his "what is it to-be-a-Latino?") And then, to be consistent, should not that question also be further relativized to times? Can time be irrelevant here, if place is crucial?

These two claims constitute the nub of Corlett's chief account of what (I think, misleadingly) he calls "Latino identity":

(C1) Someone's ancestral connection to the peoples of Iberia after 1492 is necessary and sufficient for affirmatively answering the question *whether* she is a Latina/o.

(C2) There is a certain "cluster of attributes which, when held in some combination and to some significant degree, serve to identify [some]one as being more or less a Latino." These attributes include mastery of the Spanish language, having a Spanish name, and familiarity with and appreciation for various Hispanic customs.[39] Those who, possessing the needed genealogical ties, have more of these are therein more Latina/o.

On Corlett's account, whether a person L is Latina/o depends simply on her ancestry.[40] However, "Latino identity is a matter of degree," and how Latina/o she is—the extent to which she is (a) Latina/o—varies according to various cultural and linguistic factors.[41] There is a conceptual difficulty built into any such view. For it is hard to see how someone's (or something's) having some property P could consist in her (its) having some feature $F1$, while her (its) being *more* P than another is (or than she/it used to be) consists in comparative possession of some entirely different feature $F2$. What applies here to the comparative question also applies to the scalar.

In "Analyzing Latino/a Identity," Corlett offers a "clarification" that seems to

39. Corlett consistently talks of "willful and voluntary" participation in Latina/o culture. This suggests too narrow, too active, and too voluntaristic a conception of culture and cultural involvement. Many of the habits and patterns of response that are thought to constitute someone's culture are matters of a person's beliefs, desires, likes and dislikes, preferences, etc. It is mistaken to think that, when she spontaneously possesses these responsive states as a result of her cultural environment, she is "willfully and voluntarily" participating in her culture. Nevertheless, they may be an important part of her ethnocultural life.

40. The preceding account summarizes the position taken in Corlett, "Latino Identity." Corlett, "Analyzing Latino/a Identity," *American Philosophical Association Newsletter on Hispanic/Latino Issues in Philosophy* 1 (2001): 97–104, and *Race, Racism and Reparations* (Ithaca: Cornell University Press, 2003), chaps. 2, 3, revise the ancestral condition necessary (and sufficient) for someone's being Latina/o from her having genealogical ties to past Iberian peoples to her having such ties to other Latinas/os. While he takes refuge in talk of the possibility of "virtuous circles," however, this one is plainly vicious (Corlett, *Race, Racism and Reparations,* 57–58). It requires an infinite past series of Latinas/os if there are any current Latinas/os, since A will be Latina/o only if an ancestor B was, but B will have been a Latina/o, in turn, only if some ancestor C was. And so on, ad infinitum. Moreover, this account of being Latina/o can never be usefully applied without a prior account of the same matter, possessing which renders this one unnecessary. For, according to it, in order for me to find out if someone A is Latina/o, I need to find out if some ancestor B is. However, if I already have some independent way of determining that for B, then I should be able to use that method also for A, rendering Corlett's recursive circular account otiose. If I do not, Corlett's account is still of no help, because it requires me already to know of someone precisely what it is supposed to tell me, i.e., whether s/he is Latina/o.

41. Corlett, "Latino Identity," 285.

me a different position. While defending his view that ethnicity is (an) identity on the dubious grounds that it is part of who someone is, Corlett now retreats to the claim that someone's cultural participation merely "indicates" the degree of her cultural "identification," comparing it to the way in which someone's devotion may mark how much she cares about her marriage and her spouse while it is legal facts that determine whether she is married. If this level of cultural identification is meant as a metaphysical account of being comparatively or intensively Latina/o, for example, then it cannot work because it makes being more or less Latina/o (or Latina/o to degree M) no longer the proper comparative of the quality that constitutes simply being Latina/o.

Corlett talks as if he were offering an account of being more, less, or just so Latina/o in the same sense in which (though, problematically, on different grounds from those on which) someone is simply Latina/o. It is now plain that that is not the case, and his rhetorical slide from ethnicity to ethnic identity to ethnocultural identification only obscures the fact that he is talking about two entirely different matters—what someone is and how much it matters to her. The latter is in no way a comparative or an intensity of the former. Moreover, it should be clear that his marriage analogy undermines Corlett's view more than it clarifies or supports it, because we know there is no such thing as being more or less (or this much) married. Again, being married is one thing and caring about it something quite different, not at all related as a comparative term is to its positive, unmodified form. Finally, and important for our purpose, we can ask why we should consider ethnicity an identity. Is it assumed that every quality, even every relational quality, is similarly internal to the self? If so, has not Corlett mired himself in the Hegelian doctrine of internal relations?[42]

Returning to my critique of Corlett's account of ancestry, how could a subject's being P consist in its having feature F_1, when *how* P it is—the extent to

---

42. Corlett, "Analyzing Latino/a Identity"; Corlett, *Race, Racism and Reparations,* 56. Some seem unembarrassed by such association. Thus Alcoff insists, "the Other is internal to the self's substantive content . . . a part of its own identity. . . . it is less true to say that I am dependent on the Other—as if we are clearly distinguishable—than that the Other is part of myself" (Alcoff, *Visible Identities,* 45). But if not every quality is an identity, then why should we think that ethnicity has the needed profile? Of course, it is true that many people attend to this classification of some people by others, but your view of me can hardly be what makes me me. It is just too contingent, too extrinsic to who I am. It is also true that some people invest emotionally in such classification. Still, they must exist and, being necessarily self-identical, have their identity, independently of this emotional investment. And it strains credulity to say one person can (let alone, must) be part of a second. Of course, it will be said that these matters relate to individual identity while the issue is about whether ethnicity is a social (that is, group, collective) identity. However, here I suspect many partisans of ethnic identity want to have it both ways, distinguishing someone's individual identity from her social identities, but then defining the former, as we found in Appiah, as the intersection or union of the latter. (See also Corlett, *Race, Racism, and Reparations,* 54: "My ethnic identity is part of my overall identity.")

which it is P—consists in the amount it has of some different feature F_2? If something's being P is identical with its being F_1, then its being more P (than some X) can only be identical with its being more F_1.[43] Corlett's claims, then, appear to violate the logic of comparative and scalar terms. Yet that is the form of the claims that constitute Corlett's account, if we replace "P" with "Latina/o," "F_1" with the relevant features of Iberian lineage in C_1, and "F_2" with some requisite cultural feature(s) from C_2.[44]

Any such account as Corlett's also faces a problem from the lower limit. As the level of Latina/o cultural involvement shrinks, the subject, L, approaches not being Latina/o at all, until there is no cultural involvement at all and L is not Latina/o. When the answer to the question of the degree to which something is P is "None at all," then the answer to that of whether it is P is *eo ipso* answered. There is no need to look to some other ancestral features, as Corlett wants. In this way, the 'whether' and 'how' questions are logically linked, but any account like Corlett's treats them as independent. Of course, his ally can try to block the problem by insisting that the question of how Latina/o someone is—and thus recourse to cultural involvement—cannot arise unless and until the question of whether the subject is Latina/o—the matter of her genealogy—is answered affirmatively. However, any such stipulation is ad hoc; it needs both its propriety and intelligibility to be shown.

Corlett acknowledges that, on his account, we would need to know not just *which* factors count toward someone's being Latina/o—better phrased, toward how Latina/o she is or "the *degree* to which one is a Latino"—but also *how* and *how much* each factor counts.[45] The problem is deeper than this, however, and Corlett's account can be shown to have counterintuitive implications. On it, as a Latina/o, L, Anglicizes first her Christian name, then similarly changes her middle name from Spanish, and finally her surname, her "Latina/ohood" fades; she becomes less (a) Latina/o. *Unless,* that is, over the same period, she does some things Corlett's account treats as more "Latina/o-making" (as we might say), such as gaining greater mastery of Spanish, or coming to know more Latin mu-

43. One might object: Can it not be true that being a Red Sox fan, for example, is being devoted to the Sox, but *how much* of a fan someone is remains a matter of her having more or fewer insignia merchandise, banners, bumper stickers, etc.? That is mistaken, I think. Being more of a Sox fan is *indicated* by these things, but only insofar as they are signs of greater devotion, and being more of a Sox fan consists in being *more* devoted to them, because being a fan consists in being thus devoted.

44. When I presented some of this material at the Center for Social Concerns of the University of Notre Dame, Kenneth Sayre suggested to me that, even if we take ethnicity to be biologically fixed, still, what I call "self-image" might usefully be employed to determine how Latina/o (etc.) someone is. For the general reason just offered against Corlett's account, and because of puzzles in the very idea of degrees of culturally defined ethnicity, I find problematic Sayre's rather different suggestion about how Latina/o S is might have a different basis from whether S is Latina/o.

45. Corlett, "Latino Identity," 287, emphasis retained.

sic or literature. This picture of waxing and waning ethnicity—waxing and waning across persons and times—complicated now by tradeoffs he cannot consistently deny, strikes me as unrealistic and far-fetched. More important, we must observe that waxing and waning "identity" is even odder, at the margins of coherence. Corlett also needs to provide some account of the commensurability of these very different matters.

The difficulty is not merely the one Corlett concedes, that we do not yet know *how much* Spanish a Latina/o would have to learn, for example, in order to offset what he imagines to be the de-Latinizing effects of her Anglicizing her name. Rather, I want to ask how *can L's* learning *any* amount of Spanish replace some of the Latina/ohood that she supposedly lost in changing her name? What is the metric in which this sort of commensuration could take place? What could be the relevant unit of measure?[46] Finally, we should note that Corlett's account is rather unclear about whether our person *L* also has to *like* the music for it to tend to make her more (of a) Latina/o. Corlett talks here of "respecting . . . elements of Latino culture." Suppose, however, that someone *L* comes to know more Latin(o/a) music, but likes it less.[47] Maybe the novelty wears off, or it comes to seem shallow in *L's* mind compared with Ravel, or (the no longer Lil') Romeo, or "Riverdance," or whatever it is that now captivates her. What if she gradually gains respect for, say, Spanish drama but increasingly despises Cuban poetry? How does that affect her standing as a Latina/o? I mean these questions to be rhetorical, but they point to what is unanswerable. The problem goes beyond that of assigning specific weights to the various factors. My point is that there is something highly counterintuitive in the very suggestion at the heart of Corlett's account that these cultural matters can weigh at all in the required way, tending to make someone more or less (a) Latina/o as they grow or shrink, indeed, making her Latina/o identity track this ebb and flow.

These matters are not without possible psychological consequences, we should remember, and they are not without possible normative implications. There is, of course, an ancient tradition in the West (and East, for that matter) according to which the fundamental ethical project is that of being fully what one is. Where *X* is supposed to be some deep feature of the self, as any matter

46. Note that this problem of identifying and explaining the needed units of measure (of Latina/ohood?) is a different and deeper one from the difficulty that Corlett acknowledges, which is, in effect, that of specifying *how many* of such units *L* gains in learning Spanish and how many she loses in changing her name.

47. In "Analyzing Latino/a Identity," Corlett carefully talks of someone's "respect[ing]" her Latina/o culture. This is a kind of answer to the question of what attitude, if any, is needed for being 'more Latina/o,' but it seems to me not to answer my question whether it is necessary or relevant whether the person likes the cultural elements, enjoys the music's sound, the food's taste, etc.

of identity ought to be, to say that someone is a *X,* but not much (of one), is already a normative judgment and a negative one at that.[48] Corlett denies that his comparative talk is inherently normative. This response is unpersuasive. His account explicitly holds that someone may be "more or less a Latino," and implicitly allows that some Latina/o people are more Latina/o than others. It puts some "at the core of Latina/ohood [sic]" and others at "its periphery," holds that some Latinas/os are "Latinos in a strong sense," others "Latinos in a weaker sense."[49] All this has strong normative import, including ethical, as is made clear by Corlett's insistence that "we should wear our ethnic label with pride," and his criticism of what he calls "the unfortunate disposition" and "self-deception" in someone who "seeks to completely opt out of what is clearly her genealogically based ethnicity."[50] With such stakes in the background, I think Corlett needs some stronger defense of so controversial a model, some more explicit defense against the concern that his metaphysical account is politically loaded and the worry that it is politically motivated. (I do not presuppose—or even believe—that the latter charge is, in the end, correct, only that the worry it expresses is justified.)

How can we correct the problems I have identified in Corlett's view? I have no definitive solution, but I propose, rather tentatively, that we drop what we might call Corlett's "total Latina/o score"—how Latino/a someone is, all things considered—and allow measurement (*not* grading) only of how typical of Latina/os she is in this or that respect. Rather than following Corlett in saying that someone who knows and appreciates Latino/a literature is, so far forth (or *pro tanto*) "more Latino" than someone who does not, it seems to me more appealing to stop with what is given, namely, that the former is simply *more typically* Latino/a *in* her knowledge of literature. (Or, what is different, in her preference, etc.)

It appears best to content ourselves with saying that someone is more or less typical of Latinos in her name, her linguistic competencies, and other attributes. Whether someone is a Latino/a person may in the event be, as Corlett allows, largely determined by her genetics. However, rather than then using cultural factors to determine how Latino she is, to place her near or far from the group's "core," to make her Latina/o in a "stronger sense," to fix the extent of her "Latino/a identity," we do better to allow a way simply to determine how *typ-*

---

48. Here is a putative counterexample to this claim of mine. Maybe it is not an insult to say "You're not much of liar or a thief." Still, insofar as you are a liar or a thief, there is some negative imputation in saying you are a poor one. In any case, being a Latina/o is not something presumptively bad, as being a liar or thief is, and being a liar or thief is not something deep in the responsible agent, so the purported counterexample is not relevantly similar.

49. Corlett, "Latino Identity," 285, 288.

50. Ibid., 275, 290.

ical she is of Latinas/os in this or that taste, in her knowledge of certain texts, topics, etc., in her religion, and in other such matters. We can say that person *L1* more resembles most Latinas/os than does *L2* in these or those (many or few) respects. Why do we need more than this? Why do we need, why should we accept, and how could we either interpret or verify, talk of someone's being more or less (a) Latino/a *tout court* (beyond the way fixed perhaps by mixed ancestry), still less, of one Latino/a having more Latino/a identity than another has?

In any case, whatever may be true with respect to scalar or comparative ethnicity, our concern here is more specifically with ethnic (and racial) *identity*. I think it doubtful Corlett's scalar and comparative account of Latina/ohood as a group identity, or a fortiori any such account of an ethnic (or pan-, or multi-) ethnic identity, can be saved. The notion is inherently implausible. Its two-part structure runs into problems from the lower limit. Its picture of temporally waxing and waning identity is strange. The possibility of tradeoffs and offsetting factors exposes the absence of defensible (nonarbitrary) measures and the seeming impossibility of any metric in which to conceive—let alone, execute—the needed commensuration.

The element of truth in Corlett's claims may be that, in the people he discusses, what is at the core or periphery is a particular ethnic category within their self-image (and in the self-images of some others). Pace Corlett, it is not that the person is at the periphery of the ethnic group. It remains an open question, to which I return below, whether assigning ethnicity (or race) prominence in one's identity is a reasonable or desirable course. Let us consider the most influential claim: that some people's ethno-racial identity should determine their politics.

5. Alcoff's Defense of "Identity Politics"

Linda Martín Alcoff sympathetically cites the Combahee River Collective's 1977 "Black Feminist Statement." There, she says, "identity politics emerges as a belief in the relevance of identity to politics, such that, for example, one might justifiably assume that those who share one's identity will be one's most consistent allies." Its authors "did assume that identities mattered, and that they were in some sense real."[51]

---

51. Alcoff, "Who's Afraid of Identity Politics?" in *Reclaiming Identity,* edited by Paula Moya and Michael Hames-García (Berkeley: University of California Press, 2000), 313, and *Visible Identities,* 15. The Combahee River Collective's April 1977 "Black Feminist Statement" is reprinted as chapter 7, in *Identity Politics in the Women's Movement,* edited by Audre Lorde et al. (New York: New York University Press, 2001), 59–66. I do not here dispute Alcoff's interpretation. However, it should be noted that the matter

By now it should be clear that any assertion of the reality of ethno-racial identities, or of identities of gender or sexual orientation which seem also to have interested the collective, is more complex than it looks. Its defender must show not only that ethnic, racial, and gender groups really do have members, but also that this membership merits classification as an "identity." Even the claim that races and ethnic groups genuinely have members is more problematic than it appears. More important for us, I have offered reasons to hold that these groups are not accurately and illuminatingly considered identities.

Alcoff's discussions take us through a sometimes fascinating tour of intellectual history from Hegel to Foucault and Judith Butler, offering modest, nuanced accounts of essentialism, ontological pluralism, Althusser's "interpellation," Fanon's "corporeal malediction," and much more. However, it does little to show that belonging to an ethnic group or a race, let alone having a gender or sexual orientation, constitutes someone's identity. She talks of social "processes in which identities are constructed" and maintains that "social identities are real (or not) within the social world," proceeding sympathetically to summarize the view that "identities are real in the sense of [i] being lived, [ii] of having real effects, and [iii] constituting real features of our shared reality."[52] Especially, "identity is conceived as something that belongs to a group," involving a sense of "'linked fate'" among them, "a felt connection to others of one's identity group based on the belief that their fate will impinge on one's own," which feeling "operates to tie individuals together on the basis of being subject to a certain kind of treatment."[53] That our neighbors assign you and me to the same category may, of course, affect how we are treated by them and others, how we live our lives, how each of us thinks of her/himself, and how we feel about each other. None of that, separately or together, suffices to secure the classification's accuracy, let alone make it into your identity or mine. The neighbors may be mistaken, and even if they are not, the classifications to which they attend may

---

may not be so straightforward. The statement affirms: "Our politics evolve from a healthy love for ourselves, our sisters, and our community, which allows us to struggle and work. This focusing on our own oppression is embodied in the concept of identity politics. We believe that the most profound and potentially the most radical politics come directly out of our own identity, as opposed to working to end somebody else's oppression." That seems to fit Alcoff's interpretation. On the other hand, the Statement also insists that "to be recognized as human, levelly human, is enough" (Lorde, *Identity Politics*, 61). That may suggest that the self-described Black, feminist, lesbian authors think the identity most pertinent for purposes of political morality is their identity as human, contrary to the emphasis on race, gender, and sexual orientation characteristic of the way in which identity politics seems to have developed, and the way that Alcoff construes it. The matter is, as I say, complex. For within a few sentences, the Collectives proceeds: "our situation as black people necessitates that we have solidarity around the idea of race," an affirmation more typical of the emphases we nowadays think of as identity politics.

52. Alcoff, "Who's Afraid of Identity Politics?" 324, 318.
53. Ibid., 319.

reflect little of what is most important, defining, fixed, inherent, or distinctive in either of us.

What then of the claim that ethnicity and race, whether or not identities, "matter"? What matters therein makes a difference. What sort of differences is it claimed that ethnicity and race make, and how do they make them? Alcoff talks of "the normative and epistemological implications of identity," asking "whether identities are politically healthy or reliable sources of truth."[54] By "normative" here, Alcoff seems to have in mind political or moral considerations, so she really is conjoining two very different types of issues. It behooves us to separate them. Alcoff, whose own mainstream philosophical research centers in issues of knowledge, focuses on ethno-racial identity's claimed epistemological import. She holds that "to say that we have an identity is just to say that we have a location in social space, a hermeneutic horizon that is both grounded in a location and an opening or site from which we attempt to know the world." Given that "identity . . . is something like social location," it is "plausible" to "claim that identity has epistemic salience." Indeed, so construed, Alcoff maintains, Derrida and others cannot be right to see the social categories of Black, or woman, or "gay," as identities to be claimed only as a part of the process of putting the classifications behind us. For "it is incoherent to view identity as something we would be better off without."[55]

Of course, where someone is situated relative to others will affect what and how she experiences. An interesting claim for the "epistemic salience" of race or ethnicity requires more than this. The advocates of deep identity politics, I think, do claim more than what Alcoff asserts, the mere fact that it is likely that members of a specially recognized group (call them Es) will or do think similarly about some topic, T. They claim that E1, and any E, ought to think like other Es, where this 'ought' is not merely probabilistic but is chiefly a normative political 'ought.' There is thought to be something wrong with the thinking of those who do not think like the others. Moreover, they suppose this defect to result from failings that are both intellectual and political. This is the heritage, among today's professors, of the calls from yesterday's students for consciousness-raising, solidarity, La Raza, sisterhood, Black nationalism, and similar agenda.

These stronger claims by the partisans of so-called identity politics should, I

---

54. Ibid., 334.

55. Ibid., 335. In fairness, I should point out that in *Visible Identities,* chap. 4, Alcoff offers what seems to be a substantially different account of social identity, there conceived as "interpretive horizons" with "embodied dimensions." I confess my inability to follow this combination of Gadamer's jargon with Merleau-Ponty's epistemological speculation, and concentrate on Alcoff's earlier, somewhat clearer statements.

think, be challenged on two fronts. First, even when these category-memberships may have some moral/political force in what a certain person ought to believe, feel, decide, and the like, they are not dispositive and must operate in the right way. What someone thinks, feels, or works for should not normally or substantially be a function of her desire to be like others assigned to the same group, nor emerge from group loyalty, nor reflect merely that group's interests, as if they were paramount. Rather they ought, especially, provide information for appreciation and application of moral principles and the deeper concerns and virtues they express. So, we should reject the view that how others in someone's group think, feel, and act provide her good ground for how she should think, feel, and act. Yes, experience, group-typical or not, provides both information and opportunity for sensitization. In that way, we might even be able meaningfully to talk of Black, or Latina/o, or women's "perspectives" on certain issues. Nevertheless, shared or unshared experiences, rooted in social classification or otherwise caused, only serve as occasions and opportunities to reflect, understand, and appreciate.[56] This is far from conceding what we might call the "identitarian" claim that someone's membership in a (disadvantaged) race, ethnicity, gender, sexual orientation, or whatever ought to have pride of place in shaping her moral reasoning, opinions, feelings, and commitments. Still less does it lend support to the view that conforming to the opinions, preferences, and agenda of others in the group is a desideratum, let alone, a proper goal of action.

Second, we should challenge accepted views on just what it is that the typical experiences of women, African-Americans, Latinas/os, and so on provide as a guide to thinking, feeling, and deciding. Contrary to the usual agenda, for example, someone could reasonably maintain that women have special grounds to oppose abortion, and African-Americans to reject all appeals to race prejudice and race distinctiveness. Even if ethnic and sexual categories matter morally, we need to know *how* they matter, *how much* they matter, and what is the range of their legitimate forms of impact. This is a dispute about how properly to learn from shared experiences, what lessons they ought teach. In any case, the dispute is then what it ought to be: one about moral principles, sensitivity, and virtues. In short, the issue is what we can learn from our experiences and our reflection about moral truth and value, what they are and where they reside.

56. For more on this matter of ethno-racial perspectives on normative issues, see García, "African-American Perspectives, Cultural Relativism, and Normative Issues," in *African-American Perspectives on Biomedical Ethics*, ed. Harley Flack and Edmund Pellegrino (Washington, DC: Georgetown University Press, 1992), 11–66. See also García, "Revisiting African American Perspectives and Medical Ethics," in *African American Bioethics: Culture, Race, and Identity*, ed. Lawrence Prograis and Edmund Pellegrino (Washington, DC: Georgetown University Press, forthcoming).

Of course, we can and must learn from our experience, whether or not shared with others similarly socially classified. However, everyone—and especially those from within stigmatized, silenced, and disadvantaged groups—ought to reject any claim that it is these groupings that constitute our identities (or Alcoff's "forms of identity"). It is not such factors that make us who we are.[57] It is moral conviction that shapes a decent person's political commitments, and mere group loyalty and conformity cannot shape the moral conviction of a sensible person. That holds whether the groupings are real or imagined, natural or artificial, subjective or intersubjective or objective, imposed from without or adopted within, resisted or embraced, malignant or strategic. Alcoff's lesson in intellectual history is instructive, but it does nothing to show that the self is somehow constituted by gender or race, as those classifications are used in rule-governed social practices.

To the contrary, in an old article of mine, and giving no thought at the time to issues of purported social identity, I built on a suggestion of John Searle's to propose that the canonical form of a statement of a constitutive rule is 'S should be counted and treated as P.' That requires that S exist prior to, and independent of, any rule's constitution of her *as a p*. It follows that constitution cannot go all the way down, *contra* the followers of Richard Rorty. Anyone's essence whatever it is can only preexist her social categorization and, what is different, her constitution as someone of this or that type.

There are many other troubling positions in which Alcoff's discussion finds merit. That what I am as a self is partially influenced by external forces is no news. If, however, what I am as a self is determined by external forces, especially insofar as this includes some people's malignant designs, which is what Alcoff seems to think, then we are caught in (really, we are victims of) heteronomy of the worst sort. We are other people's creatures. That is appalling, whether or not one thinks it blasphemy.

Relatedly, Alcoff's distinction between someone's public identity and her subjectivity, besides being murky and fishy, is also dispiriting and dangerous in the context of her further view that the public, in forming my public identity, also therein constructs my subjectivity, fixing its content. "The 'internal' is conditioned by, even constituted within, the 'external,' which is itself mediated by subjective negotiation. Subjectivity is indeed located." Note that the "location" of which she speaks here is my position in the social net and hierarchy that other people devise. Note also that Alcoff defines 'subjectivity' as "my own sense of myself, my lived experience of myself, or my interior life." Only the very easily pleased will find much comfort in Alcoff's concession that the external forces

---

57. Alcoff, "Who's Afraid of Identity Politics?" 312.

fixing my social location and therein forging my identity do so in a process that is "mediated by subjective negotiation." That is like your cheering because, when everyone jointly decides what clothes you are to wear each day, you also get a vote. Even if you got two votes where each of the rest gets only one, your situation is thoroughly heteronomous. More plainly put, you are oppressed. Only what is at stake here is not merely what you wear, but your identity, what you *are*.[58]

Alcoff thinks it "obvious that one's identity in this full sense, one's positional consciousness, will play a role in one's actions." She talks illustratively and admiringly of speakers at a political rally who "spoke *as* young people . . . *as* African-Americans and Latinos . . . *as* U.S. citizens."[59] Yet, we can ask, what is it for someone to speak as an *E,* that is, as a member of a certain ethnic or racial group? More important, what is it for her to reason, or believe, or feel, as one? Is it merely that she thinks or feels what she does on grounds partially affected by her belonging to that group? Alcoff says of the speakers that "their identity made a difference in what they knew about and how they approached a problem." That may be true, but it seems too modest. It will not be enough to give most partisans of robust identity politics what they want. Such partisans want these categories to dictate how we should react and what we should think.

For Alcoff, "to self-identify even by a racial or sexed designation is . . . to understand one's relationship to a historical community, to recognize one's objective social location, and to participate in the negotiation of the meaning and implications of one's identity." I have no complaint, of course, with understanding or recognition. Couching either in talk of "identity," however, suggests that this historical connection and social location capture and exhaust the real self, and I find that claim unsupported, unjustified, degrading, and dangerous. (Talk instead of "multiple identities," which some prefer, may block the monopolization, but it is of doubtful coherence and threatens the self with schizophrenia and irrevocable sundering.)

Alcoff claims that "a realistic identity politics . . . recognizes that social categories of identity often helpfully name specific social locations from which individuals engage in, among other things, political judgment" and concludes by

---

58. Ibid., 336–37. Similarly, Alcoff's rather carefree adoption of Gooding-Williams's repellent distinction between someone's "being black" and her "being a black person" is outrageous both philosophically and morally. Just what is the ontological, and thus moral, status of those people who are Black but do not undertake "to make choices, to formulate plans, to express concerns, etc., in light of one's identification of oneself as black?" (Alcoff, "Who's Afraid of Identity Politics?" 339, quoting Gooding-Williams). They are, *ex hypothesi,* Black. Are they, then, Black nonpersons, Black subpersons? Is this where the politics of identity lead us, back to the racist's rhetorical sewers?

59. Alcoff, "Who's Afraid of Identity Politics?" 340, emphases retained.

asking "What is there to fear in acknowledging that?"[60] There is nothing to fear, I suppose, in acknowledging the fact. Still, the fact that some people take their political causes from group self-interest, rather than from larger moral concerns, is an unfortunate, degraded, and antisocial phenomenon. While shared experiences can bring moral issues into sharper focus they can also obscure them, and while reflecting on them sometimes sensitizes us to certain moral considerations, they can desensitize us or narrow our sympathies.

What Alcoff asserts, then, is too narrow, generalized, and one-sided. The real dispute about identity and its place in politics is not Alcoff's concern, which seems to be that public policies need to be evaluated in part on the basis of their impact on certain groups, and that people within those groups should therefore be consulted and listened to. That is virtually beyond dispute. The deeper conflict is over whether those consulted within the groups ought to be considered its spokespersons, whether there is a special view that is peculiar to the group and that it is their responsibility (perhaps owed to the group) to articulate, whether their and others' membership in the group should be a major force in shaping their thinking and feeling and action, and whether following the group in these matters ought to be one's project in part because in so doing and only in so doing people realize and fulfill their true selves—act, and feel, and think authentically.

Alcoff sunnily remarks that here "identities had important epistemic and political roles to play precisely in ensuring and enhancing solidarity." I find this altogether too sanguine, even blasé, about the ways in which purported identities will be policed and enforced so as to "ensur[e] and enhanc[e]" the group solidarity that is politically demanded in thought as well as action. This goes well beyond the merely probabilistic anticipation of consistent alliance with which Alcoff, as we saw, began. Alcoff comes closest to what I see as the heart of the matter when she modestly allows that "the particular meaning and significance of one's identity is interpreted in many different ways." She proceeds tolerantly to suggest that "one may take one's racial identity . . . as more or less central to one's life," as if less were as eligible as more. Her allies on the front lines of identity politics are, I fear, not always so liberal and pluralistic. They invoke the rhetoric of identity precisely to make the point that their political opponent within the group needs a "reality check," that she is unaware of who and what she really and most fundamentally is, that her consciousness needs raising.

This regimen and ideological stricture are normative and ideological politics masquerading as epistemology and ontology. This is one important reason why the often false, fraudulent, and dangerous rhetoric of social identity needs un-

60. Ibid., 341.

masking for the errors and fallacies it involves. The philosopher Julius Moravscik once wrote an article titled "Who Are We, What Ought We Care About, How Should We Live?" The progression implicit in that title illustrates the sort of slide that here concerns me. We need to take care lest the partisans of identity and identity politics, ignorant of the truth or unconcerned about it, invoke the ambiguous rhetoric of identity to put in place a meretricious and indefensible answer to the first question, thereby hoping to mask and prop up insupportable responses to the second, and ultimately to turn the third question to (frequently, extreme) political agendas. Whatever one thinks of those agendas' reasonableness and morality, one ought to join in rejecting the strategy's first moves as without theoretical justification.

6. Ethno-racial Skepticism and a Deflationary Approach to Racial and Ethnic Affiliation

Alcoff's self-described "defense" of "identity politics" does little to justify either the claim that ethnicity is identity or that ethnicity has normative importance. Let us distinguish three types, not at all mutually exclusive. We can call the first *existential racialists*. (That is, metaphysical realists about race.) They maintain that humanity is really divided into a variety of races; they think races exist in reality. The second we can call *normative racialists*. They hold that for many of us, our racial affiliation *ought* significantly guide our feelings, commitments, tastes, and the like. The third are *affective racialists*. In them, what they think to be their own or others' racial affiliation *does* significantly shape their preferences, projects, specialized affections, commitments, and so on. Here I have taken no position on the first type, and I maintain an agnosticism on race's reality, in contrast to Lucius Outlaw's naturalist realism and Appiah's and Zack's antirealism.[61] Rather, I have noted that, even setting aside the controversies over whether races really exist and claims of ethnic affiliation can be adequately clarified in their content and extension, racial and ethnic membership ought not be conceived as identities. On that basis, I suggest we regard ethno-racial classification of or by ourselves or others with a certain diffidence and skepticism. In this way, I hope to have done something toward undermining the grounds on which anyone might reasonably aspire to join either of the other types, the normative and affective racialists.

61. See Lucius Outlaw, *On Race and Philosophy* (New York: Routledge, 1996); Piper, "Higher-Order Discrimination," 285–309; Appiah, "Race, Culture, and Identity" and *Ethics of Identity;* and Zack, *Thinking about Race.*

In my view, neither Black for Black, White for Black, White for White, nor Black for White favoritism is inherently immoral. However, the latter two will rightly be more suspect in a society like ours, because they are apt to conceal genuine racism, which is not mere favoritism but hostility, contempt, or disregard. Those latter forms of favoritism, pro-White favoritism, are also more dangerous in a society with a history like this one's. Still, unquestioned, unreserved, and overemphasized attention to race is a bad thing. I should extend the same concern to ethnicity. Seeing Black advancement simply as a grab for power, rather than a demand to end the injustices of racial bias, demeans the cause. Justice is a virtue, and virtue is both a kind of reward in its own right and a possibility whose pursuit is *everyone's* responsibility.

It is tempting to say that race/ethnicity should be irrelevant to beliefs and tastes. I think this somewhat too strong, since having some beliefs, tastes, and habits of feeling may stem from such vices as contempt, ingratitude, disloyalty. Surely, there is something *especially* odious in an African-American descendant of slaves endorsing slavery or unrestricted majoritarianism, or maintaining that Black people are racially inferior and merit only such treatment. The chief reason seems to be that the history of slavery and Jim Crow is so recent and egregious in many instances that we can expect almost anyone, and especially an African-American, to know this history and to draw some obvious lessons. That is less a matter of racial loyalty or "identity" than of mere moral sensitivity and educability. It is a belief process, a conviction that anyone could and should have. That makes it different from supposing that, say, an African-American ought think or feel a certain way simply because others do, or that they should all draw the same conclusions from Black history.

Cases where it seems right to say of someone that she ought to do or feel or want because of her race or ethnicity are rare exceptions rather than the rule, and usually someone's drawing moral or other beliefs from her racial affiliation threatens to introduce irrelevant and irrational elements. Allowing ethnicity to matter very much to individual beliefs and tastes may also be bad *for the group*. That is because it may discourage innovation in thinking, in beliefs, in artistic forms, in cultural expressions, and so on. This is especially worrisome insofar as it afflicts the educated, on whom the group may depend for intellectual and cultural trailblazing.[62]

---

62. Thus, I disagree with the categorically hostile reaction—found in, for example, Paul King, "A Matter of Pride," *Emerge* (October 1997): 62, 64, 65—to Randall Kennedy's suggestions that special intraracial feelings of loyalty, affection, pride, and solidarity are morally problematic (Kennedy, "My Race Problem—And Ours," *Atlantic Monthly*, May 1997, 55–65). There, King, a Black businessman responding to Kennedy in a Black news magazine, maintains that "to reject racial kinship is to embrace self-hate." He accuses Kennedy of "promot[ing] . . . mentacide—a cultural suicide, of sorts, a psychological assas-

Appiah suggests what he calls "a more recreational conception of racial identity," which allows forms of identification that are "play[ful]" and "ironic," insisting,

> It is crucial to remember always that we are not simply black or white or yellow or brown, gay or straight or bisexual, Jewish, Christian, Moslem, Buddhist, or Confucian but that we are also brothers and sisters; parents and children; liberals, conservatives, and leftists; teachers and lawyers and auto-makers and gardeners; fans of the Padres and the Bruins; . . . students and teachers, friends and lovers.[63]

We do well to reflect on some items from Appiah's list of "identities" in light of what we have said. Being Jewish, Christian, Muslim, or a member of most other religious groups already and inherently involves accepting various moral standards and trying to live by them. To treat these religious affiliations as "identities" may help to capture the importance they properly have in someone's life. Surely, someone who subordinates her religion to her politics, ethnicity, or race, is foolish. Nevertheless, to conceive them as identities dangerously downplays the subject's ability to change her mind in both her beliefs and her commitments. To treat the sexual items on Appiah's list as identities errs in ways both similar and different. Where religion seems inherently serious, many of these sexual matters may be mere personal velleities and predilections, shading over into idiosyncrasies, quirks, kinks, even perversions. To regard them as identities is often hyperbolic, melodramatic at best. At worst, such misleading thinking can pose a serious obstacle to confronting personal vice and undertaking moral reform and reorientation. (When a Hannibal Lecter adopts an "identity" as a cannibal, this self-image imports extraneous matters into his self-conception and retards his ability to see his preference as a temptation to be resisted in practice whether or not he is able to reorient his tastes.) Such "identification" is part of a flight from reality into moral complacency, self-deceit, and evasion.

---

sination." More interesting is King's quoting the great playwright August Wilson as maintaining that "race matters [because] . . . it is the largest category of identification . . . the one that most influences your perception of yourself , and . . . the one to which others in the world of men most respond." King's claim that racial kinship feelings are necessary for Black survival would matter if it were clearly true. It is not, however, and the claim itself is ambiguous on whether it is individual Black people who need kinship if we are to survive or Black culture that needs it. However, even if there is such a culture and its perpetuation would be a good thing, two dubious assumptions, we need some explanation of why that hinges of feelings of racial kinship. The claim attributed to Wilson, also unsupported, seems to be without the intended normative import. It may well be that my race does matter psychologically and socially in that I and others make much of it, without it following that either I or they should. It is only the latter, normative thesis that Kennedy's position contradicts. (This is not the place for me to register my own disagreements with Kennedy's position.)

63. Appiah, "Race, Culture, and Identity," 103–4.

Gardening and fandom are merely recreational, as Appiah says, but therein they cannot really be "identities" in any serious and proper use of the term. The term *fan* derives from 'fanatic,' and the sensible fan must always live out her attachment in a way that is playful and touched with irony. She sees herself with detachment as acting, being silly, making much out of what she must, in a calm moment, acknowledge is really nothing. Such minimal good sense is perhaps rarer at times when adults make a point of holding on to such childish things as the expensive merchandise in any Disney store, but it is a requirement of reasonableness, if not sanity.

The other items on Appiah's list move closer to the heart of our moral lives, moral selves. For, I have elsewhere argued, any moral virtues or vices or duties or prerogatives or rights or claims that we have are ones that we have in virtue of and relative to such relationships as brother, sister, parent, offspring, lover, friend, or employee or employer (to adapt from Appiah's list), or citizen, or fellow (to go beyond it) or occupant of some similar role-relationships that define and constitute our moral lives.[64] It is not from the so-called "social identities" of what are called "race" or "gender" or "sexual orientation," nor ethnicity or socioeconomic class, that our moral features emerge, and they will not play a central role in the self-image (or other-images) of the morally sober person. In the end, what reflection on the place of identity in practical rationality indicates is that we should learn from what we can term a kind of "role-centering" in which the moral claims on anyone's concern are variously and differentially distributed among people in their various tighter and looser modes of connection to her.

The personal and interpersonal categories that matter most—that determine her moral virtues and duties—are those of friend, of fellow, of citizen, spouse, parent, offspring, and so on. These morally determinative roles are analogues of friendship, most of them forms of friendship. Some of these we choose to enter and occupy. All of them pose choices. Some we discover ourselves already to occupy. That discovery is a kind of achievement of reason, to be sure. However, it is not unaided reason, but reason informed by the responses Adam Smith and David Hume called "sympathy." That sympathy, feeling what the other feels, is a starting point. In an adequate theory, the Scotsmen's "sympathy" needs to transform itself into a critical benevolence, where we want (and are therein motivated to seek) for the other not simply what we imagine we would want in her place, nor what she happens to want, but what is objectively beneficial to

---

64. For more on this conception of morality, see, among other works, García, "The Primacy of the Virtuous," *Philosophia* 20 (1990): 69–91, and "Interpersonal Virtues: Whose Interests Do They Serve?" *American Catholic Philosophical Quarterly* 71 (1997): 31–60.

her, rooted in a reflective understanding of human beings, our needs and capacities, and pursued in light of our varied connections also to others. This involves intellectual virtues that may themselves be forms of moral virtues.[65]

All this need not exclude—indeed, it recommends and even requires—forms of affection, community, pride, and solidarity.[66] Most fundamentally these will be universalized and contextually nuanced, in community with each Other, especially those close enough to work with in joint efforts against hatred, injustice, disrespect, and the effects of past hatred, injustice, and disrespect. It ought also to involve specialized emotional attachment to victims and their plight. We need not deny the possibility that race and ethnicity might sometimes serve as crude markers for some of the forms of solidarity suitable to such life. Still, no endorsement of anything that merits the name of 'identity' ought be recognized here.

Recognizing that there is a gap between the doubts I have cast on ethnicity and identity and any positive program, let me sketch some positive suggestions about identity, emotion, and ethno-racial categories. They are, I think, not merely compatible with my critique, but consonant with it and in its spirit. My suggestions are that we strive toward what might be called ethno-racial skepticism and a deflationary conception of race and ethnicity. The ethno-racial skeptic recognizes and takes account of the fact that we are very unclear about the extension and content of ethnic and racial affiliations. We do not know at this stage whether we should say races exist at all, and even ethnicity is a complicated notion, perhaps caught in unavoidable and vicious circularity with the vague notion of ethnic culture. I think we might generally do better to replace as much as possible such putative, ascribed affiliations with more restrained talk of ethnic (and, more problematically, racial) *background,* especially ancestry. We ought often simply to say that someone today is of this or that background, rather than flatly that she *is* this or that ethnicity. That is better because it seems more likely that ethnic groups used to have distinct and separate cultures and memberships than they do now.

Substituting 'What is NN's ethnic ancestry?' for 'What is NN?' (in the sense of 'What is NN's ethnic identity or ethnicity?') helps avoid some of the pitfalls that lurk here. The former question has a clearer answer (though often more complex and compound), and avoids raising such pseudo-problems as whether these collective identities are discovered or invented (by the members them-

65. It likely will also require revivified study of human nature—informed by the natural and social sciences, but resolutely philosophical—perhaps of the sort recently undertaken by Alasdair MacIntyre. See especially *Dependent Rational Animals* (Chicago: Open Court, 1999).

66. On solidarity as a moral virtue, see Pope John Paul II, *Sollicitudo Rei Socialis,* Encyclical Letter, 1987.

selves or by others). Similarly, we ought to say that this person is more typical of Latinas/os, Black people, or some other ethno-racial group than is that one—more similar to most others we assign to the group—in her name, her language, her musical, or literary tastes, among other things, instead of following Corlett in saying flatly that the one is "more Latina/o" (more Black, White, and so on), is closer to the group's core, or has a stronger ethno-racial identity. It is only the former sort of claim that we can know, and we do well to restrict ourselves to these facts rather than using them as bases for the more politically and metaphysically loaded claims Corlett wants.

Second, the deflationary approach does not comfortably fit the way some liberals talk of each individual's determining her own 'way of being' Black or Latina/o.[67] This idea is well-meaning in its fight to free individuals from imposed ethno-racial scripts, but it remains unacceptable because it suggests that being Black (or Latina, etc.) is an (ongoing) activity that can be conducted in different manners, styles, or methods. Rather, it is simply a static (and, I think, contra Corlett, nonintensive) condition of group inclusion, and something that a person cannot normally acquire or lose during her lifetime. Even if the group ceases to exist as such, through some natural or artificial calamity (e.g., genocide), it still remains true that she is of that (recently existing) people.

Third, in a deflationary account, ethno-racial special ties of pride, loyalty, fellow-feeling, and solidarity are best regarded and realized as normally morally neutral (neither obligatory nor preferable); as without major significance; as impermanent; as light-hearted and low-key when sensible; as tolerant, appreciative, and uncritical, not only with respect to others' ethnic affiliations but also to other responses/attitudes that people (within or without one's own group) do or might have to their ethnicity. Further, they should be regarded as matters to be treated not very seriously (i.e., as largely inconsequential) in their positive role (as projects, aspirations, or simply as found inclinations), but with constant and grave awareness of their potential for mischief; as external to the moral self rather than constitutive of it; as not at all determinative of moral, political, or religious commitments, but of only minor and indirect relevance to them (as when reflection on the history of African-Americans sensitizes one in general to dangers of deference to majorities); and as shallow in both the self-image (that is, what is often mischaracterized as someone's "identity") of a sober-thinking person and in her view of others. Finally I suggest that we view these ethno-racial ties as integrated with other commitments and always subordinated to universal moral projects (self-control and self-development, loving service to persons),

---

67. This is a recurrent theme in Appiah, "Race, Culture, and Identity" and, even more, in *Ethics of Identity.*

to cooperative moral partnerships, and to morally definitive role-relationships. If notions of race and ethnicity are legitimately to persist they will need to be pruned of their normative pretensions.

To say all this, of course, is only to gesture toward the work needed. A serious treatment of the supposed moral claims inherent in ethnic or racial identity would require some complexity. At least three types of 'ought' judgment, for example, seem involved in questions of whether Black people ought to have the sort of special feelings of racial kinship, pride, loyalty, and solidarity sometimes gathered (misleadingly, I think) under the rubric 'racial identity.' The first is moral, usually indicating moral obligation, but sometimes supererogation. The second is sociopolitical, perhaps distinguishable from the moral, and rooted in assumed net beneficial social effects for fighting racism or, alternatively, in the value thought to inhere in the self-realization of Black people as a people, an organic and collective self. The third type of 'ought' judgment is self-interested, and especially tied to alleged benefits to psychological health, as in some social psychologists' racial identity theory.

In addition to these differences in the source of 'ought' judgments, there are also differences in their stringency. Thus an adequate treatment of the morality of racial pride and special affection would also need to distinguish the question of whether racial kinship, and so on, are permitted or forbidden, from that of whether they are desirable (in themselves or for their effects), from that of whether they are supererogatory, and from that of whether the lack of such feelings of kinship is forbidden or even undesirable (what some have called "suberogatory"). Finally, it is likely that no overall answer can be given, especially not in abstraction from an individual's personal situation and the group's historical context. We should acknowledge that so-called "racial identity" or "racial solidarity" may need to be disaggregated for moral analysis and evaluation. Perhaps the morality of feelings of racial loyalty (and actions therefrom) is different from that of racial pride, or of special racial affection, or favoritism. This is also likely to be affected both by a group's history and social situation, and the individual's own.

The skeptical and deflationary approaches combine to capture some of the substance and goal of Appiah's call for "recreational" forms of ethno-racial identity, recognized as contingent, shaped by individual choice, lived in irony and playfulness. However, they dispense entirely with the claim, which even Appiah could not bring himself to abandon, that ethnicity and race do or ought to constitute forms of collective identity. Instead, the approach suggested here substitutes questions and claims about ethno-racial background for ones simplistically assigning someone today to this or that race or ethnicity. Likewise, it replaces the claims that someone is more Latina/o (or Black, etc.) than another, closer to the group's core or essence with the weaker and less problematic claims that one person is more typical than is another of members of their group in this or that respect. Finally, it takes some steps toward sketching and defending a more detailed strategy for collapsing the airs and limiting the dangers or ethnic and racial affiliation.

The core of anyone's self-image (and of others' image of her) should be the core of the self. That includes, first, those features of the self that do not vary across times and across possible situations (as ethnicity and race may, and are especially prone to do if, as is so commonly said nowadays, they are "socially constructed"). Second, it comprises those which have the greatest impact on moral virtues, duties, and the like. Such self-images may allow us to achieve internal coherence of self without ethnic or racial purity.[68]

This is not to endorse some fashionable cosmopolitanism. Among the problems in cosmopolitanism, and in the "irony" that attends it in Appiah, Rorty, and others, is that the cosmos, the world, is made to do the work of community in giving people a sense of belonging and of joint striving, something it is simply too large to do, unless we adopt certain special cosmological assumptions. We will need smaller or, at least, more unified groupings. However, ethnicities, especially in this age of diaspora, are ill suited to fill this role. And this is all the more true if the doubts I have raised about the very notion of ethno-racial identity have any plausibility. Another difficulty is that cosmopolitanism allows too great a role to each individual to define herself and her identity. That again, is unrealistic, especially with regard to ethnicity. Someone's choosing to be a Latina/o does nothing to make her one. Obviously it does not, if she has no Latina/o ancestors. However, even if she does, the choice cannot affect a category that inherently involves her lineage. At the extreme, this could assign siblings, even identical twins reared together, to different ethnic groups.[69]

What we need, perhaps, is a new interpersonalist personalism, stressing self- (and other-) images that emphasize the status of someone as a human being, as a rational animal, or even as a creature of God, among other concepts, with a past, an inherent nature, existing always with other persons in relationships of dependence and concern, which relationships are also normatively significant vocations, containing the clues from which someone can come to understand who she is and what suits (or behooves or becomes or fits) such a one. Glenn

68. This is what Alcoff seems to seek. See Alcoff, "Mestizo Identity," in *American Mixed Race: The Culture of Microdiversity,* edited by Naomi Zack (Lanham, MD: Rowman and Littlefield, 1995), 257–78; "Who's Afraid of Identity Politics?" and *Visible Identities.*

69. Corlett's view allows that, while someone's choice *by itself* does nothing to determine whether she is a Latina/o, her choice is likely causally to affect *how* Latino/a she is, by prompting her to act, (and to get herself to) feel, and think as Latinos/as do. Of course, I suggested above that Corlett's view is implausible conceptually and problematic in its normative guidance.

Loury has written, "The most important challenges and opportunities confronting any person arise not from his racial condition, but from our common human condition."[70] Extending Loury's point beyond race to ethnicity, we can agree that humans are "identical in essentials, different only in details. . . . It is a great—if common—moral and political error to advance the view that a person's race is his most important characteristic." Our being as persons is always being-with, being-in-relationship-to. Yet the relationships and roles that constitute our moral lives are not and ought not be seen in ethno-racial terms.

Despite what is almost routinely said, it is implausible to maintain that race or ethnicity, or the cultures with which some associate them, can give "meaning" to its participants' (members') lives.[71] There is reason to think these notions simply too vague, ill-defined, shifting, and indeterminate in content to play a central role in any self-image in which someone is well advised to invest. In any case, merely following what others have done, conforming to accepted patterns, and so on, is insufficient to justify beliefs, feelings, desires, or actions, let alone to insure their meaningfulness. (Note that it is merely a bad pun to maintain that cultures provide standards of meaningful life on the grounds that they are themselves systems of symbols and thus of meaning. One could as fallaciously argue that because we can assign semantic meaning to someone's words, s/he cannot be nonetheless chattering meaninglessly, in the sense of incoherently or pointlessly.) It is unclear just what such meaning is, but it would appear to need some higher validation than custom and an ill-justified sense of "belonging" can provide. If any immanent meaning for human life is possible, which is doubtful enough, these poor materials cannot suffice.[72]

70. Glenn Loury, "Individualism before Multiculturalism," *Public Interest* (Fall 1995): 92–106.

71. See, for example, Outlaw, *Race and Philosophy,* "Introduction"; and esp. Kuper, *Culture,* chap. 3, on Geertz; and Appiah, *Ethics of Identity.*

72. I am grateful to Linda Martín Alcoff, Lawrence Blum, J. Angelo Corlett, Sally Haslanger, and others for sharing with me their writings and thinking on these topics, and to audiences at Boston University's Institute on Race and Social Division (IRSD), University of Notre Dame, Boston College, Calvin College, Baylor University, at a session organized by the American Philosophical Association's Committee on Hispanics at the 1999 APA Eastern Division Meeting in Boston, and at the 1999 Ford Fellows Conference in Washington, for discussion of earlier versions of some of this material. Tommy Lott offered helpful commentary on some of this material at the University of San Francisco's 2001 Conference, Passions of the Color Line, and on that occasion I also profited from Paula Moya's suggestions. Jorge J. E. Gracia read and commented on an entire draft, while Jerome Veith provided research assistance. I appreciate their help and the contributions of an audience at the 2005 State University at Buffalo conference, Black Ethnicity, Latino Race? I am also indebted to Rutgers University's Competitive Leave Fellowship Program, to Boston College, and to IRSD for supporting my research on these topics over several years. This essay is dedicated to the memory of Pope John Paul II, whose splendid life ended the weekend of the Buffalo conference. His last book treated some of the issues with which my colleagues and I here wrestle.

CHAPTER 3

Individuation of Racial and Ethnic Groups: The Problems of Circularity and Demarcation

JORGE J. E. GRACIA

There is no shortage of contradictory answers to a question that is implicit in the title of this chapter: Can racial and ethnic groups be effectively individuated? The affirmative answer is particularly common among those who subscribe to an essentialistic and realistic conception of these groups. By essentialistic I mean that the members of the groups are taken to have common properties that function as necessary and sufficient conditions of group identity and membership. By realistic I mean that groups and their properties are considered to be real entities in the world, not mere concepts or imaginings. In the case of races, the properties of the racial groups or their members are frequently taken to be physical or mental, whether involving gross morphology or intellectual capacities.[1] Blacks, for example, are thought to have a certain skin color, hair texture, and intellectual capacities. In the case of ethnic groups, the properties that mark membership have been sometimes understood to be physical, but most often they involve cultural differences, such as values and attitudes.[2]

---

1. For the discussion of these views, see L. Luka Cavalli-Sforza et al., *History and Geography of Human Genes* (Princeton: Princeton University Press, 1994), 17; Stanley M. Garn, "Modern Human Populations," in *The New Encyclopedia Britannica* (Chicago: Encyclopedia Britannica, 1993), 844; M. Guibernau, *Nationalisms: The Nation-State and Nationalism in the Twentieth Century* (Cambridge: Polity, 1996), 86; W. E. B. Du Bois, *The Conservation of Races* (Washington, DC: American Negro Academy, 1897), rep. in *W. E. B. Du Bois Speaks: Speeches and Addresses 1890–1919,* ed. Philip S. Foner (New York: Pathfinders Press, 1970); Bernard Boxill, introduction to *Race and Racism,* ed. Bernard Boxill (Oxford: Oxford University Press, 2001), 7; and Pierre L. van den Berghe, *Race and Racism: A Comparative Perspective* (New York: Wiley, 1967), 9–10, and "Does Race Matter?" in *Race and Racism,* ed. Boxill, 104. Among important historical figures who have held views of this sort are Hegel, Blumenbach, Kant, Voltaire, de Gobineau, and Bernier.

2. See the discussion of these views in Anthony Appiah, "'But Would That Still Be Me?' Notes on Gender, 'Race,' Ethnicity, as Sources of 'Identity,'" *Journal of Philosophy* 87 (1990): 493–99; Clifford Geertz,

Hispanics, for example, are often thought to have darker skin than Anglo Saxons, and to put a special value on the family. From the essentialist/realist perspective, the affirmative answer to the question of individuation of these groups, then, is given in terms of these properties. Blacks are individuated by their skin color, say, whereas Hispanics are individuated by their emphasis on family values.

The negative answer is particularly common among those who conceive racial and ethnic groups as "imagined communities," to use a favorite expression in the literature.[3] There is no fixed set of properties belonging to a racial or ethnic group or their members. Rather, there is a sense of group identity that has developed among members of the groups themselves, or that has been imposed on them by others.[4] No fact of the matter characterizes these groups or serves the purpose of determining membership. Races and ethne have no essence and there is no reality that corresponds to the ideas of the groups or their presumed common properties. Races and ethne are mere concepts resulting from social construction—whence the term 'conceptualism' used to describe this position. From this perspective, individuation becomes difficult if not impossible, and many of those who agree with this judgment go on to argue that efforts in this direction are futile and must be abandoned.[5]

Recently, the tide of scholarship has favored the negative answer. Essentialism and realism with respect to racial and ethnic groups has been on the de-

"The Integrative Revolution," in *Old Societies and New States: The Quest for Modernity in Asia and Africa,* ed. Clifford Geertz (New York: Free Press, 1963), 1–26; William Peterson, "Concepts of Ethnicity," in *Concepts of Ethnicity,* ed. William Peterson et al. (Cambridge: Harvard University Press, 1982); Nathan Glazer and Daniel P. Moynihan, eds., *Ethnicity: Theory and Experience* (Cambridge: Harvard University Press, 1975), 4; Audrey Smedley, *Race in North America: Origin and Evolution of a World View* (Boulder, CO: Westview Press, 1993), 30; Fredrik Barth, ed., *Ethnic Groups and Boundaries: The Social Organization of Culture Difference* (Oslo: Universitetsforlaget, 1969); Thomas Hyland Eriksen, *Ethnicity and Nationalism: Anthropological Perspectives* (London: Pluto, 1993), 10–12; Richard Jenkins, "Ethnicity Etcetera: Social Anthropological Points of View," in *Ethnic and Racial Studies Today,* ed. Martin Bulmer and John Solomos (London: Routledge, 1999), 88; and van den Berghe, *Race and Racism,* 9–10, and "Does Race Matter?" 104.

3. Benedict Anderson, *Imagined Communities: Reflections on the Origin and Spread of Nationalism* (London: Verso, 1983; rev. ed., 1990).

4. See discussions of this position in Harold R. Isaacs, "Basic Group Identities," in *Ethnicity,* ed. Glazer and Moynihan, 34–35; Talcott Parsons, "Some Theoretical Considerations on the Nature and Trends of Change of Ethnicity," in *Ethnicity,* ed. Glazer and Moynihan, 56; Donald L. Horowitz, "Ethnic Identity," in *Ethnicity,* ed. Glazer and Moynihan, 113; Milton Gordon, *Assimilation in American Life* (New York: Oxford University Press, 1964); Anthony Smith, "Structure and Persistence in *Ethne,*" in *The Ethnicity Reader: Nationalism, Multiculturalism, and Migration,* ed. M. Guibernau and J. Rex (Cambridge: Polity Press, 1997), 27; and Michael E. Brown, "Causes and Implications of Ethnic Conflict," in *The Ethnicity Reader,* ed. Guibernau and Rex, 81–82.

5. See, for example, the sustained argument of Anthony Appiah, "Race, Culture, Identity: Misunderstood Connections," in Appiah and Amy Gutmann, *Color Conscious: The Political Morality of Race* (Princeton: Princeton University Press, 1996), 30–105.

fensive, if not altogether vanquished. Genetic discoveries seem to support the flimsiness of a biological conception of race, a fact that has also helped erode the essentialistic and realistic view of ethne.[6] Some go so far as to question the cogency of the concepts of race and ethnos. And yet talk about races and ethne is common not just in ordinary discourse, but also among academics of various stripes.[7] Moreover, this talk is not just general, that is, about race and ethnicity as such, but particular, about such racial or ethnic groups as Blacks, African Americans, Jews, Hispanics, Latinos, and Puerto Ricans. If in fact the individuation of these groups is not possible, what sense can this talk have? Could the concepts that are supposed to correspond to the linguistic terms in question have any value when the entities to which they refer cannot be effectively individuated? Add to this that many social and political projects depend on the effective individuation of these groups and identification of their members. Affirmative action policies, for example, do not seem to be able to be effectively implemented otherwise. Indeed, as Angelo Corlett has pointed out, such policies require that we "provide means by which persons can identify themselves accurately."[8]

It would appear, then, that only if there are acceptable alternatives to essentialism/realism and nonessentialism/conceptualism can we hope to account for the individuation of racial and ethnic groups. Essentialism/realism can account for individuation, but it is a discredited view. And nonessentialism/conceptualism appears to be unable to account for individuation.

One such attempt is what I call the "Familial-Historical View" of race and ethnicity.[9] However, two important objections have been advanced against this particular theory. Both question the effectiveness with which the theory ac-

6. For discussion of this view, see Appiah, "The Uncompleted Argument: Du Bois and the Illusion of Race," *Critical Inquiry* 12 (1985): 23ff., and "But Would That Still Be Me?" 496–97; Bob Carter, *Realism and Racism: Concepts of Race in Sociological Research* (London: Routledge, 2000), 157; Michael Omi and Howard Winant, *Racial Formation in the United States: From the 1960s to the 1990s*, 2nd ed., (New York: Routledge, 1994), 56ff.; David Brion Davis, "Constructing Race: A Reflection," *William and Mary Quarterly* 54 (1997): 7; Lewontin, "Race," in *Encyclopedia Americana* (Danbury, CN: Grolier), 23:116–22; Cavalli-Sforza et al., *History and Geography* (Princeton: Princeton University Press, 1994), 19–20; and Naomi Zack, "Race and Philosophic Meaning," in *Race and Racism*, ed. Boxill, 43–58.

7. The controversy about whether the scientific talk about race makes sense or not goes on. For some recent discussions, see Robin O. Andreasen, "The Meaning of 'Race': Folk Conceptions and the New Biology of Race," *Journal of Philosophy* 102 (2005): 94–106, and "A New Perspective on the Race Debate," *British Journal for the Philosophy of Science* 49 (1998): 199–225; Joshua M. Glasgow, "On the New Biology of Race," *Journal of Philosophy* 100 (2003): 456–74.

8. J. Angelo Corlett, *Race, Racism, and Reparations* (Ithaca: Cornell University Press, 2002) 16.

9. I first defended this view in the context of ethnicity in Gracia, *Hispanic/Latino Identity: A Philosophical Perspective,* (Oxford: Blackwell, 2000), chap. 3, and I further elaborate on it and develop it in the context of race in *Surviving Race, Ethnicity, and Nationality: A Challenge for the Twenty-First Century* (Lanham, MD: Rowman and Littlefield, 2005). A familial version of race has been defended by Anna Stubblefield in *Ethics along the Color Line* (Ithaca: Cornell University Press, 2005), chap. 5.

counts for the individuation of races and ethne. I call the first argument "the Circularity Objection." It has been proposed by Anthony Appiah against the use of the theory in connection with racial groups.[10] I call the second argument "the Demarcation Objection." It has been advanced by Richard Bernstein against the use of the theory in the context of ethnic groups.[11]

These two objections are important in the current philosophical conversation because they arise within two different, but significant, philosophical traditions—analytic and Continental—and yet they express related concerns. Their proponents are distinguished philosophers whose opinions carry considerable weight within the American academy, and their criticisms have had an impact on recent discussions of race. By concentrating on these objections I hope to emphasize the need to discuss the arguments used in the conversation on race and ethnicity. Frequently, discussions of these topics are centered on the value of particular views, neglecting to some extent the evaluation of the arguments used to support or undermine them.

My purpose here is to show that the Familial-Historical View is in fact immune to these objections. The aim of this essay, then, is quite limited. I do not present a full exposition of the Familial-Historical View, nor a defense of it against other kinds of objections that can be, or have in fact been, brought up against it.[12] Nor do I make a case for the way in which the Familial-Historical View accounts for the individuation of racial and ethnic groups. To do these things would require much more space than is available in an essay. I merely sketch the most pertinent aspects of the Familial-Historical View and show how it can respond to the Circularity and Demarcation Objections.[13]

1. The Familial-Historical View

The fundamental tenet of the Familial-Historical View pertinent for the discussion of the Circularity and Demarcation Objections is that racial and ethnic

---

10. Appiah, "The Uncompleted Argument." Integrated, with the title "Illusions of Race," as chap. 2, in *In My Father's House: Africa in the Philosophy of Culture* (Oxford: Oxford University Press, 1992).

11. Richard Bernstein, "Comment on *Hispanic/Latino Identity* by J. J. E. Gracia," *Philosophy and Social Criticism* 27, no. 2 (2001): 44–50.

12. For other aspects of the view and the answer to some other objections, see Gracia, *Hispanic/Latino Identity.*

13. There have been various interpretations and discussion of these objections in the literature. For a recent interesting attempt to answer the Circularity objection, see Paul Taylor, "Appiah's Uncompleted Argument: W. E. B. Du Bois and the Reality of Race," *Social Theory and Practice* 26 (2000): 103–28. Taylor's strategy is to argue that Appiah's objection is unsuccessful as long as history is not understood globally, as the history of a race, but individually, as the history of the individuals who compose the racial group.

groups are best conceived as extended historical families. Alexander Crummell and W. E. B. Du Bois were the first to make use of this notion, and they did it in the context of race. The first gives only a very sketchy idea of what he has in mind, and therefore is of no help to us here.[14] But Du Bois is more specific. After rejecting the nineteenth-century biological view of race, he presents his sociological position in an often quoted passage:

> the history of the world is the history, not of individuals, but of groups, not of nations, but of races. . . . What then is a race? *It is a vast family of human beings,* generally common blood and language, *always common history, traditions and impulses,* who are both voluntarily and involuntarily striving together for the accomplishment of certain more or less vividly conceived ideals of life.[15]

A race is a family that always has a common history, traditions, and impulses, although other things like language and blood also enter into the mix. Elsewhere Du Bois returns to the kinship provided by history:

> But one thing is sure and that is the fact that since the fifteenth century *these ancestors of mine and their descendants have had a common history;* have suffered a common disaster and have one long memory. The actual ties of heritage between the individuals of this group vary with the ancestors that they have in common with many others. . . . But the physical bond is least and the badge of color relatively unimportant save as a badge; *the real essence of this kinship is its social heritage* of slavery; the discrimination and insult; and this heritage binds together not simply the children of Africa, but extends through yellow Asia and into the South Seas.[16]

Still, this is not enough. Du Bois does not dwell much on what exactly he means by a racial family, nor is he specific about what he means by history and the pertinent aspects of it for his view. This has led to a number of criticisms and interpretations of his position. Is he an essentialist or a nonessentialist? He seems to waver.[17] If his view is essentialistic, then it would be of no help to us here insofar as we need an alternative to essentialism that is immune to the criticisms against this position. And if it is not essentialistic, then we need more than he gave us to be able to meet the Circularity and Demarcation Objections.

I propose, then, to present the version of the Familial-Historical View I have

---

14. For Crummell, see Appiah, *In My Father's House,* chap. 1.
15. Du Bois, *Conservation of Races,* 74. My emphasis.
16. Du Bois, *Dusk of Dawn: An Essay Toward an Autobiography of a Race Concept* (New York: Harcourt, Brace, 1940), 117. My emphasis.
17. See Appiah's discussion in *In My Father's House,* chap. 2.

defended elsewhere, for two reasons.[18] First, it is more developed, containing some of the specific elements missing in Du Bois, although much of it is implied by his insight. Second, I believe it can effectively answer the objections based on the difficulties posed by the individuation of races and ethne.

The fundamental tenet of the Familial-Historical View is that the members of racial and ethnic groups need not have an identifiable property (or set of properties) that is shared by all the members throughout the existence of the groups. This accounts for the lack of agreement concerning any particular conditions, or even kinds of conditions, that are necessary and sufficient for particular races or ethne. People can't agree on any because generally there aren't any. Even a superficial consideration points to difficulties in the identification of any such conditions. What are the properties common to all Blacks, or Hispanics, or Jews? Skin color has been historically paramount when identifying Blacks, but there are Blacks whose skin color is lighter than that of many Whites. Language is frequently taken as the distinguishing feature of Hispanics, but many Hispanics do not speak Spanish at all, and others speak it very badly. Religion is often cited as what holds Jews together as a group, but many Jews do not practice a religion or even believe in God. Indeed, who counts as Black or Hispanic changes from place to place. Some people who are thought to be White in Cuba, for example, are classified as Black in the United States.

In response to these difficulties, the Familial-Historical View proposes that we must abandon the project of trying to conceive racial and ethnic groups in terms of discernible common properties, and keep in mind that the properties in question are significant first-order properties. I am not speaking about trivial properties such as the property of belonging to the group, or second-order properties such as identity. I mean phenotypical or genotypical properties, such as skin color, attitudes, or genetic traits. This means, in turn, that in order to belong to one of these groups it is not necessary that one share a property (or set of properties) with other members of the group.[19] Blacks can have light skin and be Black; Hispanics can lack Spanish fluency and be Hispanics; and Jews can be atheists and be Jews. Indeed, contrary to what some philosophers and sociologists think, it is not even necessary that the members of the groups name themselves in particular ways or have a conscious sense of belonging to the group. Some of them may in fact consider themselves so and even have a consciousness, or sense, of themselves as a group, but it is not necessary that all of them do. After all, children and people suffering from Alzheimer's disease can-

---

18. As developed in Gracia, *Hispanic/Latino Identity* and *Surviving Race*.

19. This explains why, in his attempt to characterize ethnicity, Weber concluded that it is not feasible to go beyond vague generalizations. Max Weber, "What Is an Ethnic Group?" in *The Ethnicity Reader*, ed. Guibernau and Rex, 22, 24.

not be expected to have a sense of group identity and yet their membership in the racial and ethnic groups to which they are taken to belong is not questioned for that reason.

According to the Familial-Historical View, the members of a race or an ethnos are tied by the same kind of thing that ties the members of a family. There may not be any common properties to all of them, but nonetheless they belong to the same group because they are related, as a father is to a daughter, an aunt to a nephew, and grandparents to grandchildren. The metaphor of the family is helpful here, but we must be clear that this metaphor does not require genetic ties. One does not need to be tied by descent to other members of a family to be a member of the family. Indeed, perhaps the most important foundation of a family, namely marriage, takes place between persons who are not related by descent but by contract. And in-laws become members of families indirectly, again not through genesis. This seems to work well for ethne, although racial groups seem to require a genetic tie. The issue of whether they do or not will not affect the defense I will mount in response to the objections brought against the Familial-Historical View of race, however. So I will not discuss it here.

This means also that any requirements of coherence and homogeneity do not apply.[20] Families are not coherent wholes composed of homogeneous elements; they include members that differ substantially from each other and may clash in various ways. Physical features vary widely within the same family, and views of the world, politics, and religion, for example, can be quite opposed. Contrary to Corlett, descent does not appear to be a necessary condition of membership in *all* ethnic groups, even if it may be so in some and in the case of racial groups.[21] Families are related clusters persons with different, and sometimes incompatible, properties, and homogeneity of is not one of their necessary conditions.

This does not entail that other factors do not play roles in particular contexts in the constitution of racial or ethnic groups, contributing both to their creation and preservation. To deny that they do would be to be blind to reality. According to the Familial-Historical View, history generates relations that in turn generate properties among members of groups and serve to unite them among themselves and to distinguish them from others in particular contexts. The use of the Spanish language is one of the properties that unites many Hispanics and can serve to distinguish them from other ethnic groups in certain contexts. Some Hispanics in the Southwest are united by their knowledge of Spanish and this serves also to distinguish them from Anglos who live in that part of the country. These people speak Spanish as a result of certain historical events, such

20. However, it is common to use racial and ethnic labels to homogenize. For the literature on ethnicity in particular, see Suzanne Oboler, *Ethnic Labels / Latino Lives: Identity and the Politics of (Re)presentation in the United States* (Minneapolis: University of Minnesota Press, 1995).

21. For Corlett's view, see *Race, Racism and Reparations*.

as the invasion and colonization of the Southwest by Spaniards in the sixteenth century. Had these events not occurred, these people would not know any Spanish or have any claim to be Hispanics. Certain historical events, then, established particular relations that in turn generated a linguistic property.

Although historical events and relations tend to generate common properties, such properties might not go beyond certain periods, regions, or subgroups of people: a may follow b, and b may follow c, and c may follow d, implying a connection between a and d even when a has no property in common with d. Let me explain this further. Consider the case of a, b, c, and d in which a has a relation (aR_1b) with b; b has a relation (bR_2c) with c; and c has a relation (cR_3d) with d, but the relation between any two of these is not the same. This does not entail that there is an immediate relation between a and c or d, or between b and d. (In order to simplify matters I assume that the relation between a and b is the same as the relation between b and a, and so on with the others.) Now, the mentioned relations allow us to group a, b, c, and d even though there is no property common to all of them, not even a relation that unites them directly. There is, however, a relation between a and b, another between b and c, and another between c and d. At the same time, these relations allow us to separate the group $abcd$ from other groups, say $mnop$, because none of the members of $abcd$ has relations with the members of $mnop$, or because, although they may have relations with $mnop$, the relations between a, b, c, and d are different from the relations between m, n, o, and p. Group identity entails both unity and distinction in a world of multiplicity such as ours, and unity and distinction are easily understandable when there are properties common to all the members of a group, but such properties are not necessary. The unity and distinction of a group can be explained as long as there are relations or properties that tie each member of the group with at least one other member without assuming that there are common properties to all members.

This is the kind of unity in terms of which the Familial-Historical View proposes to explain racial and ethnic groups. The unity of these groups does not involve commonality; it is a familial-historical unity founded on relations and the properties to which they give rise in context. This is one reason why these groups are neither permanent nor closed communities. Races and ethne are fluid, open, and changing. In the case of ethne in particular, members come and go, enter and leave, as they forge new relations among themselves and with members of other groups, depending on particular and contingent circumstances.[22] Du Bois, then, had the right idea: a race is like a family, tied by a history. But is this view cogent?

22. The fluidity of ethnic groups has been recognized by Joan Vincent, "The Structure of Ethnicity," *Human Organization* 33, no. 4 (1974): 376; E. P. Thompson, *The Making of the English Working Class* (New York: Pantheon, 1963), 9; and Thomas Jenkins, "Ethnicity Etcetera: Social Anthropological Points of

2. The Circularity and Demarcation Objections

Now let me turn to the two objections that are the topic of this chapter: Circularity and Demarcation. Both are formulated in terms of the individuation of groups.

A. Circularity

The Circularity Objection is presented by Appiah in the context of his criticism of Du Bois's view of race. As we saw above, the core of Du Bois's position is that races are like families and need to be understood historically. A history is the key to racial identity, the distinctions among races, and racial group membership.

To this, Appiah objects that this claim is circular insofar as the individuation of a race by its history presupposes the individuation of the history by the race. He puts it thus:

> When we *recognize* two events as belonging to the history of one race, we have to have a criterion for membership in the race at those two times, independent of the participation of the members in the two events. To put it more simply: sharing a common group history cannot be a criterion for being members of the same group, for we would have to be able *to identify* the group in order to identify *its* history. . . . Du Bois' reference to a common history cannot be doing any work in his *individuation* of races.[23]

B. Demarcation

The Demarcation Objection is raised by Bernstein in his criticism of my view of Hispanic ethnicity.[24] The difficulty concerns demarcation, that is, the way to determine who qualifies as Hispanic. The Familial-Historical View, Bernstein claims, does not provide sufficient guidance in this respect. He frames the argument in terms of the use of history my theory makes.[25] History, he objects, is not specific or particular enough to be able to distinguish Hispanics from other ethnic groups. History is general: it can be your history or mine, this history or that. So the view that historical relations individuate (or "particularize," as he puts it) Hispanics and account for membership in the group fails.

View," in *Racial and Ethnic Studies Today,* ed. Martin Bulmer and John Solomos (London: Routledge, 1999), 90, among many others.

23. Appiah, "The Uncompleted Argument," 27. My emphasis, except on 'its.'
24. Bernstein, "Comment on *Hispanic / Latino Identity,*" 44–50.
25. Ibid., 49.

Bernstein is aware, of course, that when I apply the Familial-Historical View to Hispanics, I speak not of history in general, but of "our history," that is, of the history of Hispanics. But he argues that I need to point out to something that turns "history" into "our history," and that the Familial-Historical View does not effectively do this because it denies that there are common properties to the group of Hispanics and the notion of family it uses to further clarify the issue is ineffective without such properties.

From this it would seem that Bernstein's objection is similar to Appiah's: history cannot individuate ethnic groups (races for Appiah), because history itself needs to be individuated. However, Bernstein's argument is not the same as Appiah's. His objection is not that the Familial-Historical View is circular, for he believes it need not be, provided that one identifies a group's sense of history as what individuates the history of the group. In short, he accepts the Familial-Historical View's tenet that ethnic groups are individuated by their history, but he objects that this view as articulated by me does not identify a sense of history as the individuator of history.

Do the Circularity and Demarcation Objections defeat the Familial-Historical View? Before we can answer this question, we need to make sure that we understand the exact force of the objections. One major difficulty with this is the vagueness of the notion of individuation. Both objections use this notion, but we are not quite sure of what is meant by it. The reason is that individuation is not only frequently debated, but also understood in different ways in the literature. This lack of uniformity generates ambiguities that we need to avoid.[26] So let me briefly turn to individuation.

3. Individuation Clarified

Individuation is frequently understood in at least two ways.[27] In one, it has to do with the conditions that must be satisfied for something *to be* individual. This is a metaphysical understanding of it, so let us call it "metaphysical individuation." In this way, we speak of the individuation of this 2×4 card as the process involved in the satisfaction of certain conditions that establish the card's individuality.

---

26. Apart from the sources to which reference will be made later, see Ofelia Schutte's comments in her discussion of racial and ethnic identity in "Negotiating Latina Identities," in *Hispanics / Latinos in the United States: Race, Ethnicity, and Rights,* ed. Jorge J. E. Gracia and Pablo De Greiff (New York: Routledge, 2000), 61–76. Several other articles in the same collection illustrate the variety of uses to which the term *individuation* is put in the context of races and ethne in particular.

27. In a third way, individuation is also understood linguistically to refer to conditions that govern the effective use of language to pick out individuals. This is irrelevant for present purposes.

In a second sense, individuation is used to refer to conditions that must be satisfied for something *to be known* as individual. This is an epistemological understanding, so let us call it "epistemological individuation." In the case of a 2×4 card, the pertinent conditions that have to be satisfied refer to the knowledge that someone may have about the card's individuality.

The difficulties with figuring out what is meant by the individuation of racial and ethnic groups do not end here, however, for the notion of individuation is parasitic on the notion of individuality, and individuality too is a contested notion.[28] There are in fact many understandings of it, but it suffices to point to two frequently found in the literature that are particularly pertinent for present purposes. The first conceives individuality as a second-order property of things that are noninstantiable instances of instantiables, so let us refer to it as "noninstantiable individuality."[29] In this sense, "this 2×4 card" is individual, but "card" is not, for "this 2×4 card" is an instance of "card" that cannot itself be instantiated into other cards. "2×4 card," on the other hand, is not individual, for there can be instances of it, "this 2×4 card" being one of them.

In another way, individuality is conceived as a second-order property of things that are different or distinct from all other things.[30] We might say that this is a conception of individuality as uniqueness, so let us call it "uniqueness individuality." In this sense, "this 2×4 card" is individual in that it is in some sense different or distinct from everything else—that 2×4 card, this human being, and the table at which I am sitting.

There are at least two common senses of 'uniqueness,' however, that we also need to make explicit. According to one, uniqueness is a second-order property of a thing that is one of a kind. "The last Dodo bird" is unique in the sense that there can be only one of its kind (when the kind is taken precisely as "the last Dodo bird"). But when the kind is taken to be just "Dodo bird," then the last Dodo bird is not unique, for there are many other animals that qualify as Dodo birds.

There is, however, another, weaker sense of uniqueness. In this way, a partic-

---

28. The notions of racial and ethnic groups themselves are also contested, but for the sake of brevity I assume that we all understand what these expressions mean when we say that Blacks constitute a racial group and Hispanics constitute an ethnic group.

29. For a defense of this view, see Gracia, *Individuality: An Essay on the Foundations of Metaphysics* (Albany: State University of New York Press, 1988), 43–56. I am using the term *property* nontechnically to mean feature or characteristic, so it should not be confused with the technical Aristotelian understanding of it as presented in, for example, Porphyry's *Isagoge*.

30. For a very early understanding of it as distinction, see Boethius, *De Trinitate* I, in *Theological Tractates*, ed. and trans. H. F. Stewart and E. R. Rand (Cambridge: Harvard University Press, 1968), 6. For a contemporary criticism of this kind of view, see Héctor-Neri Castañeda, "Individuation and Non-Identity," *American Philosophical Quarterly* 12 (1975): 131–40. For other conceptions of individuality, see Gracia, *Individuality*, chap. 1.

ular Dodo bird is unique in the sense that there is no other bird, or any other being for that matter, that happens to be in fact quite like it, even if there are other entities that are also birds, or even Dodo birds. This is the result of the particular properties that the Dodo bird in question happens to have. Being born at a certain place, of certain parents, at a certain time, having lived in certain places and certain times, and having associated with certain other birds, eaten certain foods, and so on, gives this Dodo bird a set of properties that is not shared by any other bird, or any other being for that matter. So, it is not that the Dodo bird in question is one of a kind, for all Dodo birds belong to the kind "Dodo bird," but that it enjoys a unique, albeit contingent, set of properties that renders it different from everything else, including other Dodo birds, in particular circumstances. This is the sense of 'uniqueness' that is used in the subsequent discussion.

In sum, if we combine the two conceptions of individuality and the two conceptions of individuation we have distinguished, and apply this scheme to racial and ethnic groups, we get at least four possible ways of understanding the topic that concerns us here:

1. Metaphysical individuation of the noninstantiability of racial or ethnic groups
2. Metaphysical individuation of the uniqueness of racial or ethnic groups
3. Epistemological individuation of the noninstantiability of racial or ethnic groups
4. Epistemological individuation of the uniqueness of racial or ethnic groups

In 1, the issue involves the conditions that need to be satisfied for a group to be noninstantiable. What are the conditions that make it impossible for Blacks, considered as a group, to be instantiable into other groups of Blacks? In 2, the conditions apply to the uniqueness of the group. In this case the question has to do with what makes a group contingently different, as a group, from all other groups. What makes Blacks different or distinct from all other groups? And in 3 and 4, the question involves the conditions governing the knowledge of such noninstantiability or uniqueness. How can we know that Blacks constitute a group that is noninstantiable or unique?

4. Back to the Objections

A. Circularity

Applying the scheme we have developed about individuation to Appiah's objection, we can surmise that it concerns individuation understood as uniqueness rather than as noninstantiability. He is concerned with what makes the group "the same as" and thus different from other groups. Still, the objection could be formulated in at least two ways, depending on whether one takes him to be speaking about metaphysical or epistemological uniqueness. And there is room in his text for both interpretations insofar as he speaks both of the sameness of the group (metaphysics) and our ability to identify it (epistemology). So here are two likely formulations of the argument:

Metaphysical formulation
1. The Familial-Historical View proposes that a race is unique because it has a unique history.
2. But a history of a race is unique because it is the history of that unique race.
3. Therefore, a race cannot be unique because it has a unique history.
4. Therefore, the proposal of the Familial-Historical View fails.

Epistemological formulation
1. The Familial-Historical View proposes that a race is known to be unique because it is known to have a unique history.
2. But a history of a race is known to be unique because it is known to be the history of that unique race.
3. Therefore, a race cannot be known to be unique because it is known to have a unique history.
4. Therefore, the proposal of the Familial-Historical View fails.

Put in these terms, the objection at first appears to be impregnable. Indeed, we could illustrate Appiah's point by putting it linguistically in this way: the claim "The history of a race individuates the race" is circular because a reference to the race is already contained in the subject of the sentence.

I submit, however, that Appiah's objection is not impregnable. One weakness in it is that Appiah equivocates on the meaning of 'the history of a race.' This expression can have at least three senses. In one, it refers to the history of a race once the race is constituted, that is, the history that follows the constitution of a race. In another sense, it refers to the history within which the race becomes constituted. And in a third sense, it refers to the history that precedes the constitution of the race.[31] Races, just like other social groups, are established in time and under particular circumstances, and there is a history that precedes them, a history in which they develop, and a history that follows them. The history that precedes them consists of the set of events that happens before the race is constituted. The history in which they develop consists of the events that directly

---

31. One can also speak of the history that follows the disappearance of a race, but it would be hard to construe this as in any sense being "the history of the race."

or indirectly affect the race throughout the process of its constitution and after. And the history that follows the race consists of the events that follow after the race has been constituted.[32]

It might be helpful to present the three cases I have suggested schematically, where 'R' stands for a race and 'E_1 E_2 E_3 E_4' stand for (the events that constitute) a history, as follows:

1. The history of a constituted race:

   R E_1 E_2 E_3 E_4

2. The history within which a race is constituted:

   E_1 E_2 R E_3 E_4

3. The history preceding the constitution of a race:

   E_1 E_2 E_3 E_4 R

Let us consider the group of Whites as an example. Sense 1 of history refers to the series of events (E_1 E_2 E_3 E_4, all coming after W) that occurred after the racial group of Whites, say, became distinct from other racial groups. Sense 2 of history refers to the series of events (E_1 E_2 E_3 E_4, where W is between E_1 E_2 and E_3 E_4) within which the group of Whites became distinct from other groups. And sense 3 refers to the series of events (E_1 E_2 E_3 E_4, coming before W) that preceded the distinction of Whites as a group.

Now, it certainly makes sense to argue that a race could not be individuated by the history that follows the constitution of the race, for that history presupposes the race. However, the history that is regarded as individuating in the Familial-Historical View need not be this history, but rather it can be the history that precedes the constitution of the race or even the history within which the race develops. The history that precedes a race is not contingent on the race and can be described without reference to it, so the problem of Circularity does not arise concerning it. We can individuate that history by referring to things other than the race, such as other events, other entities, and so on. The history that precedes Whites can be distinguished by reference to the events that constitute it, for example, and not the group of Whites. So, it is possible to claim that history individuates the race without falling into circularity in that it is in the context of certain events in that history that the race emerges. Something similar could be said about the understanding of the history of a race as the history in which the race develops. A developing race may not yet be considered to be a race, and so the factors involved in its individuation do not appear to require the race as fully constituted. But this case is not as clear as the previous one.

32. Keep in mind that what I mean by history here refers to actual events that happen, rather than to what we think of what happens or to a narrative we produce about it.

So far I have been referring to races, because it is the individuation of races to which Appiah applies the Circularity Objection. But something similar could be said, mutatis mutandis, about ethne. And, indeed, the situation is even clearer in this case. As long as one can distinguish the three senses of history mentioned, one can also answer Appiah's objection if it were to be applied to the Familial-Historical View of ethnic groups.

Perhaps a more detailed example will clarify the point. Let us for a moment consider the ethnic group we call Latinos or Latin Americans. There is surely a time at which this group did not exist. Indeed, before 1492 there was no such group of people. What was there? In the Iberian peninsula there were Catalans, Spaniards, Galicians, Portuguese, Barques, and Andalucians. Some of these groups had political independence—the Portuguese, for example—but most of them did not. In pre-Columbian America also there were many groups of indigenous people: the Maya, Aztec, Inca, and so on. But surely before 1492, there was a history. Events were happening both in Iberia and pre-Columbian America. There were wars, invasions, and the formation of political units among many other happenings. And these events were individual and can also be identified and distinguished from other events. For example, the marriage of Ferdinand and Isabella brought the kingdoms of Castile and Aragon together. Montezuma became the king of the Aztecs. These events were historically unique and could be identified as such by any observer who had access to them. But neither the individuality nor the identification of these events as individual require a reference to the future that is Latin America or the group we know as Latinos or Latin Americans. Yet these very events, as well as others, set the stage for the encounter between Iberia and pre-Columbian America. And this encounter, or encounters, as I have argued elsewhere, generated events that slowly created the conditions for the development of the group of people we now refer to as Latin Americans or Latinos.[33] Latin Americans are certainly not Iberians, but they are not pre-Columbians either. So much for the history that preceded Latinos.

Now let us consider the history within which Latinos emerged. This is the history that begins in 1492 and continues to this date. At first there were no Latinos, but slowly, as a result of many events there came to be. And this happened in different places, contexts, and circumstances. In this history, there are events that can be identified without reference to Latinos. For the formation of this group is not uniform in every place in Latin America. So there may be places where historical events may be individuated and we can identify them as such without reference to Latinos. In other places, however, there are events tied to the group because the group has already emerged. So the history within which

33. Gracia, *Hispanic / Latino Identity*, chap. 5.

Latinos emerge is sometimes dependent on the group but at other times it is not. And this makes possible reference to some of this history, or part of it, without involving the group. This again precludes circularity.

Finally there is the history that follows the group's formation. And this one clearly is tied to the group. Yet even here one could speak of this history as molding and changing the group and thus as influencing the group. Consider a natural disaster in Mexico that elicits a sense of solidarity throughout Latin America. The national disaster can be indicated without reference to Latinos, or even Mexicans. But it can be a force in the formation of a feeling of solidarity between the people directly affected by the disaster in Mexico and the people not affected by it in Chile, thus strengthening Latino ties.

Metaphysically, then, the Circularity Objection fails. But does it fail also epistemologically? I do not see why not, as long as the mentioned senses of history are kept separate. In principle one can speak of the events that preceded 1492 and of the knowledge we have of them. And we can speak of those events as narrowing down and preparing the conditions for the emergence of Latinos as well as establishing the conditions for knowing the group. We can speak of the historical events that preceded the Latino ethnic group, but we only *know* that it is their history once the ethnic group has been established. More on this later.

B. Demarcation

Now let us apply the scheme of individuation to Bernstein's objection. When this is done, it becomes clear, as it was with Appiah, that he is not interested in individuality taken as noninstantiability. He is not concerned with the fact that the group of Hispanics is not instantiable into groups of Hispanics. If the group of Hispanics is composed of 300 million individual persons, the group of these persons is not instantiable into groups of 300 million individual persons. This is just as happens with this cat: it is not instantiable into other cats. Bernstein's concern is with individuality conceived as uniqueness, that is, with what makes the group of Hispanics unique, in a similar way in which Napoleon was unique. In this, the issue Bernstein addresses is similar to Appiah's. But to know this, as was also the case with Appiah, is not enough to understand the full impact of Bernstein's objection insofar as we still have to establish whether he frames the issue in metaphysical or epistemological terms.

A point to consider is that, as noted above, Bernstein makes the suggestion that the Familial-Historical View can be rendered effective in accounting for individuation when a sense or consciousness of history as "ours" is added to it. By consciously appropriating history, by identifying ourselves with certain events, he holds, we can effectively particularize history and demarcate the ethnic group to which we belong. This seems to suggest that Bernstein's claim is epistemo-logical insofar as the individuation factor to which he refers is our conscious-ness. But in fact, from something else he tells us, we can surmise that it is in fact metaphysical. In a pertinent text he states that "there must also be a sense of one's identity and pride *in being* Hispanic," for Hispanics to constitute a group.[34] This suggests that Bernstein has in mind a sense of identity ("pride in being"), or we might say self-identification, here, but this pride functions metaphysically—it is what unifies and distinguishes Hispanics, what makes them *be* Hispanic. History individuates groups, but it is history made uniquely "ours," as he puts it, through self-identification. It is history as we know it and appropriate it that is pertinent for uniqueness, not history independently of our knowledge of it. Knowledge of our history makes us who we are.

One way to render Bernstein's argument is as follows:

1. For an ethnic group to be unique, it has to have a unique history.
2. But for an ethnic group to have a unique history, its members must know the group's history.
3. But according to the Familial-Historical View, members of a group do not have to know the group's history.
4. Therefore, the Familial-Historical View fails to account for the uniqueness of the group.

Again, as with Appiah's argument, this objection appears very strong, maybe even impregnable. The key to it is the second premise, for Bernstein can claim good company. Indeed, Searle has argued along similar lines concerning the re-ality of social groups.[35] Still the argument is not convincing and its main weak-ness is precisely found in the second premise. This claim can be challenged on at least four grounds. First, the members of ethnic groups do not need to know the histories of the groups. Ethnic groups function as such even when their members lack a sense of themselves in that self-identification is a long and pro-tracted process that often depends on conditions external to a group and takes a long time to emerge. How long has it taken Hispanics in the United States, for example, to have a sense of themselves? Indeed, some even dispute they have such a sense now! Besides, even if a sense of themselves were required, this does not necessarily entail knowledge of the group's history.

Second, people can be taught to think of themselves in ways that are contrary

---

34. Ibid., 49. My emphasis. Note the similarity between this view and Paula Moya's position in "Why I Am Not Hispanic: An Argument with Jorge Gracia," *American Philosophical Association Newsletter on Hispanic/Latino Issues in Philosophy* 2 (spring 2001): 100–105.

35. John Searle, *Social Construction of Reality* (New York: Free Press, 1995).

to the facts; they can be indoctrinated, and facts can be covered up or misrepresented. Consider that children may grow up thinking they are natural offspring of their parents when in fact they are adopted. So, what members of an ethnic group may think is their history is not always an accurate reflection of that history. There is much about Latino history that is pure fabrication, or dependent on a certain take on the facts determined by ideological commitments.

Third, Bernstein's claim can be taken to refer to all members of ethnic groups or just to some members of the groups. If all, then clearly this is false insofar as children and incompetent persons may not be able to know about the history of the groups to which they belong, and even among those members of the groups who are competent to know it, it might happen that they do not know it for a variety of contingent reasons. Many members of ethnic groups in the United States, for example, have an underprivileged status that prevents them from learning about their historical roots. When one is concerned with putting bread on the table, it is difficult to think about one's heritage. And if it is only some members of the groups that need to know about the histories of the groups, how are we to identify them and on what basis are we to legitimize their authority in this matter? Who among Hispanics has been "appointed" to this task? Academics? Hardly, they disagree among themselves. So, to whom do we turn? These are tough questions to answer for anyone who holds the view Bernstein puts forth.

Last, even if one were to accept that knowledge of history is required for the individuation of groups on historical grounds, it would not be necessary that such knowledge be found in the group; it could be found in members of other groups. And, indeed, it is often the case that what others think is as important or even more important for group identity than what the group itself, or its members, think.

Of course, this does not mean that self-identification and group identification cannot be part of the conditions that play a role in ethnic unity, or that the appropriation of history by a group does not play a role in that group's self-identification. It certainly can and does. The knowledge of a fact does not alter the fact, although it may (1) produce other facts that otherwise would not have been produced and (2) modify certain facts that otherwise would not have been modified. My knowledge of who hit me over the head may alter my future conduct, but that knowledge cannot alter the hit or the identity of the person who did it. This is a distinction that is often missing in discussion of these issues.

5. The Individuation of Racial and Ethnic Groups

So much for the failure of the Circularity and Demarcation Objections to undermine the Familial-Historical View by attacking its effectiveness in accounting for individuation. This is as much as can be accomplished in an article of this size. To hope that we can go beyond this and establish the conditions of effective individuation of racial and ethnic groups is unrealistic. It is not possible to determine what things, or even what kinds of things, whether properties or relations, make racial and ethnic groups unique and account for their particular membership. Nor can we expect to establish the causal genesis of racial or ethnic groups, that is, how they are formed and the sorts of things that are responsible for their creation rather than the creation of some other kinds of groups. Such tasks would require a detailed presentation and discussion of the Familial-Historical View. Nonetheless, we can learn something from these objections and the answers that we have given to them that will allow us to say something useful about the individuation of racial and ethnic groups from the perspective of the Familial-Historical View. Although the objections turn out to be ineffective as formulated, their consideration brings to the fore some aspects of the individuation of racial and ethnic groups that merit attention and help in determining the parameters of an affective view.

The Circularity Objection reveals the need to take into account various senses of history and to understand the history of social groups in concrete terms. One of the problems with this objection is that it looks at races as fixed groups of people already constituted, without taking into account their context, development, and changing character. Another is that it ignores the variety of histories that affect these groups.

The Demarcation Objection, on the other hand, by emphasizing the sense of history in ethnic groups, uncovers the need to consider significance an important factor in the constitution of these groups, although it makes the mistake of restricting significance to mere awareness. Such individuating factors as the number of people involved or the unique spatiotemporal location of these individuals are not sufficient to account for the uniqueness of racial or ethnic groups. Racial and ethnic groups increase and decrease, and they cross spatiotemporal boundaries.

With this in mind, we can turn to the two pertinent questions for us in this context: First, what makes racial and ethnic groups unique if one adopts the Familial-Historical View? And second, how do we know they are unique at any particular time? The first question is metaphysical, the second epistemological.

A. Metaphysical Uniqueness of Races and Ethne

According to the Familial-Historical View, the uniqueness of racial and ethnic groups results from the bundle of properties, including relations, which in turn arise from historical events and apply to their members at any time during, and cumulatively throughout, their existence. These groups are unique but contingently so, because history is the key to their uniqueness, in that history generates the properties that distinguish them in context. But history is contingent. Things could have been otherwise. It is possible that Latinos could not have existed. What if the Spaniards had decided that San Salvador was not India and therefore had turned back to Spain? After all, the Vikings seem to have done something like that, and nothing came of their landing on North America. Or what if Cortez had not burned his ships? Or what if Montezuma had not been captured and the Spaniards that invaded Mexico had been killed? If any of these things had happened, history would have been very different. Perhaps pre-Columbian America would not have been unified under two empires—the Spanish and Portuguese. Perhaps the British would have invaded instead. Perhaps many nations would have developed without common languages and history. And so, perhaps there would never have been any Latinos!

Now, from the answer to the Circularity Objection we know that the history in question is complex. First, there is the history that precedes the constitution of the groups; second, there is the history within which the groups develop; and third, there is the history that follows their constitution. The first two of these histories contribute to the individuation of the groups, that is, to making them unique and thus different from other entities in context. But, of course, this by itself does not seem to explain why groups actually become constituted as unique. So what is it in history, or what is necessary in history, to accomplish this?

At least three factors need to be considered: First, historical events that affect certain people directly and not others; second, the number of events—few isolated events cannot compare to chains or clusters of many events; and, third, the significance of the events. An example might help. Consider the case of the Hispanic ethnos and the historical factors that in particular has helped constitute it into the specific ethnos it is. First, the initial encounter between the sailors aboard the Castilian ships and the natives of San Salvador affected both groups of people directly in rather obvious ways but did not directly affect Russian peasants or Chinese bureaucrats living in Russia and China at the time. Second, the Viking's landing in Newfoundland, for example, produced only a few events, whereas the landing of the Castilian ships in San Salvador unleashed a chain of events of enormous proportions. And, third, the Spaniards did not just give a few colored beads to the natives, but rather proceeded to change their way of life in significant ways, imposing a foreign model of government and a different religion, among other things, on them, while at the same time incorporating much from them into their own culture.

The three factors mentioned, when taken together, illustrate how certain historical events effectively tie some people, while at the same time separate them from others, thus rendering the group in question unique through the relations in which they are embedded and the properties that these relations generate. The relations and properties in question vary, depending on the circumstances. Often they involve experiences of particular sorts, whether positive or negative. Indeed, negative experiences such as those associated with domination, colonization, and marginalization are frequently cited as particularly significant.[36]

This is similar to what happens with a family: A marriage unites certain persons and separates them from others. History becomes ours, as Bernstein would put it, precisely because of the kind of history it is. It creates us as groups, by uniting us and by generating relations and properties that, in context, separate and distinguish us from others.

The Familial-Historical View, then, allows for the discussion of historical conditions and properties of ethnic groups at particular times and places in spite of its rejection of the need for common group properties. There is no reason why, for example, we cannot speak of certain properties of these groups at certain periods. We can, for example, speak of Hispanic philosophy or thought in the nineteenth century. It also allows for the discussion of criteria of identity within a historical context. But all this has to be understood within a relational and nonessentialistic metaphysical framework. This is why we can, without contradiction, discuss particular properties of ethnic groups in context.[37] To make this, or any other property associated with *some* members of a group, part and parcel of the nature of *all* members of the group, is to fall back into the kind of essentialism that distorts ethnicity and is responsible for much oppression and discrimination in human history. On the other hand, to reject the metaphysical framework is to give up on understanding ethne and how they work. It condemns us to a kind of superficial, and culturally biased, description of ethnic phenomena without a foundational understanding of them, or to the kind of description that is more properly undertaken in fields such as sociology and cultural anthropology.

So far I have been speaking about ethnic groups in particular. But what I have

36. See, for example, Walter Mignolo, "Hispanics/Latinos [and Latino Studies] in the Colonial Horizon of Modernity," in *Hispanics/Latinos in the United States,* ed. Gracia and De Greiff, 99–124.

37. I have done something like this with Hispanics and *mestizaje,* in Gracia, *Hispanic/Latino Identity,* chap. 5.

said could be applied, mutatis mutandis, to racial groups. Now let me briefly turn to the epistemological individuation of unique races and ethne.

B. Epistemological Individuation of Unique Racial and Ethnic Groups

Can we effectively account for the identification of racial and ethnic groups? Surely the answer is yes, provided we have access to the unique bundle of properties and historical relations that apply to them, for these distinguish them from other entities we know and tie the groups throughout their histories. Of course, we cannot account for the uniqueness of the groups merely qua races or ethne, for as such they are not unique. A race, qua race, is not unique and cannot be known to be unique insofar as there are many races. And the same can be said of an ethnos. Rather, race and ethne are known to be unique qua the particular races and ethne they are, that is, as "Blacks" or Hispanics, for example. And how can we know their unique sets of properties and histories? By the relations that can be established between them and an observer. It is by considering them in a historical grid in relation to an observer that their identification is possible.

This is not very different from the way I know you as a unique and different human being. How do I do it? Because you are located in a grid of which I am part and that is centered on me. I function as an absolute point of reference in it. You are right in front of me, or to my left, or to my right. And you are related to me in certain ways, as my friend, or a stranger, or my daughter. And you have certain characteristics that are evident from my perspective: a certain height, a certain shape, and so on. And so it is with racial and ethnic groups. A group is nothing but its members, and I can identify it through them. Of course, there are questions about how to identify members I do not presently see, but there are ways to do it, just as I can identify members of families that I do not see. "Do you know my cousin Peter? No. Well, he is very tall, and . . ." This kind of talk makes perfectly good sense, although there is much more that needs to be said about this, but the saying will have to wait for another time.

This does not mean that there may not be disputable cases. But don't most of our concepts tolerate disputable cases? This applies to even a common notion such as "most of." In a group of 50, does 26 qualify as most of the group? How about 251 in a group of 500? And what of 1,000,001 in a group of 2,000,000? "Most of" is not equivalent to "the majority," so the issue is controversial. But this does not entail that the concept of "most of" is senseless or unusable. It only means that some concepts do not stipulate strict boundaries. And this is precisely the case with racial and ethnic groups.

6. Summary

I began by briefly presenting two contrary answers to the problem of the individuation of races and ethne. Then I presented the pertinent tenets of the Historical-Familial View of racial and ethnic groups. Next I formulated two objections to this view: the Circularity Objection in the version adopted by Appiah, and the Demarcation Objection in Bernstein's formulation. The Circularity objection argues that this view cannot explain the metaphysical or epistemological uniqueness of racial groups because it falls into circularity. The Demarcation Objection argues that this view cannot explain the metaphysical uniqueness of ethnic groups because it fails to make reference to the sense of history necessary for history to be considered particular to a group. This led me to introduce some distinctions between four different understandings of individuation, which I subsequently used to understand the Circularity and Demarcation Objections. I concluded that both objections are concerned with individuality understood as uniqueness, taken broadly and contingently.

I argued then that both objections are ineffective: the first, because it fails to distinguish several senses of history and, the second, because its assumption about the need for a sense of history for ethnic groups to exist as such is misguided. However, I found that the consideration of these objections proved useful in establishing some requirements of an effective view of the individuation of racial and ethnic groups, although I have not attempted to provide any list of necessary or sufficient conditions of it here. Indeed, I have not said anything either about the kind of history that generates racial and ethnic groups as opposed to other social groups, although I added some general conditions concerning the relevance of the events in question. This is an important issue, but one that will have to wait for another occasion.[38]

---

38. I have read versions of this paper in many forums and have frequently received interesting criticisms and suggestions from the audience. I am particularly grateful for the audiences at Department of Philosophy at the University of Iowa, the conference on "Black Ethnicity, Latino Race?" that took place at the University of Buffalo in April 2005, and the Central Division Meetings session in Chicago, April 2006. I especially would like to thank Steve Tammelleo, who commented on the paper in Chicago, for his insightful criticisms.

CHAPTER 4

Ethnicity, Race, and the Importance of Gender

NAOMI ZACK

Often when Americans intend to affirm race, they affirm a distinctive ethnic way of life, and when they practice racism, they substitute facile ideas and images for meaning and understanding. It is difficult to hate people whose culture is understood, but easy to hate people who are imagined to embody a label that means "inferior" or "dangerous." In the United States, ethnicity can work within groups to pattern peaceful social relations, while race often works across groups to disrupt or destroy the ethnic patterns of "Others."[1] Ethnicity is particular in myriad ways, whereas race is abstract. Ethnicity is like sand, race is like fog. The difficulty in constructing grand theories of ethnicity is synergistic, because it makes us focus on specific histories and existing individuals. But race militarizes our thinking from ideal general types, outward and downward. If we disabuse ourselves of false biologistic theories of race, we are left with ethnicity in all of its multiple concrete forms.

Before going further into the architectonic of racial and ethnic discourse, I should explain that the main work of this article is about race and gender. Part 1 is an analysis of the recalcitrance of scientifically discarded ideas of race among several contemporary philosophers. Part 2 addresses ongoing political racial mechanisms that are more broad than the pettifogging disputes of academics. The resilience of bogus notions of race and the zeal with which they are defended would be cause for despair if we had to resolve theoretical disputes about race to achieve freedom and peace in our times, or if solving them would be sufficient to bring about those ends. However, I've recently come to the con-

1. As Falguni Sheth pointed out at the Buffalo conference, ethnic identities can be chauvinistic as well as benign, a point which I do take up in part 2 of this essay.

clusion that gender is now the necessary and sufficient liberatory fulcrum, and in part 2 I suggest that changing the gendered nature of political leadership might offer greater promise for deep structural changes in our society.

Returning now to the theoretical issues, sand and fog are good metaphors for race and ethnicity, because sand and fog are real things in the world. We can talk about them directly without having recourse to people's false beliefs. Most of the things that people believe about ethnicity are true. But what is ethnicity? An informative universal definition of what constitutes an ethnic group would seem to be impossible, because the criteria for membership in ethnic groups vary according to group. They may be based on cultural traditions, ancestral origin, religion, common language, physical appearance, nationality, ideology, geography, politics or common history, either singly or in any combination thereof. It would seem that all that can be generally said about ethnic groups is that their members self-identify in distinctive ways and that they are recognized in distinctive ways by others, usually members of contending, dominant or subordinate, and sometimes culturally appreciative groups; there is no necessity for a match between criteria for self-identification and identification by others. Also, ethnic groups tend to be composed of families, and commonality among members of an ethnic group is expected to be taught to future generations, because it has been transmitted generationally in the past.

Given these considerations, the best way to define ethnic groups would seem to be via ostensive definition, that is, lists of existing and historical groups. Indeed, ever since the great waves of immigration to the United States during the early twentieth century, social scientists have studied ethnicity as the histories and life experiences of specific groups: Polish, Italian, Jewish, Irish, Chinese, East Indian, Mexican, Ghanaian, Dominican, Puerto Rican, and myriad others. This literature is too vast to even properly gesture toward here.[2]

However, the study of ethnic groups in the United States, and perhaps other nations as well, is conditioned by realities within society, whereby those groups specifically designated as "ethnic" have subordinate status related to their non-white racialization, histories of immigration, or varied degrees of assimilation to dominant culture or dominant ethnic groups. It is therefore very useful to distinguish between ethnic groups as bare identities of people and ethnic groups as identities forged or assigned within contentious power structures. This sec-

2. On problems with defining ethnic groups, see Jorge Gracia, *Hispanic/Latino Identity: A Philosophical Perspective* (Oxford: Blackwell, 2000). See also Naomi Zack, *Thinking about Race,* 2nd ed. (Belmont, CA: Wadsworth, 2005–6), 35–43; Stephen Thernstrom, ed., *Harvard Encyclopedia of American Ethnic Groups* (Cambridge: Belknap Press, 1980); F. Fred Wacker, *Ethnicity, Pluralism, and Race* (Westwood, CT: Greenwood, 1983); and Werner Sollers, ed., *Theories of Ethnicity: A Classical Reader* (New York: New York University Press, 1996).

ond sense of ethnicity enables us to understand that in the United States, European ethnic groups no longer suffer oppression on the grounds of their ethnicity, whereas those from Africa, Asia, the Middle East, and the Americas still do, and it destabilizes any useful notion of ethnic groups that can be captured in descriptions of bare identities. Linda Alcoff, Jorge Gracia, Angelo Corlett, Gregory Velazco y Trianosky, and Susana Nuccetelli, have all made incisive and substantial contributions to thought about these issues. All, except perhaps Linda Alcoff, might have hopes for a general philosophical theory of ethnicity, based on the histories of oppressed groups. To the extent that such theoretical work is successful, it can anchor a philosophical perspective on ethnicity that would also be a theoretical contribution to the social science treatment of the subject. And, I should add that I think it countervails my opening view here, that grand theory in ethnicity is not possible.

Now for race. What is race? Most that is commonly believed about race is false because race does not exist in the way that even the most innocent beliefs about it imply. What is false is the pervasive underlying assumption that the human species is biologically, which is to say physically, or "naturally," divided into races. The contemporary scientific information about the lack of this natural taxonomy is based on evidence that precludes the possibility of scientists ever discovering a natural basis for racial divisions in society. At this point, we can say a priori that, if the existence of human races entails that there is a biological basis that determines social divisions, then it is impossible that races exist. There are two reasons why this is so. First, there is nothing in human physiology, in blood or anything else of that sort, that could constitute determining racial essences for distinctive racial groups. And second, human biological variety within recognized social racial groups, which is greater than the variety between groups, precludes the possibility of necessary and sufficient conditions for racial membership. Let's look closer at these claims.[3]

The possibility of a race gene or a race chromosome, which could count as a determining essence or even a marker for this or that race is precluded by both the distribution of racial phenotypes or those observable traits considered racial ones in society, and by what is known about human genetics, or the processes that determine the phenotypes of individuals. According to Mendelian heredity, phenotypes are determined by genotypes that do not get inherited together but are subject to dispersal and recombination at conception. While some phe-

---

3. In the rest of the discussion in this section, I draw on my analyses and conclusions from Naomi Zack, *Philosophy of Science and Race* (New York: Routledge, 2002). All of the scientific sources for the claims about human heredity and natural history are listed in the endnotes and bibliography of that book. Also, in the critical discussion that follows in the next section of this chapter, there are specific references as the general claims in this section are applied to a current controversy in the literature.

notypes occur more frequently in some populations than others, there has been no agreed-upon method, which is independent of social racial taxonomy, for determining the number of human populations; estimates have varied from single digits to hundreds of thousands. Moreover, social racial taxonomy varies, both historically and from culture to culture, as did the number of races posited by scientists of race. Aside from a population basis for race, the other promising anthropological candidate has been geographical origin. But, the genetic material used to track geographic ancestry bears no causal relation to the genetic material that determines phenotypes deemed racial. Even the prevailing African-origins hypothesis about modern Homo sapiens does not guarantee that the original African population had traits that later came to be associated with Africans. And its competing multiple-origins hypothesis is based on assumptions that there was travel and genetic mixtures between different continental populations.

The impossibility of physical race has implications for how careful people, especially philosophers, should talk about race. It is disingenuous to assume that races exist, solely because the idea of race has been used and felt so widely and deeply, and to proceed from that assumption to a new and better definition of race that will "save the phenomena." The phenomena that need to be saved are social, and the only thing that can save them is the biological impossibility. Even if a new and better definition of race could be constructed, it would not be the same as the historical definitions in use, and given the problems with those definitions and usages, it is not clear what the purpose of the new and better definition could be. It is not necessary to be able to talk about race as though race were real, in order to address racism, because everything that can be said about racism as proceeding from beliefs held by human beings can be stated in terms of those beliefs and their consequences, without supporting the truth of the beliefs.

False beliefs may have real consequences and much that is true can be said about false beliefs. When beneficial personal and community identities, which exceed reactions to racism, are based on false beliefs about the existence of biological race, the same epistemic mechanism is at work, although the consequences are different. The false beliefs have real consequences that in this case, unlike the case of racism, may be beneficial, but that in itself has no effect on the falsity of the beliefs. To refuse to critically examine beliefs about what exists, because they are held by the majority is to abrogate a philosophical responsibility that goes back to Socrates: *Nomos* is not *physis;* convention is not reality. And to assume that because a term such as *race* can be used in meaningful discourse within a society, there must be a real entity to which that term refers, is to persist in allowing oneself to be confused by grammar in ways that have been blocked for philosophers since Bertrand Russell. Enough about the biological emptiness of human racial taxonomy has been explained by biological anthropologists, as well as philosophers, to justify being quite firm about these points, even though those who should know better may still refuse to acknowledge them. Such recalcitrance concerning notions of race merits close examination whenever possible and I offer an extended example of both the recalcitrance and an examination of it, in the next section.

1. *The Journal of Philosophy* and Race

In recent articles published in *The Journal of Philosophy* (*JP*), Michael Hardimon and Robin Andreasen have presented biological taxonomies of human races, while neglecting this crucial philosophy of science question:[4] Is a taxonomy of human biological races scientifically justified at this time? Also in *JP*, Joshua Glasgow criticizes "the new biology of race," as previously proposed elsewhere by Philip Kitcher and Andreasen, without taking up the question of whether this "new biology of race" is scientifically justified.[5] The omission of this crucial question is problematic because Hardimon, Kitcher, and Andreasen seem to assert that their biological notions of race are compatible with science, in cases where the current data and conclusions of relevant scientists indicate otherwise.[6] If these writers believe that the question of whether science justifies race is irrelevant to studies of race, then they should give reasons for the irrelevance, which they do not. If they believe that the question of whether

4. Michael O. Hardimon, "The Ordinary Concept of Race," *Journal of Philosophy* 100 (2003): 437–55; Robin O. Andreasen, "The Meaning of 'Race': Folk Conceptions and the New Biology of Race," *Journal of Philosophy* 102 (2005): 94–106.

5. Joshua M. Glasgow, "On the New Biology of Race," *Journal of Philosophy* 100 (2003): 456–74; Robin O. Andreasen, "A New Perspective on the Race Debate," *British Journal for the Philosophy of Science* 49 (1998): 199–225, and "Race: Biological Reality or Social Construct?" *Philosophy of Science* 67 (2000): S653–66; Philip Kitcher, "Race, Ethnicity, Biology, Culture," in *Racism,* ed. Leonard Harris (Amherst, NY: Humanity, 1999), 87–120.

6. The omission of the question of whether race is scientifically justified is in addition puzzling to me as someone who has previously written on the subject of race and science, because Hardimon makes numerous references to my 2002 book, *Philosophy of Science and Race,* and Glasgow refers to my 1993 *Race and Mixed Race* (for his claim that there is greater variation within than among races), but neither author appears to recognize that this question of a scientifically justified foundation for race has been central to all of my work on race. See, for instance, the books cited in Hardimon and Glasgow's *Journal of Philosophy* articles: *Philosophy of Science and Race* (New York: Routledge, 2002), and *Race and Mixed Race* (Philadelphia: Temple University Press, 1993). Hardimon refers to *Philosophy of Science and Race* in footnotes 2, 3, 27, 43, 44, 47 in his article; Glasgow refers to it in footnotes 15 and 23, and in the text he refers to *Race and Mixed Race.* Also Kitcher in "Race, Ethnicity, Biology and Culture," refers to conversations with me at a conference on race held at Rutgers University, fall 1994, in endnotes 1 and 14 and includes *Race and Mixed Race* in his reference section.

science justifies race is relevant to studies of race, then any "new biology of race" ought to be consistent with contemporary science, which the "new biology of race" is not. In this commentary I will show how "the new biology of race" is inconsistent with science.

The present subject is the ordinary or common sense idea of race. People who have this idea and use it in discourse and behavior often believe that data and conclusions in the biological sciences support the existence of human races. Where there is dispute among scientists about whether data supports the existence of human races, philosophers may be of assistance by checking whether race terms are used with consistent meanings by scientists, and explaining the empirical justifications for competing theories and interpretations of data; that is, they might apply philosophy of science to 'race.'

Biological anthropologists and population geneticists have minimalized their race concepts since psychic (psychological, moral and cultural) notions of race were separated from physical notions during the early decades of the twentieth century, beginning with the work of Franz Boas and his cohort. But what is presented to the public in popularizations of scientific findings sometimes gives the impression that the concept of race has more life in science than it presently does, or given what is already known, ever could again. The present scientific consensus appears to be that there is no scientific justification for ordinary ideas of race, insofar as those ideas are based on the assumption that human biological races exist.[7] Given this consensus, treating biological notions of race as though they were scientific, would seem to require showing how current scientists are mistaken about the connections between available evidence and the conclusions they have drawn from that evidence. Hardimon, Kitcher, and Andreasen have nowhere (to my knowledge) undertaken that project.

Late-nineteenth-century white supremacist theories of race were replete with both specialist and nonspecialist speculations about race, and philosophers should take care to stay close to the ground concerning the scientific research of the twentieth century, lest their scientifically ungrounded creations be passed on to those less scientifically informed than they. This is a matter of seeking and presenting the strongest approximations to truth. When it comes to questions about physical reality, our best choice is to turn to the results of well-established expertise in the relevant sciences. The question of whether a biological taxon-

---

7. For statements of the current consensus in biological anthropology that there is no scientific foundation for a race concept, see, for example, John Relethford, *The Human Species: An Introduction to Biological Anthropology* (Mountain View, CA: Mayfield, 1997), esp. part 4, "Human Variation," 351–77; American Anthropological Association, "1998 AAA Statement on 'Race,'" *Anthropology Newsletter* 39 (1998): 3. See also the preceding year of discussions about race in American Anthropological Association, *Anthropology Newsletter*.

omy of human races is real is thereby a question to be answered by findings in biological anthropology, transmission genetics, and population genetics, subfields of human biology that underwent extensive revision over the last half of the twentieth century. The question of whether beliefs about race in ordinary life, and the actions based on them, are real, is another matter. Of course, people believe and act as though race is real, and of course, their beliefs and actions result in all manner of social facts.[8] This should go without saying because the important questions concern justification: Are the beliefs themselves held to be justified by science? Yes. Does science justify the beliefs? No.

The legitimacy of race in science is important because the modern idea of race, which began with the development of biology as a science in the eighteenth and nineteenth centuries, has always been accompanied with deference for the science of biology. So if ordinary people in their usage of what Hardimon calls "our" ordinary concept of race assume that racial taxonomy has a foundation in science which it does not have, this is a big problem for the ordinary concept of race in critical terms—although not necessarily in sociological, political, or rhetorical ones. To explain how science fails to uphold a concept of race on which the ordinary concept could justifiably depend, I will begin with Hardimon's *JP* article and then consider Kitcher and Andreasen's claims about a genealogical notion of race.

A. Hardimon's Conception of Our Ordinary Concept of Race

Hardimon is aware that the ordinary concept of race entered history as a racist concept (positing a moral hierarchy of races), with links to scientific theories held in the eighteenth and nineteenth centuries, but he claims that it has a coherent core of claims, which is independent of the scientific concept of race as well as racism, although not necessarily incompatible with either one.[9] Hardimon therefore proposes a "conception" of our ordinary concept which has three components: (1) human groups have distinguishing "visible physical features of a relevant kind"; (2) human races are linked by common ancestry; (3) racial groups originate from distinctive geographical locations, usually continents.[10] I think it indisputable that "we," as ordinary people, do have this conception of race. What is disputable is the legitimacy of the conception insofar as each of its components is based on past scientific notions of race that are no longer acceptable to scientists as a scientific foundation for race. And if we, as ordinary

---

8. See Zack, *Philosophy of Science*, chap. 7, pp. 103–18, for discussion of race as a social construction.
9. Hardimon, "Our Ordinary Concept of Race," 449–51.
10. Ibid., 451–52.

people who have this conception, also believe that its components are grounded in a scientific notion of race, which many do believe, then something is wrong with our ordinary concept of race.

Here are the current scientific problems with Hardimon's three components of our ordinary concept of race. First, Hardimon's (1). The distinguishing "visible physical features of a relevant kind" presupposes a social system of racial attribution that has not always existed historically in human societies and that first originated during the modern period of European exploration and colonization. Indeed, as late as the sixteenth century, some English traders expressed qualms about enslaving those who had "the same shape" as they did, and Queen Elizabeth expressed concern about the consent of those enslaved. Also, John Locke in his *Letter on Toleration* considers discrimination based on "differences in complexion" as an example of a cause for rebellion.[11] Of course, by the time we get to Hume and Kant, racial differences are "self-evident" (with Kant relying on Hume as an authority).[12] So it is not timelessly the case, independently of history and culture, that those visible differences that count as racial differences are as Hardimon claims, naturally "striking." Hardimon writes:

> It is undeniable that these visible features are striking—from a *human* point of view. The proof being that human beings *find them* striking.... It seems to me likely that they would still be striking—*physically* striking—in a world free of racism.[13]

The nineteenth-century anthropometric attempts to correlate quantitative physical differences with differences in social races were later repudiated by biological anthropologists and shown by historians and scientists, such as Stephen Jay Gould, to have been biased, with some data outright falsified.[14] But nineteenth-century anthropometry probably contributes as much to the present ordinary concept of race—and its resultant perceptions—as it suggests the falseness of that concept for educated people at this time. What we find striking in our perceptions of other human beings is not necessarily natural, unlearned, or

11. For a discussion of ideas about race in Locke's times, see Zack, *Bachelors of Science: Seventeenth-Century Identity Then and Now* (Philadelphia: Temple University Press, 1996) chapter 12, "Slavery without Race," 168–81. The references for the traders qualms about "same shape," and Elizabeth's egalitarianism, and Locke on discrimination, respectively, are: Nigel Tattersfield, *The Forgotten Trade* (London: Jonathan Cape, 1991), 11; W. O. Blake, *The History of Slavery and the Slave Trade* (New York: Haskell House, 1958; reprint 1969), 168; and John Locke, *A Letter Concerning Toleration*, ed. James H. Tully (Indianapolis, IN: Hackett, 1983), 52.

12. For a full discussion of how Hume accepted the existence of human races as self-evident and Kant sought to shore this up by reasoning that because there were hybrids, there must be races, see Zack, *Philosophy of Science*, chapter 1, "Philosophical Racial Essentialism: Hume and Kant," 9–24.

13. Hardimon, "Our Ordinary Concept of Race," 454–55.

14. See Stephen J. Gould, *The Mismeasure of Man* (New York: Norton, 1996).

independent of culture. That we find those physical traits of others that we take to be racial differences "striking" is an important sociological and psychological fact, but it is not a justification for those conceptual underpinnings, or beliefs, that are at least partial causes of our finding what we understand to be racial differences, "striking."

Hardimon's (2) and (3) are interrelated. Both the common ancestry link and the geographical origins hypothesis rely on discarded scientific foundations of race. The consensus of biological anthropologists at this time (now frequently and conspicuously broadcast by popularizers of science in publications such as the *New York Times*)[15] is that all modern Homo sapiens originated from the same common ancestors, in Africa, no more than 100,000 years ago.[16] There is evidence that this original population may not have had the characteristics of skin, hair, and bone structure that came to be associated with Africans during the modern period, insofar as there is evidence that they had very fair skin hues and were hirsute.[17] There is furthermore widespread doubt among evolutionary theorists that what have come to be considered distinctive racial traits of skin, hair, and bone were necessarily adaptive to distinctive environments, because the remains of ancient people with varieties of distinctive racial traits have not been exclusively found on the continents with which those distinctive racial traits are associated.[18] Furthermore, in tracking the migration of the original African ancestral population, nonprotein coding genetic material (which has no relation to bod-

15. As of this writing, the latest popular article is: Nicholas Wade, "DNA Study Yields Clues on Early Humans' First Migration," *New York Times* (International), May 13, 2005, A7. Looking back for further examples, the following articles highlight the contemporary anthropological consensus on the *out-of-Africa* thesis: John Noble Wilfred, "Skulls in Caucasus Linked to Early Humans in Africa," *New York Times,* May 12, 2000, A1, and Nicholas Wade, "The Human Family Tree: 10 Adams and 18 Eves," *New York Times,* May 2, 2002, F1.

16. Luigi Luca Cavalli-Sforza, *Genes, Peoples, and Languages,* trans. Mark Seielstaad (New York: Northpoint Press, 2000), 57–66. Blackburn explains that the out-of-Africa thesis is partly based on the unlikelihood of the independent development of similarities among Africans, Asians, Caucasians, and Amer-Indians: Daniel G. Blackburn, "Why Race Is Not a Biological Concept," in *Race and Racism in Theory and Practice,* ed. Berel Lang (Lanham, MD: Rowman and Littlefield, 2000), 3–26, esp. p. 18.

17. See Nina G. Jablonski and George Chaplin, "The Evolution of Human Skin Coloration," *Journal of Human Evolution* 39 (July 2000): 57–106.

18. That is, human remains of all racial types have been found on all continents. See my discussion of the Kennewick Man controversy relative to this issue in Zack, "Philosophical Aspects of the 1998 AAA [American Anthropological Association] Statement on Race," *Anthropological Theory* 4 (2001): 445–65. On problems for easy assumptions that racial traits are evolutionary adaptations to climate, see my discussion in *Philosophy of Science and Race,* 39, and for the scientific sources, see Alain Corcos, *Myth of Human Races* (East Lansing: Michigan State University Press, 1997), 83–88; Ashley H. Robins, *Biological Perspectives on Human Pigmentation* (Cambridge: Cambridge University Press, 1991); C. Loring Brace, "Nonracial Approach toward Human Diversity," in *The Idea of Race,* ed. Ashley Montagu (Lincoln: University of Nebraska Press, 1965), esp. 107, where Brace sums up the independence of racial traits in terms of selective pressures.

ily traits), such as mitochondrial DNA, is used, so there is no empirical evidence to support the claim that there is a correlation between what we now consider to be physical racial traits, or phenotypes, and any continental location.[19]

Hardimon does not appear to be aware of these scientific problems with the genealogical and continentally based ideas of race. If he is aware of the problems, then insofar as these ideas are imbedded in our ordinary concept, it is not clear why he thinks there is any truth or cognitive validity to that concept. However, he states that the case for "eliminativism" pertaining to this ordinary concept rests in part on the simple idea that "without *race* there would be no *racism*."[20] He goes on to say that racism does have a "toehold" in reality and to argue that preservation of the core idea of race (through the conception of it he offers in (1)–(3)) is necessary in order to address racism.[21] This is debatable once we distinguish between justified belief and unjustified belief. On the level of justified belief we can mention unjustified beliefs without ourselves holding or using them. Consider religion. One can study religion, reason with religionists, and argue against their claims without believing that their ontological commitments are justified. American society used to be very religious, then it became secular, and now seems to be becoming more religious. But one does not have to believe that Jesus is her personal savior to talk about born-again Christians or the intolerance of homosexuality evinced by some of them. Similarly, one does not have to believe that an ordinary concept of race that depends in its core on now-discredited scientific ideas is a justified concept in order to talk about that ordinary concept of race or about the racist beliefs and behavior of some of those who think that the ordinary concept of race is fine. Finally, in addition to antiracist goals of social justice, there is the question of truth, namely: as best we know, does our ordinary concept of race have a basis in physical reality if physical reality is what scientists say it is in a particular domain? The answer is, "No." As to Hardimon's claim that this concept is compatible with science, it is not compatible with *contemporary* science.

B. Kitcher's New Idea of Biological Race

Although Kitcher's 1999 anthologized article was not published in the *JP*,[22] Glasgow cites it as an authority for "the new biology of race" in his *JP* article.

---

19. Cavalli-Sforza, *Genes, Peoples, and Languages*, 61–66. In addition to the nonprotein coding nature of genetic tracking material, the relatively ephemeral quality of soft tissue further complicates hypothesis about what we would call racial traits in ancient peoples.

20. Hardimon, "Our Ordinary Concept of Race," 455.

21. Ibid.

22. Kitcher, "Race, Ethnicity, Biology and Culture," n. 2.

Moreover, Andreasen, in her critical defense against Glasgow's criticism of her cladistic idea of race, referring to herself and Kitcher, writes in the *JP*:

> We have independently argued that . . . most problems faced by earlier biological conceptions can be avoided by defining race genealogically. Kitcher and I are not alone in defining race this way; there is a growing number of biologists who endorse similar definitions.[23]

Let's examine Kitcher's claims first.[24] Kitcher has two sets of claims about race. First, he believes that the geographical isolation of human populations in the past was sufficient to establish the existence of ancient races that were, he says (more or less), "pure." These "pure races" were closed breeding groups for the most part and can be understood as individuals who were descended from ancestors of the same race. Thus, Kitcher advances (R1) below as a necessary condition for a concept of race, with (R2) stipulating heredity of racial characteristics:

> (R1) *A racial division consists of a set of subsets of the species* Homo sapiens. *These subsets are the pure races. Individuals who do not belong to any pure race are of mixed race.*
> (R2) *With respect to any racial division, the pure races are closed under reproduction. That is, the offspring of parents both of whom are of race R are also of race R.*[25]

To accommodate what is known about racial mixture among groups such as African Americans, Kitcher further notes, "Socially disadvantaged races may consist of a pure core together with people any of whose ancestors belong to that core."[26]

Kitcher offers two important qualifications to this first set of claims, the first moral, the second (for want of a better word) epistemological. First, Kitcher carefully disavows all associations between his proposed concept of race and hu-

---

23. See Andreasen, "The Meaning of 'Race'," 94–95, n. 5, for this "growing number" of biologists. Andreasen gives no evidence that the views held by her sources are gaining more adherents, that is, that the number of biologists defending notions of race are indeed "growing." If it is, one would like to know how the new adherents present their case against the scientific views they are replacing, i.e., what the arguments are.

24. Although Kitcher's article appeared after Andreasen first published in this area, his ideas appear to be the background for all of the recent attempts to resurrect viable notions of biological race published in the *Journal of Philosophy*. I also think that Kitcher's views might predate Andreasen's because I remember another version of them from a paper he gave at a conference on race at Rutger's University in the fall of 1994. Although, as I quote Andreasen in my text, here, and according to Kitcher's unpublished remarks to me [in January 2006], each has arrived at the genealogical approach independently.

25. Kitcher, "Race, Ethnicity, Biology and Culture," 92–93.

26. Ibid., 93.

man worth or intellectual abilities, before proposing the concept and throughout his article. And second, Kitcher accepts that in-breeding intergenerational groups not otherwise considered races, such as the English aristocracy, would qualify as races according to his concept.[27]

Now let me turn to Kitcher's second set of claims. Kitcher proposes that his concept of biological race is useful to explain high rates of intraracial breeding among descendants of races in physical proximity in American society. He claims that relatively low rates of intermarriage between descendants of different pure or relatively pure races, particularly in the case of blacks and whites, may be evidence of "incipient racial division" on a local level. Kitcher supports his notion of "incipient races" with what he relates as Ernst Mayr's "non-dimensional" notion of species:

> Populations at a given place at a given time belong to different species if they are not exchanging genes. In exactly parallel fashion, we could recognize "non-dimensional" races, groups at a particular time that are not exchanging genes at substantial rates.[28]

Kitcher's notion of "incipient racialization" is a new notion of biological human race. It has problems of multiplying entities in unpredictable ways and does not match present anthropological notions of human races or possible human races. Kitcher is aware that social factors, such as slavery, segregation, and class structures, may be important causes of what he calls "incipient racialization," but he maintains that, nonetheless, the results of social strictures are biological in a way that justifies a biological concept of race. Kitcher then concludes that race might be biologically real and socially engineered:

> We might say that races are *both* socially constructed and biologically real. Biological reality intrudes in the objective facts of patterns of reproduction, specifically in the greater propensity for mating with other "blacks" (or other "whites" respectively); the social construction lies in the fact that these propensities themselves have complex social causes.[29]

Kitcher uses the terms *social construction* and *biological reality* in novel ways here. Usually when "race" is called a social construction, it is not meant, as he seems to assume, that some human beings are responsible for creating the phenomenon they call by that name. Indeed, if this were all that were meant by "social construction," then water made by combining hydrogen and oxygen would

27. Ibid., 87–90 and throughout the article, 103–4.
28. Ibid., 102.
29. Ibid., 106.

qualify as a social construction. Rather, to say that something is a social construction is in part, at least in this case, to correct an earlier view that it was natural. And when race is called "biologically real," this is not a reference to human mating preferences in a particular society (which are presumably physically realized), but rather a reference to whether or not a taxonomy of human races is supported by independent genealogical and phenotypical evidence that applies to the whole of humankind.

But overall, the main problem with Kitcher's concept of race is its lack of scientific justification, even though it is presented in quasi-scientific language. If we begin with the modern commonsense notion of three major human races, the scientific task is to find some independent evidence for this taxonomy. It is debatable that there ever were pure genealogical groups corresponding to the three major races, which had the phenotypic traits associated with those races in the modern period. At best, a taxonomy of pure ancient races is a hypothesis, whereas Kitcher seems to treat it as a premise. There is not only the problem of evidence that the traits now associated with races may not have been present in the ancestral populations of those groups, but the highly relevant implications of the two current competing stories of human history, the *out-of-Africa* thesis, and *multiregionalism*.

According to the out-of-Africa thesis, which is now the dominant view among biological anthropologists, all modern humans originated in Africa and some of their descendants left that continent for Asia and Europe. Insofar as traits associated with modern races may not have been present in the original African population, but may have developed after migrations, and not necessarily as adaptations to geographical conditions (some may have been adaptively-neutral mutations),[30] at best one can hypothesize a foundation for racial purity based on time spent by an in-breeding population in a particular place. This is not sufficient to ground the ordinary racial taxonomy that posits the three main races as stable natural kinds, because it leaves vague the amount of time necessary to form a race. Although any amount of time spent by a group in reproductive isolation could be massaged by Kitcher's application of what he presents as Mayr's dictum to justify calling that group a race, or even a species, the result would be a large, indeterminate number of relatively temporary human races. While few anthropologists doubt that there is a large, indeterminate number of relatively temporary human populations, nothing empirical is added by calling these populations "races," especially given the connotations of 'race' in ordinary language, which include more essentialist properties limited to far fewer groups.

---

30. There is, for example, some dispute about whether light skin color does facilitate the absorption of vitamin D in cold climates. See Corcos, *Myth of Human Races,* n. 18.

The second account of human history and variation, the multiregional thesis, holds that Homo sapiens originated in Africa but spent at least 1 million years in multiple geographical locations, and that from the beginning, the different groups interbred. Interbreeding, as a scientific concept in this context, has a far lower threshold to establish population mixture and maintain a common species (as well as block scientific ideas of racial purity) than does what Kitcher would call "impurity" or interbreeding as a social concept. The multiregionalists require evidence of only one exogamous mating per generation in a small population.[31] In other words, Kitcher's notion of pure ancestral populations corresponding to ordinary notions of race has no empirical basis, even on the multiregional hypothesis. In addition, contemporary researchers believe that Homo sapiens share all but 0.2 percent of their genes, and of that 0.2 percent, 6–15 percent, or 1/5000 of all genes has been assigned to differences that line up with social racial designations.[32]

As for Kitcher's claim about incipient racial formation, it is unlikely that population geneticists would accept it, because there is less in the present situation to support the existence of pure races than there is in the historical record, and the historical record is not taken by them to support the existence of pure races. Even on a demographic level, according to the 2000 census, 7 million Americans self-identified as multiracial. If one adds to this the incidence of mixed race among existing self-identified African Americans, which some sources place as high as 90 percent, and also evidence that a significant percentage of whites have nonwhite ancestry, even a nonscientific case for roughly pure races in the United States is very weak.[33] The present mixture in the black and white populations, and also within Hispanic, Native American, and Asian groups, guarantees continued genetic mixture even without intermarriage. Furthermore, if we are not beginning with pure or even roughly pure races, what occurs with racial interbreeding is not racial to begin with. That is if races were never pure, then it is not coherent to talk about racial mixture as though that were a new racial phenomenon.[34] Another way of putting this is that if racial taxonomy lacks a scientific basis, then so does mixed race.

31. See John H. Relethford, "Models, Predictions, and the Fossil Record of Modern Human Origins," *Evolutionary Anthropology* 8 (1999): 7–10; Milford H. Wolpoff, John Hawks, and Rachel Caspari, "Multiregional, Not Multiple Origins," *American Journal of Physical* Anthropology 112 (2000): 129–36.

32. On these figures and sources, see Relethford, *The Human Species,* 357–58; Alan R. Templeton, "Human Races: A Genetic and Evolutionary Perspective," *American Anthropologist* 100 (1998): 632–51. A common error in reporting this information is to skip the first number of overall human variation and then state the variation that lines up with social race as though there were 6–15 percent variation in *total* human genes that line up with social races.

33. For discussion of ideas of race and mixed race in the United States according to the 2000 census, see Zack, "American Mixed Race: Theoretical and Legal Issues," *Harvard Blackletter Law Journal* 17 (2001): 33–46.

34. That is, the grounds for recognition of mixed race identities are social, not scientific. Although

What Kitcher's concept of race does successfully describe is in-breeding ge-nealogical groups, of which there are probably many hundreds of thousands among humankind today and throughout its history. That these groups are de-termined by social factors and historical circumstances is indisputable, but to claim that they offer a scientific foundation for what the ordinary person thinks of as race, much less a "new biology of race," is misleading. It is misleading be-cause it falsely appears to provide contemporary scientific justification for the ordinary concept of race.

C. Andreasen's Claim That Races Are Clades

The problems with both Hardimon's and Kitcher's proposals are evident in a different form in Andreasen's proposal of "cladistic races" as a "new biology of race." Andreasen reports that she and Kitcher have "independently argued that most problems faced by earlier biological conceptions can be avoided by defin-ing race genealogically."[35] She explains that the term *clade* in systematic biology means a *monophyletic group*, which is a group composed of an ancestor and all of its descendants. The concept of clades is traditionally used for defining higher taxa and not for intraspecies divisions, but Andreasen asserts:

> Nonetheless it is possible to apply these ideas to race. A number of research groups have proposed branching diagrams that aim to represent evolutionary relationships among reasonably reproductively isolated human breeding populations. I maintain that races can be defined as monophyletic groups of such populations.[36]

Andreasen's assertion that clades are races begs the question of whether evolu-tionary scientists who have provided the data for human evolutionary branch-ing believe that it supports ordinary ideas about racial taxonomy. Strictly speaking, insofar as all present humans are descendants of mitochondrial Eve, we and she form one clade, call it "Eve's Clade." Clearly, "all its descendants" is too strong a requirement if we are to think about subclades within Eve's Clade, because the evolutionary story so far suggests that after some original members of an African population left Africa for Asia, some members of the resulting Asian population left Asia for the Americas. So, to define a subclade within Eve's Clade, we would have to stipulate that only the subclade members who remained in a geographical area were part of that subclade, because the other descendants will

---

not everyone agrees that such recognition is liberatory. See Ranier Spencer, *Spurious Issues: Race and Multi-racial Identity Politics in the United States* (Boulder, CO: Westview, 1999).

35. Andreasen, "The Meaning of 'Race,'" 94.

36. Ibid., 95.

be among those who have left. This means that from the start, Andreasen's notion of human clades as "monophyletic groups" is not a purely genealogical notion as she claims. It is a notion that requires the addition of continental geographical restrictions. A clade is therefore an inbreeding group on a continent. Thus the genealogical concept of race does not resemble a concept of race until it is also a geographical concept. And even that combination is probably not sufficient, because a race-clade of Asians would not count unless they were, in what we recognize as "racial" terms, different from their ancestral race-clade of Africans.

The question that further arises in the context of scientific justification for a cladistic race concept is: How long must the inbreeding group remain on a continent to be a race, if some of its descendants are to be considered a different race in virtue of having moved to a different continent? This question is pertinent because the evidence is not conclusive that what are considered to be physical traits in a commonsense concept of race are adaptations to continental geographical conditions. An additional complication is that the genetic material used to track human populations bears no relation to the genetic material associated with traits of skin, bone, or hair, because it does not code for protein. Indeed, Luigi Cavalli-Sforza, from whom Andreasen derives her notion of clades, has said the following about his own data, which makes it clear that genealogy itself cannot ground race:

> The classification into races has proved to be a futile exercise for reasons that were already clear to Darwin. Human races are still extremely unstable entities in the hands of modern taxonomists, who define from 3 to 60 or more races. To some extent, this latitude depends on the personal preference of taxonomists, who may choose to be "lumpers" or "splitters." Although there is no doubt that there is only one human species, there are clearly no objective reasons for stopping at any particular level of taxonomic splitting. In fact, the analysis we carry out . . . for the purposes of evolutionary study shows that the level at which we stop our classification is completely arbitrary.[37]

Quite possibly, Andreasen is not concerned with the lack of a scientific justification for ordinary concepts of race, because she views the ordinary and scientific concepts as both historically interlapping and independent of each other. She writes, "While providing biological definitions of 'race,' scientists often use CS [common sense] as a starting point. Likewise, CS conceptions of race have

37. Luigi Luca Cavalli-Sforza et al., *History and Geography of Human Genes* (Princeton: Princeton University Press, 1994, abridged paperback edition), 19.

been greatly influenced by science."[38] And, "who decides the NK [natural kind] meaning of 'race' or any other NK term, when scientific and folk meanings diverge?"[39] If Andreasen had begun with the question of whether a concept of race is now justified in science, she could not simply assume that human clades are natural kinds, as she does. However, after she posits human clades as races and then as natural kinds, she returns to the apparent incompatibility between commonsense racial taxonomy and her cladistic system, which as Glasgow points out, omits Asians as a distinct race-clade.[40] She then claims that she does not support semantic deference for science, and that therefore both commonsense and cladistic notions of race can coexist, if we accept that they are different and serve different purposes. She sums up:

> In CS, race helps to explain human social relations, racist beliefs and practices, and the like. Because its explanatory role is different in each case, 'race' has come to function as a NK term in one context and a social kind term in another. Its meaning as a NK term is given by science; its meaning as a social kind term is given by CS. Since there is significant overlap between these uses, both deserve the label 'race.'[41]

Andreasen is right that the word *race* is used in society and also has been used in science. This raises philosophical questions about how both ordinary people and scientists connect their different usages, as well as questions of reference.[42] However, Andreasen then goes on to develop her "argument for the relative autonomy" of scientific and ordinary conceptions of race. As sociological observations (perhaps advanced in a democratic spirit), the multiplicity of contradictory claims about science and race accepted and asserted by Andreasen reflect long-standing popular confusion about race.

Philosophers can sort out this popular confusion about race by attending to the part of the ordinary concept of race that has always had a built-in semantic deference for science. And if we track that deference to its current target in science, that part of the ordinary concept of race evaporates in second-order discourse, and we are obligated to move on to more accurate examinations of human history and identity to take its place. Regardless of how well-intentioned

---

38. Andreasen, "The Meaning of 'Race,'" 100.

39. Ibid., 96.

40. Glasgow, "On the New Biology of Race," 459–60.

41. Andreasen, "The Meaning of 'Race,'" 105.

42. On the difficulties of applying the "new theory of reference" to concepts of race, see Zack, "Race and Philosophic Meaning," *American Philosophical Association Newsletter on Philosophy and the Black Experience* 94 (1994): 14–20, reprinted in *Race and Racism,* ed. Bernard Boxill (Oxford: Oxford University Press, 2001), 43–58.

is the semantic deference held by some philosophers for ordinary confusion about human biological race, they may do substantially more harm than good with speculative, amateur biological attempts to resurrect or support humanistic beliefs in the reality of biologically based human physical racial taxonomy. Politically conscious members of disadvantaged so-called racial groups are not the only "activists" who may want to believe that race is biologically real, as a foundation for social identities, even though it is not difficult to explain that one need not believe that race has a foundation in science in order to combat racism. Some observers think that American society may now be losing basic respect for individual liberty and goals of equality. If egalitarians can make up "scientific" theories of race to accommodate cherished, but scientifically unfounded beliefs, then so can others. Again, human populations are of course real, as are types and even clusters of physical hereditary traits, but nothing new is added to information about them by calling them "races."

2. Postracial Uses of Race and Why Gender is Important

The philosophers discussed in part 1 are not alone in committing what might be called "the fallacy of the ontological obligation" to offer grounding or objective reference for both racism and ordinary ideas about race. With a mind toward the title and theme of this book, I want to suggest that when Hispanic/ Latino scholars speak of race, they are allowing themselves to be hypnotized by postbiological notions of race, whereby everyone knows that the real subject is ethnicity once one brackets both old and new forms of discrimination that work as racisms. Latin Americans, particularly Mexicans, have had a concept of *la raza* which has meant a stable identity of what, based on nineteenth-century racial divisions, would be considered mixed indigenous, European, and sometimes African, races. But when the U.S. government via the census during the late twentieth century, designated Hispanic/Latino as a unified category, the bureaucratic intention was to refer to an ethnicity, because respondents have been expected to be Hispanic/Latino and either white or black. However, even though those who are Hispanic/Latino and white are presumed to be racially white, the fact that many bureaucratic forms have boxes for "white—non-Hispanic" means that white Hispanics, although whites, are not "pure" whites, in some sense. Thus, after bureaucracy created, as a new census category,[43] with one hand an ethnicity, it creates with the other, a race. I call this postracial race,

---

43. Jorge Gracia makes the important point that, of course, the existence of Hispanics and Latinos was recognized before the group was created as a census category.

because it does not directly rest on ideas about biology, as race did, but comes into being by default, in the ongoing wake of white supremacy. Whiteness continues to be constructed as a special kind of biological race, while at the same time, as many have pointed out, whites continue to pretend that they themselves have no "race."

There are other examples of postracial racial mechanisms. The understanding after September 11, 2001, that Saudi Arabians, Iranians, Afghanis, Iraqis, Palestinians, Moroccans, Jordanians, Syrians, and many others from suspect geographical locations could be racially identified, crept into the media unchallenged. However, I don't think that even the most wildly speculative pseudoscientists of race and their followers have hazarded a biological foundation for this group. And by comparison, the category of Asian has within it similar disparities although longer historical antecedents through the nineteenth-century categories "Oriental" or "Eastern."

Returning to the driving social force of white supremacy, the machine of racialization continues to process people, because new forms of discrimination are necessary in order to protect old forms of privilege that are increasingly being threatened. Nonetheless, I submit that it is a grave error to buy into this confusion and attempt to fulfill the fallacious ontological obligation. The title of the conference at the University at Buffalo, from which this book has evolved, "Black Ethnicity, Latino Race?" brilliantly cuts through the fog that continually arises from the shifting sands of ethnicity. Black ethnicity is real. It always has been real as the host for parasitical notions of black race. Latino race is a reactive possibility for identity based on white supremacist discrimination. There is a delusion of alchemy at work here, as though wherever there is discrimination that people falsely believe is based on something like race, which oppressors think they can detect, there must be, and there then is, race, as a well-grounded locus for resistance. Believing that something exists, as in the case of human biological races, is not sufficient to call that thing into existence. A fortiori, acting as though one believes that something exists, as in the case of racist behavior toward a group that is at the same time not believed to be a race, does not call race into existence. Race is an historical idea about real human biology and no matter how justifiably aggrieved victims of racism may be, their real complaints and complaint do not make race exist.

What I am implying here is that there is no necessary or inevitable link between racist attitudes and behavior and the existence of races. To insist on such linkage in the name of liberation runs the danger of being locked into a situation of conflict that cannot be resolved because injured parties perpetually strive to provide an ontological basis, which can only be a false one, for the attitudes and behavior of aggressors and oppressors. That is the theoretical and to a large extent, practical situation in which many participants in identity politics and race studies and critiques are now stuck. It works like a classical dialectic with no synthesis. Because racist behavior and attitudes are an effective form of oppression given current hierarchies of power, opposing them by constructing new ontological bases for them perpetuates them. Resisting racism on the grounds of race is like resisting quicksand—with fog.

We are living in an age of exhaustion of ideas of race, while the wheels of resistance spin on the basis of such ideas. And yet, there is still racism and oppression. I think that we need some new liberatory ideas. For a while I thought that widespread knowledge of the biological emptiness of social racial taxonomies would tip a critical balance. One way in which this could still happen would be through more education about the biological emptiness of race, which would, in effect, reduce ideas of race to ideas of ethnicity, in first-order discourse. Such a reduction could not be a matter of definition or fiat decision but would have to reach deeply into what ordinary people thought about ethnic differences and how they behaved as a result of their beliefs. Because of the rhetorical difficulties in launching that reduction, and because it divides up the human world in ways that ignore a more well-grounded human difference, I don't think that even a successful antiracist project based on understanding the biological emptiness of race could in itself solve the major social problems of our times. The success of the antiracist project could leave intact disparities in power, with the same hands exercising the same kind of control. Oppressors would simply identify new markers for their victims. That is, the fundamental problem of oppression is probably not a question of who or what some people are, but a matter of what other people are permitted to do.

I now think that the *axis* of oppression should be reconfigured from a liberatory perspective in ways that focus on gender. During the centuries of old-style racial oppression—old-style, because based on false physical essentialisms—patriarchy was the form of social organization among the ruling classes. White men ruled, not only over white women but over nonwhites, as well. Gender roles were strictly delineated to support forms of patriarchy within the ruling classes. Gender roles in subordinate classes were always distinctive insofar as poor and nonwhite women were expected to labor outside the home and were not accorded the same honored female virtues as white upper- and middle-class women. However, gender has historically been more than the patterning of men's and women's roles and culturally constructed traits. White ruling class men have historically ruled through enactments of specific constructions of masculinity, mainly violence, exploitation, and domination generally, not just over women, but over nature and men in ethnic groups different from their own. Western racial systems were invented by white European men and for the most part, implemented by them, as a way of ranking and organizing preexisting ethnic groups. That is, racial taxonomies have worked as an ideal system super-imposed on real differences in ethnicity in order to rank and organize people so that profits from labor and the honorific dimensions of human achievements remained in the hands of white rulers. The story of white male rule, like the story of men's rule over women, is not new. But what is new are recent ways in which gender taxonomy has changed along with changes toward postracial race. These gender changes highlight the importance of gender for the theoretical reconfiguration I am proposing.

Women's liberation in Western democracies has brought women into the workplace and civic life. However, women's formal equalities have not funda-mentally changed the structure of gender inequalities. Women retain traditional subordinate roles in their private lives and continue to reproduce traditional pa-triarchal roles through disproportionate shares of parenting and domestic sec-ond shifts. But, they are no longer women, as women have been historically understood, after they enter public life and succeed there. Successful women in public life function as androgynes. Men in public life, however, have not toned down their traditional constructions of masculinity but rather, especially on the highest levels of politics, have recently exaggerated them.

Public life and the conduits of real politics and real power have since the year 2000 become more aggressive, more exploitative of natural environments, less nurturing, less compassionate, and perhaps through the new mechanisms of post-race and white supremacy, even more racist. But I am suggesting that the root of the problem is not only false beliefs about race, but perhaps more important, real social constructions of masculine gender. Men not only continue to rule the world, along with a few female androgynes, on the highest political levels, but they do so as though only exaggerated stereotypical masculine values are important. For there to be real concern for families, individual well-being, and protection of natural beings and environments, on the highest levels of power, something else is necessary. There needs to be a displacement or transvaluation of public values and the valuation of priced goods compared to unpriced and perhaps unpriceable goods, which are largely still produced for free, as gifts, by women in their private lives, or simply "given" in and by natural environments.

To be effective historically, the kind of transvaluation called for would need to take the form of rule by women on the highest levels of national and inter-national politics. And it would have to be women as they have been understood historically, with their traditional concerns and traditional roles. There has been a small degree of political implementation of this kind of political gender re-balancing in the third world and a more substantial implementation of it in Norwegian high politics since the 1970s.[44] Citizens and subcitizens of the one

44. By law, the Norwegian parliament must have 40 percent female membership and the political

remaining and so-far continually ascending superpower have not yet shown credible signs of their ability to imagine such a shift. I have written at greater length about this matter in my book, *Inclusive Feminism,* and will continue to do so.[45]

Let me close with some further (avowedly nonscientific) speculative observations. The entry of women into public life with formal but not substantive equality parallels the assimilation of members of some ethnic and racialized groups into the white European ruling class. As the androgynes gain acceptance and recognition, men become more exaggeratedly masculine, thus reconstructing the androgynes as imperfect males, who, not coincidentally, still mother children and clean toilets in their other lives. As successful erstwhile ethnics assimilate to white life, the preexisting whites recalibrate their self-definitions so that subtle discriminations in the allocation of power persist. The theory, as well as the practice, which would short-circuit these unresolved dialectics are what need to be created. I have suggested a transvaluation of the most basic public social values. The test of whether such a transvaluation will represent a genuine further state in the dialectics of white and male power will be whether it blocks the logic and structure of the old status quo, by preventing the old players from protecting their privilege by redefining their identities. In other words, it must become both ideationally and practically impossible for whites to become whiter and for men to become more masculine as a basis for continued injustice. There are further questions here of the links between identities and actions that issue from them. We may have to devise new ways for ethics to determine not only politics, but social custom as well. And as intellectuals we should be less diffident in making both intellectual and moral judgments about our real lifeworld.[46]

---

concerns of women are recognized to be specific to their historical gender roles, among the political elite. See Hege Skjeie, "Credo on Difference—Women in Parliament in Norway," first published in the International IDEA, *Handbook: Women in Parliament: Beyond Numbers* (Stockholm: International IDEA, 1998). Web posting at www.idea.int (accessed May 2005). For more discussion of these issues, see Zack *Inclusive Feminism: A Third Wave Theory of Women's Commonality* (Lanham, MD: Rowman and Littlefield, 2005), chapters 7 and 8.

45. Zack, *Inclusive Feminism,* chaps. 7 and 8.

46. I thank Jorge Gracia for conscientious and incisive editorial assistance toward the final draft of this article. I am also grateful to him for organizing, with great panache, a splendid and highly enjoyable conference on race, which included many of the same participants who attended the Rutgers University conference on race more than ten years ago in the fall of 1994. I read parts of the introduction and part 2 of this article at this Buffalo conference. (I also read a longer account of the movie *The House of Sand and Fog,* which is not in this chapter, but which I will happily make available if anyone wants it.) Part 2 is an expansion of remarks with which I ended the first section in my conference paper. I wrote it after the conference, and a revised part of it was included in my December 2005 American Philosophical Association Eastern Division Conference paper in New York City, "A Philosophically Serious Comparison of the Ontologies of Race and Gender." Earlier drafts of part 2 of this essay benefited from critical comment for which I am extremely grateful to Bradford Z. Mahon, Rodney C. Roberts, Jason Hill, and Scott Pratt.

CHAPTER 5

Ethnic Race: Revisiting Alain Locke's Neglected Proposal

ROBERT BERNASCONI

In her essay "Is Latina/o Identity a Racial Identity?" Linda Alcoff argues that there is an inevitable racialization of Latina/o identity in process and that it is on that basis that Latinas/os have been shut out of the melting pot.[1] At the same time she acknowledges an ethnicization of Black identity in the sense that blackness has been deessentialized and that self-identification is becoming an important part of its meaning (H/L 40). In other words, on her analysis, the expression "Black ethnicity, Latina race" refers to an identifiable and ongoing historical process. By contrast, many contemporary philosophers treat the concepts that they employ as if they did not have a history, and in particular they assume that racial identities are inherently essentializing. The historical evidence does not support this latter claim, although there has been at times a clear tendency in that direction. Alcoff's sensitivity to this historical process as well as her hope that "race" might change its meaning (H/L 40) leads her at the end of the essay to advocate David Theo Goldberg's notion of "ethnorace." distinguishes "ethno-race" from "race," on her understanding of the term, is that ethno-race does not imply common descent. More positively, it suggests an identity that is at least in part the product of self-creation, while at the same time, as Alcoff also observes, being in some measure visible on the body.

Goldberg's notion of "ethnorace," which he employs in *Racial Subjects* particularly with reference to Hispanics, but with more theoretical detail in *Racist Culture,* is not only a possible resource, but also a symptom of shifts in our way of conceptualizing race.[2] It is a notion that arises from the recognition that it is

1. Linda Martín Alcoff, "Is Latina/o Identity a Racial Identity?" in *Hispanics/Latinos in the United States,* ed. Jorge J. E. Gracia and Pablo Dde Greiff (New York: Routledge, 2000), 41. Henceforth H/L.

2. David Theo Goldberg, *Racist Culture* (Oxford: Blackwell, 1993), 75. Henceforth RC. See also *Racial Subjects* (London: Routledge, 1997), esp. 64–67.

simply false to suppose that what defined racial ascriptions in the past and to-day can be "inevitably reduced to a single, essential claim about biological inheritance" (RC 74). He argues that where physical attributes are assigned a significance, the significance must be considered cultural. Thus the choice of some natural kind as a criterion for group construction is a social choice. In addition, it is always a complicated and highly significant issue as to who makes the choice, whether it is imposed from outside or not, and this too will shift historically.

How far Goldberg's notion of "ethnorace," or similar notions, might succeed in disturbing the notions of race and ethnicity is still an open question. However, Goldberg touches on a crucial issue that helps to explain the divergence between the approach taken to these issues by analytic philosophers and that adopted by so-called continental philosophers when he reminds us that whereas we can distinguish analytically what we have learned to call "race" from what we have learned to call "culture," these are not separated phenomenologically. Like Alcoff, Goldberg emphasizes the role played by appearance in ethnic as well as racial identification: when we identify someone racially or culturally, the so-called physical characteristics are presented as part of a whole that is seen alongside "modes of dress, bearing, gait, hairstyle, speech and their relation" and is not seen as separate from them (RC 74). Jean-Paul Sartre already made this point in *Anti-Semite and Jew* and recollection of it here moves us tentatively toward thinking of race, as Sartre would say, as a form of facticity, rather than as either a biological fact or a social construction.[3] But whereas Alcoff seems to argue for the notion of ethno-race on the grounds that both the notions of race and of ethnicity are needed to understand Latina/o identity in the United States (H/L 42), Goldberg seems to be promoting ethno-race as a way of highlighting the way that employing racial identities in order to determine groups, as well as the formation and selection of which identities constitute races, is a matter of cultural choice (RC 75).

In order to free up our thinking of race and culture to new ways of conceptualizing them, we need to go more deeply into the history of the notions of race and ethnicity themselves. If we are to grasp what possibilities for transformation these terms bear, we need to have a fuller historical understanding of how they came to take on the meanings they have, in addition to an openness to the phenomenology of race. This undertaking far exceeds what is possible in

---

3. Jean-Paul Sartre, *Réflexions sur la question juive* (Paris: Gallimard, 1954), 73–77; *Anti-Semite and Jew*, trans. George J. Becker (New York: Schocken, 1976), 61–64. Sartre does not employ the term *facticity* in that book, but it determines his approach. See Robert Bernasconi, "Can One Understand Race in Terms of Facticity? On Sartre's and Fanon's Conceptions of Race," in *Rethinking Facticity*, ed. François Raffoul and Eric Sean Nelson (Albany: State University of New York Press, forthcoming).

a brief chapter. However, in the present context I will try to explore the potential of a notion parallel to Goldberg's "ethnorace": Alain Locke's notion of "ethnic race." Locke's introduction of this term in "The Concept of Race as Applied to Social Culture" not only offers an opportunity to explore latent possibilities in the notions of race and ethnicity, but also, given the way in which he proposes it during a decisive period in the formation of our current conceptions, provides an opportunity to survey the way in which those conceptions came to be formed.

Alain Locke published "The Concept of Race as Applied to Social Culture" in June 1924 in what was only the second issue of *The Howard Review.*[4] Published by Howard University, this was not a specialized journal but a general periodical on whose editorial board Locke served. The issue in which Locke's essay appeared included E. Franklin Frazier's study of the colored longshoremen in New York City, as well as articles on Shakespeare, on Byron, and on the origins of Roman Satire. This perhaps helps to account for the fact that, so far as I can tell, Locke's essay was largely lost from the broader academic community until Leonard Harris's indispensable collection of Locke's essays, *The Philosophy of Alain Locke,* republished it in 1989.[5] However, even then, the deep significance of this major text went largely unrecognized. This was not helped by the fact that in 1989 there were only a few thinkers ready to break with the relatively new orthodoxy that race is not real. Furthermore, Locke is not entirely consistent in his claims. The overall argument of Locke's essay that race and culture are not in a fixed relationship, but instead are variables that for the most part are not even paired, is presented by him as capable of bringing down a significant portion of what passed for social theory at the time. Nevertheless by the end of the essay, his commitment to pluralism led him to present his account as an addition to modified versions of the theories initially opposed, and not as a replacement for them (PAL 198). One can also see this as a characteristic display of modesty on Locke's part about his own achievement. However, I believe that, even if this one essay by Locke was the only text by him available to us, his stature as a major thinker would be secured, by virtue of the sheer originality of the conceptual framework presented in it.

There is no clearer indication of Locke's originality than the concept of "ethnic race" that he introduced in this essay (PAL 190). To Locke's contemporaries, familiar, for example, with Joseph Deniker's distinction between ethnic groups

4. Alain Locke, "The Concept of Race as Applied to Social Culture," *The Howard Review* 1 (1924): 290–99.

5. Leonard Harris, ed., *Philosophy of Alain Locke* (Philadelphia: Temple University Press, 1989). Henceforth PAL. Locke's essay was reprinted earlier by Jeffrey C. Stewart in *The Critical Temper of Alain Locke* (New York: Garland, 1983), 423–31. Unfortunately this useful volume had only limited circulation.

and races, it would have sounded paradoxical, as it does to us also, although the terms now have a different sense.[6] But we are perhaps more puzzled than they would have been by his claim that race itself (and not just a specific concept of race) is "a culture product" (PAL 193), which to our ears, at least initially, tends to sound nonsensical. Both the concept of ethnic race and the idea of race as a culture product arise from Locke's readiness to allow for some significant connections between race and culture. It is, he says, "Too early" to deny all connection between them. Today, by contrast, these two terms have been dissociated: race is attributed to nature and studied by biology, whereas culture is studied by anthropology. However, this distinction is a historical achievement and a questionable one at that, as is clear from the difficulty anthropologists have had excluding the idea of race from their studies. As Locke said, just because one prominent account of the interrelation of the terms was wrong does not mean that there is no interconnection between them (PAL 188–9). One can read Locke as if he was simply resisting the inevitable dissociation of race and culture, but that would be anachronistic. Locke has much to offer contemporary thought about race and culture, not only because he was addressing the topic at a time when these concepts were fluid, but also because he was, on account of his own experience as a member of an oppressed minority, almost inevitably more struck by the process of reciprocal cultural interchange than members of the dominant culture; he had a different perspective on the process.

One way of negotiating Locke's difficult conceptions would be to read him as a proto-deconstructionist, a deconstructionist *avant la lettre*. There is some precedent for doing so, albeit not with reference to his writings on race, so far as I am aware. In 1988, Ernest D. Mason wrote an essay, "Deconstruction in the Philosophy of Alain Locke."[7] His focus was on the so-called relativistic dimension of Lockean thought. Furthermore, in the afterword to his collection in 1989, Leonard Harris referred to Locke's "subterranean deconstructive project," albeit again with reference to values. Recalling the almost formalistic conception of deconstruction that was prominent in its early years, deconstruction identifies a binary opposition, reverses the hierarchy, and then passes to a new term that is undecidable between the terms of the binary opposition. So, with reference to the opposition between speech and writing, the Western philosophical tradition is said to promote a priority of speech over writing because in speech the speaker is present, whereas the writer is absent from what is written. Deconstruction in response locates within the very texts that pronounce

6. J. Deniker, *Les races et les peoples de la terre* (Paris: Schleicher Frères, 1900), 3; *The Races of Man* (London: Walter Scott, 1900), 3.

7. Ernest D. Mason, "Deconstruction in the Philosophy of Alain Locke," *Transactions of the Charles S. Pierce Society* 24 (1988): 85–106.

the priority of speech a hitherto unrecognized concept of writing that promotes over speech a certain priority of writing. This writing is not the same as the writing that is opposed to speech. It can be called a proto-writing, in the sense that it is prior to the opposition between speech and writing. That is to say, proto-writing is undecidable between them.

Proto-writing thus succeeds in "disorganizing the entire inherited order."[8] Similarly, one could say that Locke, faced with the opposition between race and culture, where race is traditionally presented as determining culture, reversed the hierarchy, presenting race as a product of culture. However, this was merely preparatory to abandoning the oppositional sense of these terms, culminating in their conjunction in the notion of ethnic race. It should also be recognized that, from this deconstructive perspective, abandoning the notion of race and relying solely on the notion of ethnicity would not ultimately liberate us from the inherited notion of race, as intended; the modern notion of ethnicity was formed by its association with a very broad concept of race before being transformed by being brought into opposition to a narrow concept of race and remains marked by it. That is to say, the notion of ethnicity belongs to the same lexical space as race and invariably invokes it, if only in its attempt to distinguish itself from it. To attempt to disorganize the entire inherited order by denying race as an exclusively biological concept in order to rely entirely on a concept of ethnicity is, from a deconstructive perspective doomed to failure, because it does not do enough to disturb the dominant conceptual framework. It merely promotes one side of an opposition at the expense of the other. Nevertheless, even if one could say in this way that Locke formally deconstructed racial essentialism, one would still be left with trying to make some sense of what he had accomplished. The deconstruction has not taken place until the operation has some hold over us. We must read Locke's text closely to see if the deconstruction can take hold.

In "The Concept of Race as Applied to Social Culture," before presenting his own position, Locke provides a snapshot of how the distinction between race and culture was imagined in the first quarter of the twentieth century. We see immediately that both terms were a great deal more fluid then than they are now. This fluidity is possible only because the assignment of "race" to biology, like that of "culture" to anthropology, had not yet taken place at the time the essay was written. For the last fifty or sixty years, "race" has been assigned to na-

---

8. Jacques Derrida, *Positions* (Paris: Minuit, 1972), 56–57; *Positions,* trans. Alan Bass (Chicago: University of Chicago Press, 1981), 41–42. To flesh out this formulaic account one would need to read carefully Derrida's discussion of Rousseau: See *De la grammatologie* (Paris: Minuit, 1967), 203–445; *Of Grammatology,* trans. Gayatri Chakravorty Spivak (Baltimore: Johns Hopkins University Press, 1976), 141–316.

ture, in part in an attempt to dispel one of the ideological conditions of the racism that governed the genocides of the Second World War. Biology thus becomes the sole arbiter of questions involving race and so it can unilaterally decide to deny the reality of race. With the notion of race so rigorously policed within the academy in the postwar period, African-American philosophers attempting to talk about race were made to feel very much on the defensive. They were going against dogma and their use of terms was heretical. That view still seems dominant but with the pendulum swinging back, now is the time to give Locke another reading.

We will understand very little of the history of the concept of race, and thus be confused also about how race was lived, if we do not recognize that for most of their history the terms *race* and *culture* were not easily separated. The term *race* was, from its first definition in the late eighteenth century, used to talk about specific peoples who were as readily identifiable by their behavior as by their physical appearance.[9] The question was not which physical characteristics correlated with what forms of behavior. Observers did not so much find a correlation between the physical and the moral (or, as we might say today, between the biological and the cultural); they saw, or thought they saw, only peoples who looked, acted, and perhaps even thought differently from themselves. Early in the nineteenth century the term *race* was beginning to take hold to describe broad groupings of such peoples and this led to questions about their origin, their number, their destiny, and the effect of race mixing between such groups. It was the task of anthropology to address such questions; what retrospectively we think of as biology—human biology—was included within it, as it would be well into the twentieth century. Most thinkers in the nineteenth century saw the racial as manifesting itself in both physical aspects and "moral" or cultural aspects. In other words, for them, race was as visible in behavior and in dispositions or talents as it was in physical appearance.

In our time the distinction between the cultural and the racial tends to be regarded as the great achievement, the solid rock on which all thinking on this

---

9. See Robert Bernasconi, "Who Invented the Concept of Race?" in *Race,* ed. R. Bernasconi (Oxford: Blackwell, 2001), 11–36. I argue there that Kant supplied the first definition of race. One could also argue that Herder was largely responsible for developing the term *culture* in its specifically modern sense. Kant did not so much characterize the different races by their different cultures, as he separated the races into those that had culture, those that did not but could be given culture, and those incapable of receiving it. Herder objected to the tendency to restrict culture to some peoples. He preferred to think of cultures. He also specifically denied the (Kantian) idea of race. This shows how the full story of the relation of this pair of terms would be a great deal more complex than I have been able to indicate here. Johann Gottfried Herder, *Ideen zur Philosophie der Geschichte der Menschheit,* ed. Martin Bollacher (Frankfurt: Deutscher Klassiker, 1989), 255.

topic must be based, but we need to understand its history better.[10] The decisive form of the distinction is usually attributed to Franz Boas. Legend has it that
he introduced the distinction between race and culture, which freed anthropology from biology and thereby opened the way for the renunciation of race
as a biological category. However, this is not the true story about Boas; it certainly does not reflect Boas's position in the 1920s; and, finally, it does not reflect how Locke saw Boas's contribution. It is clear from *Race Contacts and
Interracial Relations* that Locke valued Boas's book *The Mind of Primitive Man* for
its rejection of the permanency of race types.[11] Boas presented ample evidence
for this thesis in his extensive study for the United States Immigration Com-
mission, and he had summarized some of the conclusions in his contribution
to the First Universal Races Congress held in London in 1911, a conference
Locke may have attended.[12] Boas believed that environmental conditions, social growth, and development impacted racial types, but he presented his findings in a discourse and using methods which by no means illustrate the division
between anthropology and the biological sciences that was subsequently attributed to him.[13] It was therefore entirely appropriate that Locke would cite
Robert H. Lowie, not Boas, as arguing for "a complete disassociation of the concept of race from the concept of culture" (PAL 190). Lowie had studied with
Boas at Columbia University, but he was very clear that he did not want to be
considered one of Boas's followers.[14]

In his 1917 essay, "Culture and Race," Lowie explained that, if culture is defined in terms of social acquisition, then racial characteristics, precisely as innate,
could not by definition determine culture.[15] One need only accept this definition, which seems today so innocuous, to have dissolved one of the more widespread forms of racial determinism. To put it another way, Lowie recognized that
the terms *race* and *culture* were at that time in the process of being redefined
or transformed in such a way that a certain relatively recent form of racial essentialism was being discredited. This was accomplished by assimilating race

10. In what follows I have been greatly stimulated and helped by Kamala Visweswaran's "Race and
the Culture of Anthropology," *American Anthropologist* 100 (1968): 70–83.

11. Alain Locke, *Race Contacts and Interracial Relations,* ed. Jeffrey C. Stewart (Washington, DC: Howard
University Press, 1992), 75–76.

12. Franz Boas, *Changes in Bodily Form of Descendants of Immigrants* (New York: Columbia University
Press, 1912); "Instability of Human Types," in *Inter-Racial Problems,* ed. G. Spiller (London: P. S. King, 1911),
99–108; and for the supposition that Locke attended the congress, *Race Contacts,* xxxciii.

13. John S. Allen, "Franz Boas's Physical Anthropology: The Critique of Racial Formalism Revisited,"
Current Anthropology 30 (1989): 79–84.

14. Robert F. Murphy, *Robert H. Lowie* (New York: Columbia University Press, 1972), 12.

15. Robert Lowie, *Culture and Ethnology* (New York: Douglas C. McMurtrie, 1917), 17. Henceforth
CE.

to nature and culture to the social, following the seventeenth- and eighteenth-century understanding of the relation of nature and society, where nature is necessary, but the social is, by contrast, the site of contingency. Nevertheless, even Lowie did not exclude some influence on culture of heredity traits.

It was only in 1940 with Ruth Benedict that race and culture became antonyms. For her, race is transmitted biologically: culture is acquired after birth and "is not a function of race."[16] One can clearly see how Benedict radicalized Lowie's sharp division between race and culture when she proposed the methodological experiment that one "hold culture as the constant, employing race as a variable" (RSP 22), which is a perspective that would not have occurred to earlier generations, whose starting point was always race or what came to be called "race." To be sure, her conclusion that, often in history, races combine, although not necessarily biologically, to form cultures, was not new. The idea that races are fixed permanently rather than produced was already widespread in the second half of the nineteenth century; but this did not yet lead to a dissolution of the tie binding specific races to specific cultures.

Although Locke explicitly acknowledged Lowie's contribution in dissociating race and culture, so that there could be great changes of culture without any change of race and that relatively minor changes of hereditary ability might produce major cultural differences (PAL 190; see CE 41), he identified a defect in Lowie's position: the fact that Lowie presented no account of why many "culture traits" are so persistent to the point where they come to be thought of as ethnically characteristic. That is to say, Locke acknowledged that the attempt to explain race in terms of culture, or vice versa, had been discredited, but he also realized that the existence of stable cultural characteristics within a group could not simply be explained "as mere historical combinations" (PAL 191). To provide the terms in which an explanation might be offered, Locke introduced the notion of "ethnic race" (PAL 190).[17] This is the heart of Locke's dynamic and social interpretation of race, according to which race is "social in manifestation and derivation" (PAL 198). Locke has what might be called a functional and dynamic definition of race: "Race operates as tradition, as preferred traits and values, and when these things change culturally speaking, ethnic remoulding is taking place" (PAL 195). In other words, Locke tries to retain a place for inheritance, but without thinking of it primarily in physical terms.

Locke's notion of ethnic race is not without its dangers, at least in the way he

16. Ruth Benedict, *Race, Science, and Politics* (New York: Modern Age Books, 1940), 19. Henceforth RSP.

17. Locke equates his idea of ethnic race with Gault's term *sociologic type* (PAL 193). Although I have not succeeded yet in locating in Robert Gault's work any use of this phrase it is worth noting that Gault rejects all idea of a social or group mind.

presented it. The problem can easily be demonstrated by observing Locke's attempt to avoid Lowie's "*extreme* cultural relativism" (PAL 190, my emphasis). Of course, Locke himself with increasing clarity came to embrace cultural relativism and formulated a version of it at the end of the essay (PAL 198).[18] Nevertheless, he tried to qualify it. Already in *Race Contacts and Interracial Relations* he anticipated the development of an account of basic culture types that would constitute "a real science of human society which can account for the superiorities—the real, the admitted, and the unchallenged superiorities at certain periods, of certain ethnic groups and certain civilization types" (RCIR 11). To be sure, in "The Concept of Race as Applied to Social Culture," Locke acknowledged that the basis for doing so was lacking at that time, nevertheless this confirms the limits of his pluralism, in the absence of any justification for his "standard of value for relative culture grading" (PAL 194), albeit we are already led to understand that the judgment is to be made with reference to cultural origins, cultural assimilation, cultural survival, and concrete institutional contributions (PAL 196). One can only express relief that Locke did not go further down this road.

Locke's position is that, instead of culture expressing the race from which it arises, race is a cultural product in the sense that "the cultural conditions must explain the race traits" (PAL 194). It is in this way that Locke reversed the relation of race to culture. He saw not only that each ethnic group is "the peculiar resultant of its own social history" (PAL 194) but also that a broad sense of race is one of the operative factors in a culture (PAL 194). This point readily accommodates our sense that a group's own sense of itself is a major part of its identity. In this way, ten years before Julian Huxley and A. C. Haddon proposed the term *ethnic group*, Locke explicitly rejected the idea of using the term *culture group* in place of the term *race*.[19] Retrospectively we see Locke as swimming against the tide, but his motivation and inspiration came from his experience. He conceded that "concrete culture types as often as not are composite racially speaking, and have only an artificial racial unit of historical deprivation and manufacture" (PAL 194), but he did not conclude from this that reference to race had in consequence lost all relevance or significance. Locke's view of cultural assimilation was such that, even though a relatively "pure" race could have a

18. See further Ernest D. Mason, "Alain Locke's Philosophy of Value," in *Alain Locke. Reflections on a Modern Renaissance Man*, ed. Russell J. Linnemann (Baton Rouge: Louisiana State University Press, 1982), 10–14.

19. Julian S. Huxley, A. C. Haddon, and A. M. Carr-Saunders, *We Europeans: A Survey of 'Racial' Problems* (London: Jonathan Cape, 1935), 108. The term *ethnic group* was also subsequently adopted by Ashley Montagu in an effort to leave behind the notion of race: *The Concept of Race* (London: Collier Books, 1964), 25.

highly mixed culture, and even though "blood intermixture" or "physical assimilation" might or might not accompany or even precede cultural assimilation, race itself, that is, what he called social or ethnic race, was ultimately nothing else than a culture-type understood in terms of culture heredity (PAL 192). This was reflected some years later in his accounts of the process of hybridization, a process that was reflected in the name "Afro-American," which he understood as the title of a cultural hybrid (PAL 213).[20]

Locke cited Lowie again to lend authority to this account of the transmission of cultures, according to which the Western and North American cultures take credit for the way they are taken up elsewhere but are slow to acknowledge their own debts (CE 33, quoted at PAL 196). Of course, Locke did not need Lowie to tell him that, but he was not averse to using Lowie's authority to make a point that can in fact still be made today with some purpose. One must be clear, therefore, that the term *culture-types* is not acting as proxy for an idea of pure races. The basis of Locke's conception is the idea of cultural intermixing. So when Locke equated race with "culture-heredity," it was to insist that "in its blendings and differentiations" it be "properly analyzed on the basis of conformity to or variance from culture-type" (PAL 192). In this context Locke recognized that "blood intermixture" also played a role in cultural assimilation.

Locke's conception of race is based on the recognition that races, insofar as they exist as defined populations, are not so much given as produced. The notion was fairly widespread by Locke's time but had not been fully thought through. What seems to have led Locke to do so, thereby leading him closer toward the idea of "ethnic race," was his 1923 review of Roland B. Dixon's *The Racial History of Man* under the title "The Problem of Racial Classification." Dixon had readily conceded that the "actually existing groups of people" we call "races" do not coincide with the "pure types" as usually described because the races are usually blends.[21] Furthermore, Dixon acknowledged that what are taken to be pure types are themselves "purely abitrary types" (RHM 401, quoted at PAL 166). However, Locke recognized that Dixon was inconsistent in the application of these insights. Locke evoked Keller's *Race Distinction* where it is argued that the concrete descriptive reference of the physical racial types should be abandoned in anthropology as "imaginary forms" (PAL 18).[22] At this point

20. Surprisingly African-American identity is often considered a synonym for Black identity, but it does not call for much reflection to recognize that the two terms are only equivalent in a strictly limited context, specifically the United States. If the topic of this volume had been framed in terms of "Latino race and African-American ethnicity," and if we focus on the numerous Blacks in the United States who nevertheless do not consider themselves, nor are considered, African-American (recent immigrants from Africa, for example), it already appears less paradoxical.

21. Roland B. Dixon, *The Racial History of Man* (New York: Charles Scribner, 1923), 502. Henceforth RHM.

22. Locke, who mistakenly cites *Race Distinction* as *Race Distinctions*, also mistakenly cites Keller as say-

Locke advocated divorcing "the idea of race in the physical sense from 'culture-group' or race with respect to ethnic traits" (PAL 168). It is this latter conception that becomes in "The Concept of Race as Applied to Social Culture" what Locke calls "ethnic race." However, to adopt it is not to abandon all reference to the biological. Indeed, it amounts to an attempt to pass from physical or anatomical anthropology to what he calls biological anthropology which, he says, adopts a "more general morphological approach" (PAL 165).

Dixon's acknowledgment that "actually existing groups of people" do not conform to the "pure types" that are not so much discovered as constructed and identified as the fundamental races was nothing new. Paul Topinard in his *Anthropology* in 1876 had already openly conceded that races were an ideal type.[23] Rudolf Virchow and A. H. Keane would present the concept of race as too broad, too compromised by racial mixing, and fundamentally too indeterminate to be of much help to those wanting to classify the various populations before them at that time.[24] Like most scientists today, they denied that race is a (useful) scientific concept, but because the notion of race was not thought to be solely, or even preeminently, based on scientific evidence, the idea persisted in anthropology for some time to come. It needs to be remembered that the idea that "the concept of race is purely biological" became orthodoxy only in 1964 with the UNESCO *Proposals* long after those biologists who were largely responsible for the *Proposals* had renounced the term *race,* proposing instead the term *ethnic groups.* This was an attempt to abolish racism by fiat and, of course, it failed, as the adherents of this view soon discovered. These efforts are monuments to a time when people thought one could change the world simply by changing the way we talk about it. This was, at best, a half-truth, but the important point here is that race was not first assigned to biology and then denied by biologists. As I have shown, one can already find biologists at the end of the nineteenth century arguing that "race" fails to identify determinative populations in a useful way and that it was no solution to the growing complexity of the data available to them simply to multiply the number of races they recognized.[25]

Ashley Montagu, a student of Boas, like Lowie and Benedict, played an im-

ing "imaginary forms" rather than "imaginary norms." See A. G. Keller, *Race Distinction* (New Haven: Department of Anthropology, Yale University, 1909), 7. The misprint is in the original: Alain Locke, "The Problem of Race Classification" *Opportunity* 1 (1923): 263.

23. Paul Topinard, *L'Anthropologie* (Paris: C. Reinwald, 1876), 471. Henceforth A.

24. Paul Topinard, "De la notion de race en anthropologie," *Revue d'anthropologie,* series 2, no. 2 (1879): 589–660; Rudolf Virchow, "Rassenbildung und Erblichkeit," in *Festschrift für Adolf Bastian* (Berlin: Reimer, 1896), 19; A. H. Keane, *Ethnology* (Cambridge: Cambridge University Press, 1896), 4–6, and *Man Past and Present* (Cambridge: Cambridge University Press, 1899), 31–33.

25. For more information on this, see Robert Bernasconi, "General Introduction," *Race and Anthropology* (Bristol: Thoemmes, 2003), 1:xii–xvi.

portant role in removing the term *race* from biology. A brief examination of his vocabulary shows how the debate was shifting. In 1942 he rejected the idea of cultural races, proposing in its place the idea of cultural castes. At the same time he discarded the idea of biological races, albeit at this early stage of the campaign his resolve was somewhat half-hearted as he conceded elsewhere in the book that human races do exist in the biological sense.[26] Montagu, also, like Locke, described races as culturally produced, but he meant something different by it. Increasingly determined to expose the fallacy of race as a biological concept, he located the origin of the concept of race in the illegitimate transfer of a correlation between social status and physical appearance to biological difference. In other words, "a culturally produced difference" was mistakenly given a biological status (MM 21–22). Montagu presented the idea of race as a false deduction based on correct observations of what had been cultural produced. He outlined the process whereby slaveholders, looking for reasons to justify their conduct, tied differences in social or caste status, via obvious differences in physical appearances, to biological differences.[27] It thus treated as permanent and legitimate what was merely stable and contingent. It is not important here to challenge Montagu's narrative of the cultural production of race, but it is worth noting that, for better or worse, Locke's approach was more general. He focused on how certain cultural practices exaggerated, lent significance to, and even created differences. These differences came to be supported by what one might call "breeding practices" that were institutionally encouraged or tolerated. We ourselves today can see how the significance given to racial purity in North and Latin America played a decisive role in the cultural production of the White, Black, and Hispanic "races."

In conclusion, and returning to my earlier question of whether one can say that the essentialist concept of race was deconstructed in the Lockean text some eighty years ago, the best I can offer is to say that I think it is yet to be decided. The deconstruction will not have taken place until Locke's conception takes hold and, while it has the potential to do so, some of Locke's own subsequent reservations about the notion of culture in his 1950 essay "Frontiers of Culture" serve as a warning. Even if one judges that Locke was too harsh on himself when he said that the cultural effort and self-expression associated with the idea of the "New Negro" died from a misconception of culture (PAL 232), in saying that "culture has no color" and that "there is no room for any consciously main-

---

26. Ashley Montagu, *Man's Most Dangerous Myth: The Fallacy of Race* (New York: Columbia University Press, 1942), 71–72 and 74. Henceforth MM.

27. In the second edition of *Man's Most Dangerous Myth* (Cambridge: Cambridge University Press, 1946), Montagu at page 20 cites for support Gunnar Myrdal's *An American Dilemma* (New York: Harper and Brothers, 1944), which had just been published (citing Myrdal, 89 and 94).

tained racialism in matters culture" (PAL 233), Locke seemed to have largely forgotten his own ideas of race from 1924. One could say he was responding to a changed situation, but as the situation continues to change, the reasons for advocating a dynamic conception of race grow.

To my mind what is most problematic about the current rigidity of philosophical thinking on race is the dogmatic air of those who insist that race has no warrant except as a biological concept and that it is a concept that biology has renounced, with the obvious consequence that the term should be summarily abandoned. By throwing light on the fluidity of these concepts in the 1920s, showing how recent the decision to distinguish race as biological from culture was, Locke invites us to renew our thinking on this topic. His account better accommodates the complexities under consideration than the somewhat simplistic approach that limits itself to culture, following the artificial division between biology and anthropology fashioned in the course of the last century. However, because this approach relies parasitically on the kind of self-identification that it has formally renounced, just to be able to distinguish the different groups, race is reimported to the extent that it is part of a group's self-consciousness.

If, as Linda Alcoff reminds us, the same forces that compel us to think of Black ethnicity in place of a Black race or races lead us to think of Latina/o ethnicity as a race, then we need to respond to this situation by examining how the terms *ethnicity* and *race* are not only both indispensable, but are also dialectically connected, and have become increasingly so to the extent that they have been treated as antonyms. We inherit a model according to which race is permanent and culture is changing. This model conceives race in terms of arbitrary ideal types whereas no population seems ever to conform to them because of the fact of race mixing. Locke fully acknowledges the fact of race mixing, just as he highlights cultural exchange, but he also sees a certain stability across these changes. Races are as much products as culture is: race is a cultural product (PAL 193) and culture has roots and grows in that social soil which, for want of a better term, we call 'race' (PAL 206). Nevertheless, race is about "proprietorship" and "vested interest" (PAL 203), that is to say, about belonging, and this too must be taken into account. Finally, the concept of ethnic race, as opposed to simple ethnicity, also addresses the factical resistance that frustrates attempts to re-create identities on our own initiative. What we are used to calling "ethnicity" cannot be reduced to biological inheritance, nor is it simply a matter of choice.

There are many reasons why one might reject the idea of thinking of Latina/o identity in racialized terms, but all too often a caricature of the concept of race is employed to suggest that no group fits the racial model and that Latinas/os fit it less well than anyone. This caricature usually deploys notions of essentialism, of purity, and of continuity across spatial and temporal boundaries that have in fact played much less a part in the history of racial thinking than most people, especially philosophers, imagine. Linda Alcoff's essay with which I began is a valuable corrective to this picture. She focuses largely on the political reasons why one might want to resist considering Latino/a identity as simply an ethnicity, but when finally she proposes that what is called for is "an identity that is the product of self-creation—at the same time that it acknowledges the uncontrolled racializing aspects associated with the visible body" (H/L 42) and when she adopts Goldberg's "ethnorace," she moves in the direction of the notion of ethnic race as Alain Locke presented it. Locke's notion is not without its difficulties and problems, but as the logic of Latina/o identity and of African-American identity edge a little closer together and as the question of whether these identities are races or ethnicities becomes more undecidable, I believe there is much to be said for exploring the resources of Locke's dynamic conception of group identity to see how far it captures the reality of African-Americans and Latinas/os in the United States of America today.

CHAPTER 6

What Is an Ethnic Group?
Against Social Functionalism

SUSANA NUCCETELLI

Prominent among the philosophical issues raised by ethnically diverse societies are questions concerning the collective identity of the groups of people
that constitute them. Here I argue that ethnic-group identity depends in part
on external factors grounded in a people's history of interactions with others
and with the environment. This externalist thesis can be made out, however,
only if it meets a number of challenges, one of which is brought by 'social functionalism,' a view advocated by Akeel Bilgrami (1995). Although originally offered as a thesis about religious-group identity, social functionalism would
mutatis mutandis also apply to ethnic-group identity. After showing that Bilgrami equivocates between two identity theses, I reconstruct social functionalism as a doctrine about ethnic-group identity. Given that doctrine, it is the
fundamental commitments of members of an ethnic group that determine their
collective identity. Furthermore, such commitments, even when negotiable and
context dependent, amount to a group-identity-constituting factor that fulfills
a certain social function for each member of an ethnic group. But, as I argue
here, there are reasons to reject social functionalism. For one thing, 'Twin Earth'
cases show that it provides neither a necessary nor a sufficient condition for the
identity of ethnic groups. And it cannot accommodate some plausible intuitions
about the semantic features of the words used to talk about ethnic groups. But
externalism accommodates both the Twin Earth cases and those plausible semantic intuitions. In addition, it better captures the fact that, in the case of
Hispanics and many other ethnic groups, whether or not members share a fundamental commitment is irrelevant to their being collectively who they are.

1.

Can someone who holds no religious beliefs at all be a Muslim? In a personal anecdote, Bilgrami recounts how he was 'a Muslim for five minutes' during an unfriendly encounter in a Hindu neighborhood in India.[1] It is not difficult to see that the force of this anecdote rests on an equivocation between two possible construals of the noun, 'Muslim.' Although this word is often used to indicate adherence to a certain religion, it is sometimes also used to indicate membership of an ethnic group. As a religious-group term, *Muslim* can be truly applied to all and only those whose religion is Islam. If interpreted in this narrow sense, Bilgrami's story is simply false: no person with no religious beliefs at all can be a Muslim for any period of time. But religious-group terms such as *Muslim, Jewish,* and *Christian* also admit another construal under which they are ethnic-group terms (hereafter, EGTs). That is why, for instance, we may truly say that Albert Einstein and Karl Marx were Jewish, even though by no stretch of the imagination can they be counted among those whose religion is Judaism. Thus, charity requires that we understand Bilgrami's anecdote in this broader sense: it is as an EGT that he means it, not a religious-group term at all.

Understood in this way, the question 'What is a Muslim?' turns out to be a question about the identity of Muslims as an ethnic group—rather than as a religious group. Nonetheless, on Bilgrami's account, it is adherence to Islam that determines the ethnic identity of Muslims.[2] Furthermore, Islam is taken to be an identity-constituting commitment of Muslims that fulfils a function for all members of that ethnic group. Underwriting this claim is the social functionalist's thesis that

> SF 1: *Whatever determines membership of an ethnic group is a factor that fulfills a social function for the members of the group.*

Assuming that adherence to Islam is the factor that determines the collective identity of Muslims, we may now ask: What, if any, is the social role Islam fulfils for the members of that group? Bilgrami has it that to fundamentalist Muslims, Islam is *the only* basic value they uphold—while to moderates it is but one value among others. This appears to lead to the conclusion that there might be no sin-

---

1. Bilgrami recalls saying, to his surprise, "I am a Muslim," when looking for accommodation in a Hindu neighborhood in India—even though he was not a believer in Islam. "It was clear to me that I was, without strain or artificiality, a Muslim for about five minutes. This is how negotiable the concept of identity can be." See A. Bilgrami, "What Is a Muslim? Fundamental Commitment and Cultural Identity," in *Identities,* ed. K. A. Appiah and H. L. Gates, Jr. (Chicago: University of Chicago Press, 1995), 199.
    2. Ibid., 198–99.

gle, overarching social function of Islam that is one and the same for each member of that group.

But, on Bilgrami's view, this is *not* so. He holds that there is a nonreligious, overarching social function Islam fulfills for all members of that ethnic group, since it has the role of providing Muslims with a sense of autonomy from the West and a sense of dignity—which are contingent on the historical, social, and material circumstances faced by members of the group. As a fundamental commitment of all Muslims, Islam has "recognizable historical sources and has a vital function in a people's struggle to achieve a sense of identity and self-respect in the face of that history and the perceptions formed by it." Moreover, such a commitment can be understood as "a defensive reaction caused not only by scars and memories of Western colonial rule but by the failure of successive governments to break out of the models of development imposed on them by a dominating neocolonial presence of the superpowers through much of the cold war."[3]

Whether or not this line of thought can account for the social function of Islam is, of course, a matter for empirical investigation by the social sciences. For the issue of concern here, however, let us note that Bilgrami's social functionalism is a philosophical doctrine suggesting how to go about determining the identity of Muslims. If sound, this doctrine can, mutatis mutandis, be put at the service of suggesting how to account for the collective identity of other ethnic groups. As far as I can tell, Bilgrami's proposal consists of *SF 1* above, together with the thesis that

> *SF 2: The identity of ethnic groups is determined by no criteria other than the fundamental commitments of their members.*

Such identity-constituting commitments can be construed as inclinations and preferences underlying some choices of relationships, moral principles, values, and norms common to all members of an ethnic group. If we think of them in terms of related psychological attitudes, we may call such commitments "proattitudes" and take them to be very general psychological dispositions to accept certain relationships, principles, values, and norms. (Although fundamental commitments likewise underwrite the negative psychological attitudes of rejection toward certain relationships, principles, values, and norms, we shall for brevity's sake ignore these here.)[4] Given social functionalism, proattitudes that count as fundamental commitments are identity-constituting for ethnic groups.

---

3. Ibid., 209.
4. I would like to thank Gary Seay for discussions of the notion of a fundamental commitment.

For this reason, their loss is group-destructive, in the sense that it undermines the collective identity of the group they sustain. The notion of a fundamental commitment as being constitutive of the self-identity of each moral agent is, of course, Bernard Williams's.[5] At the personal level, a fundamental commitment has a role similar to that suggested by Bilgrami for group-identity—namely, that of helping to establish a sense of our own selves as the sort of persons we are. But to put fundamental commitment at the service of accounting for the identity of Muslims as an ethnic group, Bilgrami gives a twist to Williams's notion while keeping its essential feature of being identity-constituting for the person.

We are now in a position to state *SF,* the conception of ethnic-group identity presupposed by social functionalism:

> SF *A group of people constitute an ethnic group if and only if,*
>> *(a) Its members share at least some commitments which, though context dependent, are nevertheless fundamental in the sense that they establish who those people collectively are, and*
>> *(b) Such fundamental commitments fulfill a historic social and/or cultural function for the people who have them.*

Given condition (a), if any proattitudes that amount to the fundamental commitments of those who have them were lost, that would be identity-destructive for them (they would then cease to be who they are as a group). Given condition (b), the fundamental commitments of a people have cash value for the members of that ethnic group, since they fulfill a need of its members (even though their function is always contingent on that group's history and context).

Note, however, that any account of the collective identity of ethnic groups along these lines would have an objectionable epistemic consequence. For it would follow from that account that the members of an ethnic group must have some special awareness of, or privileged epistemic access to, the fundamental commitments constitutive of their collective identity. Any fundamental commitment is, after all, some person's mental state although it need not be a psychological attitude with full propositional content, such as a belief or a desire, it is nonetheless at least an inclination or preference leading to the acceptance of certain relationships, values, norms, and the like. Such fundamental commitments must then be either conscious states or at least dispositional states of individuals (i.e., states that, although in the "back" of a person's mind, are accessible on reflection). Either way, inclinations and preferences have a psychological reality, and must therefore be epistemically accessible in a special, first-person way

---

5. See Bernard Williams, *Moral Luck* (Cambridge: Cambridge University Press, 1981), and *Ethics and the Limits of Philosophy* (Cambridge: Harvard University Press, 1985).

to those who have them. According to a long tradition in philosophy, each person has privileged epistemic access to her own mental states and events—a view that is weaker, and therefore more plausible, than the standard Cartesian conception of self-knowledge from which the tradition derives. Social functionalism, then, has the consequence that each person must have special epistemic access to the fundamental commitments she shares with other members of her ethnic group.

It seems, therefore, that social functionalism now faces two objections: one metaphysical, the other epistemic. If compelling, these objections amount to a reductio ad absurdum of the doctrine. The metaphysical objection would be well supported if an examination of a representative number of ethnic groups revealed that no fundamental commitment of their members was either necessary or sufficient to the identity of a certain ethnic group. The epistemic objection follows from the metaphysical one: if it turned out that no fundamental commitment were needed for the collective identity of a people, then a fortiori they need have no epistemic access to such commitments. This would be consistent with the externalist view. In fact, as we shall see, if social externalism is correct, a people need have no epistemic access *at all* to crucial factors that determine their collective identity.

2.

The metaphysical objection to social functionalism is grounded on evidence from a representative selection of ethnic groups. Consider the case of Latin Americans and their descendants abroad, an ethnic group known in the United States as "Hispanics" (or "Latinos"). First, let's not confuse this EGT with *hispanos,* a word used in Spanish to denote *anything or anyone fundamentally related to either Spain or its former overseas Empire.*[6] In fact, not only the content but also the history of the term *Hispanics* is quite different from that of its Spanish false cognate: although it existed before the mid 1970s, it acquired its present use in U.S. English then, when it began to occur instead of 'Chicano' in some contexts. The latter term was at the time increasingly employed by public officials to refer to *anyone of Latin American ancestry, whether or not the person was of Mexican descent.*[7]

---

6. Spanish dictionaries follow the Spanish Royal Academy in defining 'hispano' as "Spanish or of Spanish origins." See, for example, Ramón M. Pidal and Manuel Gili Gaya, *Diccionario general de la lengua española* (Barcelona: Bibliograf, 1970), 896, and Julio Casares, *Diccionario ideológico de la lengua española* (Barcelona: Gustavo Gili, 1987), 450.

7. The word *Hispanic* figures in standard dictionaries dating before the 1970s—e.g., *Webster's New World Dictionary of the American Language* (Cleveland, OH: World, 1962). But those dictionaries attest that

Never entirely accepted by those to whom it was applied, 'Hispanics' nevertheless came into general usage, in spite of persistent attempts to replace it with 'Latinos,' a term that has caught on among some members of the group.

A close scrutiny of the content of 'Hispanics,' 'Latinos,' and other genuine EGTs can be seen to support the metaphysical objection against social functionalism, for it reveals that in fact no fundamental commitment of those denoted by each term is either necessary or sufficient for the collective identity of their group. For the record, note that social externalists and functionalists may both agree on what the semantic content of any genuine EGT is: namely, that any such term expresses a predicate and picks out a property, where the latter is understood in a broad sense according to which any meaningful predicate expresses a property. On this view, tokens of 'Hispanic' could be said to express the property of *having Hispanic ethnicity, being of Hispanic descent,* or simply, *being Hispanic*—and similarly for tokens of 'Muslim,' 'African-American,' 'Inuit,' 'Maori,' and so on.

Social externalists and functionalists may also agree in two further claims:

1. *A people's instantiating any such a property need not depend on either genetics or race, since the property could instead be construed as a complex one grounded in deep-lying factors responsible for the group's distinguishing collective identity.*
2. *To constitute an ethnic group, a people must (even when they are quite diverse) at least have one feature in common.*

On both doctrines, any loss of individuating properties is destructive for the identity of the ethnic group they sustain. Yet these doctrines offer competing accounts of the relevant properties. That is, a conflict arises between social functionalism and social externalism when it comes to determining the precise sort of deep-lying feature that all members of an ethnic group must have in common. As we've seen, given social functionalism, (a) those features are the fundamental commitments of members of an ethnic group, and (b) such commitments must be readily accessible to all group members. But (a) and (b) turn out to be false of a number of actual ethnic groups. For example, it is false of Hispanics—a group that therefore amounts to a counterexample to social functionalism. Since in their case, it can be shown that no fundamental commitment determines their collective identity, a fortiori, members of the group need have

---

the term was considered synonymous with 'Spanish' or 'of Spanish origins.' Nixon's officials are often credited with introducing the current usage of the term, in response to concerns that the government was wrongly applying 'Chicano' to people who were not of Mexican descent. See, for example, P. Schmidt, "The Label 'Hispanic' Irks Some, but Also Unites," *Chronicle of Higher Education* 1, no. 14 (November 28, 2003):A9. Yet whether or not this is historically accurate does not affect my line of argument.

no access to such commitments. Doctrine (a), as a putative claim about what determines the identity of Hispanics, is in fact refuted by demographics: well-known evidence suggests that there is *no* religion, values, view of history, perception of the Other, moral norms, etc., common to all members of the group. Whether construed as attitudes or as proattitudes, there is nothing on such counts that all Hispanics have in common.

Furthermore, Hispanics appear to share *no* relevant superficial features at all, as is evident from a closer look at their diverse racial backgrounds, cultural practices, and social preferences. Although some Hispanics have European ancestry (which may or may not be Spanish), others are entirely of Amerindian, African, Middle Eastern, or East Asian descent. Some speak European languages, mainly but not uniquely, Spanish, Portuguese, and English; others, Amerindian ones such as Quechua and Guaraní. Some have dark skin, others light; some listen to classical music, others to salsa, tango, or *chamamé*.

Must we then conclude that there is *no* property *at all* that Hispanics share and that determines their identity? No, for even though they share no superficial feature, deep-lying factors responsible for their ethnic identity are not difficult to find. Arguably, Hispanics share a wealth of communal experiences, including some very characteristic past events and states. There is now logical space to maintain that it is precisely these that constitute their identity and make them the people they are. There is, for instance, a common history Hispanics share, consisting in their quite idiosyncratic relations with other nations and with their physical environment. Although we would expect that a mature social science would provide a detailed account of these factors relevant to Hispanic identity, we may tentatively list among them the fateful encounter of Amerindian civilizations with Europeans in 1492, three centuries of Iberian colonial domination, the bloody nineteenth-century wars of independence, and some salient episodes in Latin America's perennially uneasy relationship with the United States and with other Western powers (including some notorious episodes of overt political, economic, and military interference by those nations).

On this account, it is a history of conditions and events connecting Hispanics to others and among themselves, as well as a certain relationship to their physical environment, that in part determines what it is *to have Hispanic ethnicity, to be of Hispanic descent*, or simply, *to be Hispanic*. An account of ethnic-group identity along these lines is externalist, for it understands 'being Hispanic' as a property of a people that presupposes the existence of others (i.e., those with whom Hispanics have historically been related in such-and-such ways).[8] The same

8. It has become conventional to define external properties by contrast with those that are internal. While the latter do not presuppose the existence of anything other than that the thing that has them,

point can be made in a variety of equivalent ways. We may say that, on social externalist assumptions, being Hispanic supervenes on external factors, since it supervenes on a people's relations to things 'outside' that ethnic group. But we could also hold that being Hispanic is an external property because it does not preserve across internal replicas. However construed, these claims can be supported by a 'Twin-Earth' thought experiment, to which we now turn.

Imagine a possible world, w_2, superficially identical to the actual world, w_1. In w_2, there is a continent referred to in vernacular as 'the Americas' that is partly inhabited by a people referred to as 'Hispanics.' These have superficial properties (nonintentionally described) indistinguishable from those of Hispanics in w_1 (including their physical, social, moral, cultural, religious, and practical features and preferences). We shall call that continent, 'Twin Americas,' and the people just described, 'Twin Hispanics.' Twin Americas differs, however, from the Americas in a number of ways relevant to the identity of Twin Hispanics. First, it is a continent of quite recent creation since it resulted from geological developments that took place, say, in the twelfth century. In addition, the people who inhabit it have had historical experiences that differ radically from those of Hispanics in the actual world. At this point, we may imagine that the Aztecs, Mayans, and Incas never existed in Twin Americas, nor did the Spaniards and Portuguese ever arrive there. But suppose that conquerors of another national group did: say, the Chinese, who ruled for three centuries, imposing Confucianism instead of Scholasticism—so that the peoples called 'Hispanics' in w_2 have never stood in any relationship to Aristotle, Aquinas, the Fathers of the Church, or any of the other 'authorities' imposed on Hispanics during more than three centuries of Iberian rule.

Often, in discussions of what determines the identity of natural and biological kinds, we come to the point where we must test our metaphysical intuitions and try to determine what we should say in the counterfactual scenario. In a similar way, we must now test our metaphysical intuitions by asking what we should say about the identity of those peoples? Are they Hispanics? Should we call them 'Hispanics'? Were we to answer (as I think we should) that it is *not* possible for them to be Hispanics, and that it is not possible to use the EGT 'Hispanics' in either speech or thought involving them, our intuition would then be

---

the former do. (For instance, the property of *being west of Central Park* is relational or external by definition: whether an object has it depends on how that object is geographically related to Central Park.) Similarly, external properties differ from internal ones in that the former may *not* preserve across internal replicas. Thus, the external property of *being west of Central Park* does not preserve across internal duplicates: when I am at the Museum of Natural History, I have it, while any possible replica of mine who is at the Metropolitan Museum, lacks it. Either way, these are the possible construals of 'external properties' I am invoking here.

supporting social externalism of the sort underlined above. For the intuition underwriting our answers is that, given those peoples' interactions with others and with their environment, even though everything else remains the same, it is simply not possible, in the metaphysical sense, that they should be Hispanics. If this thought experiment is compelling, then so is the following principle of group identity for Hispanics:

> HGI. *For every possible world and for every person in a possible world, a person is Hispanic if and only if she is a member of an ethnic group individuated by the same factors that individuate the group of Hispanics in the actual world.*

The Twin Earth case suggests that, in w_2, the people superficially identical to the Hispanics in w_1 lack the property of being Hispanic. Since, by hypothesis, the two groups differ only in their histories of communal relations to others and to the physical environment, it follows that these are the deep-lying factors that determine the collective identity of the group.

Similarly, the Twin Earth thought experiment entails that the ethnicity of a group does not supervene on some internal properties of the group—an externalist thesis that may be expressed as

> E. *Necessarily, two groups of people x (in any possible world) and y (in any possible world) could have the same superficial properties but differ in their ethnicity.*

That would be the case whenever x's and y's histories of interaction with others and with the environment differ substantially—which amounts to saying that the property of having a certain ethnic identity may not preserve across groups that are internal replicas. In short, any such property is relational—in other words, it supervenes on external factors. I submit that a closer look at what determines membership of the group of Hispanics supports each of these conclusions, which can be summarized in this way

> H. *The ethnicity of a people supervenes on their history of relations with others and with the environment.*

That individuals identified as Hispanics do share a heritage marked by past acts and events in the way suggested above is, however, completely independent of whether or not those individuals themselves have explicit knowledge of the historical experiences of their group. This provides another reason for rejecting social functionalism in light of the epistemic consequences of that view noted above.

3.

Externalist intuitions also appear plausible for other ethnic groups. Consider the property picked out by 'Eskimo' and 'Inuit,' both EGTs conventionally used to talk and think about the people of a large traditional culture in the arctic regions of North America, Asia, and Greenland. The term *Eskimo* (in vernacular, *eaters of raw meat*) was introduced by Algonkian Indians to refer disparagingly to certain people whom they encountered as neighbors. That EGT was never accepted by some members of the denoted group, and there was, in the late 1970s, an attempt to replace it with 'Inuit,' a term that seems to have caught on among certain communities in Canada and Greenland. Were we to ask, to what, if anything, 'Eskimo' applies, the best candidates would, again, be a property: that of *having Eskimo ethnicity, being of Eskimo descent,* or simply, *being an Eskimo.* Either way, there is no denying that the members of this ethnic group, despite their diversity, share an ethnic identity that distinguishes them from other Northern peoples. Although it would be a nonstarter to make that property depend on either genetics or race, we may construe it as an external property along the externalist lines suggested above. Our account, in that case, would begin by noting that for the Eskimo too, deep-lying factors seem responsible for their being who they are. Although we shall in the end look to social science for a detailed account of such factors, we can in the meantime run a Twin Earth case to isolate the putative factors scientists should look at. Once again the thought experiment will point to the history of the ethnic group and its relations to the environment: the Eskimo interactions with others (including the Algonkians) in the arctic regions of the world are the factors that have made possible their being who they are, with their characteristic seminomadic culture, their art, their ways of life, and their language (Eskimo, a major branch of the Eskimo-Aleut family). Salient in that history are, of course, their being the descendants of indigenous peoples of the far north, and also their contacts with seagoing Norsemen in the thirteenth century, and finally their causal commerce with an especially severe physical context in the arctic regions of North America, Asia, and Greenland.

But externalist intuitions along these lines are not evoked exclusively by the cases of the Hispanics and the Eskimo. As yet another instructive example, consider the Romani. In their case, an externalist account of their ethnic identity appears the *only* sound option available. As before, the account first considers the content of the EGT commonly used in speech and thought involving this ethnic group: namely, 'Gypsy,' which resulted from a mutation of a misapplied French term for Egyptians. This EGT plainly testifies to the misconception of Westerners about the group's origins, wrongly believed to be in Egypt. Even today, a number of biased connotations such as those of *wanderers* and *fortune tellers* are still associated with this and other EGTs for the Romani, such as 'Travelers,' the term preferred in Britain (which clearly connotes a way of life that is simply false of many members of the group).[9]

In any case, to account for the collective identity of the Romani, we may construe the property of being Romani as an external one, provided we have a sound intuition that some external deep-lying factors appear responsible for their being who they are. And again we shall be tentative in our conclusions, since it is up to the social sciences to produce the final account of such factors. As with previous examples, we may run a Twin Earth thought experiment to support our intuitions, holding constant the superficial properties of the Romani in the counterfactual situation while varying the history of causal interactions of the group with others and the environment. If it is, then, only those variations that determine our different judgments about the identity of the group, we may confidently confirm the presumption that it is indeed something external that is responsible for the collective identity of the group. I expect that salient among such external factors would be the Romani's diaspora from India to Europe in the fourteenth and fifteenth centuries, their development of a characteristic nomadic culture with particular folkways and language (Romany), and their ability to maintain a migratory way of life, chiefly in Europe and America, for centuries.

Again in this case, it could be held that the members of this ethnic group, despite their diversity, share a property that distinguishes them from other peoples of the world—which need not depend on either genetics or race. As in the cases of being Hispanic or being Eskimo, the property of being Romani is a complex one, grounded in some past states and events of their common experiences with others and with the environment. If I am right about this, it follows that it is not a fundamental commitment accessible to all Romani, but rather their history of relations with others and with the environment that determines their collective identity.

If the above accounts of Hispanic, Eskimo, and Romani identity are plausible, then the thesis of constitutive social externalism (CSE) also is, since it maintains

CSE. *It is a people's history of interactions with others and with the environment that determines their identity as an ethnic group.*

9. In "The Time of the Gypsies: A 'People without History' in the Narratives of the West," in *Identities,* ed. Appiah and Gates, Jr., 338–79, Katie Trumpener reports that the designated peoples themselves prefer tribal EGTs, such as 'Sinti' and 'Roma' in Germany and 'Vlax' in the Balkans.

In other words, such relations determine the type of ethnicity a group instantiates. The explanatory counterpart of this thesis, explanatory social externalism (ESE), is the claim that

> ESE. *Any correct account of the identity of an ethnic group must consider its history of relations with others and with the environment.*

That is, any correct account of the identity of an ethnic group must consider relational properties of that group. Further support for each of these externalist theses is provided by a well-supported account of the semantic features of ETGs, to which we now turn.

4.

   Among important questions about ethnic-group words are not only what counts as a proper use of such terms but also how to account for their meaning and denotation. In popular discourse, the proper use of ethnic-group terms is often the central issue.[10] Philosophers have shown some interest in both the proper-use and the semantic question. The former is principally addressed by those who write on political and social philosophy and often also involves discussions of other group terms, such as racial-group terms and nationality terms. For example, Ofelia Schutte attempts an answer to the proper-use question in the course of discussing whether the use of EGTs undermines or contributes to the struggle of minority groups for their rights in the United States.[11] But the semantic question is, of the two, the most relevant to my interest here. Unfortunately, the literature addressing it is by no means abundant. Frege has written on the role of 'Turk' in sentences such as 'The Turk besieged Vienna.'[12] Yet his remarks are limited to logical form, urging that the semantic contribution of an EGT to the propositions in which it occurs is that of a singular term— without providing sufficient support for this claim.[13]

   Jorge Gracia (2000) has made a current attempt to answer the semantic question. After offering some pragmatic reasons in order to justify the use of ethnic

---

10. For instance, see discussion on the adequate terms for the peoples of traditional societies in P. Keal, *European Conquest and the Rights of Indigenous Peoples: The Moral Backwardness of International Society* (Cambridge: Cambridge University Press, 2003).

11. Ofelia Schutte, "Negotiating Latina Identities," in *Hispanics/Latinos in the United States: Ethnicity, Race, and Rights,* ed. Jorge J. E. Gracia and Pablo De Greiff (New York: Routledge, 2000), 61–76.

12. Gottlob Frege, "On Concept and Object," in *Philosophical Writings,* ed. P. Geach and M. Black (Oxford: Blackwell, 1952), 42–55.

13. Nuccetelli, "Reference and Ethnic-Group Terms," *Inquiry* 6 (2004): 528–44.

groups terms, he looks at the semantic properties of "ethnic *names.*" His account of such properties is rooted in Wittgenstein's family of resemblance approach to the meaning of words, which amounts to a cluster theory of meaning. On this theory of EGTs, there is a cluster of different meanings speakers associate with those terms and such meanings determine their denotation. Yet since the cluster theory of EGTs can be shown to be a variant of Fregean semantics, it is also vulnerable to objections that undermine the latter. Call 'descriptivism' a semantic account of EGTs that is either Fregeanism or the cluster theory. In "Reference and Ethnic-Group Terms," I have offered a number of objections to descriptivism. I shall rehearse neither the objection nor commentaries on the literature connected with this theory of EGTs semantic properties.[14] It is sufficient to note that, of the two major semantic accounts of the content of EGTs, descriptivism and the causal theory, it is only the latter that avoids some puzzles that arise from certain scenarios involving communication by means of such terms.[15] Semantic descriptivism takes the property picked out by tokens of an EGT to be the speakers' *nondemonstrative* conception/s of an ethnic group. This has the implausible consequence that, whenever the speakers's only conception of the property denoted by an EGT is true, not of all and only the members of the intended group, but of the members of some *other* group, then the extension of the speaker's tokens of that term would be the property of belonging to that other group. Furthermore, as we've seen in the cases of 'Hispanic,' 'Eskimo,' and 'Gypsy,' although speakers may have erroneous and sometimes even opposite ways of thinking about the property of belonging to a given ethnic group, they may still succeed by conventional linguistic means in expressing propositional attitudes involving that group.

14. In "Race Culture, and Identity: Misunderstood Connections," in *Color Conscious: The Political Morality of Race*, ed. K. A. Appiah and A. Gutmann (Princeton: Princeton University Press, 1996), Anthony Appiah looks closely at both the direct-reference and the descriptivist semantic account of racial-group terms. Although he remains neutral between these accounts, on his view any such term would turn out to be empty under either account. For in the case of racial-group terms, he contends, neither essences nor descriptions are plausible candidates that might contribute to the grounding of their extension. Yet, on Appiah's view, racial-group terms do have a role to play in explanation and prediction of action, no less than 'witchcraft,' 'phlogiston,' and other empty words. A number of reasons, however, precludes Appiah's discussion for being of any help for the topic of concern here. First, his arguments attempt to undermine each of the two best semantic accounts for the case of racial-group terms without proposing an alternative theory. Furthermore, his appeal to a racial-term's role in explanation and prediction of behavior is a pragmatic move that falls short of addressing the semantic question. In addition, neither his rejection of Fregean semantics and the direct-reference theory nor his conclusion about the role of racial-group terms in folk-psychology can apply to EGTs' case unless it is shown that these and racial-group terms are relevantly analogous.

15. In Nuccetelli, "'Hispanics,' 'Latinos,' and 'Iberoamericans': Naming or Describing?" I proposed a version of referentialism about ethnic-group terms that is stronger than the causal theory I now favor. For more on the latter, see Nuccetelli, "Reference and Ethnic-Group Term."

These arguments support a causal theory of EGTs. At the same time, they also provide reasons for construing the property of belonging to an ethnic group in the externalist way suggested above. For instance, in the case of the Eskimo, the causal theorist may hold that when the Algonkians dubbed their neighbors 'Eskimo,' they had causal contact with a group of individuals constituted by a certain property cashed out along externalist lines. Our deference to a referential usage going back to the Algonkians' interaction with those people (whose eating habits they disdained) is what grounds the content of that EGT for us.

One difficulty with my proposal, however, is that it appears to imply that a person belongs to an ethnic group or groups "no matter what." That is, I seem committed to holding that someone who has no sense of belonging to a certain group is nonetheless a member of the group provided there is an historical chain, however remote, linking that person with a group individuated along the lines suggested above. But I can meet this objection. For when it comes to ascribing ethnicity to *individuals,* externalism is consistent with a plausible principle such as

AEI. *Any individual belongs to a certain ethnic group if and only if her sensing membership of that group figures in at least some intentional description of that individual,*

where the latter includes ascriptions of beliefs, desires, fears, hopes, and the like. For the purpose of concern here, the intentional description that matters involves attitudes presupposing the *empathy* of those who have them with an ethnic group they sense to be their own. Such attitudes often underlie some of their actions and must therefore be invoked in any folk explanations or predictions of them—as when we explain why some Armenian Americans boycott Turkish-made products or Rosa Parks refused to sit in the back of the bus. By contrast, other actions are explained and predicted in terms of attitudes that presuppose the rejection of a certain ethnic group, which is sensed as antagonistic. They can only be explained or predicted by invoking a person's *antipathy* toward a certain ethnic group—as when we explain Le Pen's reactions to Muslims in France, or the use of 'Sudaca' as a derogatory nickname for Latin Americans in Spain.

Attitudes of both types are ordinarily invoked in intentional description, which is crucial to ordinary folk-psychological explanations and predictions of behavior. It is not uncommon to link a commonsense explanation of someone's action to her membership of a certain ethnic group. For example, an explanation of why Phong went out of his way to show the Carnegie Hall to some tourists may very well invoke his being East Asian, and his discovering that the tourists were from South Korea. Similarly, after learning that I'm Argentinian, the gym clerk from Honduras told me I need not worry if I forgot my ID. Why did she believe then that I could be an exception to the rule? A plausible answer here would consist in intentional description that invokes ethnicity. Yet neither Phong nor the gym clerk need be aware of (let along have special epistemic access to) the deep-lying factors responsible for ethnic identity in either case. After all, the issue at stake is metaphysical, not epistemic.

Finally, let's consider the following case: a South American ambassador to the Organization of American States in Washington brought his two daughters with him to the United States.[16] These young women then grew up in Washington, developing *no* psychological attitude at all presupposing empathy to Hispanics— but had instead some attitudes that presuppose either total indifference or antipathy to them (such as the belief that they do not belong to that ethnic group, the hope that they would not be mistakenly taken for a member of the group, and the desire to avoid interaction with anyone whose ethnicity was Hispanic). Given AEI, since no intentional description in this case need invoke the daughters' sensing their being Hispanic at all, it seems to follow that these young women cannot be said to have that property.

Yet social externalism can accommodate scenarios of this sort, in which individuals drop out of an ethnic group. It can also make room for the fact that membership of ethnic groups is a matter of degree. Moreover, it is clearly consistent with the evidence that members of an ethnic group often lack reflective knowledge of either their membership of it, or of the deep-lying factors that determine the identity of their group, or of both. At the same time, social functionalism has been shown implausible. For although fundamental commitments and historical recollection are often important elements for communities and find their expression in a great variety of symbolisms, the counterexamples proposed here show that they cannot determine the identity of ethnic groups. In addition, social functionalism was found to have unacceptable epistemic consequences, and this result amounts to indirect support for social externalism. Ethnic identity, then, has much to do with a people's legacy from the past. It is the history of their interaction with others and their environment that makes them who they are, and it is in this way that they are constituted as a people.

---

16. This anecdote is based on a real-life case. I would like to thank Bill Cooper and Gary Seay for their input on this example.

RACISM, JUSTICE, AND PUBLIC POLICY

CHAPTER 7

Racial Assimilation and the Dilemma of Racially Defined Institutions

HOWARD McGARY

1. Racism and Race Talk

The evidence is overwhelming in support of the claim that people have been assaulted, denied opportunities, enslaved, and even killed because they were perceived to be members of a particular racial group. The legacy of racism, particularly antiblack racism, still shapes economic, political, and social relationships in contemporary American society. People of good will claim that the goal of the good society should be to eliminate all of the vestiges of a system of racial discrimination. Unfortunately, there is not a consensus about what the present social reality is regarding racism and what steps, if any, should be taken to eliminate it.

The nature of racism and what should be done to eliminate it is complicated by the disagreements over the nature and value of racial identities.[1] Contemporary political thought has focused on the role race should play in our lives. One group of theorists claims that races are natural kinds. For them, races are real. Some of these theorists make an inference from the reality of race to the

---

The ideas developed in section 3 of this essay were originally presented in my "Douglass on Racial Assimilation and Racial Institutions," in *Frederick Douglass: A Critical Reader*, ed. Bill E. Lawson and Frank Kirkland (Malden, MA: Blackwell, 1998), 50–63.

1. See, e.g., Kwame Anthony Appiah, *Ethics of Identity* (Princeton: Princeton University Press, 2005); Appiah and Amy Gutmann, eds., *Color Consciousness: The Political Morality of Race* (Princeton: Princeton University Press, 1996); Bernard R. Boxill, *Blacks and Social Justice* (Lanham, MD: Rowman and Littlefield, 1992); Howard McGary, *Race and Social Justice* (Malden, MA: Blackwell, 1999); Charles W. Mills, *Blackness Visible: Essays on Race and Philosophy* (Ithaca: Cornell University Press, 1998); Lucius T. Outlaw, Jr., *On Race and Philosophy* (New York: Routledge, 1996); and Tommie Shelby, *We Who Are Dark* (Cambridge: Harvard University, 2005).

conclusion that a person's race is a morally relevant characteristic of persons. While others admit that races are real on the ontological level, they deny that they have any moral relevance.

According to both positions, because race is real it can be sensibly used as a subject term in our discourse. On this view, because races are natural kinds, they are seen as causally efficacious. A person's race can causally affect things like attributes, characters, and mental abilities. However, not all those who view races as natural kinds believe that some races are superior to others nor do they intentionally support the position that some people should be denied opportunities because of their racial identities.

However, the critics of races as natural kinds have argued that these things will be the unintended consequences of adopting such an account of the nature of racial identities. Anthony Appiah, has described these views on racial identity as racialism, and, for him, racialism cannot be defended on ontological or moral grounds.[2]

The worries associated with races defined in naturalistic terms lead some theorists to defend the view that races as natural kinds do not exist.[3] In the recent spate of literature on race, this position has been characterized as racial eliminativism.[4] According to this position, a just or a good society should strive to eliminate race talk from our moral, political, scientific, or social discourse. For the racial eliminativist, race talk just doesn't make sense.

Obviously, racial naturalists reject the eliminativist position. But there is also a group of critics who reject racial eliminativism, but do not believe that racial naturalism is nonsense, and as such, it need not be eliminated from our discourse and theorizing.[5] They defend what they describe as racial constructivism. According to this position, races do exist but they lack a natural essence. This is the view that many attribute to W. E. B. Du Bois in his classic paper, "The Conservation of Races."

2. Kwame Anthony Appiah, "Racisms," in *Anatomy of Racism*, ed. David Theo Goldberg (Minneapolis: University of Minnesota, 1990), 3–17.

3. For excellent philosophical discussions of the reality of races, see Kwame Anthony Appiah, *In My Father's House* (New York: Oxford University Press, 1992); Bernard R. Boxill, introduction to *Race and Racism*, ed. Boxill (Oxford: Oxford University Press, 2001); Joshua M. Glasgow, "On the New Biology of Race," *Journal of Philosophy* 100 (2003): 456–74; Michael Hardimon, "The Ordinary Concept of Race," *Journal of Philosophy* 100 (2003): 437–55; Sally Haslanger, "Gender and Race: (What) Are They? (What) Do We Want Them to Be?" *Nous* 34 (2000): 31–55; Philip Kitcher, "Race, Ethnicity, Biology, Culture," in *Racisms*, ed. Leonard Harris (Amherst, NY: Humanities Books, 1999): 87–117; Ronald R. Sundstrom, "Race as a Human Kind," *Philosophy and Social Criticism* 28 (2002): 91–115; Paul C. Taylor, *Race: A Philosophical Introduction* (Malden, MA: Blackwell, 2004); and Naomi Zack, *Race and Mixed Race* (Philadelphia: Temple University Press, 1993).

4. See Frederick Douglass, "The Future of the Colored People," in *Negro Social and Political Thought 1850–1920*, ed. Howard Brotz (New York: Basic Books, 1966), 308–10.

5. See, e.g., Outlaw, *On Race and Philosophy*, 135–57.

It is not my purpose in this chapter to resolve the dispute over the concept of race. My goal is to examine the tension that some racial eliminativists experience when they support social institutions that are defined in terms of racial categories.

2. Nineteenth-Century Racial Eliminativism

In the nineteenth century, an important segment of black social and political thought focused on the debate between racial eliminativists and black nationalists. Frederick Douglass was an ardent supporter of the eliminativist point of view,[6] whereas Alexander Crummell was an early advocate of black nationalism.[7]

Douglass and Crummell strongly disagreed over the importance of racial identity, racial pride, and the role that race should play in any strategy for achieving social justice. Douglass believed that racial identity did not have any intrinsic value, and that taking pride in one's race indicated a misunderstanding about the nature of pride. As far as social justice was concerned, Douglass believed that the only way for people designated as black, or any other downtrodden racial group, to be treated justly required the elimination of races altogether. In other words, he supported biological amalgamation. But having said this, we also find that Douglass also believed that institutions of a complexional character would be necessary for a time until the society could eliminate racial distinctions.[8]

Crummell, on the contrary, believed that blacks or any other racial group should acknowledge and take pride in their racial identities and that doing so was a crucial component of any program that would lead to treating all people justly. He also believed that blacks must leave the United States in order to flourish as a group.[9]

The dispute between Douglass and Crummell in the latter part of the nineteenth century is similar in many respects to the present dispute between Anthony Appiah and Lucius Outlaw. Of course, the dispute between Appiah and Outlaw has been shaped by findings in biology, genetics, and social anthropology that were unavailable to Douglass and Crummell. So where Douglass and Crummell saw races as natural kinds, Appiah and Outlaw both agree that races

6. Douglass, "The Claims of the Negro Ethnologically Considered," in *Negro Social and Political Thought,* ed. Brotz, 226–44.

7. Alexander Crummell, "The Relations and Duties of Free Colored Men to Africa," in *Negro Social and Political Thought,* ed. Brotz, 171–80.

8. Douglass, "An Address to the Colored People of the United States," in *Negro Social and Political Thought,* ed. Brotz, 211.

9. Crummell, "The Race Problem in America," in *Negro Social and Political Thought,* ed. Brotz, 180–90.

are socially constructed. However, like Douglass and Crummell, they disagree about the value of acknowledging racial identities.[10] Appiah's goal is to reach a time where racial identities do not exist, while Outlaw's goal is to reach a society where people can be respected and treated justly in spite of their racial identities. Their dispute is not over whether races are real on the ontological level, but over whether races should have any moral or political relevance in our actions and theorizing.

Perhaps we can gain insight into the dispute between contemporary eliminativists and noneliminativists by examining Frederick Douglass's reason for thinking that he could consistently support racial eliminativism and what he called "institutions of a complexional character."

3. Douglass on Racial Institutions

Although Douglass gave an eloquent defense of the dignity of human beings, he did not believe that all humans act in dignified ways. For Douglass, every human being is deserving of rights and respect, irrespective of characteristics like race, religion, or gender.[11] According to him, morality sets the bounds of political and social action, and thus it should govern the means and strategies adopted by political and social activists.[12] It should be noted, however, that Douglass recognized that justice is an important part of what we mean by morality, but that it does not exhaust the concept. So even though a political leader may not be required by the constraints of justice to show compassion and generosity, more general moral requirements may obligate him to do so. However, Douglass's position raises an interesting question: If justice does not exhaust the demands of morality, can a morally decent person distribute social benefits and burdens by using race as a criterion of distribution?

Douglass resists giving a blanket condemnation of racial classifications. He writes: "We shall undoubtedly for many years be compelled to have institutions of a complexional character, in order to obtain this very idea of human broth-

10. Appiah and Outlaw have had public exchanges over the view that Appiah expressed in his important article "The Uncompleted Argument: Du Bois and the Illusion of Race," reprinted in *"Race," Writing and Difference,* ed. Henry Louis Gates, Jr. (Chicago: University of Chicago Press, 1986), 21–37.

11. Douglass, "The Claims of the Negro Ethnologically Considered," 226–41.

12. Douglass, "Love of God, Love of Man, Love of Country: An Address Delivered in Syracuse, NY, September 24, 1847," in *The Frederick Douglass Papers,* ed. John W. Blassingame (New Haven, CT: Yale University Press, 1982), 2:105; Douglass, "Of Morals and Men: An Address Delivered in New York, NY on May 8, 1849," in *The Frederick Douglass Papers,* ed. Blassingame, 2:170–74; Douglass, "The Color Question: An Address Delivered in Washington, D.C. on July 5, 1875," in *The Frederick Douglass Papers,* ed. Blassingame and John R. McKivigan (New Haven, CT: Yale University Press, 1991), 4:420–21.

erhood."[13] As a racial assimilationist, Douglass condemns distinctions on the basis of race, but he reluctantly accepted voluntary self-segregation of the races in certain institutions as a possible step to the racially assimilated society.[14] By a racially assimilated society, he meant a society where a person's race is legally, morally, politically, and socially irrelevant. According to Douglass, racial assimilation is a requirement of a morally good society.[15]

Douglass was weary about recognizing racial distinctions because race had been used to cause needless pain and suffering. He rejected racial divisions in society, but he stopped short of claiming that race is never a relevant characteristic of persons. While Douglass clearly believed that people made too much of race, he refused to categorically reject the significance of race.

Douglass was clearly ambivalent about the value of drawing racial distinctions. As I quoted earlier, Douglass saw a need for black institutions only as a temporary means for navigating between a racist society and a racially assimilated society. Even though it is clear that he believed this, he still spoke in a mocking manner of people who took pride in their race. According to him, it is a mistake to take pride in one's race because to do so is to take pride in something over which one has no control.[16]

Douglass's argument against racial pride is controversial. If I understand his position, African Americans will need institutions organized on the basis of race for a time, but they should not be proud of the need to develop and support these institutions. Their attitude should be that of persons who take an awful tasting medicine; they do so only because it is the most effective means of curing some ailment. It is not done out of a sense of pride or delight, but necessity.

In the real world, this is a difficult posture for any group of people to take, especially a group that has been despised and oppressed over a long period of time. Organizing and supporting black institutions is not analogous to taking distasteful medicine. In order for institutions to be effective, the people who populate them (as a matter of motivation) often feel that there is something of value in the institutions themselves. Frequently they reject the view that the value of these institutions strictly lies in the ends to be achieved.

As an intellectual exercise, Douglass's view does make sense. People can in thought see black institutions as a necessary evil. However, in practice it is hard to build and support institutions that you think only have instrumental value. I

---

13. Douglass, "An Address to the Colored People," *Negro Social and Political Thought,* ed. Brotz, 211.

14. Douglass, "Letter to Harriet Beecher Stowe," in *Negro Social and Political Thought,* ed. Brotz, 220–26.

15. Douglass, "The Future of the Colored People," in *Negro Social and Political Thought,* ed. Brotz, 308–10.

16. Douglass, "The Nation's Problem," in *Negro Social and Political Thought,* ed. Brotz, 316–17.

don't think there is any conceptual confusion in Douglass' position, nor am I sure that his view is psychologically impossible. However, in a racist society most people won't be able to do what is required to build and support such institutions if they cannot claim that such institutions have some intrinsic value that can serve as a source of pride for the parties involved.

Douglass's argument against racial pride is very controversial, and Bernard Boxill has given fairly compelling reasons for thinking that it is unsound.[17] My purpose, however, is not to challenge the soundness of Douglass's argument against racial pride, but merely to explore some of the consequences of Douglass's reluctance to rule out the significance of racial identity in decision making.

Douglass's views about the relevance of race in decision making came under attack from a variety of sources. Antiassimilationists argued that he failed to appreciate the importance of race[18] and some racial assimilationists[19] flatly denied that race should have any significance. Who is right?

Douglass's position was clearly influenced by his own experience of slavery. Slavery presented a stark example of how race could be misused. American slavery was clearly an institution that denied certain human beings their rights because of their race. But we should be careful here. The basic wrong of slavery is not that it makes some people slaves and others not. The moral wrongness of slavery is that it makes any human being a slave. Even if slaves were not singled out for slavery because of their racial identity, slavery would still be a profound wrong. The case of American slavery does not show that distributing benefits on the basis of race is, in itself, wrong. Or, put in another way, the case of slavery does not show that race is never morally relevant in making moral and political judgments. But one thing is clear: Douglass was extremely reluctant to accept race as a morally relevant characteristic.

Douglass's reluctance to see race as morally relevant seems to be based on something like the following principle: likes should be treated alike unless there is some morally relevant reason(s) for treating them differently. Of course, Douglass would add that race is rarely, if ever, a morally relevant difference between persons. Since Douglass did not take a categorical stance against the relevance of race, how does he justify the use of race in our moral decision making? Douglass tells us that for a period of time we must make decisions on the basis of race in order to reach a time where such decisions are unnecessary. But what is the structure of his argument?

17. Boxill, *Blacks and Social Justice,* 176–77.

18. See, e.g., Martin R. Delaney, "The Condition, Elevation, Emigration, and Destiny of the Colored People of the United States," in *Negro Social and Political Thought,* ed. Brotz, 37–111.

19. See, e.g., Henry Highland Garnet, "The Past and the Present Condition, and the Destiny of the Colored Race," in *Negro Social and Political Thought,* ed. Brotz, 199–202.

It might appear that Douglass is giving a utilitarian argument in support of his position. According to such an argument, we use race as a means for creating a future good or to avoid some future harm for society as a whole. On this view, it is not the individual good but the aggregate good that matters. The rights of individuals matter only to the extent that respect for these rights promotes greater good for society as whole than any of the other available alternatives. However, there is a strong reason for thinking that this was not the structure of Douglass's argument. Over and over again, Douglass tells us that slavery and racial discrimination are wrong because they violate the natural rights of human beings, not because these practices fail to promote the greatest good for society as a whole.

Douglass uses a natural-rights argument to defend the position that we can use race as a means to secure a racially assimilated society.[20] In other words, acknowledging race as relevant in decision making is necessary to secure equal human rights for all. So, for Douglass, ex-slaves are justified in self-segregating or building African-American institutions as a kind of self-defense against the denial of their humanity. As is normally the case with self-defense, the potential victim is justified in causing harm to another person if there is no other recourse open to him. This is most apparent when the victimization is due to wrongdoing.

However, some theorists believe that we have a right to defend ourselves against innocent threats.[21] If they are correct, Douglass may be on firm footing if he maintains that ex-slaves and their descendants have a moral right to make racial characteristics relevant provided that doing so is the only way to defend their natural rights as equal human beings against innocent and noninnocent threats. Remember that Douglass believed our ultimate goal should be to completely rid our society of racial classifications, although we may have to use these classifications for a time in order to reach this goal. Basically, he believed that racial classifications were a hindrance to the individual and the society. Douglass's argument has some appeal, but his provisional reliance on institutions of a complexional character is still the source of considerable controversy.

One wonders how long institutions of a complexional character will be needed. Are they needed until all the laws that prohibit African Americans from participating are wiped from the books? Or perhaps they are needed only until the spirit, as well as the letter, of civil rights laws has been achieved.

Answers to these questions are not simple. A system of prolonged racial op-

---

20. Douglass in *Life and Writings of Frederick Douglass,* ed. Philip S. Foner (New York: International, 1975), 4:136, 147, 162–164.

21. Some pro-abortionists believe that even if a fetus is an innocent person, a woman has a right to defend herself against it if it threatens her life.

pression like the one in the United States has profound effects. It not only assigned positions and roles in society, but it shaped the way we think about others and ourselves. It produced harmful stereotypical attitudes and beliefs, and it bred deep-seated distrust and suspicion between people perceived to be of different races. If it is reasonable to believe that the harmful consequences cited above did occur, and that they were an assault to the human dignity of African Americans, then we need to have a clear account of why Douglass felt that African-American institutions were necessary to avoid these harmful effects and to secure the natural rights of African Americans.

When African Americans were legally barred from participating in important institutions that were necessary for their development and self-respect, it is clear why there was a need for separate institutions of a complexional character. Because they were legally prevented from participating in white institutions that were crucial for their self-development, they needed their own institutions to fill this void. But what happened after Jim Crow laws were formally abolished? Did this eliminate the need for African-American institutions? I think not. Even though segregation laws were no longer on the books, this was a far cry from opening up American institutions to all under conditions of fair equality of opportunity. The repeal of Jim Crow did not eliminate the need for African Americans to struggle to become true participants. Even today, many would argue that African Americans still have a second-class status when it comes to fully participating in American life.

Would Douglass urge African Americans today to abandon institutions of a complexional character or would he think many of the current cultural, economic, and political obstacles still make such institutions necessary? Perhaps Douglass's views on African-American emigration proposals after the Civil War can be of some use to us here. Martin Delany and other African-American activists urged African Americans to leave the United States and to establish residency in Africa and other places. Douglass vigorously opposed these proposals.[22]

Douglass believed that the emigrationist position was based on an unwarranted pessimism about the future of race relations in the United States. According to Boxill, the primary reason for Douglass's optimism was his confidence in the power of moral persuasion.[23] In other words, Douglass believed that white racists could be convinced that African Americans were deserving of human rights. In fact, Douglass believed the legitimacy of the claim by African Americans for human rights was so self-evident that the denial of such rights would

---

22. Douglass, "African Civilization Society," in *Negro Social and Political Thought,* ed. Brotz, 262–66.

23. Boxill, "Two Traditions in African-American Political Philosophy," *Philosophical Forum* 24 (1992–93): 125–31.

eventually become a source of shame for white people. And this shame would lead them to change their behavior.[24]

Should Douglass's optimism be applied to the present situation of African Americans? If we do, what should follow from such optimism? Should this optimism lead us to embrace a racially assimilationist ideal which requires that we reject all racial classifications, including those of a transitional sort? Remember that in Douglass's argument against African-American emigration proposals, he urged African Americans to stay in the United States to struggle to achieve their rights as American citizens. He believed that their resistance would serve to confirm their humanity to themselves and others. But if we employ this reasoning in the case of present-day race relations in the United States, a racial eliminativist like Douglass should not endorse the creation of institutions of a complexional character. He should urge people to be optimistic about eliminating racial distinctions instead of forming racial defined institutions. Given that there has been some progress in race relations, the assimilationist recommendation should be to fight for the opportunity for all to participate in common institutions rather than any kind of separation based on race.

Will racial assimilationists who share Douglass's belief about racial institutions face the pain of inconsistency if they provisionally defend racially defined institutions as a means to achieve a racially assimilated society? Can these provisional institutions be defended without giving race a significance that assimilationists claim that they should not be given? Although this racial significance need not be understood in biological or genetic terms, it must be acknowledged if racially defined institutions are to be sustained in the present cultural, economic, political, and social climate. If racial institutions, even ones of a temporary nature, are to be defended, then any such defense will require an account of the significance of race that is socially viable and consistent with democracy and justice. Whether or not such an account can be provided is still a matter of controversy.

4. Contemporary Eliminativists and Racial Institutions

What stance should contemporary racial eliminativists take toward black colleges and other black institutions and organizations? Should they adopt the view that I have attributed to Douglass or can they justify making a person's race morally and socially significant in designing institutions and organizations? Some white conservatives and liberals have argued that there is a glaring inconsistency in recognizing black institutions and organizations while at the same

24. See Foner, *Life and Writings of Frederick Douglass,* 162–64.

time rejecting white institutions. However, the supporters of institutions like historically black colleges are quick to point out that these colleges do not bar white applicants. They also add that these colleges acknowledge and highlight specific cultural and historical experiences, but they do not exclude people from exploring these experiences because they are members of a particular racial group.

Does such a reply silence the critics of black colleges? It clearly does not silence the critics who believe in racial separatism, but who think that black separatism is accepted as morally permissible while white separatism is seen as morally unjustified. But it is also unconvincing to some nonseparatists who think that the best way to end racism and treat all people justly is to be colorblind. They do not question the motives of the supporters of black colleges, but they do believe that the means that they have adopted to achieve their ends are morally impermissible. The supporters of black colleges innocently and unwittingly embrace what Appiah describes as racialism. For Appiah, racialism even in its most innocuous form, breeds racial essentialism and normative beliefs about how people should behave and think if they are to be racially authentic. On this view, there is danger in claiming that race is a morally relevant characteristic even when this is understood in a purely instrumental way. Acknowledging racially defined institutions helps to perpetuate a way of thinking that has caused too much pain and suffering.

5. The Defense of Race and Race Talk

The critics of racial eliminativism point out that it is not wise to throw the baby out with the bath water. They argue that if we properly acknowledge race, and use it appropriately, then we can avoid racism. Lucius Outlaw appears to take this position. Outlaw believes that something good would be lost if we completely eliminate the idea of races.[25] For him, acknowledging races is not intrinsically bad. The harm does not come from acknowledging races, but from some races believing that they are entitled to use other races as unwilling means to satisfy their ends. According to Outlaw, it is possible to recognize racial differences without supporting oppression and subjugation.

Outlaw's view has a great deal of support in the general public, but I don't want to try to defend it here. My concern is with people who believe that our ultimate goal should be to eliminate race talk and race thinking, but that it is permissible to recognize races as a means to reach that goal. However, I do won-

25. Outlaw, *On Race and Philosophy,* 151–57.

der about the scope of the eliminativist view. In the United States, people have been unjustly discriminated against on the basis of a variety of characteristics, for instance, height, weight, and facial appearances among other things. Does the eliminativist believe that justice cannot be achieved without eliminating each of these characteristics?

In a recent book, Appiah use John Stuart Mill to give us an argument for using the state to eliminate morally unacceptable identities, and he thinks that racial identities count as morally unacceptable identities.[26] He imagines a society where people are not overtly denied opportunities because of their perceived racial identities. In such a society, he urges morally decent people do away with harmful racial and ethnic identities. Why? He gives two reasons: such identities cause more harms than good to others and such identities cause self-inflicted harms. The first reason is clearly utilitarian within John Stuart Mill's brand of utilitarianism. However, the second reason is more controversial. In order to show that the state is justified in interfering with self-inflicted harms, Appiah may have to weaken Mill's negative reaction to legal paternalism. Since Mill's aversion to paternalism is an important part of his liberalism, it is hard to see how using the state to get people to eliminate racial identities can be described as liberal if we must embrace a moderately strong form of legal paternalism to do so.

From the perspective of Douglass, we are morally justified in giving relevance to racial identities only when doing so is necessary for self-defense. So, if the eliminativists can show that we don't need race to defend people against unacceptable harms, then Douglass's argument is no longer persuasive. Thus the dispute between the eliminativists and the noneliminativists appears to turn on empirical facts. Namely, are there reasonable ways to prevent unacceptable harms to human beings that don't involve giving significance to racial identities? If the answer is no, then like Douglass we must continue to give significance to these identities until they are no loner needed.

Clearly in the nineteenth century the harms that Douglass had in mind were the economic, legal, political, and social barriers to black advancement. But if he were alive to day, would he side with Appiah or would he think that there is still work to be done before we can abandon using race in a purely defensive way? Remember that Douglass's goal was to eliminate races unless they were a necessary form of self-defense, not to conserve them in a benign form. Is a black or African-American identity necessary as a kind of self-defense?

The root idea of the self-defense argument seems to be that we cannot allow blacks to needlessly suffer until we can reach a time when race does not mat-

26. Appiah, *Ethics of Identity* (Princeton: Princeton University Press, 2005), esp. chaps. 1, 4, and 5.

ter. To do so would be to ignore or devalue their pain and suffering. But this argument only makes sense if we view things in consequentialist rather than deontological terms. A Kantian, for example, would ask whether it is right or just to tolerate the undeserved suffering of some rational beings. If we cannot answer in the affirmative, then we should not treat any rational beings this way. On the contrary, a consequentialist might argue that we can tolerate such suffering if it will bring about a greater amount of happiness or well being into the world.

However, there is another form of the self-defense argument that has been advanced by supporters of racial essentialism. The idea is that there are certain things that people are unable to know or appreciate because they are members of particular racial groups. Some racial essentialists have argued that the white race is blind to the natural equality and worth of the black race. They claim beliefs and feelings of white superiority are deeply woven into the consciousness of white people.

Given this version of the self-defense argument, no amount of racial interaction will create a state of affairs where black people as a group will be treated fairly because social institutions are dominated by white people. There are no rules or regulations that can be put into place in a liberal society that will totally prevent antiblack attitudes and practices from causing harmful effects. But this type of racial essentialist argument has been judged to be unsound because it is thought to rest on a discredited racial essentialism. Since biological or genetic accounts of the meaning of races are in disfavor, any attempt to explain human behavior and thought by reference to naturalistic accounts of race are also rejected.

6. Racial Institutions and Nonessentialist Accounts of Race

Can the self-defense argument be recast where race is not thought of as some natural property of persons? The definition of race is not rooted in biology, but in social and historical experiences. On this reading, racial differences are not characterized in naturalistic terms. Put in terms of racially defined institutions, these institutions are not necessary because blacks and whites cannot see each other as moral equals because of genetic differences. Nor are they necessary because most whites and blacks by their very natures harbor ill feelings toward each other. On this reading, blacks and whites have very different experiences and these experiences create or cause them to have different epistemic standpoints.

This view is very different from the position proposed by feminist writers like

Sandra Harding. Harding has argued that in the case of women their very bio-logical natures give them insight into the world that is physiologically based. For her, women can know things to which men cannot have access.[27] Charles Mills attributes similar arguments to black writers.[28]

The epistemic standpoint position that I present here is understood in causal terms, but not biologically or physiologically. The position, instead, rests on so-cial causation. In his book, *Blackness Visible*,[29] Mills examines arguments about how society can cause people to have certain beliefs. He focuses on Marx's cri-tique of a priori and innate ideas about the way society should be organized. Marx challenged the idea that capitalism is the only system compatible with man's nature. For Marx, there is no natural subordination or inequality. These things are caused by the mode of production in a given society and the ideas or beliefs that dominate in a given society are not natural but socially induced.

But even if we accept Marx's view about the social determination of belief, this would not show that people who are designated as black have a different epistemic standpoint than whites. If society causes us to believe the way we do, then this would not explain why black people who live in predominantly white environments have different epistemic standpoints. Shouldn't a view of eco-nomic standpoints based on social causation of beliefs be able to address this concern?

This concern is thought to be especially relevant in our times because of the widespread belief that there is much greater interaction between blacks and whites today than there was before the 1954 Brown decision and the civil rights act of the 1960s. If this is true, it seems reasonable to suppose that blacks and whites today have quite similar life experiences, and the idea of a racial stand-point based on radically different life experiences does not seem viable.

However, the supporters of racial standpoints question the premise that there is significantly more interaction today between blacks and whites and the con-clusion that blacks and whites no longer live very separate and unequal lives. They point to the work of sociologist William J. Wilson to support their posi-tion.[30]

But we should be careful here and specify what the supporters of the racial standpoint view are really saying. Are they claiming that blacks and whites, be-cause of their different experiences, have different beliefs? Or are they claiming something more radical, namely, that because of different experiences, whites

---

27. See Sandra Harding, ed., *The Feminist Standpoint Theory Reader: Intellectual and Political* (New York: Routledge, 2003).

28. Mills, *Blackness Visible*.

29. Ibid.

30. William Julius Wilson, *Declining Significance of Race* (Chicago: University of Chicago Press, 1978).

are incapable of knowing things that blacks can know? If it is the latter view, then the racial standpoint view challenges the objective view of reality.

Let us consider a true-to-life case that might help us to understand better the racial standpoint position. In New Jersey, racial minorities, especially blacks, have complained for decades that the State Police use race as a reason for stopping minority motorists.[31] Poll after poll has shown that black motorists, regardless of their ages and economic backgrounds, believe that racial profiling exists, while the polls also show that the exact opposite is true for white motorists. How do we explain this disagreement over whether racial profiling exists?

An objectivist would claim that there is a fact of the matter and that this fact is knowable to all people irrespective of their racial identities. But defenders of racial standpoints based on social experiences would argue that a person's racial identity has a bearing on what they think about the issue.

But in our racial profiling case, doesn't the fact that a significant number of white people in the polls believe that racial profiling exists show that there are no racial standpoints? Don't these people demonstrate that the racial identity of persons does not prevent them from believing or knowing something that many members of their race don't believe?

The supporters of racial standpoints would say no. They believe that when we examine this group, we find that they really don't hold this belief. A significant segment of this group consists of people who have a general grudge against the police, and so they are willing to believe anything negative about them. You also find among this group those who don't really believe that there is a pattern of white officers singling out black motorists, but due to their general sympathies for the historical plight of black people, they join blacks as a kind of show of solidarity. So, as the argument goes, when we closely examine these statistics we find that the disagreement over the actual existence of racial profiling pretty clearly breaks down along racial lines.

Here are four possible responses to the racial profiling case.

(1) The white population believes that racial profiling exists, but they don't care because the victims are black.

(2) The white population simply needs more evidence than blacks to conclude that racial profiling exists, because they are more objective about these matters and thus are not as favorably disposed as blacks to believe these things about white police officers.

---

31. For good philosophical discussions of this issue see the papers by Arthur Applebaum, Howard McGary, and David Wasserman in *Handled with Discretion: Ethical Issues in Police Decision Making,* ed. John Kleinig (Lanham, MD: Rowman and Littlefield, 1996), chap. 5.

(3) The evidence for racial profiling is sufficient to believe that it does exist, but from their racial standpoint whites at this time cannot see it.

(4) The evidence for the existence of racial profiling is sufficient to believe that it does exist, but from their racial standpoint whites will never be able to see it.

It seems that only position (4) challenges the objectivist view of reality. All of the other positions allow for the possibility that blacks and whites can one day come to have the same knowledge about racial profiling.

In conclusion, what does all of this have to do with the racial eliminativist's defense of institutions of a complexional character? If there is such a thing as a racial standpoint that is socially determined, then black people may have to depend on black institutions as a means of self-defense against black victimization that cannot be readily seen by the majority white population, for instance, black police organizations and black protest organizations that focus on police abuses. But if what I have argued for above is sound, racial eliminativists may have to accept that the existence of racial standpoints for the foreseeable future may force them to temper the racial assimilation that Douglass so hopefully envisioned.

7. What about Racial Identities That Don't Harm Others?

Remember I said that Appiah (an eliminativist) seems to want to do away with racial identities even when the harm that results because of them is only harmful to the persons who embrace such an identity. Are there such cases? Or do racial identities always result in harm to others because they prevent us from being coherent in our assessment of moral reasons? It seems as though Appiah might be sympathetic to the latter position. If he does adopt this position, then this would allow him to avoid the criticism that his form of liberalism is too paternalistic.

Here, I won't explore whether in our present society adopting an African-American identity can be benign or whether it might only cause harm to the holders of such an identity. This raises complex and interesting issues. As Appiah recognizes, a thorough examination of them will generate fascinating questions about the relationship between culture and racial identities and the more general moral question about what we owe to others.[32] In the not too distant future, I plan to take up these issues and Appiah's thinking about them because they must be answered if we are to correctly decide if racial eliminativism is the only morally defensible position.

32. Appiah, *The Ethics of Identity* (Princeton: Princeton University Press, 2005), 26–35 and chap. 6.

CHAPTER 8

Comparative Race, Comparative Racisms

LINDA MARTÍN ALCOFF

In an article entitled, "Top Colleges Take More Blacks, but Which Ones?" the *New York Times* reported in June 2004 on an increasing discomfort among some leaders in ethnic studies about the overly generalized racial categories used in affirmative action policies. Henry Louis Gates, Jr., is quoted as expressing concern about the fact that many of the black students accepted to Harvard are not of U.S. origin but come from the Caribbean or Africa. Mary C. Waters, the chair of Harvard's Sociology Department and author of the influential books *Black Identities* and *Ethnic Options,* is quoted as saying, "If it's about getting black faces at Harvard, then you're doing fine. If it's about making up for 200 to 500 years of slavery in this country and its aftermath, then you're not doing well."[1]

The controversial essayist Richard Rodríguez registers a similar complaint about the broad brush strokes of U.S. census categories, which are listed as "Black, White, Asian/Pacific Islander, Native American/Eskimo, and Hispanic." He imagines each category as a "drafty room" in which "statisticians in overalls" move India "over beneath the green silk tent of Asia" and direct "Mayan Indians from the Yucatan . . . to the Hispanic pavilion," which is styled in Spanish Colonial. Here, he says, the Mayans must share quarters with "Argentine Tangoistas . . . and Russian Jews who remember Cuba from the viewpoint of Miami."[2] The existing census categories, Rodríguez seems to be suggesting, are incapable of doing justice to the ethnic, linguistic, cultural, political, and experiential differences that are lumped together within these broad identity groupings.

There are two interestingly similar questions being raised here by Gates, Wa-

---

1. Sara Rimer and Karen W. Arenson, "Top Colleges Take More Blacks, but Which Ones?" *New York Times,* June 24, 2004.

2. Richard Rodríguez, *Brown: The Last Discovery of America* (New York: Viking Press, 2002), 105.

ters, and Rodríguez. The first question, which is raised in regard to African-American and black identity, asks whether ethnicity makes a difference within the racial category of blackness, and if so, what kind of difference it makes. The second question, which is raised in regard to Latino identity, asks whether race makes a difference within ethnic categories, in particular the ethnic category of "Hispanic" or "Latino," and if so, what kind of difference it makes. Thus both questions raise the issue of difference *within* a category, either racial difference within an ethnicity, or ethnic difference within a race.

Each of these questions (or sets of questions) indicate two further, and two different, types of concerns. One concern is about social ontology, and asks how adequate a description can be that uses such wide and amorphous classifications. The second concern is moral and political, and asks whether the differences that these classifications skip over are in fact morally and politically significant, especially in the application of laws meant to redress past injustice and/or bring about future equality. Pressing the question of difference within a category might be motivated by either ontological or moral or, what is most likely, both types of considerations.

Of course, one might ask whether the law is a fine enough instrument to be able to parse out such distinctions as might be necessary if we want to achieve more ontological adequacy and moral fairness. The law seems more like a blunt instrument, handy and dangerous in equal measure.

In this chapter I will leave to my betters in moral and political philosophy the discussion of policy and legal matters, and address the two questions about the social ontology and moral significance of differences within racial and ethnic categories as general ontological questions rather than as policy questions. In philosophy, of course, unlike in law, social ontology can be practiced with as fine a set of distinctions as we have the patience to develop, but in my view, it should ideally be practiced in such a way that our aim is higher than mere accuracy; rather, our ultimate aim in doing social ontology should be to establish useful distinctions that are connected to common linguistic and cultural practices and that might elucidate our political realities and moral responsibilities. This means that going back to Leibniz's definition of identity as indiscernibility is not terribly useful in getting at the problems we have with identity concepts today, or arguably, with identity concepts as they occur in ordinary languages at any time (there are exceptions, of course). Further, I would argue that the questions of social ontology and moral significance—although they are conceptually distinct questions—cannot be completely disentangled, given the normative implications that follow from our formulation of the ontological tasks before us. How hard we will want to work the distinctions of social ontology, for example, will mostly depend on their moral implications.

Let me make one further preparatory note: I am going to approach the ontological questions primarily through considerations of sociological positionality and political practice, which is something philosophers rarely do and requires some explanation. I believe we can discern the contours of our present day social ontologies precisely through this lens of empirically based practical analysis and sociological ethnographies.[3] Given that ethnicity and race *only* figure as *social* kinds of entities, I suggest that we can learn about *what* they are from *how* they operate in communities and *what effects* they have on practice. In other words, given that their only locus of existence is the social realm—which includes practices, structures, and beliefs—we must look to find them here, and not in an imagined presocial realm through intuition or conceptual analysis.[4] Empirically based analysis may not yield an exhaustive or completely adequate account, but it is indispensable in order to draw out important aspects of the social ontology of race, ethnicity, and their interrelations.

I will not take up here the general ontological questions about whether "race" or "ethnicity" are legitimate or meaningful categories, since I have addressed each of these questions in previously published work.[5] For the purposes of this chapter, I will take race to be a very real aspect of social identity, one that is marked on the body through learned perceptual practices of visual categorization, with significant sociological and political effects as well as a psychological impact on self-formation. All of this is true despite the fact that race is a historically variable phenomenon and subject to change. But changing the meanings of race is not susceptible to individual agency, only collective. (Individuals might try to surgically alter their appearance, but this in itself does nothing to alter racialized categories, and probably simply reinforces their power). In contrast to race, I will take ethnic terms as principally referring to groups that are demarcated by historical events, cultural practices, and structural formations, rather than by the phenomenological experience of identities that are marked on the body. Ethnic terms signify a group's relationship to historical experiences and cultural practices, and they are indicated more by practices than by physical appearance. Ethnic identities are "real" despite the fact that such narratives and practices are endlessly subject to reinterpretation and change. In my view, the narratives and practices that demarcate ethnic identities are not scripts we

---

3. This method would not work for all of the kinds of entities that ontologists concern themselves with, and I don't believe it even works fully for gender, but it does work with ethnicity and race.

4. Such an approach as I am advocating for here is developed extremely well by Paul C. Taylor in *Race: A Philosophical Introduction* (Malden, MA: Blackwell, 2004).

5. See especially "Toward a Phenomenology of Racial Embodiment," in *Race,* ed. Robert Bernasconi (Malden, MA: Blackwell, 2001), 267–83; and "Against Post-Ethnic Futures," *Journal of Speculative Philosophy* 18 (2004): 99–117.

are forced to follow, as Anthony Appiah fears, but real historical events and structures with an impact on our lives, families, and communities, with which we each must grapple.[6]

1. Black Racial Identity and Ethnic Difference

Gates raises the issue of honesty, and this is often an important concern that people have for wanting to contest the currently available categories for self-identification. In the literature on multiracial identity, for example, there are many first-person accounts that argue that we need to allow for multiracial categories because monoracial categories require multiraced people to be "dishonest" about their family genealogy, as well as their experience (or lack of experience) of discrimination.[7] Exclusivist categories cannot express the experience or complex family allegiances of multiracial people. The context of Gates's statement—his call for people to be honest—does not indicate whether his concern is about self-disclosure, or simply about honest discussions, but it is clear that what he wants us to be honest about is the variability of identity within the rough racial categories used, for example, in admissions. Those broad categories may conceal differences that make a morally and politically relevant difference, and he wants to have an honest discussion that names those differences.

The differences that Waters thinks are relevant within blackness are spelled out in her statement that "if its about making up for 200 to 500 years of slavery in this country and its aftermath, then [our admissions policies] are not doing well." To make visible the distinction that she is alluding to here, we need to put the emphasis in her statement on the phrase "in this country." Slavery in the New World was not exclusive to the United States, of course, nor have U.S.-based institutions become enriched only by the enslavement that occurred exclusively on U.S. soil, but have also become enriched by slavery committed elsewhere. Nonetheless, the implication of Waters's statement is that affirmative admission policies need to clarify whether they are aiming toward redressing slavery here, or redressing slavery against all people of the African diaspora, or attempting a future-oriented remedy for the ongoing onslaught of antiblack racism.

These distinctions bear on the types of arguments used to justify affirmative action, but they also bear on whether we are assuming a focus that encompasses

---

6. See, e.g., Appiah's arguments in *Color Conscious: The Political Morality of Race,* by Appiah and Amy Gutmann (Princeton: Princeton University Press, 1996), 97–99.

7. See, e.g., Maria P. P. Root's anthology, *The Multiracial Experience: Racial Borders as the New Frontier* (Thousand Oaks, CA: Sage, 1997).

black identity generally or only African-American identity. The generic term *black,* used today intentionally by many critical race theorists such as Patricia Williams, Robert Gooding-Williams, Charles Mills, Lewis Gordon, and others, signifies a transnational grouping that crosses geographical and national boundaries but shares, at minimum, the obstacle of antiblack racism and the legacy of colonialism.[8] So one way to understand this debate is that it concerns how we define what is the more salient feature of identity: being black, and thus being the target of antiblack racism, or being African American with a relation to a specific historical experience of U.S. slavery.

It would seem that only a backward-looking justification for affirmative action that aims to redress U.S. slavery would be relevant for the distinction Waters is invoking. Forward-looking justifications may not be as troubled by these distinctions within blackness, unless one can show that antiblack racism works differently for different ethnicities that share blackness. This idea—that ethnic difference can have an impact on antiblack racism, by perhaps diluting or softening it—is probably the key claim behind the concern Waters articulates, that is, that racism is not equally distributed across the various ethnicities in the African diaspora. That claim itself requires empirical study.

Sociologist Ramón Grosfoguel and historian Chloé S. Georas have analyzed the way in which Caribbean immigrants negotiate the racial categories of the United States after their arrival to the New York metropolitan area. Their study indicates how U.S. racial categories can erase the otherwise salient ethnic differences among people of color, but also how various ethnic identities can offset the impact of certain kinds of racisms. Thus, they show how the available categories of social identity can have real material effects. For example, they argue that

> in many instances the racism experienced by Afro-Puerto Ricans is more profound than that experienced by lighter Puerto Ricans. However, no matter how "blonde or blue-eyed" a person may be, [and no matter how successfully he can "pass" as white], the moment that person self-identifies as Puerto Rican, he enters the labyrinth of racial Otherness [in which] Puerto Ricans of all colors have become a racialized group in the imaginary of white Americans, whose racist stereotypes cause them to see Puerto Ricans as lazy, violent, stupid, and dirty Although Puerto Ricans form a phenotypically variable group, they have become a new "race" in

8. See Patricia J. Williams, *Seeing a Color-Blind Future: The Paradox of Race* (New York: Farrar, Straus and Giroux, 1997); Robert Gooding-Williams, "Race, Multiculturalism, and Democracy," *Constellations* 5 (1998): 18–41; Charles W. Mills, *Blackness Visible: Essays on Philosophy and Race* (Ithaca: Cornell University Press, 1998); Lewis Gordon, *Bad Faith and Antiblack Racism* (Atlantic Highlands, NJ: Humanities Press, 1995).

the United States. This highlights the social rather than biological character of racial classifications.[9]

Their claim here is that the ethnic (or national) category "Puerto Rican" has become racialized in the sense that it has come to signify shared essential and inherent traits. Certain negative traits are essentialized across the identity category of "Puerto Rican" in the same way that so-called "racial traits" are essentialized across racial groups. Based on this kind of example, some theorists today are developing combinatory ethno-racial concepts to signify this slippery overlap between racial, ethnic, and cultural identity categories. To understand how ethnic traits can be essentialized as permanent traits and dispositions one needs recourse to a concept like race. How else could the concept of ethnicity, defined as a cultural rather than biological grouping, be viewed as the grounding for innate traits, unless some biology-like notion of race is operating as a kind of "stealth" foundation for the identity? The category "Puerto Rican" is a classic case of an identity with both racial and ethnic meanings, where the racial meanings—the racist negative attributions—extend beyond similarities of skin color.

There are many such examples of stealth racial arguments, from the "culture of poverty" as an explanatory thesis for the persistence of African-American poverty, to Samuel Huntington's hysteria about the impact Latino, and in particular Mexican, immigration is having on Anglo-Saxon values. Huntington's argument is that Latinos must assimilate—linguistically, culturally, and politically—to Anglo-Saxon culture or democratic values will be in jeopardy. Ominously, he declares that the continuation of Mexican immigration represents "a major potential threat to the cultural and possibly political integrity of the United States."[10] "There is no *Americano* dream," he claims. "There is only the American dream created by Anglo-Protestant society. Mexican Americans will share in that dream and in that society only if they dream in English."[11] Con-

9. Ramón Grosfoguel and Chloé S. Georas, "The Racialization of Latino Caribbean Migrants in the New York Metropolitan Area," *CENTRO Journal of the Center for Puerto Rican Studies* 8 (1996): 195. Grosfoguel has emerged as one of the leading analysts of migratory identities within colonial contexts; hence my reliance on his analysis here. See also *Migration, Transnationalization, and Race in a Changing New York,* ed. Héctor R. Cordero-Guzmán, Robert C. Smith, and Ramón Grosfoguel (Philadelphia: Temple University Press, 2001); Ramón Grosfoguel, *Colonial Subjects: Puerto Ricans in a Global Perspective* (Berkeley: University of California Press, 2003); and *The Modern / Colonial / Capitalist World-System in the Twentieth Century: Global Processes, Antisystemic Movements, and the Geopolitics of Knowledge,* ed. Ramón Grosfoguel and Ana Margarita Cervantes-Rodríguez (London: Praeger, 2002).

10. Samuel Huntington, *Who Are We? The Challenges to America's National Identity* (New York: Simon and Schuster, 2004), 243.

11. Ibid., 256.

sider the metaphysical assumptions embedded in Huntington's claim that Latinos cannot remain Latinos in any meaningful sense and uphold democratic values, the rule of law, or a work ethic, all of which he defines as antithetical to Latino cultures.[12] The category of Latino is thus operating much less like an ethnicity for him and more like a race, with intractable tendencies and dispositions. Mexican identity is so deeply different, even antithetical, to Anglo-Protestant identity that Mexicans must lose their Mexican identity in order to accept and live by the values Huntington attributes to Anglo-Protestant culture, what he calls the "American creed." He does not imagine the possibility of *Mexican* identity itself adapting and changing (even if we were to accept his premise that it needs to). Such intractability is a hallmark of the concept of race.

Huntington is out to civilize us, and perhaps we should be grateful that he thinks it is at all possible, but it is at the price of self-erasure and historical amnesia. Huntington's proposal is to educate U.S. Latinos in the same manner as Fanon described his own education in French colonial Martinique, where through the inculcation of French language, history, culture, and literature, to the exclusion of anything else, the Martinican was made into a sort of "second best" Frenchman. In the colonies there was no place for an unassimilated or independent Martinican identity, and yet the irony was that a black Martinican could never *fully* assimilate and so remained peripheral, imitative rather than authentic, and therefore suspect. The end result, as Fanon explains, is that "the educated Negro suddenly discovers that he is rejected by a civilization which he has none the less assimilated."[13]

In all of the cases just discussed—Fanon, Huntington, Grosfoguel, and Georas—ethnicity and race mingle. The lesson of Fanon is that French ethnicity is essentially white and cannot be black. The lesson of Huntington is that Mexican ethnicity is really a race: it is unchangeable and has set features that have to be left behind because they cannot be reformed. Both of these lessons support the claim of Grosfoguel and Georas that at least some ethnic categories are racialized, subjecting all members of the group to racial essentialism.

What does this merger of race and ethnicity indicate in regard to our two

---

12. Within a few weeks of the publication of Huntington's book (March 2004) on the threat Latinos pose to "American democracy," the Associated Press reported that Mexican workers employed by U.S. companies within the United States are four times more likely to die in work-related accidents as U.S.-born workers. These death rates have been rising faster than their population increase, to a peak of 420 in the year 2001. The AP reported also that the main causes of this inflated work-related death rate are, first, the Mexican workers' "third world" work ethic and, second, the flagrant disregard for safety laws by the companies that hire them. So much for the superiority of Anglo-Protestant cultural values and respect for the rule of law.

13. Frantz Fanon, *Black Skin, White Masks,* trans. Charles Lam Markmann (New York: Grove Press, 1967), 93.

questions about the social ontology and moral significance of differences within racial and ethnic categories? It suggests, oddly, that some ethnicities experience racism. This would mean that the difference that ethnicity makes within a race (as in Afro–Puerto Rican or Jamaican) may not always remove or decrease racism because racism is attached to the ethnicity itself. Such a locution requires an account of racism that would not make all racism supervenient on antiblack racism, but that would understand racism as the idea that essentialized traits are traceable to a variety of physical features or to genealogical origin.[14] Two important caveats here: not all Latino ethnicities, obviously, are racialized in the way that "Puerto Ricans" are in New York, and it is also obvious that Afro–Puerto Ricans must experience a multiple onslaught of antiblack racism in combination with this specific anti–Puerto Rican racism.

Further, the merging of race and ethnicity (of which I give more examples in chapter 10 of *Visible Identities*), suggests that we should seek the *operative* meaning of identity terms, and not simply their *conceptual or abstract* meaning. That is, although "Puerto Rican" is a nationality and an ethnic term of identity, operationally, it signifies race in a way that is not the case for all other ethnic terms, such as "French" or "Danish." Part of the causal story behind this operational tie to race may be traced to the history of terms such as *culture* and *people,* which stood in for what we think of as ethnicities today but were demarcated as genealogical groups in the past with common ancestors and a common geographical location and common traits. Thus, before the biological conception of race emerged (some say, with Kant) with an *explanation* of the intractability of traits, cultural identity groups carried the weight of these claims of inherence.

Now let me return to the Grosfoguel and Georas study for a different, and what might seem, an opposing argument. Their study also looked at the relations between Jamaicans and African Americans in New York, which were initially very close: they lived in proximate neighborhoods and Jamaican immigrants relied at first on "African American social networks for job opportunities." Yet ultimately Jamaicans avoided the "labor market marginalization of African Americans" and "were successfully incorporated into the host labor market in well-paid public and private service jobs . . . [and] are currently portrayed by the white establishment in New York as a model minority." Such success was made possible by the fact that the post-1965 immigration from Jamaica generally came from a "more educated and skilled" sector of the population, including "professionals, managers, secretaries, administrative personnel, and skilled workers." Their accent also provided a distinguishing mark giving them

---

14. I develop the beginnings of such an expanded account in chapter 11 of *Visible Identities: Race, Gender, and the Self* (New York: Oxford University Press, 2006).

some distance from "the negative symbolic capital of African Americans." Grosfoguel and Georas thus argue overall that "the Jamaican community's strategy
was to emphasize ethnic over racial identity. The fact that Jamaicans were not
subsumed under the categorization 'African American' avoided offsetting the
positive impact of their skilled background."[15]

Here we have a different lesson about difference: that ethnic differences can
help some groups to alter their class or labor market position and to offset antiblack racism. Perhaps Jamaican ethnicity is still being racialized, but in a different way than non-Caribbean African Americans are racialized.

Of course, the empirical studies of Grosfoguel and Georas that I've cited
(which are only a small part of their larger empirical work) are meant to be more
illustrative than conclusive. How far can we generalize from the case of Jamaicans in post-1965 New York? Certainly, their success in altering their class
position in New York may not be replicable in every part of the country, say, just
to make a wild guess, Mississippi. This would again need empirical study, but in
some contexts antiblack racism may simply trump every other group or individual feature. Also what is clearly important in this case study is the class status of this particular immigrant generation, without which the difference of
accent alone may well have been insufficient to maintain an ethnic distinction
in the eyes of white or nonblack employers. But what *can* be claimed from this
study is that some black non–African Americans are able to develop and maintain a distinct identity at least in some contexts, thus making it possible for them
to be generalized (or essentialized) differently, for example, as having a higher
skill level or a different "work ethic." In this way they might be able to temper
their experience of antiblack racism.

I believe that it is also important that black non–African Americans do not
figuratively invoke by their very presence the history of U.S. slavery, which can
elicit a host of white guilt and shame responses to the memory of this lengthy
state-sponsored mass atrocity that has obvious after-effects in the economic position of African Americans today.[16] Fanon argued that such guilt responses to
the reminder of mistreatment often lead to racism as a psychic strategy to as-
suage and absolve guilt. So for this reason, also, a reason that has nothing to do
with the intentional choices or practices of any immigrant group, black non–
African Americans may experience reduced reactions of racist hysteria.

I want to underscore the contingency of this lesson about the differences that
ethnicity can make, and acknowledge that sometimes, as the Amadou Diallo and
Abner Louima cases painfully illustrate, such ethnic differences make no differ-

---

15. Grosfoguel and Georas, *The Racialization of Latino Caribbean Migrants,* 197.
16. Native Americans also invoke guilt responses, and in some locations Mexicans may as well.

ence at all. (The Wen Ho Lee case is another interesting case to study, because there racialization trumped education, cultural assimilation, and class.)[17]

So I have at this point provided both confirmation and complication of the claims that ethnicity makes a difference within a race and that race makes a difference within an ethnicity. Grosfoguel and Georas show both that ethnicity can offset or at least alter the form of some racisms, though their study would indicate that ethnicity alone may be insufficient to accomplish this unless class and education advantages are also present. But their work also complicates the very distinction we might make between ethnicity and race, showing how ethnicities can also become nearly indistinguishable from race.

The only general conclusion we can make at this point is that even further fine-tuning of our social ontologies will need to be made if we want to get to the morally and politically significant differences. In other words, ethnic differences within a given race may or may not make morally significant political differences in the amount of racism a group is subjected to, depending on the presence or absence of other factors. Having an ethnic identity itself, then, does not necessarily mean that one has escaped racialization. Black non–African Americans may escape the extremities of antiblack racism, or they may face specific forms of it that are just as extreme, such as anti–Puerto Rican racism in combination with antiblack racism. To identify morally and politically significant differences within a racial group, such as differences that would impact racism and social discrimination, the presence of the category of ethnicity by itself is insufficient.

2. Differences and Solidarities

I will take up the complicated relationship between ethnicity and race again in the final section of this chapter through an analysis of Richard Rodríguez's concept of "brown." But first, I want to explore the issue of cross-ethnic and cross-racial relations further by approaching it from a different direction, from which we might discern some practical solutions.

In a small and nonrandom discussion with union organizers and leaders, I was given the following picture of organizing and contract negotiating among a wide racial and ethnic range of health care workers across the state of New Jersey, involving primarily hospitals and nursing homes.[18] In many workplaces, as

17. See the discussion of Lee's case in Frank Wu, *Yellow: Race in America beyond Black and White* (New York: Basic Books, 2002).

18. Obviously, this is not sufficient evidence for conclusive results but suggests some of the questions that should be addressed in a more adequate sampling.

well as in larger public domains, there exist what seasoned organizers call "communities of solidarity." These communities of solidarity share a high level of trust among members, a sense of what political scientists call "linked fate," and a more or less well-defined common political agenda. Communities of solidarity may engender, and be engendered by, organizational networks that operate like kinship systems: by enhancing communication, sharing useful information, providing support of various kinds, and spreading ideas.

In many workplaces, communities of solidarity do not spontaneously cross ethnic lines. Hence, in order to build an alliance between communities of solidarity among different ethnicities in the African, Asian, or Latin-American diaspora, for the purpose, for instance, of an organizing drive or a contract battle or a strike, union organizers must make concerted efforts to build that solidarity just as they have to work to build solidarity between white and nonwhite workers. In any given struggle, a decision has to be made collectively about which issues will take priority: Which issues will launch a strike, for example, or which issues will become the centerpiece of an organizing drive? These issues include things like wage scales for different sectors of the work force, rules about how internal transfers can be applied for, and specific work rules on different types of jobs that can lead to discipline and dismissal. Because the work force is so often segmented into jobs in ways that line up with race, gender, and ethnicity, the arguments over how these issues will be prioritized often involve conflicts across communities of solidarity.

Efforts to create solidarity and coalition between various ethnicities can obviously appeal to shared experiences, for example, the shared experience of anti-black racism among black ethnicities, or of anti-immigrant prejudices among immigrants. But they also must overcome a variety of antagonisms between nationalities as well as anti-immigrant prejudices, linguistic chauvinism, and anti-black racism across groups. Alliances and conflicts do not always line up on one axis or another, but vary. For example, immigrant workers sometimes buy into the racist stereotypes of African Americans, whether they themselves are light or dark-skinned. Immigrant workers may, like the Jamaicans Grosfoguel and Georas studied in New York City, try to position themselves as better than African Americans, in order to gain economic and social advantage, and this may lead them to oppose the prioritizing of internal transfers.[19] Domestic (that is, U.S.) ethnicities sometimes will side with management to support rules that restrict the use of any language other than English in the workplace, rules that

---

19. Allowance of internal transfers—where a janitor, for example, can apply to become a maintenance technician—are critical tools in overcoming racism. It is often easier for a person of color to be hired into a facility as a janitor than as a maintenance technician, and if internal transfers are not encouraged that person may remain at the lowest job rung for their entire work life.

fine and otherwise penalize workers who occasionally speak in their first language. Domestic groups may also resent the common request among immigrant workers to make four-week vacations a contract battle, which the immigrant workers see as a necessity so that they can return home to visit their family, including even their children or spouses.

Despite the variety of the conflicts, it is clear that nonwhite immigrant workers face an intersectional form of discrimination: they face racism as well as prejudice against perceived "foreigners" as well as colonialist attitudes about their countries of origin as well as restrictions on their right of speech if they speak Creole, French, Spanish, Tagalog, or any language other than English. They thus experience an intersectional version of oppression that combines and puts into play several axes of first world chauvinism and divisiveness.

Employers, of course, often can and often do exacerbate such divisions. For example, nursing home and hospital employers sometimes bring in Filipina nurses from overseas, paying them at a different and higher wage rate and moving them more quickly into nurse manager positions. Employers may also initiate severe restrictions on language use and build solidarity across labor and management lines on the basis of nativist preferences. They may, and often do, create ethnic-based hierarchies in the workplace. But arguably, these employer-initiated actions would not work if there were not already various kinds of divisiveness and chauvinisms among workers that the shop stewards and union leaders must challenge and make a concerted effort to overcome.

These workplace examples show that ethnic differences do make a difference within racial categories in the creation of communities of solidarity and for the purposes of political mobilization. Although I have mentioned the problems of chauvinism, it is also clear that the obstacles that organizers encounter in their efforts to create alliances across communities of solidarity are sometimes the natural result of the way in which experience and objective positioning in the segmentation of the labor force have an impact on trust and understanding. Why should Dominican nurse aides have solidarity with white male skilled tradesmen, who often dominate the maintenance positions in hospitals and nursing homes, or trust that the tradesman will be able to understand the conditions of work for a nurse aide if elected to the bargaining committee? It is not simply ingrained chauvinism that is at work here in creating obstacles for solidarity, but also natural lines of demarcation based on life experience and work experience.[20]

20. Some of these ideas are discussed in "Is Organizing Enough? Race, Gender, and Union Culture," by Bill Fletcher, Jr. (former Education Director of the AFL-CIO) and Richard W. Hurd (Director of Labor Studies at Cornell University), *New Labor Forum* 2000.

These examples suggest that we should be skeptical toward the claim that immigrant groups are always or even generally better off than domestic groups. In some cases immigrant groups can make solidarity with white racism, while in other cases they will be subject to a cross-racial alliance based on first world chauvinism. So the distinction that Waters might want to make would need to be drawn differently if the intent is to mark differences in the *intensity* of oppression (which may not be her intention). Rather than assuming that immigrants will always leapfrog over domestic groups, we need to study the intersectional oppressions immigrants face in order to assess and compare experiences of racism and discrimination. To combat divisiveness, in fact, we should all consider the ways in which U.S. nationalism, what we used to call "Great Nation Chauvinism," is affecting and infecting the contemporary efforts, in the labor movement as well as elsewhere, to achieve equality and fairness and civil rights for all.

This is not to say that domestic U.S. minorities have no disadvantages vis-à-vis immigrants or foreign nationals. I well remember a dinner of the APA Committee of Hispanics/Latinos where we went around the room counting how many of us Latinos in the philosophy profession were born outside the United States versus how many were U.S.-born Latinos: the ratio was something like 8–1. For a variety of reasons that have to do with class as well as nationality, the foreign-born sometimes have significant advantages. But when class advantage does not exist, nor educational advantage, nor a difference in racialized identity, as is true for many recent immigrants from poor nations, there is little leapfrogging, and in fact, class status tends to move downward, not up; because the United States does not recognize foreign credentials, degrees and skills cannot transfer without a proficiency in English. The overall point here is that, just as all domestic minorities are not equally oppressed since there are variations of class and visible appearance (especially for Latinos, lightness), so too all immigrant groups are not equally advantaged over them for the same reasons.

Clearly, differences within categories of identity *can* have moral and political relevance. But the complication is that we need a complex grid with multiple axes to understand those "differences within," rather than a single yardstick by which differences can only be marked as "more" or "less than."

3. Black, White, and Brown All Over

As a way to further complicate the grid of comparative racisms, I want to look at the comparative claims about black, white, and Hispanic identities that Richard Rodríguez advances in his latest book, *Brown,* which has the ambitious subtitle: *The Last Discovery of America*. Rodríguez sees himself, I suspect, as the

H. L. Mencken of the Latino community: the lone iconoclast exposing the shibboleths and illogic of our time in essay form. Like Mencken, Rodríguez takes his iconoclasm and isolation as a badge signifying intellectual independence and integrity; thus he likes to recount with humor and evident pride the many rebuffs and attacks he experiences from Latinos who attend his lectures around the country. Also like Mencken, Rodríguez mistakes conservatism for common sense.

Rodríguez's argument looks on the surface to be in favor of maintaining the complexity of ethnic specificity in any schema of identity, as indicated by his sarcastic rendering of the census takers quoted in the beginning of this chapter. He also insists that brown is irreducible to either black or white, a claim that goes some way toward maintaining specificity against the racial reductionism of the black/white binary. But as I will argue, his real thesis is one of alarming simplicity.

The ostensible thesis of the book is that "the future is brown." What he means by this is that an honest retelling of the racial story of the United States and an honest acknowledgement of where the United States is heading will show that, in both cases, brown dominates. Rodríguez explains that this is not because Latinos are becoming the "largest minority," a phrase he rightly finds oxymoronic, but rather, because Hispanics (as he calls us) are brown, because black people are really brown, and because the facts of erotic attraction will mean that eventually everyone will become brown. On the one hand, this thesis must remind us of José Vasconcelos, Franz Boas, and the contemporary theorist Randall Kennedy, all of whom argued in one way or another that the "problem of race" will be resolved through a cross-racial coupling that eliminates racial differences and creates new hybrid peoples with familial connections in every direction.[21] However, Rodríguez's claim actually reminds me more of Francis Fukuyama's book, *The End of History and the Last Man,* which dreams of a final and absolute end to social change and revolutions.[22] Where Fukuyama thinks capitalism is bringing an end to ideology and thus ideological clashes, Rodríguez hopes the browning of the United States will bring an end to race, to racial conflict, and to our "obsession" with difference.

Rodríguez makes two other claims, besides the intermarrying claim, that he

21. See José Vasconcelos, *La raza cósmica* /The Cosmic Race, trans. Didier T. Jaén (Baltimore: Johns Hopkins University Press, 1997); Randall Kennedy, *Interracial Intimacies: Sex, Marriage, Identity, and Adoption* (New York: Random House, 2003); and Franz Boas, *Race, Language, and Culture* (Chicago: University of Chicago Press, 1940). Vasconcelos is the only one in this group who does not argue in favor of hybridity on the grounds that it will reduce or even eliminate racism, but he does argue that the future will be dominated by superior hybrid rather than inferior "pure" identities.

22. Francis Fukuyama, *End of History and the Last Man* (New York: Free Press, 1992).

thinks lend further support to this hope. The first is that Hispanic identity is based on the illusory belief that past historical attachments will continue to prevail in the future. He says "Hispanicity is culture. Not blood, Not race. Culture, or the illusion of culture—ghost-ridden. A belief that the dead have a hold on the living."[23] Since Hispanic identity has no racial or "blood" essence, he suggests that it is based in culture, but the culture one had before coming to the Anglo-dominated world of the United States. However, Rodríguez believes that cultural assimilation is both desirable and unavoidable.[24] Thus, Hispanicity is without foundation and bound eventually to deconstruct.

Rodríguez's assumption here is that Hispanic or "brown" identity has no racial basis because it is the product of heterogeneity and is essentially variable. He is correct, of course, that Latinos come in every possible race. However, the racial variety within Hispanicity—or its lack of racial foundation—does not actually entail a transcendence of considerations of what he quaintly calls "blood." If we adopt Angelo Corlett's genealogical definition of Latino identity, in which *latinidad* is based on a familial relationship that can be traced to Latin America, then *latinidad* is not reducible to a cultural practice that anyone can adopt but is an unchosen category of identity based on blood ties. Corlett's account has the virtue of explaining how racial variety can coexist with a biologically based identity: through genealogical and geographical rather than racial reference points.

Rodríguez does not consider this possibility. He presents our options as a mutually exclusive choice between invoking racial commonality or acknowledging the amorphousness of history. Since there is no real Hispanic culture that meaningfully incorporates all Hispanics, he holds the category as metaphysically corrupt, although he acknowledges its current political (though socially constructed) reality. To illustrate this idea, Rodríguez uses the faded and indistinct connotations that the color brown signifies as a metaphor for the state of Hispanic identity. "Brown confuses," he claims; it is "a color produced by careless desire, even by accident." Brown represents a "complete freedom of substance and narrative." Thus, in saying that the future is brown, he is suggesting that in the future, there will only be, in his words, the muddy sign of decomposition, the color of fog, of maggots, and faded celluloid.[25] The color of nothing substantial.

Brown is thus used by Rodríguez in the same way that Derrida used the concept of *differance* as that which cannot signify but can only disrupt the attempt

---

23. Rodríguez, *Brown*, 128–29.
24. I discuss this aspect of his claim in *Visible Identities*, chap. 7.
25. Rodríguez, *Brown*, xi.

to stabilize meanings or establish reference. Black and white are distinct, firm, and substantive, but brown is accidental, careless, unsubstantial. Here, Rodríguez is maintaining the idea that hybridity cannot have definite form, that the combination of strains can only be a dilution, not a new form in itself. But why *must* brown be a sign of decomposition, no clearer than fog, unless one assumes that combinatory identities cannot have any integrity unto themselves? In reality, many sorts of "brown" or hybrid identities have become self-standing, substantive cultural forms, with collective meanings and specific histories, such as Mexican, Nuyorican, or Chicano identities.

Rodríguez makes interesting contrasts between white and brown, on the one hand, and between brown and black, on the other. When explaining whiteness, Rodríguez refers mainly to white self-constructions or self-understandings. "White" identity, he tells us, "is an impulse to remain innocent of history," whereas "Brown marks the passage of time." This is because brownness is a visible reminder of a history of erotic encounters. Whiteness, by contrast, reveals that there is nothing truly interesting in one's history, in the sense of erotic boundary-crossing, so one might as well ignore it. Now on the one hand, Rodríguez makes clear that he doesn't really buy this white claim of ahistoricity, and he makes fun of the metaphorical bleaching and occasional acid baths that whites must resort to in order to absolve their memories and empty their history. But he then turns around and voices a surprising admiration for this feckless attempt to escape, on the grounds that it furthers the "freedom to become" which is "the freedom to imagine oneself free."[26]

Here we might be reminded of Nietzsche, for whom strategic forgetting is a necessity of the will to life. Rodríguez seems similarly to believe that forgetting is required for self-transformation. Thus he gives whites a certain amount of credit for forgetting, as an impulse that has good effects even if its motivated by cowardice or denial. The idea, however, that forgetting will enhance the possibility of self-transformation is open to debate. Isn't it more likely that forgetting will limit self-transformation, by removing important motivations (the desire to avoid abusive histories)? Can the ability to be free to think and act differently really require a pathological denial or a repudiation of one's forbears?

Rodríguez thinks blackness also involves a denial, but one he shows no sympathy for, not even the amused sympathy he shows for white denials. He argues that African Americans are really brown, that is, the product of black and white relations. He realizes that their reasons for not wanting to acknowledge their brownness are different from whites: with different motivations and different political effects, more understandable and less morally troubling. (Who wants to

26. Ibid., 139, 140.

acknowledge the paternity of a rapist?) But it is similarly, Rodríguez insists, a denial of the truth of history. He then says: "The last white freedom in America will be the freedom of the African American to admit brown. Miscegenation. To speak freely of ancestors, of Indian and Scots and German and plantation owner. To speak the truth of themselves. That is the great advantage I can see for blacks in the rise of the so-called Hispanic." He also adds, amazingly, "What I want for African Americans is white freedom. The same as I wanted for myself."[27] In this book, which is his third, Rodríguez exemplifies the same desire to shave off the color of his skin as he admitted to in his first memoir of childhood, *Hunger of Memory*.

By the end of *Brown,* Rodríguez presents the reader with a monoracialist futuristic vision that is actually identical to a nonracialist future, the sort of imaginary color-blind world that some whites still believe they live in. On Rodríguez's account, brownness is both more true than anything else and, to repeat, wholly unsubstantial. So in the end, Rodríguez's "brown" is really just a form of whiteness in drag since it aims to deny the legacy of history that remains in cultural identities, as well as the specific substance of racial identity, and it lends credence to the ideal of color-blindness. Where blackness irresponsibly denies truth, and brownness signifies only the lack of substance, whiteness, as it is lived and imagined, represents freedom and the possibility of self-determination. Although his ostensible thesis is that the future is brown, Rodríguez's real thesis is that the future will be, and should be, white.

Rodríguez's real aim in *Brown* is not sociological as much as it is psychological: his aim is to help us toward an imaginary refiguration of the powerful symbol of race. Brownness is merely a stage in that process: by deflating the substance of race, it leads to a lightening—or whitening—of the burden of race. There are many inconsistencies in his reinterpretation of the historical narrative of racialization (e.g., the fact that he both rejects and embraces racial denials, and the fact that he both defends and erases brown identity). These inconsistencies do not constitute a flaw, but rather an aid to his real goal, which is to muddy the definitions of race so much that the categories lose their intelligibility.

However, where does this really take us? The boundaries between groups and between group concepts can be vague and arbitrary without losing their operational force. The Nazis tried very hard to objectify Jewish identity and to develop technical instruments by which its presence could be detected even in the absence of self-disclosure, visible physical signs, or any genealogical information. They failed in this task, yet nearly succeeded in genocide nonetheless. Human

---

27. Ibid., 142.

variability does not admit of either clarity or precision, yet it structures our social relations and causes, or excuses, oppression. And miscegenation has not always led to an elimination of categories of difference, as much Latin-American
history reveals, but more often to their proliferation into more variegated maps
with hierarchies intact.

4. Conclusions

So what can be learned from the debate over ethnic differences within the
category of blackness and from Richard Rodríguez's ruminations on brown
identity? Several observations can be made. Perhaps most obvious is that we are
living through a cultural moment of profound transformation in the way our
society thinks about, conceptualizes, and categorizes racial and ethnic identities.
The black/white binary is undergoing deconstruction, the assumed homogeneity of blackness is undergoing transformation, and the way in which Latino
identity relates to either ethnicity or racial categories is up for debate. Obviously, the epiphanies people are having about the complexity of all these categories are not equally shared: some groups have been thinking and living these
complexities for some time, while others are new to the whole discussion. Yet
the fact that the current moment is one of debate, transformation, and no small
amount of confusion means that perhaps philosophers might make a real world
difference if we can use our skills to help clarify the options.

A second observation is that the weight of old ideologies can be seen pulling
heavily on the attempts at new thinking and new categories. Rodríguez may
look as if he is queering brownness, or using brownness to queer race, and thus
providing a sophisticated new take on the postmodern fluidity of identity formations. However, I have tried to show in my reading that white supremacy still
structures his aesthetic. Whiteness as the freedom to forget the past, and to ignore its effects on the political economy of the present, is the only ideal he can
imagine. But this is not an equal opportunity ideal. I would also suggest that the
sort of concern about who is benefiting from affirmative action that motivated
the first half of this chapter—the concern that would circumscribe reparations
within a nationalist framework that stops at the border—is also weighed down
by old ideologies. As the theorists in Latin-American studies have been emphasizing, globalization as a transnational political economy is hardly new; it is
more than five hundred years old, and we need to develop transnational rather
than national accounts of economic enrichment, identity formation, as well as
moral and political responsibility. Nonwhite third world peoples coming to the

United States out of economic desperation have a long and complicated historical tie to the United States government and multinationals; very few are genuinely new to the adverse effects of this orbit of power.

What I ultimately want to argue for, then, may appear to go against the grain of much commonsense thinking, but I think it is our best plan. I want to argue for identity proliferation, which is what some people see as analogous in its harm to nuclear proliferation. Wouldn't it be better, some think, to stem the tide of identity categories, if not immigration, and adopt either a racial eliminativism or some pan-national or otherwise amorphous category like "brown" under which we can all be subsumed? No, not while our labor markets are still stratified by race, ethnicity, nationality, and gender, and not while the global culture wars continue to heat up. To understand the complexities of global identities and global markets, we need specificity. Analyzing and accounting for the specificities of our complex differences in no way entails an increase in conflict but should enhance our ability to see more clearly where we need to negotiate and compromise and thus how we might more effectively make common cause.

Rodríguez thinks that the metaphysics of difference is hopelessly muddy, that the political effects of naming our differences always undermine justice, and therefore we should all become neutral, meaning brown, meaning white. He is not alone in thinking this way. Yet in the real world, communities of solidarity will continue to grow organically, demarcated by misplaced chauvinisms at times, but also based on real and not only imagined shared experience. The task of the organizer is not to convince everyone that neither race nor ethnicity are real, but to show precisely and accurately how, precisely because of their very identities, workers have in some cases common enemies and common problems and can thus make common cause. Perhaps we philosophers can help.

CHAPTER 9

Recognizing the Exploited

KENNETH SHOCKLEY

1. Exploitation

At least when applied to other persons, "exploitation" signals a particularly pernicious sort of act. One need not look very hard to see that racial and ethnic groups have provided the basis for many institutionalized wrongs that surely constitute exploitation. Historically, one racial or ethnic group has often exploited another. American slavery and South African Apartheid provide all too apparent examples. Certainly exploitative practices often utilize persons thought of as "the other" in a particularly pernicious way. Given the salience of racial and ethnic groups, and their ties to power differentials, these groups often serve as the unfortunate locus of exploitation. However, while recognition of those in different races as "the other" serves as the basis for abusive practices, there is something particular to the exploitation that goes beyond institutionalized abusive practices based on group-oriented power differentials. Shared practices with those considered as "other"—living together with difference—puts us at risk of exploiting one another. But how might we avoid this morally depraved practice? To know how to prevent, avoid, or judge whether one group exploits another, we need a better understanding of the particularly pernicious form of exploitation that takes place between those individuals who share a practice. Not every moral wrong, even if particularly atrocious, constitutes exploitation. So this leads us to the question, what separates exploitation from other acts of abuse?

A caveat is in order from the outset. We use the term *exploitation* in a variety of ways. One important distinction involves separating the sense in which a person is exploited from the way in which a situation is exploited.[1] It may be the

---

1. For an exposition of this distinction see Robert E. Goodin, "Exploiting a Situation and Exploit-

case that we treat people as mere things and exploit them in the latter sense. In this sense to exploit a person contains what may be the grave wrong of failing to treat them as an agent at all.[2] But there is another sense in which acts of exploitation do not deny the agency, even the moral significance, of the exploited. It is with this sense that I am here concerned.

In what follows I shall not consider in any detail questions concerning the group dynamics and social pressures that allow for individuals to exploit others by means of institutions. I understand exploitation to apply to individual actions, actions made possible by a certain arrangement of institutions and practices.[3] Neither will I consider the interesting question of whether a group per se is capable of exploitation.[4] Rather, through the defense of a position advanced by Lawrence Thomas, I hope to shed light on the nature of exploitation more broadly.[5] I shall argue that for exploitation to be possible the exploiter must acknowledge, tacitly or explicitly, both a commonality shared with the exploited and the normative significance of the vulnerability being exploited, whether this vulnerability is related to restricted employment options, unjust social institutions, or some other vulnerability-producing situation or institution. Intuitively it might seem that the particular wrong attached to exploitation is that the exploiter recognizes various needs of the exploited and uses those needs to take advantage of the individual (or individuals) exploited. Of course, there is great subtlety and contextual variance in the various acts of exploitation. Moreover, it might seem as counterintuitive to claim that exploiters recognize some commonality with those exploited as it is intuitive to claim that exploiters take advantage of the needs of those exploited. Lawrence Thomas has gone some way toward untangling these complexities. In several works he has argued that a common humanity, or at least a common status of some moral significance, is

---

ing a Person," in *Modern Theories of Exploitation,* ed. Andrew Reeve (London: Sage, 1987), 166–200. The cases with which we are interested are those which involve the exploitation of a person, which will be taken to be inherently wrong.

2. This was the issue underlying early debates involving the humanity of indigenous peoples in North America and Africa. For example, the debate between Las Casas and Sepúlveda in 1550 focused on whether the Indians were human at all, and therefore even capable of moral responsibility. (I owe this example to Jorge Gracia.)

3. When we refer to the "exploitative practices" of individuals I take that to be elliptical for "acts of individuals constituting exploitation in accordance with the norms of a social practice." As the analysis I here present should make clear, the more expansive expression is almost entirely redundant.

4. I would think this is only possible in the case where the group constitutes a collective agent. Generally, I would expect groups provide the means to create and maintain institutions which allow the exploitation of others who are identified according to group membership.

5. This chapter was written prior to the publication of Thomas's "Moral Equality and Natural Inferiority," *Social Theory and Practice* 31 (2005): 379–404, which addresses some of the same issues as a means to the larger issue of Kant's treatment of race and moral equality. In "Moral Equality" he maintains his focus on personhood and common humanity.

often presupposed by those interacting in many relationships notable for their inequitable nature.[6] The case of racial slavery, one of the two social evils with which Thomas is particularly interested, surely constitutes an extreme case of exploitation.

After considering exploitation more generally, I shall defend Thomas's view from a charge raised by Margaret Urban Walker. However, the conclusions I draw will have implications not only for the viability of something closely akin to Thomas's position, but for understanding the wrong of exploitation more generally. I shall argue that the harm of exploitation can be characterized by the recognition of a common moral status, found within shared practices of moral significance, and a willingness to use vulnerabilities made available by that practice to advance one's interests in a matter that is in tension with that recognition. Institutionally generated vulnerabilities grounded on racial difference provide fertile ground for exploitation. In presenting this argument, I shall point to a crucial distinction between recognizing a morally significant status, and evaluating or appraising an individual or action on the basis of that status. However, we should begin by considering the general form of exploitation.

Whether we take it to be a matter of unfair treatment[7] or simply a matter of taking advantage of a situation or person, the charge of "exploitation" captures a paradigmatic moral wrong. When an employer is accused of exploiting his employees we take that charge to amount to a claim that the employer is intentionally taking advantage of some vulnerability on the part of his employees to further his own ends by means of that vulnerability. Similarly, when one group exploits another, some vulnerability is used to create an advantage for the exploiting group. While much of the work on exploitation has focused on economic issues, if we take the basic wrong of exploitation to be a matter of inappropriately taking advantage of a situation or person, it is clear that while economic exploitation is a common variety of exploitation, the underlying moral wrong is much more widespread.[8] Generally, acts of exploitation involve

6. While Thomas argues for the presumption of a common humanity, I will argue that it would be better put as the presumption of a common moral status. Laurence Thomas, "Evil and the Concept of a Human Person," *Midwest Studies in Philosophy* 20 (1995): 36–58; "Power, Trust, and Evil," in *Overcoming Racism and Sexism,* ed. Linda A. Bell and David Blumenfeld (Lanham, MD: Rowman and Littlefield, 1995), 152–71; and *Vessels of Evil* (Philadelphia: Temple University Press, 1993).

7. For example, Justin Schwartz, "What's Wrong with Exploitation," *Nous* 29 (1995): 158–88.

8. For the general focus on economic issues see, for example, G. A. Cohen, "The Labor Theory of Value and the Concept of Exploitation," in *Marx, Justice, and History,* ed. M. Cohen, T. Nagel, and T. Scanlon (Princeton: Princeton University Press, 1980), 209–38, and G. A. Cohen, *History, Labour, and Freedom* (New York: Oxford University Press, 1989); Jon Elster, "Exploitation, Freedom, and Justice," in *Nomos XXVI: Marxism,* ed. Roland Pennock and John Chapman (New York: New York University Press, 1983), 227–52; Schwartz, "What's Wrong with Exploitation"; Alan Wertheimer, *Exploitation* (Princeton: Princeton University Press, 1996). For the basic characterization of "exploitation" I offer in this section,

taking *unfair* advantage of another person and are such that "if successful, [confer] certain perceived benefits upon the exploiter."[9] The wrongfulness of exploitation involves the inappropriate use of other people. But it is not the mere *use* that is particular to exploitation, for we do not necessarily exploit the bank teller when we use his services. Exploitation requires an abuse of power, an abuse enabled by shared practices.[10]

While the abuse of power is essential to exploitation, it is also the case that "exploitation implies some measure of co-operation, unwilling or involuntary though it may be, on the part of the exploited."[11] So while it seems appropriate to consider the actions of the con artist exploitative it seems less appropriate to so consider the actions of the mugger. Exploitation requires that both parties recognize they are participating in some form of social practice. "There is nothing about acts that make them intrinsically exploitative. It all depends on the context in which they are performed—on the nature of the game that people think they are playing."[12] The social practice shared by exploiter and exploited make possible acts of exploitation.

Acts of exploitation are instances where someone, the exploiter, plays for advantage, utilizing a practice to advance their interests, where it is inappropriate to do so. In terms of shared practices, instances of exploitation are cases of using a practice, on which one person (the exploited) depends, to advance one's

---

and for the claim the we should cast the net somewhat more broadly in considering what might constitute exploitation, I follow the work of Robert E. Goodin in "Exploiting a Situation." We can accept the basic analysis of exploitation Goodin presents without necessarily taking onboard either his particular brand of utilitarianism or the particulars of his position that protecting the vulnerable plays a key role in moral theory (see Goodin, *Protecting the Vulnerable* [Chicago: University of Chicago Press, 1984]). Of course on an intuitive level it seems clear that in exploiting the vulnerabilities of others, exploiters are violating a duty to protect the vulnerable. I merely wish to remain agnostic as to how we spell out this duty.

9. Goodin, "Exploiting a Situation," 168. Also, "taking advantage of other people's honesty or blindness to steal from them constitutes exploiting people tout court, whereas taking advantage of those attributes for [securing an otherwise unenforceable contract or conducting taste-tests uncontaminated by visual cues] does not. Exploiting a person is, then, essentially a matter of 'taking unfair advantage' of that person" (171). See also Joel Feinberg, "Noncoercive Exploitation," in *Paternalism,* ed. R. Satorious (St. Paul: University of Minnesota Press, 1984), 201–235, and *Rights, Justice, and the Bounds of Liberty* (Princeton: Princeton University Press, 1980).

10. "Exploitation . . . consists essentially in an abuse of power" (Goodin, "Exploiting a Situation," 184). See also J. R. S. Wilson, "In One Another's Power," *Ethics* 88 (1978): 299–315. The abuse of power is also a central theme in Thomas's "Power, Trust, and Evil" and in Schwartz's "What's Wrong with Exploitation."

11. Goodin, "Exploiting a Situation," 175. See 181–82 for the distinction between being exploited and being badly exploited: there may be degrees in which one is exploited, but whether or not one is exploited is not itself a matter of degree, it is a modal property. This ties nicely to the contrast between recognition respect and appraisal respect.

12. Ibid., 183.

interests at the expense of the exploited's dependence on that shared practice.[13] Let us then understand exploitation, for our purposes here, to be an inappropriate advantage taking of an individual in a state vulnerable relative to the exploiter. While I do not claim that all relationships commonly taken to be exploitative necessarily fall under this model, it does captures a wide swath of paradigmatically exploitative relationships, a swath which includes cases where a society and its institutions reinforce a set of social practices that enable one group to take advantage of the vulnerability of another group.

2. Thomas and the Presumption of Common Humanity

Thomas's work on the evils of slavery and the Holocaust is both illuminating and intriguing, and I can do scant justice to its full significance here. Thomas notes that while the evil attached to slavery may be unparalleled, the power arrangement associated with slavery is not capricious.[14] Not so for the relationship between the Jews and the Nazis during the Holocaust. Of course, this in no way indicates that one of these evils is, as a type of evil, worse than the other; and Thomas goes to great lengths to avoid such a comparison. Indeed, much of the project of his book, *Vessels of Evil,* involves showing that they constitute evils of interestingly different kinds. The distinction between capricious and noncapricious relationships, however, is helpful when we consider the particular evils involved. In what follows I will focus on exploitive relationships that are noncapricious.

Thomas points out that noncapricious practices are expectation generating. That is, to those parties involved, whatever irregularities or asymmetries in power there might be, both parties rely on one another. While this practice may manifest gross injustices, the expectations produced by their relationship generate a moral base level.[15] Of course, this base level may be so low that it is of little comfort to the exploited. But it will provide *some* comfort by means of a reasonable (but certainly not infallible) expectation that they will not be harmed *capriciously.* This is not to lessen the evil of exploitation. As I argue below this moral base level also helps characterize the particular evil attached to exploitation.

Of particular interest for my purposes here is Thomas's claim that even in that

13. Here 'inappropriate' may be spelled out in terms of vulnerability, and we can then clearly see Goodin's motivation for appealing to a duty to protect the vulnerable as that particular duty violated by acts of exploitation. See his *Protecting the Vulnerable.*

14. The crucial distinction between capricious and noncapricious institutions is a pervasive theme in much of his work, but it is made perhaps most concisely in "Power, Trust, Evil," 154–58.

15. Thomas refers to this base line as a "moral floor." See "Power, Trust, and Evil," 161.

paradigmatically exploitative institution, American race-based slavery, there may arise some level of trust. To put the point sharply, trust may arise between two people in dramatically different positions of power within an unjust social institution *because* of the practices of that institution, not *despite* those practices. We can find this capacity for trust in the mutual expectation required of any noncapricious power arrangement. One individual expects that the other will behave in a certain way, in accordance with terms set by their common shared social practice, no matter how depraved that practice. Such a practice may not require a rich conception of trust, but it does require that there be some level of mutual reliance and some possibility for mutual goodwill on the basis of that reliance.[16]

For this mutual reliance to exist, even in an institution as paradigmatically unjust as slavery, some commonality must be recognized. We might even say that for slavery to exist as a social practice those who enslave recognize the *humanity* of those who are enslaved. Thomas argues that "certain forms of oppression and hostility carry in their wake moral sentiments which, far from denying the humanity of those being oppressed, logically presuppose the humanity of the oppressed."[17] Thomas takes this recognition of a common humanity to be a necessary precondition of the practice of slavery. Of course, just because some commonality is recognized we should not expect that individuals in these sorts of radically unjust institutions (or even in comparatively just social institutions with asymmetrical power arrangements) to treat one another as moral equals. Indeed, slaves and slave owners may have very different conceptions of humanity, but they do recognize a commonality, else the institution of slavery would be capricious.[18] And there is this evidence as well: slave owners in the South regularly assigned slaves to care for their children. This alone indicates to Thomas that there was not only a level of trust, but also recognition of common humanity. For surely one would not give the care of one's children to someone or something which one did not trust with intimate knowledge of that child; and it would only be appropriate to give this responsibility to someone with whom one shared common humanity.[19] In general and with only the rare exception

16. For the difference between trust and mutual reliance, see Annette Baier, "Trust and AntiTrust," *Ethics* 96 (1986): 231–60; and Karen Jones, "Trust as an Affective Attitude," *Ethics* 107 (1996): 4–25. Thomas provides the following explication of trust: "Minimally, trust is understood to mean giving another reason, aside from self-interest, to believe that one will refrain from harming the other, though one could do so without loss. Or, trust is a matter of giving another reason to believe that one will benefit him or her though one could refrain from doing so without an loss whatever" (*Vessels of Evil,* 136).

17. Thomas, "Evil and the Concept of a Person," 51.

18. Of course it would be foolish to deny that it often did take capricious forms, but for reasons well rehearsed by Thomas, and exemplified by the domestic roles assigned slaves in the antebellum South, it did not take this form generally.

19. See Thomas, "Power, Trust, and Evil," 161–63.

of a few conflicted individuals, those who enslave do not take the slave to have the status of a moral equal.[20]

A caveat is in order: the evil of exploitation comes in many forms, and the trust that underlies them requires the recognition that something is held in common on which to ground that trust. Thomas takes humanity to be this commonality, but it need not be the case that a thick notion of humanity underlies any and all relationships of trust had within exploitative practices. All that Thomas needs is that the recognition of a common status is presupposed by participants of a shared practice, and that this is so because of the very nature of that practice. Slaves were held responsible for their actions, and whatever basis is used to ground this responsibility serves as the source of a commonality between enslaver and slave. Both recognized that they were subject to certain expectations, even if those expectations were markedly different and manifestly unjust. Even though this arrangement is undeniably and paradigmatically immoral, the commonality indicates that both parties, willing or not, were party to a social practice that they expected to govern the actions of one another and within which they tacitly recognize one another as beings capable of trust. Again, this is so even if behaviors permissible within that practice were morally reprehensible. In short, even in what is nearly the most unequal of practices, the practice of slavery, a commonality of some normative significance must be presupposed by the practice participants share.

According to Thomas, the wrong of slavery (or at least the particular wrong of slavery as an exploitative practice) is just that the "master" must recognize that the slave is the sort of being who may be worthy of trust and is, therefore, a moral being.[21] But the master treats that slave in a way at tension with his status as a moral being. We need not presuppose anything particularly thick about what it is to be a moral being to see this point. The institution of slavery requires that individuals be recognized as having a moral status and yet also requires that they be treated in ways incongruous with that status.

3. Walker's Worry

Margaret Urban Walker argues that Thomas dangerously oversimplifies the complexities surrounding moral recognition. Moreover, presuming that individuals must recognize even those they exploit as having equal moral signifi-

---

20. In the language of Kenneth Goodpaster, while slaves might be recognized as being worthy of moral consideration, the level of moral significance they receive is generally quite low. "On Being Morally Considerable," *Journal of Philosophy* 75 (1978): 303–25.

21. Thomas, "Power, Trust, and Evil," 161–65, and "Evil and the Concept of a Human Person," 51–53.

cance may blind us to the nature of truly horrific cases where there is no such recognition. Her initial objection is that Thomas does not recognize the way in which "trust relations can be nonsymmetrical, selective, contextual, and sliding scale." She continues,

> I might very well trust you, all the while making very different assumptions about what is expected of you, why you will be moved to performance, and what capacities in you are presumed necessary and what conditions surrounding you are presumed salient such that my expectations and reliance make sense. Trust relations need not be symmetrical, even if they are reciprocal: A and B may be bound together by relations of trust, but that in which and with which A trusts B may not be that in which and with which B trusts A. Nor must A trust B on the same grounds, for the same reasons, or with the same assumptions of ability and motivation that B trusts A. Nor can we assume that trust relations between individual masters and slaves were similarly, much less uniformly, defined and based.[22]

The thrust seems to be this: since the trust that arises between slave and master does not require *mutual and equal* recognition the attitude it requires cannot serve as the sort of moral floor which Thomas takes it to serve. There would not arise the requisite sort of equal recognition between slaves and masters, nor, one would expect, between most individuals in such paradigmatically unequal exploitative relationships. Such individuals may trust one another, but not for the same reasons, or with the same assumptions. The expectations generated by a given practice are different for those in different positions in the power relations institutionalized by that practice. If the relevant moral status is the product of expectations that generate some equal moral footing, then there *is* no relevant moral status. The position Thomas advocates relies on an equality in our affective responses to one another that simply is not there. The very power relationships which he hopes to explain by means of this equal recognition undermine the possibility that those in different power positions within the institution will recognize one another as equals. Walker thinks this mistake is frequently made, and that it constitutes an unrealistic hopefulness about human moral interaction.[23]

Walker notes that Thomas and others do not argue that "certain interactions

---

22. Margaret Urban Walker, "Ineluctable Feelings and Moral Recognition," *Midwest Studies in Philosophy* 22 (1998): 74. Both Walker and my critique of her position follow Karen Jones's view of trust, outlined in "Trust as an Affective Attitude."

23. In "Ineluctable Feelings," Walker applies her general critique, that presupposing universal moral recognition between humans is unwarranted, against positions advanced by Christine Korsgaard, Martha Nussbaum, and Patricia Greenspan as well. The position I present here may be adjusted, in part or in whole, to allow for a defense of at least Nussbaum and Greenspan. I am not as confident that the position I advocate is consistent with Korsgaard's Kantian line.

between human beings *produce* proper moral recognition. Rather, they claim these interactions commit their parties to *tacit* acknowledgment of each other's moral standing, such that the parties then pay a price for not recognizing this standing explicitly."[24] Thomas does not claim that interactions within the institution of slavery, for example, invariably *produce* moral recognition between slaves and "masters" but rather that the institution of slavery *presupposes* that all parties involved acknowledge one another's moral standing.

Rather than taking this to support the presupposition-approach of Thomas, Walker thinks this makes explicit an even more serious problem: the assumption that there is a tacit acknowledgment of a common humanity leads us to presume a moral goodness in humanity that is not borne out by history. Indeed, the illegitimate denial of equality because of racial difference seems to lie at the root of race-based exploitation. Hoping that there is some underlying commitment to equality despite racial difference may seem mere wishful thinking. People simply do not acknowledge, tacitly or otherwise, one another's humanity as often as we might like to believe. This is especially true in extreme cases of exploitation. Moreover, Walker holds that the presumption of equality may lead us to obscure oppressive power relationships. Such accounts may be not merely inaccurate, but pernicious, for they may prevent us from recognizing morally depraved relationships. The taskmaster enforcing the long hours and isolation of illegal workers, or the "coyote" smuggling illegal immigrants across the Mexican border in inhumane conditions, or the smugglers packing human beings into shipping containers, or the drug smuggler preying on the dreams of young "mules" certainly do not seem to recognize the humanity of those they exploit. Presupposing the recognition of a common humanity obscures and obfuscates the evil that humans do to one another; and this Walker rightly holds to be dangerous.

4. Recognition and Appraisal

As Walker notes, trust between those on opposite ends of exploitive relationships may not be completely symmetric: the exploiter and exploited do not trust one another in the sense of having a deep respect for one another *as equals*. The inequalities essential to exploitation make this impossible.[25]

A slave might trust his master to forebear cruel treatment in certain cases and feel gratitude for meeting those optimistic expectations; another slave might trust his

---

24. "Ineluctable Feelings," 76. The claim is with respect to all four of the positions criticized (see previous note).
25. A point emphasized in Schwartz's "What's Wrong with Exploitation."

master to forebear cruel treatment in confidence that he has demonstrated to the master the ineffectiveness of lashing, with gratitude quite out of point. A master might trust her slave to obey and be loyal, where the thought of gratitude to the slave for being loyal is preposterous.[26]

However, in an important sense, they *do* trust one another to abide by the practice, for that is what makes noncapricious practices noncapricious. The fact that they have a particular form of relation, shaped by a practice (whether morally reprehensible or not) sets the possibility for the sort of appraisal of that relationship on which Walker relies for her criticism. There is a common practice, else there would not be anything to set the unequal and variant "trust" relations which Walker rightly finds so troubling. If, following Karen Jones's insightful analysis, we characterize trust as "optimism about the goodwill of another," then, while there may be a wide variety of forms trust might take one would expect this optimism to be grounded, at least in part, in the expectations generated by a shared practice.[27] One would expect that when trust forms, it forms on the basis of the goodwill generated by common expectations. The symmetry of their expectations and reliance and, indeed, occasional trust, forms as a consequence of the tacit recognition of the authority of their shared practice. Insofar as they both constrain their behavior to abide by the norms of a noncapricious practice there is just this tacit recognition. The form taken by their expectations may, as Walker notes, fail to be symmetric, but the tacit recognition *is* symmetric. It is here that we find the foundation for noncapricious practices; it is here that we find the particular atrocity of exploitation: the unfair use of others despite recognition of a common status.

As her focus on inequality *within* a shared practice makes clear, Walker focuses on appraising the respect and affective responses formed within that practice, not on the basic recognition individuals have of one another as participants of that practice. It is the latter point on which Thomas's account is focused when he indicates that an attitude of trust is tacitly assumed by those involved in noncapricious institutions. To be fair, Walker's criticism of Thomas is markedly tempered, and her concern lies more with his lack of focus on the complexities of trust. But the particular complexities with which Walker is rightly concerned are matters of moral appraisal.

Walker's analysis appears to confuse recognition of a common status with

26. Thomas, "Ineluctable Feelings," 74.
27. Jones, "Trust as an Affective Attitude," 11. Jones is careful to point out that we should not read too much into "optimism." In particular we should not take "'optimism' to suggest a general tendency to look on the bright side" (6).

evaluation on the basis of that status. Thomas focuses on showing that there is a common status had by individuals who share a common practice. Of course, sharing a practice does not presuppose equality *within* that practice. As Thomas points out,

> Non-punitive practices are supposed to be affirming—though not necessarily to the same extent, at the same time, or in the same way—for all who participate in them; and affirmation presupposes that on some account or in some context, a person is entitled to or deserving of an expression of good will—be it no more than praise or an expression of satisfaction for a job well done, even though the person was forced to do it.[28]

A common practice requires that there is the expectation of some degree of goodwill, commonly endorsed by those participating in that practice. While mutual and equal recognition is had with respect to one's participation in a certain practice, Thomas explicitly points out that the mode and form of affirmation might be dramatically variable. Indeed, this very variability is what gives rise to what Thomas refers to as the "morally incongruous institution" of slavery.[29] Incongruity results from recognizing the slave as an entity worthy of moral consideration while simultaneously using that practice to advance one's interests without regard to that moral significance. For the evil of slavery to take the form it does, and as I will suggest is the case for exploitation more generally, this incongruity is required. That there is a common practice need not require a common *mode* of expectation. Mutual expectation that all parties will recognize the authority of the practice does not ensure that the modes of behavior within that practice will satisfy some other moral criterion, such as fairness or the respect of autonomy.

Indeed, while Thomas focuses on the "common humanity" of the exploiter and the exploited, the force of his position comes from appeal to a presupposition of the practice. Appeals to common humanity have the air of an evaluation of the practice, and so claiming that there is a recognition of this common humanity seems to be an assumption that is simply not borne out in real human relations. Such an appeal may be mistaken for a claim that exploitative practices run afoul of some general moral norm that has no necessary or constitutive connection to the practice. Of course one would expect that any exploitative practice *does* run afoul of other moral norms. However the distinctive wrong of exploitative practices arises from the fact that they presuppose a commonality

---

28. Thomas, *Vessels of Evil,* 143.
29. Ibid., 147.

as a matter of the very nature of the practice. The appeal to common humanity is built into the very practice of slavery (as the child-caring point makes clear), just as an appeal to common expectations is built into exploitative practices more generally. These expectations are made possible by the common status of being party to a noncapricious, even if morally reprehensible, practice.

The conflation of recognition with status and the evaluation of that status is strikingly similar to the distinction between recognition respect and appraisal respect. On the standard view, recognition respect "consists in giving appropriate consideration or recognition to some feature of its object in deliberating about what to do."[30] Recognition respect involves recognizing a particular status. Applying this to Thomas's position, recognition respect would apply to the status of being party to the relevant institutionally defined practices—such respect would be symmetric even if positions within that practice are far from symmetric. Individuals, even in insidious and exploitative (but noncapricious) practices recognize one another as having a particular status in common, namely, bring party to a shared practice. Where that practice has moral weight, in general so does the status of being a participant in that practice. Appraisal respect, on the other hand, involves evaluation of some aspect of an individual or their actions. "Appraisal respect is an attitude of positive appraisal of a person either judged as a person or as engaged in some more specific pursuit."[31] Whereas recognition respect is an all or nothing affair—one either has a given status or not—appraisal respect can be a matter of degree and need not be reciprocal. One person may be appraised as more meritorious, according to some standard for praise, than another. However we should notice that appraisal, or evaluation, only makes sense if the person being appraised is already recognized as having the status they have, a status which gives some basis for appraisal. One may be appraised as a good or bad person only if one is already recognized as a person.

Walker's core criticism, that presuming there is some affective component between those in exploitative practices is a dangerous idealization, focuses on matters evaluative and comparative, and so seems more appropriately a matter of moral appraisal than of moral recognition. Thomas, on the other hand, appears focused on moral recognition. The tension Thomas identifies results from a practice requiring the recognition of a status at odds with what is required of participants in that practice. We have already seen that there may be a common status between individuals situated in dramatically unequal positions. Of course, this common status may make power inequalities and morally contemptible interactions between these individuals yet more morally blameworthy. But this

30. Stephen Darwall, "Two Kinds of Respect," *Ethics* 88 (1977): 38.
31. Ibid., 44.

sort of blameworthiness is a matter of evaluation and requires some recognition of status for blame to be meaningful.

To be clear, I am not here arguing that Walker's position is inconsistent or even untenable, but rather that it is misdirected and so does not undermine Thomas's position or the general claim that exploitation requires the recognition of a commonality. Indeed, Walker's claims reinforce Thomas's point: when we consider the great wrong of exploitation, the fact that exploitative practices require that one presuppose the moral status of the exploited in one's exploitation gives an additional dimension to the wrong.

5. Exploiting Shared Practices

In recent work Philip Pettit and Michael Smith have argued that individuals who engage in something as thin as conversation with the purpose of coming to an (honest and earnest) agreement cannot help but recognize one another as fellow participants in a practice and incur commitments to one another on the basis of that participation.[32] Participants subject themselves to the norms of conversation and, in doing so, must recognize one another as holding a normatively significant status. This, I claim, amounts to taking a form of recognition respect toward one another. Now it is ludicrous to claim that slaves are morally obligated to abide by the claims of their "masters"; the Pettit and Smith account relies on a level of voluntarism that is paradigmatically absent in the case of slavery and exploitative relationships more generally, and which therefore accommodates this concern. However the point remains that from a commonality presupposed by sharing a practice participants will recognize one another as having a normatively significantly status. And sharing a practice need not require an explicit acknowledgement of the authority of that practice, or even an explicit awareness of the practice itself. All that is needed is that one recognize that there is reason to constrain one's behavior in accordance with that practice.

This point sheds light on the nature of exploitation more generally. Thomas claimed that the practices of American racial slavery presuppose recognition of common humanity. Within this common humanity we find both the foundation of trust and the roots of optimism about the goodwill of others in the practice. However, the humanity of slaves was recognized and utilized (exploited) in the pursuit of the slave owner's ends with little or no regard for the slave. Slave

---

32. Philip Pettit and Michael Smith, "The Truth in Deontology," in *Reason and Value: Themes from the Moral Philosophy of Joseph Raz,* ed. Philip Pettit, Samuel Scheffler, et al. (New York: Oxford University Press, 2004), 153–75.

owners must be disposed to think of slaves both as human beings and, at the same time, simple tools. Using someone to advance one's ends in virtue of common status requires the recognition of that status—slavery required the inappropriate use of humans while at the same time requiring those who use other humans to recognize them as humans. More generally, insofar as an institution is exploitative, practices within that institution will require participants to recognize one another as participants.[33] I suggest that the distinctive wrong of exploitative practices is that they require participants to presuppose a commonality of some normative significance (which I have spelled out in terms of shared expectations), and then enable the inappropriate use of people on the basis of that commonality.

This analysis shows the particularly pernicious form that exploitation takes in the case of noncapricious hierarchical power relationships. In such arrangements, systematically, one person is vulnerable to another. Indeed, in a rough sense, this vulnerability is a direct implication of the power inequality inherent in hierarchical power arrangements. Any inequality of power provides a vulnerability; only through acting on that vulnerability, in the manner outlined above, do acts become exploitative. However, as I have argued, in any noncapricious institution practices associated with membership in that institution, whether those practices are abusive or not, will be shared by all those subject to the institution. Individuals sharing these practices have a common status, which provides for the basis for a limited form of trust, of optimism about the goodwill of another. And yet these practices give the means for exploitation.

The tension that Thomas saw in the attitudes held by slave owners is a feature of exploitative practices more generally. Exploiters must recognize a common status which they then utilize to advance their own interests by exploiting the power differential made possible by that common status. They recognize a commonality, a status of moral significance, and then use that commonality in a way that emphasizes the inequality. Exploiters rely on expectations shared with those they exploit. These expectations indicate a commonality, a shared practice according to which both parties constrained their behavior. The commonality is used by exploiters to access a certain vulnerability in order to advance their own interests. This is the essence of *using* someone—the exploiter treats the exploited only strategically.[34] We can see this in the actions of con artists, slavers, "coyotes," and smugglers. Such individuals use the fact that they share a prac-

---

33. This is no way lessons the reprehensibility of exploitative institutions, as Thomas went to great lengths to point out in *Vessels of Evil*.

34. This point is made in Goodin's "Exploiting a Situation and Exploiting a Person," and Schwartz's "What's Wrong with Exploitation."

tice with those made vulnerable by that practice to advance their own interests in a manner inconsistent with the status they cannot help but recognize in virtue of that shared practice. This inconsistency requires attitudes in tension: the exploited must be seen simultaneously as someone with whom a status is shared, and as a "mark," as a thing to be used.

Let us return to Walker's concern, that presupposing individuals in vastly different power positions must recognize one another as having a common status was wrong, first, in that it seems an implausible claim that there must be such equal recognition and, second, in that such a presupposition would blind us to grave injustices. Against the first claim I argued that there is a commonality that cannot but be recognized. Now we can see this is a general feature of exploitation. Against the second claim, we can see that far from blinding us to evil Thomas's analysis of slavery points toward a way of characterizing the moral wrong of exploitation. Indeed, Walker's concern, if warranted, would make it difficult to see the particular wrong of exploitation, for the pernicious nature of exploitation is such that it requires the exploiter to recognize a commonality that can be exploited. Such recognition of a common status, far from being implausible, is required for the very possibility of acts of exploitation.

However we can see the motivation for Walker's concern if we consider the appraisal of actions on the basis of that common status. If we presume that individuals in noncapricious but exploitative institutions recognize one another as moral equals, then we risk trivializing the deep moral wrong in acts of exploitation, acts which are all too real. We might take Walker's critique as a warning, therefore, not to conflate the recognition of status with the moral appraisal of individuals on the basis of that status. One might very well recognize that a status is shared without treating others in that status in a fashion that is even minimally morally acceptable.

At the outset I claimed that living together in difference puts us at risk for exploiting one another. In living together we share practices, even where those practices mean very different things to different people, even when those practices are very much unjust, and even where those practices are only tacitly acknowledged. But many of these practices still constrain our actions. As Plato wrote in a similar vein,

We have shown that just people are cleverer and more capable of doing things, while unjust ones aren't even able to act together, for when we speak of a powerful achievement by unjust men acting together, what we say isn't altogether true. They would never have been able to keep their hands off each other if they were completely unjust. But clearly there must have been some sort of justice in them that at least prevented them from doing injustice among themselves at the same time as they were doing it to others. And it was this that enabled them to achieve what they did.[35]

There are normative constraints in even the most unjust social arrangements—even though, given their injustice, those social arrangements ought to be changed or eliminated. While a practice might involve a gross injustice, an inexcusable institutionalized harm that cannot be tolerated under any circumstances, there are normative constraints that take place within any such practice taken by practitioners to guide their behavior. Without such constraints the practice would be capricious, and would fail to generate expectations in the relevant way. These normative constraints, which might be judged to be contemptible from without a practice (as Thomas intimated when he made reference to "common humanity"), demonstrate that there is normative force within that practice. And it is this internal normative pressure, I suggest, that makes exploitation possible. I would suggest that we might characterize exploitation as a violation of a pro tanto obligation generated in virtue of a shared practice—in raising expectations, reliance, and even trust, we set normative conditions both on ourselves and those who share those practices.

In conclusion we should consider the obvious fact that, historically, racial differences have served as the basis for a great many exploitative practices. This analysis does not rely on any particular conception of race and is certainly not committed to the claim that there is anything substantial (or even real) about race or racial groups. All it requires is that participants in a practice take some members as having a different moral worth, and that some vulnerability is available such that the exploited might be inappropriately used. I have argued that one characteristic wrong of exploitation (the *in*appropriateness characteristic of exploitation) is a result of recognizing a common status and yet treating the exploited in a manner at tension with that common status. Race-based exploitation relies on taking members of a different racial group as being equals, and yet inappropriately using members of that racial group in a manner at tension with that equality. Those in the exploited racial group may be recognized as equals only insofar as that recognition allows the presumed difference to be exploited—that is, used to advance the interests of the exploiter without regard to the commonality with the exploited. According to the analysis presented here, exploitation requires that exploiters share a practice with the exploited. If exploiters are distinguished from the exploited on the basis of race, then there must be the presumption of a moral inequality according to one's race. Once

35. Plato, *Republic* I, 352b–c.

this contrast is complemented by vulnerability (generally a power differential of some sort), the seeds of exploitation are sown.

But the attribution of race has no essential pride of place as a means of exploitation, apart from its unfortunate historical prominence. Recognition of "the other" as sharing a practice while yet taking them to be different in a morally significant way is required for exploitation. While "race" has constituted a common historical means by which this difference-within-commonality has been referenced, we might replace "race" in the above treatment with "ethnicity," "linguistic group," "gender," "sexuality" or any other category that might be given a putative moral status and serve as a means of differentiating and exploiting those seen as "the other."

CHAPTER 10

Racial Justice, Latinos, and the Supreme Court: The Role of Law and Affect in Social Change

EDUARDO MENDIETA

Traffic between ethnicity and race in the United States has often been arbitrated by law. That race and ethnicity have waxed and waned into each other, race turning into ethnicity and ethnicity turning into race, has been to a large extent determined by the way in which the law has displaced one and privileged the other. The law that has performed this work has been produced by the Supreme Court through the interpretation of the Constitution. A history of either race or ethnicity in the United States is incomplete if it does not take into account the role the Supreme Court has played in codifying, legislating, and granting legitimacy to racial prejudices. Today we have come to take for granted that race is a social construct, but we often overlook the way in which the law has contributed to the social construction of race. As legal scholar Ian F. Haney López put it, "To say race is socially constructed is to conclude that race is at least partially legally produced."[1] As most Supreme Court decisions involving race attest, law influences the way in which we view race because of judicial deference to and reliance on science, and when science fails to arbitrate, by credence being given via the judiciary to quotidian prejudice.[2] The science from

---

1. Ian F. Haney López, *White by Law: The Legal Construction of Race* (New York: New York University Press, 1996), 10.

2. The most recent cases in which the Supreme Court deferred to science and made use of it visà-vis race is the Michigan Affirmative Action case. Interestingly, it was Justice Clarence Thomas who in his dissenting opinion made the most extensive use of the most recent social science research to call into question the overall usefulness of testing to measure the ability and success rates of African-American students entering law school. In addition to Haney López's discussion of the uses of science in justifying exclusionary practices codified into law by the Supreme Court in the book here being discussed, see also John P. Jackson, *Science for Segregation: Race, Law, and the Case Against Brown v. Board of Education* (New York: New York University Press, 2005), which studies the ways in which eugenics and science was used

one period turns out to be another's crass prejudice, and law contributes to our naïveté about science's involvement in justifying racism and genocide. And Haney López adds: "The legal system influences what we look like, the meanings ascribed to our looks, and the material reality that confirms the meanings of our appearances. Law constructs race."[3] To this I would add that *law constructs race* primarily by giving content and latitude to the way in which citizenship is allocated to different subjects—who may become citizens, what rights are granted to citizens, and the degree to which citizenship is fully enforceable— for these are determined differently, depending on race. In tandem, race is granted solidity by being inscribed within the primary way in which agents are granted access to the body politic, namely citizenship.

Rogers Smith has documented in exemplary fashion the ways in which citizenship in the United States has been closely tied to the racial activism not just of White supremacists, but also the courts, which in turn has left an ignominious trail of decisions on which Jim Crow was justified and tolerated.[4] We need only look at decisions of the Supreme Court to realize that this institution has contributed to the "construction" of race by establishing the way in which citizenship is allotted.[5] Unfortunately, the Supreme Court has contributed substantively and enduringly to the tradition of "legalized racial oppression" that has defined so much of American racial history. This history reveals that the writers of the Constitution refused to recognize Blacks as full citizens, thereby sanctioning slavery, and Congress sanctioned the "removal" of Native Americans from their lands into reservations, annexed foreign lands by appealing directly to racial ideologies (the Mexican-American and Spanish-American Wars were both examples of racial expansionist policy and ideology),[6] and excluded Chinese and Japanese immigrants from citizenship. In addition, the first Congress refused non-Whites the possibility of naturalization; local and federal authorities turned their backs on the lynching of Blacks and Asians. Further, the

to challenge the legality of the Brown ruling. See also Stephen Jay Gould, *The Mismeasure of Man* (New York: W. W. Norton, 1996); and Philip Kitcher, *Science, Truth, and Democracy* (New York: Oxford University Press, 2003).

3. Rogers Smith, *Civic Ideals: Conflicting Visions of Citizenship in U.S. History* (New Haven: Yale University Press, 1999).

4. Ibid., 19.

5. Mark S. Weiner, *Black Trails: Citizenship from the Beginnings of Slavery to the End of Caste* (New York: Alfred A. Knopf, 2004).

6. See the classic study by Victor G. Kiernan, *America: The New Imperialism. From White Settlement to World Hegemony* (New York: Verso, 2005); see also Howard Zinn's indispensable *A People's History of the United States: 1492–Present* (New York: Harper Perennial Modern Classics, 2003). Another work that still remains a breakthrough, though it has fallen off the field of vision of contemporary scholars, is Benjamin B. Ringer's massive *'We the People' and Others: Duality and America's Treatment of Its Racial Minorities* (New York: Tavistock, 1983).

Supreme Court ruled in *Dred Scott* that Blacks were inferior and thus unworthy of citizenship, and with *Plessy v. Ferguson* the court ruled that "separate but equal" institutions were legal, thus condemning Blacks to unequal treatment and a regime of apartheid segregation. In *Korematsu v. United States* that the court found that racial minorities could be interned on the basis of racial profiling.[7]

One may argue along with Haney López that the Supreme Court has contributed to the construction of race by the way in which it has made laws that have directly affected the "material geography of social life."[8] This is a good way of talking about race, for race must be measured and quantified by the ways in which social agents are able, or unable, to transverse the "geography" of social space. Indeed, when we speak about race, we are dealing with the ways in which racially marked social agents are either allowed or disallowed to transverse the geography of political space. Segregation, separate but equal, ghettos, prisons, and slums involve coordinates in a social topography.[9] We can discern race by the way in which social space is marked and distributed. As Eric Yamamoto put it:

> When we talk about race in the US we are talking not just about skin color but also the cultural shape and content of our polity [that is, what López called the material geography of our social life]. Color and culture, intertwined, influence who gets in (immigration), who participates politically (electoral districting and multilingual ballots), who gets incarcerated (three strikes and you're out), what languages are spoken (English only legislation), what customs are allowed (housing arrangements, spiritual practices), how educational opportunities are parceled out (slotting according to "cultural traits"), and how social services are delivered (medical care, welfare). Designations of cultural difference are used effectively by some in dominant power positions to justify excluding racialized groups from the polity.[10]

Social space, however, is also delimited and circumscribed by its social weight and density, and it is marked by what I like to call "affect," or the "emotive." Race is also a matter of affect, of how we feel about racially marked agents. If we are racist, it is not primarily because we are convinced of the validity and

---

7. See Eric K. Yamamoto, "Critical Race Praxis: Race Theory and Political Lawyering Practice in Post–Civil Rights America," *Michigan Law Review,* 95 (1997): 821–900; and Louis H. Pollak, "Race, Law, and History: The Supreme Court from Dred Scott to Grutter v. Billinger," in *Daedalus: Journal of the American Academy of Arts and Sciences* 134 (2005): 29–41.

8. López, *White by Law,* 17.

9. I develop this argument at length in Eduardo Mendieta, "Plantations, Ghettos, Prisons: US Racial Geographies," *Philosophy and Geography* 7 (2004): 43–60. See also the book I co-authored with Angela Y. Davis, *Abolition Democracy: Beyond Empire, Prisons, and Torture* (New York: Seven Stories Press, 2005).

10. Eric K. Yamamoto, "Critical Race Praxis," 821–900.

eloquence of racial prejudices, but often because we feel racism, we feel hostility against the racially marked.[11] Race and racism are primordially about affect, about the ways in which we feel and thus emotively map social space. And the Supreme Court has contributed to the emotional education of citizens by regulating the ways in which they can be intimate.[12] As counterintuitive as this may sound, one of the most fundamental ways in which citizens are socialized as citizens is by socializing their affect, that is, by educating their emotions. Indeed, patriotism and nationalism are reflections of the way in which citizenship is related to the emotional life of citizens and a nation.[13]

Citizenship is not just a matter of rights and duties; it is also an institution sustained by a series of moral assumptions and attitudes expressed in affect. Affect and the moral psychology of a polity condition and reflect each other. One may say that national character—what makes different nations and people distinguishable and discernable—is precisely the combination of affect and their corresponding moral psychology. To citizenship, therefore, corresponds a moral psychology that adds moral values to certain emotions. Emotions such as regard, respect, gratitude, admiration, solicitude, anger, fear, contempt, disgust, shame, even hate can, must, or may be experienced with regard to some members of the polity. Indeed, it is this moral psychology that the politics of virtue seeks to educate and modify. Within this moral psychology we find respect, gratitude, sacrifice, loyalty, and deference, but also contempt, disregard, arrogance, and derogation.[14] This moral psychology regulates the way in which strangers and co-citizens interact in the life-world of democratic public space.[15]

At the heart of U.S. citizenship are a series of laws that have instigated, muted, and quieted racial affect by regulating intimacy among citizens. I argue in what follows that no decision of the Supreme Court illustrates better this insight than *Brown v. Board of Education*. This decision, fifty years old in 2004, epitomizes brilliantly that law contributes to the construction of race by mapping social geography and by conditioning civic affect. Law constructs race by regulating the

11. Paula M. L. Moya, "'Racism Is Not Intellectual': Interracial Friendship, Multicultural Literature, and Anti-Racist Moral Growth," unpublished manuscript (2005), 1–33.

12. See Randall Kennedy, *Interracial Intimacies: Sex, Marriage, Identity, and Adoption* (New York: Pantheon, 2003); Rachel F. Moran, *Interracial Intimacy: The Regulation of Race and Romance* (Chicago: University of Chicago Press, 2001); Eduardo Mendieta, "The Erotics of Racial Power or the Technologies of the Racist Self," in *Passions of the Color Line*, ed. David Kim (forthcoming).

13. Eamonn Callan, *Creating Citizens: Political Education and Liberal Democracy* (Oxford: Clarendon Press, 1997).

14. Danielle S. Allen, *Talking to Strangers: Anxieties of Citizenship since* Brown v. Board of Education (Chicago: University of Chicago Press, 2004).

15. David Haekwon Kim, "Contempt and Ordinary Inequality," in *Racism and Philosophy*, ed. Susan E. Babbitt and Sue Campbell (Ithaca: Cornell University Press, 1999), 108–23; Martha Nussbaum, *Hiding from Humanity: Disgust, Shame, and the Law* (Princeton: Princeton University Press, 2004).

ways in which social agents can enter and transverse the geography of society and by determining the kinds of affect they can and must feel, whether covertly or overtly. The argument does not end there, however. I also discuss different takes on the legal and historical significance of *Brown* in order to derive some lessons about how to think about Latinos and their agenda for racial and social justice in an age in which judicial activism is being enacted from the right and the civil rights agenda gains of the Warren Court are under attack.[16]

1. The Quest for Racial Justice

On May 17, 1954, the Supreme Court announced two decisions that have assumed landmark status: *Brown v. Board of Education* and *Bolling v. Sharpe*. *Brown v. Board of Education* is the catchall title given to a group of four lawsuits that sought to challenge segregation in four different states: Kansas, South Carolina, Virginia, and Delaware. This fact must be recalled because otherwise one might think that the Supreme Court was responding to one challenge, and that its decision was therefore more magnanimous and fair than it actually was. *Brown* represents the convergence point of a long series of litigations across states; it was not one plaintiff, but many, knocking at the doors of the Supreme Court. Only this much is uncontested, but the rest has come under severe scrutiny, particularly because the decision recently celebrated its fiftieth anniversary. This anniversary was accompanied by the publication of some important works of social and legal history. I would like to rely on at least two of these in order to support the general theses I defend here about the relationship between law, citizenship, social geography, and civic affect.

One of the most noteworthy books dealing with *Brown* is Richard Kluger's *Simple Justice*. It was first published in 1975, and reprinted in 2004 with an additional final chapter that looks back on the fifty years of *Brown*.[17] Kluger's book is social history, that is, history from below. The book is made up of several, very closely and thickly narrated stories of the main protagonists that converged to bring to fruition the Supreme Court's *Brown* decision. Behind every great legal decision stand the moral and civic courage of many citizens. In the case of *Brown,* Kluger thought that the protagonists were ordinary citizens who confronted every imaginable and unimaginable kind of threat and harassment, survived, prevailed, and continued to fight for their rights. In Kluger's gripping narrative we

16. Margaret Talbot, "Supreme Confidence: The Jurisprudence of Justice Antonin Scalia," *New Yorker* (March 28, 2005): 40–55.

17. Richard Kluger, *Simple Justice: The History of* Brown v. Board of Education *and Black America's Struggle for Equality* (New York: Alfred A. Knopf, 2004).

encounter the stories of Reverend Joseph Albert DeLaine, who initiated the litigation to dismantle Jim Crow and "separate but equal" apartheid segregation. Chapter 1 of the book, entitled "Together Let Us Sweetly Live," opens with the following passage:

> Before it was over, they fired him from the little schoolhouse at which he had taught devotedly for ten years. And they fired his wife and two of his sisters and a niece. And they threatened him with bodily harm. And they sued him on trumped-up charges and convicted him in a kangaroo court and left him with a judgment that denied him credit from any bank. And they burned his house to the ground while the fire department stood around watching the flames consume the night. And they stoned the church at which he pastored. And fired shotguns at him out of the dark. But he was not Job, and so he fired back and called the police, who did not come and kept not coming. Then he fled, driving north at eighty-five miles an hour over country roads, until he was across the state line. Soon after, they burned his church to the ground and charged him, for having shot back that night, with felonious assault with a deadly weapon, and so he became an official fugitive from justice. In time, the governor of his state announced they would not pursue this minister who had caused all the trouble, and said of him: Good riddance. All of this happened when he had decided the time had come to lead.[18]

In Kluger we also read about Thurgood Marshall, "Mr. Civil Rights," and the ways in which he became a titanic figure by arguing civil rights cases and encouraging other Blacks to litigate against segregation. We also learn about Justice Warren, and how he was the arbiter and author of the *Brown* decision, and how he worked diligently to ensure complete unanimity in the decision. Warren understood that a momentous decision such as *Brown* would have to be pronounced with one loud and unambiguous voice, even if brief, unhurried, and unemotional. In general, Kluger's book 2004 reissue gives us the opportunity to revisit the question raised by *Brown*. The book is one of the few works that has placed at the center of its social narratives not only the moral and political courage of citizens but also the way in which this courage transformed the very moral fabric and image of our society. As Randall Kennedy put it in *The New Republic* (July 5–12, 2004), Kluger showed eloquently that "*Brown* was not simply a legal declaration from on high. It was also a response to a moral demand from below."[19] In more than one way, then, Kluger showed that citizens can transform society.

During 2004 Michael J. Klarman also published *From Jim Crow to Civil Rights:*

---

18. Ibid., 3.
19. Randall Kennedy, "Schoolings in Equality," *New Republic* (July 5–July 12, 2004), 7.

The Supreme Court and the Struggle for Racial Equality.[20] Like Kluger's book, Klarman's work will also surely become a classic of legal and social history, but unlike the former, Klarman's book takes a different approach. Their general conclusions converge, but whereas the focus of Kluger is more circumspect and delimited, namely the activity of those persons most directly linked to the conditions that resulted in *Brown,* Klarman aims to paint a larger canvass. An analogy may be useful here. Klarman's work is reminiscent of that of French *Annales* school historians, and particularly of Fernand Braudel. Like these historians, Klarman is interested in the way in which minor historical details form part of larger social historical trends, or what *Annales* historians called the *longue durée,* the long view.[21] Thus, Klarman's *From Jim Crow to Civil Rights* offers us a social history of *Brown,* but in the process we learn about the shape and trends in post–World War II United States. There are no heroes in Klarman's book, as there are in Kluger's, nor is there a rational logic of legal enlightenment in it. Concurring with Derrick Bell, Klarman attributes less power and consequence to legal precedent and coherence and more power to legal fortuity. Indeed, Klarman explicitly denies any primacy or autonomy to what he calls "the legal axis" in Supreme Court decisions. Court decisions are not possible without prior civic activism, and once they have been pronounced, they are not self-enforcing. They must be translated into legislation by either Congress or by presidential fiat. To echo David Hume, the law does not move citizens to action, but the passions of moral outrage and its consequent civic activism do.

Yet, as Kluger is adamant in his almost hagiographic narrative of racial uplift and slow but deliberate triumph over the forces of racial prejudice and White supremacy, Klarman is sanguine about the cumulative effect of *Brown* on race relations in the United States. Klarman's book is one of the most meticulously researched works on the Supreme Court, but it is animated by a series of questions that once answered leave us with a massive act of deconstruction and demystification. Klarman asks at the outset the extent to which *Brown* educated the American citizenry about race relations: Did *Brown* have the direct effect of jump-starting the civil rights movement in the sixties that led to massive demonstrations? Did *Brown* contribute to the desegregation of the South? To what extent did *Brown* bring about a peaceful social revolution in American society by legal enactment? And to what extent can we attribute to *Brown* the power to bring about racial justice on the basis of the unfolding inner logic of the law? In other words, to what extent can we attribute to law, and in particular consti-

---

20. See Michael J. Klarman, *From Jim Crow to Civil Rights: The Supreme Court and the Struggle for Racial Equality* (New York: Oxford University Press, 2004).

21. Fernand Braudel, *Las Ambiciones de la Historia* (Barcelona: Crítica, 2002).

tutional law, a positive, progressive, enlightening power that if left to its own de-
vices would bring about transformative results?

Klarman is unequivocal in his answers. *Brown,* like other momentous decisions by the court, did little to educate U.S. citizenry about race relations. *Brown*
expressed legally what had become common knowledge by the fifties, namely
that the doctrine of racial supremacy with a polity racially divided was intoler-
able. *Brown* did little to desegregate the South, as the statistics reveal too clearly.
Of the 1.4 million Black children in that part of the community, not one attended a desegregated school by 1960, and by 1964 only one in a hundred attended.[22] Notwithstanding almost two decades of litigation by the NAACP, the
results were meager and the decision unenforced. In fact, Klarman suggests that
Brown may have slowed the emergence of a militant civil rights movement by
giving Blacks the hope that litigation, the way of the courts, could bring about
racial justice.

Klarman is also quite explicit about what might be called the determinacy of
law. Given the constitutional precedents available in 1954, *Brown* was hardly a
decision that was consequent or easily derivable. Klarman puts it this way:

> We have seen that all judicial decisions are the products of the intersection be-
> tween the legal and the political axes. When the legal sources are relatively deter-
> minate, the justices tend to adhere to them, unless their political preferences to the
> contrary are very strong. The justices invalidated the grandfather clause in *Guinn*
> (1915) and the phony false-pretense law that supported peonage in *Bailey* (1911)
> because these were transparent evasions of constitutional constraint, because the
> justices had no personal inclination to reach contrary results, and probably because
> they believed that public opinion supported the outcomes. . . . Yet constitutional
> clarity is itself an ambiguous concept. Whether the transitional sources of consti-
> tutional law are thought to plainly forbid a particular practice depends on the per-
> sonal values of the interpreter and on the social and political context. . . . Because
> constitutional clarity lies in the eye of the beholder, no judicial interpretation can
> ever be a result simply of the legal axis; rather, all such interpretations are inevitably
> a product of the intersection of both axes. *Brown* illustrates the same point. To the
> justices who were most committed to traditional legal resources, such as text, orig-
> inal intent, precedent, and custom, *Brown* should have been an easy case—for *sus-
> taining* school segregation. Jackson candidly conceded that barring segregation
> could be defended only in political, not legal, terms. Thus, the legal axis alone can
> never determine a constitutional interpretation, as judges always have to choose
> whether to adhere to that axis. When their preferences are strong, the justices may
> reject even relatively determinate law, because they are unable to tolerate the re-

22. Kennedy, "Schoolings in Equality," 6.

sult it indicates. In 1954, most of the justices considered racial segregation—the doctrine that Hitler had preached—to be evil, and they were determined to forbid it, regardless of whether conventional legal sources sanctioned that result.[23]

This is a sobering conclusion for all those who believe in the blind innocence and benign impartiality of the law. It certainly gives tremendous credence to Derrick Bell's notion of legal fortuity, namely the idea that Blacks derive a modicum of racial justice from the courts only when other extralegal factors are aligned to make a certain legal result desirable, independent from whether this result actually benefits Blacks directly.

Klarman's answers prove most enlightening and demystifying when he turns to the relationship between *Brown,* the emergence of a militant, direct-action civil rights movement, and the building of a consensus in the North and in Washington to intervene directly and actively on the side of Blacks. Klarman postulates that *Brown* did have the following direct result: it emboldened southern racists to be more vocal and explicit about their ideologies of White racial supremacy and their contempt toward Blacks. *Brown* was taken by the South as a direct and insolent assault on the culture and social fabric of the southern way of life. It radicalized southern Whites to become defiant of the court and the federal government. Many southern politicians rode their political candidacies on the cart of a defiant posture to the North and the Supreme Court. This defiance, instigated by certain politicians, turned into grotesque violence against Blacks: lynchings, assassinations, riots, and beatings. And all of this was aided and abetted by the forces of law and order. According to Klarman it was this spectacle of racial hate and violence that galvanized northern opinion to side actively with Blacks in their quest for racial justice: "*Brown* was less directly responsible than is commonly supposed for the direct-action protests of the 1960s and more responsible for ensuring that those demonstrations were brutally suppressed by southern law enforcement officers. . . .Violence, when communicated through television to national audiences, transformed racial opinion in the North, leading to the enactment of landmark civil rights legislation."[24] Or, as he put in a more lapidary fashion, "By helping to lay bare the violence at the core of White supremacy, *Brown* accelerated its demise."[25]

Klarman's provocative thesis demonstrates the role of affect in bringing about certain indirect results of *Brown.* One must ask why southern Whites would resist with such vehemence attempts to integrate public facilities. As Klarman, along with Bell, Ogletree, Kennedy, and many other legal scholars have noted,

23. Klarman, *From Jim Crow to Civil Rights,* 447.
24. Ibid., 364.
25. Ibid., 442.

the White southern response was so vehement and virulent because *Brown* took direct aim at one of the pillar institutions of racial segregation, namely grade school segregation.[26] Most important, as was made patently clear by the many pronouncements by southerners, *Brown* took aim at dismantling a barrier that hindered civic intimacy between the races. The thought of Black and White children growing up and socializing together in their formative years was abhorrent to racist southerners. To many, such closeness and intimacy smacked of miscegenation.[27] *Dread Scott* and *Plessy* had already established that Blacks should live in the American polity as abject subjects, with suspended or abridged citizenship, and marked with the scarlet letter of racial opprobrium. *Brown* sought to dismantle the wall that fractured the intimacy and affect among U.S. citizens.

The witnessing and broadcasting on television of the brutal violence against Blacks on the part of Whites and officers of the law, accompanied by the almost military discipline by Blacks in taking on the onslaught of White mobs, galvanized northern, and some southern, public opinion. It has been claimed that the Vietnam War was lost on the screens of American televisions. One could say that the Civil Rights movement was partly won because of the same television screens. The moral, however, should be quite clear: the militant civil rights movement was less about litigation or political gain, and more about the moral education of U.S. citizens by instigating their affect. What we can learn from Klarman, then, is that the law is at the intersection between two different forms of affect that condition the emotional life of the citizens of a nation: it either legitimizes and instigates an affect of abjection, derogation, and contempt, or it grants voice to a type of racial solidarity and empathy by dismantling legal boundaries that hinder interracial intimacy. As Randall Kennedy noted with respect to the salutary effect that Klarman's overall approach may have on the study of the interaction among the law, race, and culture in the United States: "An educated citizenry aroused by decent passions will usually provide a more secure foundation for freedom than judges to whom we defer too much."[28]

Klarman's overarching conclusion is that *Brown* can only be properly understood if we put this ruling on a larger historical canvas, one that gives sufficient attention to the variety of forces at play during the second half of the twenti-

26. Derrick Bell, *Silent Covenants: Brown v. Board of Education and the Unfulfilled Hopes for Racial Reform* (New York: Oxford University Press, 2004); Charles J. Ogletree, *All Deliberative Speed: Reflections on the First Half-Century of* Brown v. Board of Education (New York: W. W. Norton, 2004); Randall Kennedy, "Schoolings in Equality."

27. Klarman, *From Jim Crow to Civil Rights*, 456, and Robert J. Cottrol, Raymond T. Diamond, and Leland B. Ware, Brown v. Board of Education: *Caste, Culture, and the Constitution* (Lawrence: University of Kansas Press, 2003), 5.

28. Kennedy, "Schoolings in Equality," 12.

eth century. *Brown* cannot be understood if we do not factor in the determining, if external, forces that converged both to compel and to educate the
Supreme Court to rule against the doctrine of separate but equal. As Klarman
avers, *Brown* was the result of the pressure exerted by a series of social factors
that we too frequently neglect and overlook: "the Great Migration, the rising
prosperity and political clout of Northern Blacks, the ideology of World War
II, and the Cold War imperative for racial change."[29]

2. Latinos and Racial Justice

Schools and prisons are two large social institutions that either make or break
citizens of a polity. In the United States, poor, segregated, underfinanced, and
unsupported schooling has been met proportionately by the growth of what
Angela Davis calls "the prison industrial complex," and the severity of sentencing for differentially punished drug and violent crimes. The ways in which
schools and prisons differentially affect racial minorities is another way to see
how the law maps social space. For this reason, I would like to turn to the ways
in which Latinos have been adversely affected by the failures of school desegregation, and the ways in which they face a hostile criminal system that is bent
on punishing them at higher rates than Whites and at similar rates to Blacks.

In a report issued in July 2001, sponsored by The Civil Rights Project of Harvard University, entitled *Schools More Separate: Consequences of a Decade of Resegregation,* Gary Orfield, the author of the report, notes laconically that "from 1988
to 1998, most of the progress of the previous two decades in increasing integration in the region was lost. The South is still much more integrated than it
was before the civil rights revolution, but is moving backward at an accelerat-
ing pace."[30] Orfield proceeds to tell the short-lived story of the drive to desegregate the South. By 1964, when President Kennedy asked Congress to prohibit
discrimination in programs sustained by federal aid, 98 percent of Blacks in the
South were still in almost fully segregated schools. This is ten years after *Brown*!
By 1968, with the election of Nixon, the tide for desegregation began to reverse
with a conservatively packed Supreme Court, and with pressures from the Justice Department to slow down and even halt all desegregation requirements.
During the seventies, the Supreme Court failed to judge on desegregation cases,
basically stalling or hindering litigation to force desegregation. During Reagan's

---

29. Klarman, *From Jim Crow to Civil Rights,* 444.
30. Gary Orfield, *Schools More Separate: Consequences of a Decade of Resegregation* (Cambridge: Harvard
University Press, 2001), 2.

presidency, a new impetus to roll back civil rights and school desegregation was given free reign. As Orfield put it, "The Reagan administration brought a rapid repeal of the federal desegregation assistance program and a shift in the Justice Department to a position of strong opposition to desegregation litigation, opposing even the continuation of existing desegregation plans."[31] Finally, between the 1988 and 1998, the slow gains attained in the prior two decades in desegregation began to be rolled back.

Orfield's report focused particularly on the effects of segregation in Latino communities. Whereas Black-White desegregation was commanded by the Supreme Court in 1954, Latino-White desegregation was only acknowledged in 1973, almost two decades later. By then, under the Nixon administration, such court rulings faced an unsympathetic if not entirely hostile legislature. There was no serious effort to enforce the 1973 *Keyes v. School District No. 1 Denver, Colorado* ruling. In fact, the executive branch sought to trade off bilingual education for desegregation, offering the former rather than seek to enforce the later.[32] What Nixon enforced, namely bilingual rights, was rolled back by Reagan. The attack of Reagan's administration on bilingual education affected disproportionately those states with large Latino populations.

Orfield notes that the 1990s brought a reversal of desegregation, sliding it back to the levels of the 1970s when less than a decade of any serious effort to desegregate had been made on the part of local and federal agencies. While this roll back is serious enough by itself, Orfield discovered that resegregation had affected Latinos even more adversely. He notes: "While intense segregation for Blacks is still 28 points below its 1969 level, it has actually grown 13.5 points for Latinos. Little more than a fifth of Latino students were in intensely segregated schools in 1968, but now it is more than a third, remaining slightly higher than the rising Black level throughout the 1990s. . . . By 1998, more than three-fourths (75.6 percent) of Latinos were in predominantly minority schools, and less than a fourth in majority White schools. By this measure Latinos have been substantially more segregated than Black students since 1980, although Black resegregation gradually narrowed the gap in the 1990s."[33]

Orfield's findings have been corroborated by no other than Jonathan Kozol, surely the best-known pedagogue in the United States, who has been covering and researching the lives of children in the United States for the last forty years. In an article published in the 2005 September issue of *Harper's* magazine, which is adapted from his book *The Shame of the Nation: The Restoration of Apartheid*

31. Ibid., 2, 4.
32. Ibid., 5.
33. Ibid., 32.

Schooling in America,[34] Kozol writes: "Schools that were already deeply segregated twenty-five or thirty years ago are no less segregated now, while thousands of other schools around the country that had been integrated either voluntarily or by force of law have since been rapidly resegregating."[35] While Orfield's statistics give us a picture of the national trend, those gathered by Kozol zoom in on the urban character of this resegregation. Some of Kozol's finding demand that we quote them, as they underscore the general point that I am articulating:

> In Chicago, by the academic year 2002–2003, 87 percent of public-school enrollment was black or Hispanic; less than 10 percent of children in the school were White. In Washington, D.C., 94 percent of children were black or Hispanic; less than 5 percent were White. In St. Louis, 82 percent of the student population were black or Hispanic; in Philadelphia and Cleveland, 79 percent; in Los Angeles, 84 percent, in Detroit, 96 percent; in Baltimore, 89 percent. In New York City, nearly three quarters of the students were black or Hispanic.[36]

The other major indicator of racial status in the social geography of the United States is prison population. In a report issued in July 2003 by the Bureau of Justice Statistics, it was noted that the prison population had grown 2.6 percent over 2002, despite a decline in serious crime. In 2002, there were 2,166,260 prisoners in local and federal prisons and in juvenile detention centers throughout the United States. In July 25, 2004, the same organ of the U.S. Department of Justice released another report that stated that there were almost 6.9 million Americans on probation, parole, or incarcerated in U.S. prisons, jails, and correctionals. The report calls this group of citizens and adult residents "correctional population." Statistically, the report continues, this "correctional population" breaks down more or less in the following way: 13 percent are women, 41 percent are Black, 40 percent are White, 18 percent are Hispanic, and 2 percent are of other race or ethnicity.

This report confirmed a scandalous reality that had already been reported earlier by the same organ of the state. On May 27, the Bureau of Justice Statistics released a report that stated that nearly 2.1 million adult residents and citizens were inmates in prisons and jails. Within a correctional population of almost 13 million, Hispanics constituted an inmate population of over 2 million. The re-

34. Jonathan Kozol, *The Shame of the Nation: The Restoration of Apartheid Schooling in America* (New York: Crown, 2005).

35. Jonathan Kozol, "Still Separate, Still Unequal: America's Educational Apartheid," *Harper's Magazine* 311.1864 (September 2005), 41–54, quote at 41.

36. Ibid., 41.

port also noted that this prison population is made up of 43.6 White non-Hispanics, 39.2 percent Blacks, and 15.4 percent Hispanics. The distinction between White non-Hispanic and Hispanics in the report signals the racialization of Hispanics (as discussed by Linda Alcoff in a chapter of this book). In general, the report affirms, "sixty-eight percent of prison and jail inmates were members of racial or ethnic minority groups." Moreover, as has been documented by sociologists Darrell Steffensmeier and Stephen Demuth, Latinos are suffering harsher penalty sentences than non-Black and White defendants.[37] Like Blacks, Latinos are marked by the racial opprobrium that brands them criminal, while they lack social and political resources. That Latinos are predominantly immigrants also makes them particularly vulnerable to harsher sentences. As Steffensmeier and Demuth found out, "First, noncitizen defendants receive harsher sentences than do citizen defendants across all racial/ethnic comparisons. Second, noncitizen Hispanic defendants are sentenced more harshly than are noncitizen Black defendants and especially, noncitizen White defendants."[38]

Education and punishment are two major functions of the state, and they are obviously regulated by the law, in most cases a law that is directly generated by rulings of the Supreme Court. Thus it would make sense to argue that an important item on the Latino agenda for social justice should be to engage the courts in order to revive a civil rights agenda. However, I will argue that Latinos face not just an unsympathetic and hostile Supreme Court, but also a legal culture that has decoupled, as Eric Yamamoto put it, the quest for racial justice from lawyering and civil rights litigation. The last two decades have soured the American dream of unstoppable social improvement. Whereas events in the fifties and sixties led Americans to believe that progress in racial relations was inevitable, if slow and difficult, countertrends in the eighties and nineties have led to the awakening that neither the moral compass of the nation nor the law of the courts is guaranteed to be on the side of minority groups most in need of their sympathy and protection. Even when we expect the law to be neutral, because of its putative blindness it has been used at the discretion and interest of dominant minorities. As Klarman notes:

> Constitutional law generally has sufficient flexibility to accommodate dominant public opinion, which the justices have little inclination, and limited power, to resist. For example, the conventional sources of constitutional law did not plainly bar segregation, which in 1896 seemed like progressive racial policy given escalating White-on-Black violence and the strong commitment of most Whites to preserv-

37. Darrell Steffensmeier and Stephen Demuth, "Ethnicity and Sentencing Outcomes in U.S. Federal Courts: Who Is Punished More Harshly?" *American Sociological Review* 65 (2000): 705–29.
38. Ibid., 712.

ing "racial purity." The upshot is that courts are likely to protect only those minorities that are favorably regarded by majority opinion. Ironically, when a minority group suffering oppression is most in need of judicial protection, it is least likely to receive it. *Groups must command significant social, political, and economic power before they become attractive candidates for judicial solicitude.*[39]

The fact is that Latinos command little social, political, and economic power in such a way that they can either attract the solicitude of the court or the convergent interest of White America. In addition to this post–civil rights decoupling of racial justice from juridification, there are some other additional factors that will make it even more difficult for Latinos to advance their agenda for social justice. Let me mention three factors that may present obstacles for Latinos.

First and most important, and in contrast to Blacks but like Asian Americans, Latinos are made up of a variety of minority groups, all of them with very different histories of racial discrimination in the United States. Latinos constitute almost 13 percent of the U.S. population making them the largest minority, and thus overtaking Blacks. Yet, this number has to be divided: Mexican Americans make up 60 percent of the total Latino population, while Puerto Ricans and Cubans make up 9.6 percent and 3.5 percent respectively. The remaining 25 percent is made up of Central and South Americans. Each of these groups brings a very different history to the United States, and the United States has had very different histories of interaction with each Latino group.[40] Their claims on American society are therefore very different and in some cases almost incommensurate. Only Mexicans and Puerto Ricans can be said to have suffered the long-lasting effects of legalized segregation. Cubans are in a category of their own, as they are emblematic of the uses of ethnic politics for Cold War ends. It is difficult at first blush to see how a unified legal and civil rights strategy could be developed out of this plethora of histories, needs, and dreams.

Second and just as important, Latinos are neither a race nor an ethnicity, but a combination of both imbricated and complicated by nationality. Thus their claims cannot be solely articulated in the language of race. Nor can they be articulated solely in the language of ethnicity.[41] Whether they are named Latinos or Hispanics, they constitute a demographic fiction constructed for political

---

39. Klarman, *From Jim Crow to Civil Rights,* 450. Emphasis added.

40. I discuss this in greater detail in Eduardo Mendieta, "La latinización de 'América': Los latinos en los Estados Unidos y la creación de un nuevo pueblo," in *Relatos de Nación: La construcción de las identidades nacionales en el mundo hispánico,* ed. Francisco Colom (Madrid: Iberoamericana and Vervuert, 2005), 975–98.

41. Here I am making reference to the fact that Latinos, within the United States, occupy a very distinct place in the matrix of ethno-race, which is suggested by the fact that we are beginning to see the unusual nomenclature of "White non-Hispanic" in official documents. I am also relying on Jorge Gra-

purposes at a time when a conservative countersurge sought to roll back the civil rights agenda inaugurated by Blacks.[42] The ambiguity and duplicity of the labels interestingly is not just ascribed. It is also avowed. While 42 percent of Latinos identify themselves as "other race," 48 percent claim they are White.[43] These percentages of racial self-identification surely vary widely from one to another Latino group. Mexicans, for instance, not only identify themselves as either a race or an ethnicity, for many their *Mexicanidad* is a national identity. In addition, during the sixties, Mexicans and Puerto Ricans developed contestational identities that are pseudoracial. Aztlan and Borinquen are mythological constructs that allowed Chicanos and Puerto Ricans to develop positive panethnic identities around which narratives of resistance could be woven. Cubans also exhibit this racial ambivalence. The postrevolution exiles, picked by Washington to play a central role in the diorama of Cold War racial politics, were predominantly White, but after the Marielitos arrived in the early eighties, a racial divide sundered Cuban identity. Similarly many Central and South Americans claim Indian ancestry.

As the 2000 census has demonstrated, to the chagrin of Census Bureau social scientists, Latinos think of their identity along two lines: an ethnic and a racial one. In addition to the national background of Latinos, one can discern multiple racial self-ascriptions. We find White Hispanics, Latino Hispanics, and Black Hispanics, Jewish Hispanics, and even Chinese Hispanics. The groups that identify either as Latino Hispanics or Black Hispanics articulate a fascinating dynamic. Latino Hispanics think of their Latinity not as an ethnic label, but as a racial one.[44] Thus Latinity racializes Hispanicity, in the way that Black, a presumptively unequivocal racial marker, racializes Hispanicity. Of course, White

cia's *Surviving Race, Ethnicity, and Nationality: A Challenge for the Twenty-First Century* (Lanham, MD: Rowman and Littlefield, 2005).

42. This is a seemingly alarming claim; yet, upon closer inspection it is rather innocuous. First, and foremost, I am making reference to the fact that ethnic labels have to be circumscribed to U.S. politics. By this I mean that while "Hispanic" may have a long semantic history, its use and appropriation within U.S. legislation has very specific consequences. Ethnic labels in the United States have very specific political consequences; their use and deployment are motivated by unique assumptions and premises encrusted in the racial dynamics of the country. Second, the use of the term *Hispanic* by the Nixon administration was both politically motivated and a necessary compromise. We cannot dismiss the conservative, and anti–civil rights agenda, of the Nixon administration, even if the label "Hispanic" has come to be used as a political flag around which to gather a pan-ethnic movement. I dealt with some of these claims in my essay "The 'Second Reconquista,' or Why Should a 'Hispanic' Become a Philosopher? On Jorge Gracia's *Hispanic/Latino Identity: A Philosophical Perspective,*" *Philosophy and Social Criticism* 27 (2001): 11–19.

43. Ian F. Haney López, *Racism on Trial: The Chicano Fight for Justice* (Cambridge, MA: Belknap Press, 2003).

44. For documentation of this claims see Ian F. Haney López, "Race on the 2010 Census: Hispanics and the Shrinking White Majority," *Daedalus: Journal of the American Academy of Arts and Sciences* 134 (2005): 42–52.

Hispanic, also racializes, but differently than Black. It is the Latino sandwiched in between that destabilizes the solidity of both race and ethnicity.[45]

From all this it should be clear that a Latino politics of social justice can hardly be waged exclusively on a politics of civil rights litigation based on race claims. If Latinos have suffered legal racism it has been primarily as a result of legal racism enacted against Blacks. Anti-Latino racism is collateral damage of anti-Black racism. Only in the case of Mexicans is there an extensive and specific history of legislation and law that has sought to segregate them. We have to be clear, however, that the dynamics of racialization of Latino groups are affected, but not determined, by the racial matrix of the one-drop rule, which naturalized and froze into law anti-Black racial segregation and exploitation. United States' cultural historian David A. Hollinger has noted that the one-drop rule has been countered by the principle that all racial oppression is White oppression qua White supremacy.[46] Thus, just as a complex ethno-racial consciousness is required in order to understand the differentiated status of Latinos in the United States, we also need a more nuanced understanding of the sources of ethno-racial discrimination that Latinos have differentially suffered.

The challenge for Latinos in their quest for social justice is to embrace a civil rights agenda that benefits all oppressed minorities while at the same time not betraying the quest for racial justice that was part of the Black civil rights movement in the second half of the twentieth century. Part of this challenge is to recognize that the Black quest for racial justice has advanced, although its gains stand under continuous threat, and therefore must be protected, supported, and respected. At the same time we must have the candor to acknowledge that the Latino quest for social justice cannot supplant or eclipse the Black quest for racial justice. In this case, Latinos will have to see that their interests in racial justice converge with those of Blacks. They stand to be beneficiaries of Black gains, although Latinos themselves are not the primary targets of the claims of racial justice. But such gains are neither assured nor enduring. As Bell put it, "Racial justice, then, when it comes, arrives on the wings of racial fortuity rather than hard-earned entitlement. Its departure, when conditions change, is preordained."[47] After fifty years of *Brown,* Latinos should learn that legal battles are symbolic rather than substantive. As Kluger and Klarman show, behind barely a dozen pages of Supreme Court legal opinion stand decades of political activism and the civic heroism of community leaders. To quote Bell again, "*Brown* teaches

45. Eduardo Mendieta, "The Making of New Peoples: Hispanizing Race," in *Hispanics / Latinos in the United States: Ethnicity, Race, and Rights,* ed. Jorge J. E. Gracia and Pablo De Greiff (New York: Routledge, 2000), 45–59.

46. David A. Hollinger, "The One Drop Rule and the One Hate Rule," *Daedalus: Journal of the American Academy of Arts and Sciences* 134 (2005): 18–28.

47. Derrick Bell, *Silent Covenants,* 9.

that advocates of racial justice should rely less on judicial decisions and more on tactics, actions, and even attitudes that challenge the continuing assumptions of White dominance. History as well as current events call for realism in our racial dealings."[48]

3. The Moral Psychology of Democratic Vulnerability

I began this essay with some general reflections on the relationship between affect, law, and citizenship. I claimed that the rules and norms of citizenship both presuppose and project a moral psychology. This moral psychology maps, grids, and triangulates what López calls the "material geography of social life."[49] This moral psychology has this effect on our social life because it determines the moral life and the social intimacy of our everyday interaction with each other. The force of the law and the coercion of the state step in when the background and moral norms that regulate the social intimacy of citizens breakdown and collapse due to mistrust, arrogance, or outright contempt. The moral psychology of citizenship entails particular ways of feeling about our consociates, our co-citizens. Indeed, citizenship presupposes a type of reciprocity that is prior to the reciprocity of the law; this is the reciprocity of trustworthiness. As citizens we may be anonymous to each other, but such anonymity is granted on the condition of mutual trust, and thus respect. Unfortunately, the law is a poor educator of the moral psychology and moral imagination of citizens. In fact, the law, as the mechanism that regulates by juridifying the interactions of citizens, echoes the moral norms that are enacted in particular acts by citizens. Rarely, does the law seek to educate citizens that have not already experienced some moral education through praxis. Danielle S. Allen's *Talking to Strangers: Anxieties of Citizenship since Brown v. Board of Education* has articulated brilliantly and movingly what I have called here the moral psychology of citizenship.[50] In a true tour de force, Allen argues for the centrality of affect in the political life of democracies. She articulates this thesis by arguing against Aristotle, Hobbes, and Habermas's self-defeating quest for a politics of perfect citizens, political interaction-speech without rhetoric or perlocutionary effects, and regard for the economy of benefit and sacrifice that all polities must negotiate.

There are two central theses in Allen's work that need to be emphasized here. First, Allen defends the insight that democracy and democratic citizenship require sacrifice at the core, what she calls the negotiation of benefits and sacri-

48. Ibid., 9.
49. Haney López, *White by Law,* 17.
50. Allen, *Talking to Strangers.*

fice in the distribution of social wealth and political power. But, if this is one of its preconditions, it also entails that reciprocity be the other face of sacrifice. A polity in which only some benefit all the time, and most sacrifice themselves all the time, is not a democracy, but rather an oligarchy at best and a tyranny at worst. This reciprocity must be accompanied by trustworthiness. Citizenry trustworthiness means that citizens grant each other the prerogative to choose because in some and perhaps most of their choosing they will also do so in accord with and regard for other citizens' interests.

This leads us to the second central insight in Allen's work that I want to draw attention to, namely that "Democratic citizenship requires rituals to manage the psychological tension that arises from being an often *powerless sovereign*."[51] Democratic citizenship, therefore, is based on mutual vulnerability. As citizens of a polity, we are vulnerable to the selfishness of some constituencies and the partiality of a particular administration. But we are also vulnerable to the solicitude and deference of other groups. The sixties illustrated the two sides of this democratic vulnerability. Political friendship, one that results from civic education, and the education of the moral imagination of citizens, be it through national myths or through literature, is thus fundamental to nurturing that vulnerability while making sure that it does not become a permanent politics of victimization and exploitation.

Latinos, whether as an ethnicity or a race, can contribute inordinately to a politics of friendship because of their complicated and articulated national, ethnic, and racial histories. As an ethnic/racial group that has emerged from over half a century of racial mixing, they have unique insights into racial intimacy and interracial friendship. As an ethnic/racial group that has suffered differential discrimination in the United States, they also have learned priceless lessons about racial trust and betrayal. As children of *mestizaje,* we have a greater intimacy with interracial friendship than most Whites, and other ethnic minorities. Yet, Latino histories of discrimination and racial segregation cannot compare to that of Black Americans. Latinos can and should learn from fifty years of *Brown v. Board of Education* that the law does not educate a citizenry, rather it is gratuitous and valiant acts of interracial friendship that transform the moral psychology and moral imagination of citizens. Racial justice may be enacted through the law, but its true ground is political friendship, in which we reciprocate our trustworthiness and mutual vulnerability as powerless sovereigns of democracy.[52]

51. Ibid., 113. Emphasis added.

52. I would like to thank Linda M. Alcoff, Paula Moya, Ron Sundstrom, and Martin Woessner for comments, suggestions, and criticisms to an early draft of this essay. I would also like to expressly thank Jorge Gracia who through an early exchange of e-mail got me going on the path that led to this essay and also made substantive criticisms and suggestions that I think have made this a better work.

CHAPTER 11

Race, Ethnicity, and Public Policy

J. ANGELO CORLETT

> Whoever avoids paying his due for his wrongdoing, is and deserves to be
> miserable beyond all other men, and that one who does what's unjust is
> always more miserable than the one who suffers it, and the one who avoids
> paying what's due always more miserable than the one who does pay it.
> —Socrates, in Plato, *Gorgias,* 479e

This chapter briefly summarizes the genealogical conception of ethnicity
as a replacement for the biologically based ideas of race ("primitive race theories") I have presented elsewhere and clarifies and defends the differentialist
conception of affirmative action that underlies my genealogical conception of
ethnicity. Furthermore, I respond to various concerns that have been raised
about my views.

Race and Ethnicity

In *Race, Racism, and Reparations,* I argued, first, that the purely biological conception of race is highly problematic and a poor means by which to identify
people for purposes of positive public policy administration, and second, that
we instead ought to follow sound social science in adopting the more nuanced
ethnic categories.[1] Unlike race, ethnic categories can and do recognize the importance of culture, language, names, self-identification, and out-group and in-
group identification, among other things, in describing who and what we are.
Moreover, ethnic categories, numbering well over one hundred, do not face the

1. J. Angelo Corlett, *Race, Racism, and Reparations* (Ithaca: Cornell University Press, 2003).

problem that the few race (excluding mixed race) categories do in not being able to find room for us Latinos, indigenous Americans, and the like. In short, the concept of ethnicity is much more nuanced than that of race, and perhaps ethnicity has done less damage to promote racism than race has, at least in the United States of America. Besides being able to best, though not unproblematically, categorize us into ethnic groups for purposes of positive public policy administration, genealogically based ethnic categories when properly construed can serve as proper sources of ethnic pride as well as the basis of certain ethnically based medical research, such as sickle cell anemia.

Some have pointed out, however, that the retention of race talk has an important value. At the very least, even this metaphysically empty concept can play a crucial role in helping to describe the problem of the color line in U.S. society. I certainly concur with this astute observation and had no intention of downplaying (or denying) it in my book. However, I would caution that race is still an incoherent concept, for reasons that Jorge J. E. Gracia, Naomi Zack, myself, and others have argued at some length, and with significant plausibility.[2] That the concept of race is helpful in explaining the current state of racism in the U.S. and perhaps elsewhere in no way implies that race is a metaphysically sound notion. After all, myths can serve a positive function in life, so long as we do not think that there is an ontological essence to them. And if the myth is harmless, then there is no problem. But if the concept in question prohibits us from adequately categorizing us for positive and worthwhile purposes, then there is sufficient reason to replace the concept with a better one for that purpose. It is for these reasons that I rejected race categories in favor of ethnic ones. We simply cannot use race as a way to adequately categorize people into groups for purposes of positive public policy administration. "Black" will not suffice to identify the groups of persons who deserve reparations based on the U.S. slave trade, for example. For in this category would be included those who are not African Americans who by my definition are all of those whose genealogical roots trace to U.S. slavery, excluding many Native Americans who were not Africans but were nonetheless enslaved. It would include those with black or dark skin, whether or not their roots trace to U.S. slavery. And it might, on some accounts, exclude those of lighter skin color yet whose ancestry indeed traces back to U.S. slavery. The first group would pose serious difficulties for anyone interested in reparations for U.S. slavery. Just as in a legitimate class-action lawsuit one cannot include as plaintiffs those who have not been harmed by the defendant's harmful wrongdoings, inactions or attempted actions, one

2. Jorge J. E. Gracia, *Hispanic/Latino Identity: A Philosophical Perspective* (Oxford: Blackwell, 2000); Naomi Zack, *Thinking About Race* (Belmont, CA: Wadsworth, 1998).

cannot rightfully include as plaintiffs Blacks whose ancestry does not trace back to U.S. slavery, though such folk might well be included in a legal action against the U.S. or other countries on different charges. Blacks whose roots do not trace back to slavery in the U.S. would pose a problem of a different sort, namely, that of arbitrarily discriminating against a subgroup of African Americans in the pursuit of reparations for the enslavement of their forebears. In short, the concept of race is highly problematic in public policy contexts. Moreover, it is too crude to include such major categories as Latinos, indigenous Americans, and certain other groups because they are not Negroid, Caucasoid, or Mongoloid. And race cannot serve well to categorize people for purposes of positive public policy administration. *Race, Racism, and Reparations* analyzed ethnicity in terms of Latino identity and argued for a conception of how we ought to categorize ourselves for purposes of positive public policy administration, while recognizing that the discussion of these issues relies on social constructs.

In the end, I claim to have demonstrated that the best way to classify Latinos/as for purposes of affirmative action, for instance, is by way of genealogy, following the way various Native Americans have classified themselves for generations for purposes of public policy administration in dealing with the U.S. government. What makes me a Latino is that I am, genealogically speaking, a Latino. And this just means that my parents were predominantly Latinos, as were my grandparents, and so on. The reason why this is somewhat circular, though it remains to be seen whether or not it is viciously as opposed to virtuously so, is because what it means to say that my parents and grandparents are Latinos is contingent on the social construction of that ethnic category. Indeed, I am not confident that we can escape circularity regarding this matter. And I owe this important insight to Gracia, among others. Now, if leftists genuinely believe in reparations and affirmative action for racial injustice, then they seem to have no alternative but to adopt something like my genealogical conception of how people are to be classified, ethnically speaking. Still, it will be true that the concept of race can assist public policy in understanding how the racism that leads us to the need for public policy programs and court-ordered awards of reparations originates. Race assists ethnicity in terms of public policy administration, turning Jim (and Jane) Crow upside down. Race best enables us to understand the racism that warrants and requires compensation, whereas genealogically based ethnic categories best assist us in identifying those who ought to be compensated, and to what degree.

However true it is that genealogical considerations place us predominantly in a particular group for purposes of public policy administration, it is also true that existential considerations play a role, not in actually "placing" us into the group, but rather in understanding the depth to which we belong to it.[3] The result is that we cannot only understand the depth to which one is, say, an African American versus a Latino (or both), but also the ways in which it is reasonable to classify African Americans and Latinos differentially in terms of how much each group has (on balance) experienced harmful wrongdoing in U.S. society. This in turn facilitates development or revision of public policies that can better address historic racist injustices within the bounds of fairness.

What does it mean to be an African American? What does it mean to be a Latino or a Latina? In terms of public policy administration, it means that one has a predominant genealogical tie to members in that group as that group has been socially understood. If I have a Brazilian grandfather and an Argentinian grandmother each on my mother's side, and great grandparents also from those countries, then I am predominantly (at least 50 percent) Latino to the extent that they are Latinos. Recent breakthroughs in genetic research demonstrate it to be quite possible to verify or falsify ethnic claims by way of mitochondrial DNA examination. Indeed, much can be done to trace one's genealogy by scientific investigation. Howard McGary, for instance, is an African American to the extent that his parents and grandparents trace back to the enslavement of Africans in the U.S. To be sure, there is some incongruity here, as I have defined "Latino" in terms of genealogy, while I have defined "African American" in terms of genealogically based historical injustice, namely U.S. slavery. But this need not overly concern us now, as the point simply reemphasizes the role that genealogy plays in positive public policy administration.

Furthermore, no amount of ideological politicization ought to affect how we categorize ourselves and others in terms of public policy administration. Whether or not McGary is a rightist or a leftist on social issues, he is what he is (ethnically speaking) in terms of his genealogical ties to some U.S. enslaved Africans. Whether or not I am a moral or social/political leftist, I am a Latino in terms of my genealogical ties to my parents and grandparents who are Latinos of this or that kind. Metaphysically, race and ethnicity are problematic concepts. But insofar as public policy administration is concerned, my genealogical conception of ethnic identification serves as a reasonable and plausible method of philosophical analysis of the very conception of ethnicity at work in the identification of Native Americans for purposes of dealing with the U.S. government, a conception that has been at work for generations with reasonable success.

---

3. See Corlett, *Race, Racism, and Reparations,* chap. 2.

Public Policy

But what role would the genealogical conception of ethnicity play in determining, for purposes of positive public policy administration, a differentialist conception of reparations and affirmative action? As Malcolm X once said concerning matters of justice: "Of all our studies, history is best qualified to reward our research."[4] I would add that philosophy, especially normative ethics, must be our guide along with history. Nonetheless, the role of history in assessing who we are and what we deserve can hardly be exaggerated.

Assuming that affirmative action programs are morally justified, there are several kinds of theories of affirmative action, based on competing notions of what justifies such programs on moral grounds. Backward-looking approaches seek to justify affirmative action based on the need to rectify historic racist harmful wrongdoings, while forward-looking approaches justify it based on considerations of distributive justice and fairness. Perhaps a synthesis of these views is more plausible, using both backward- and forward-looking reasons to ground affirmative action. Whichever of these views of affirmative action one adopts, it might employ either an inclusionistic or a differentialist strategy insofar as the identification of affirmative action beneficiaries is concerned. An inclusionistic view is most common in the literature, and it holds that there is one conglomerate of groups that for backward, forward, or backward and forward-looking reasons ought to be the recipients of affirmative action programs.[5] Accordingly, "blacks and women" are included in the same category for affirmative action purposes. A differentialist view holds that, insofar as affirmative action programs are at least in part a collective response to racist harmful wrongdoings in the past and present, and insofar as groups experience such racist harmful wrongdoings to varying degrees,[6] then each group ought to receive affirmative action benefits to the extent that it has experienced racist harmful wrongdoing, all relevant

4. For discussions of the social ideas of Malcolm X, see James Cone, *Martin and Malcolm in America* (Maryknoll: Orbis, 1992); Corlett, "Political Separation and the African American Experience: Martin Luther King, Jr., and Malcolm X on Social Change," *Humboldt Journal of Social Relations* 21 (1995): 191–208.

5. This view is clearly the one that has been employed throughout the past few decades in which affirmative action has been at work in the United States, and is assumed in such writings as Barbara R. Bergmann, *In Defense of Affirmative Action* (New York: Basic Books, 1996).

6. As one commentator puts it: "not all oppressive structures are equally harmful, and they should not all be regarded with the same degree of concern" (Sally Haslanger, "Oppressions: Racial and Other," in *Racism in Mind,* ed. Michael P. Levine and Tamas Pataki, 120 [Ithaca: Cornell University Press, 2004]); and as another states: "We need to think clearly about oppression" and "it is perfectly consistent to deny that a person or group is oppressed without denying that they have feelings or that they suffer" (Marilyn Frye, "Oppression," in *Race, Class, and Gender in the United States,* 2nd ed., ed. Paula S. Rothenberg, 54 [New York: St. Martin's Press, 1992]).

things considered. This implies that, based on U.S. history there must be a ranking of the severity of experienced racist harmful wrongdoings, and that this ranking ought to determine which groups receive which benefits and in what amounts.[7] Groups and their respective harms ought to be differentiated from one another based on a plausible principle of proportional compensation already at work in U.S. law.

The differentialist conception of positive public policy administration rests on notions of kinds and degrees of experienced harmful wrongdoings by members of ethnic groups, along with the principle of proportional compensation wherein each compensated party is to receive no more or no less remedial benefits than what they deserve in albeit rough (but adequate) proportion to the harms they have experienced wrongfully. The implication of this principle for affirmative action programs and their beneficiaries is that groups such as Native and African Americans ought to receive far greater affirmative action benefits than any other groups in U.S. society based on the history and current harmful wrongdoings experienced by them, while far fewer and much lower levels of affirmative action benefits ought to be made available to Latinas, Latinos, Asians, and others residing in the United States, based on the kinds and levels of actual harmful wrongdoings experienced by members of these groups. Since no one, on balance, ought to be permitted to benefit from her own wrongdoing, quite surprising (to some) results follow from this line of thought. It follows, for example, that Anglas, being a group currently counted in the collective that constitutes legally legitimate targets of affirmative action benefits, ought to be removed from this group of beneficiaries. It does not follow, however, that well-qualified Anglas ought not to be hired, any more than it would follow that their well-qualified Anglo counterparts ought not to be hired when it comes to employment matters. By "Anglos" and "Anglas" I mean what most refer to as "white" men and women, or "European American" men and women, respectively. The implication of this line of thought for employment, educational, and other affirmative action contexts is that whatever monies are set aside for such programs ought always to be reserved for the most deserving, rather than for those who are least deserving. This is especially the case in light of the inadequacy of the resources available for affirmative action programs.

---

7. Some of the many respected sources along the lines of documenting the racist oppression of African Americans include Randall Kennedy, *Race, Crime, and the Law* (New York: Vintage Books, 1997), chaps. 1–3. Of the numerous trustworthy sources documenting the racist oppression of Native Americans, see Corlett, *Race, Racism, and Reparations*, chap. 8.

Objections and Replies

Now I turn to various concerns that might be expressed about my genealogical conception of ethnic identity and my differentialist strategy for affirmative action. Both the Circularity Objection and the Socialization Objection are aimed at my genealogical conception of ethnicity, whereas the other concerns pertain to my differentialist conception of affirmative action.

Circularity and the Genealogical Conception of Ethnicity

It might be objected that I have said nothing to expound on the notion that some circular arguments are more virtuous than others in that the latter provide a more informative account of reality than the former. For if sense cannot be made of this notion, then there is good reason to reject my analysis. Let me answer by pointing out, first, logically speaking, every argument can be traced to its "first principles" or assumptions, which afford no argumentative support. In this sense, most every, if not every, argument will be to some extent circular. Still, Alvin Goldman, following William P. Alston, has noted that epistemically speaking some circular accounts are more virtuous than others.[8] Consider the well-known example of a viciously and unvirtuously circular argument: "The Bible is the word of God because God wrote it." But insofar as epistemic coherence is a necessary though insufficient condition of knowledge, and insofar as coherence is contingent at least in part on how informative the philosophical account provided is, it seems reasonable to infer that an analysis of ethnicity or race that provides the most informative account of who we are is, other things being equal, the better analysis.

With this in mind, I have argued at length in various sources the following: knowing, speaking, and respecting a Spanish language or dialect is neither necessary nor sufficient for Latino identity; having a traditional Latino name is neither necessary nor sufficient; participating in and respecting a Latino culture is neither necessary nor sufficient; and self-in- or out-group identification are neither necessary nor sufficient. This reasoning provides a via negativa account of Latino identity. And it goes a long way, perhaps further than any competing positive account, in capturing the nature of Latino identity regarding public policy considerations.

Additionally, I have argued that geneaology is both necessary and sufficient for Latino identity as the analysis is indexed precisely to public policy contexts.

---

8. Alvin Goldman, *Knowledge in a Social World* (Oxford: Oxford University Press, 1999). This point is a well-accepted truth in philosophy more generally.

This means that I am, for instance, a Latino to the extent that my parents, grand-parents, and great grandparents, say, are Latinos. I have already conceded that this is in the end circular, but again I am not confident that such circularity can be avoided. Still, perhaps the notion of the social construction of ethnic concepts may further rescue them from the charge of vicious circularity. For when I say that I am a Latino, I mean to convey that I am a Latino according to what a ma-jor segment of society has, rightly or wrongly, named Latinos. More precisely, what I mean to express is that I sufficiently satisfy the description of what groups refer to as Latinos, especially others who refer to themselves and certain others as Latinos. As history progresses, the social notion of a Latino evolves but also crystallizes into a notion with which increasing numbers of people concur. Some agree with the notion of what a Latino or Latina is for purposes of racist domination or exclusion, whereas others make use of this social construct for purposes of ethnic pride and the like. So when I refer to myself as a Latino, I am adopting for the most part what societies have constructed over time as the identity of those of us with Iberian ancestry.[9] Now if it turns out that this so-cial notion, like other ethnic concepts, is a myth without ontological basis, then so be it. But this fact hardly discounts the influence of this concept on people's lives. In short, this is hardly a viciously circular account of ethnic concepts, even though it is circular. In this it contrasts with the well-demonstrated unvirtuously circular traditional analysis of race.[10]

Socialization and the Genealogical Conception of Ethnicity

A second concern that might be raised about my analysis of ethnic identity is that genealogy is not a necessary condition of it. This argument insists that a child of Anglo ancestry who is raised in, say, Mexico for the entirety of her child-hood and who has adopted the Mexican culture as her own, is indeed a Latina. Yet my account denies this.

My reply to this concern is that my analysis is not a metaphysical one, but ethically oriented for purposes of public policy. I fully concur with Gracian and Zackian observations that lead to a kind of metaphysical skepticism about racial and ethnic identities. I have made this doubly clear elsewhere.[11] But I also make it clear that I am, insofar as the ethics of ethnicity is concerned, a realist. I do not believe that the Angla child of the example is (read: ought to be construed

---

9. For a brilliant philosophical discussion of the nature of Latinohood along these lines, see Gracia, *Hispanic/Latino Identity*.

10. See Corlett, *Race, Racism, and Reparations*, chap. 1; Gracia, *Hispanic/Latino Identity*; Zack, *Thinking About Race*.

11. Corlett, *Race, Racism, and Reparations*, chap. 1.

as) anything but an Angla. The reason is that public policy cannot handle well such a convoluted practice of ethnic identification. Fraud would abound and the basic reasons for ethnic-oriented public policies, such as affirmative action, would be defeated. I still believe that my reasoning here is correct, and to deny it would court disaster for affirmative action policies.

It is genealogy that places us into this or that ethnic group, as the cases may be. But if it is true that, after genealogy, what distinguishes ethnic groups from one another is their diverse experiences in the world, then this surely becomes a focal point of differentiating between groups insofar as what they deserve in the administration of public policy.

The Whitewashing of Affirmative Action

Several well-meaning leftists have for decades supported what turns out to be a conspicuously flagrant violation of justice and fairness as it pertains to the administration of affirmative action programs. Lumping all ethnic groups together (except Anglos) into what many (and at times myself) refer to as "people of color," and deeming them "oppressed," they affirm a blanket support for them. But this leads to the categorization of Anglas as oppressed. This has the adverse effect of minimizing the oppression of, say, Native and African Americans and simultaneously inflating the levels of oppression of Anglas. Indeed, it ignores Kimberle Crenshaw's insight that "Black women," for example, "can experience discrimination in ways that are both similar to and different from those experienced by white women and Black men," and often experience "double-discrimination."[12] Moreover, she argues that Angla feminism often "overlooks the role of race. Feminists thus ignore how their own race functions to mitigate some aspects of sexism, and, moreover, how it often privileges them over and contributes to the domination of other women."[13] I would add that it is also true that Anglas on average, on balance, and as a class have served as oppressive forces against Native and African American men in particular. This is true both in terms of their overt acts of racist oppression, but also in terms of their moral negligence in failing to do the right things when the most oppressed needed their support.[14]

12. Kimberle Crenshaw, "Demarginalizing the Intersection of Race and Sex: A Black Feminist Critique of Antidiscrimination Doctrine, Feminist Theory, and Antiracist Politics," in *Feminist Legal Theory,* ed. Katharine T. Bartlett and Rosanne Kennedy (Boulder, CO: Westview Press, 1991), 63.

13. Ibid., 67.

14. For philosophical analyses of responsibility for failures to act, see Joel Feinberg, *Freedom and Fulfillment* (Princeton: Princeton University Press, 1992), chap. 7; John Kleinig, "Bad Samaritanism," in *Philosophy of Law,* 5th ed., ed. Joel Feinberg and Hyman Gross (Belmont: Wadsworth, 1995), 529–32.

Now the reason for affirmative action programs for Anglas is typically construed as assisting the least advantaged group in order to improve the condition of society as a whole. But this "whitewashing of affirmative action" has deleterious effects on U.S. society, and more importantly, on the compensatory rights of the most wronged persons in society to receive what is their due according to morally required backward-looking considerations. Moreover, by ignoring such compensatory rights it harms society as it says, in effect, that certain rights can and should be trumped for the greater good, which effectively nullifies the very notion of a right to begin with.[15]

A plausible ethic must take seriously what people deserve both in terms of considerations of distributive justice and compensatory justice.[16] Furthermore, if it is true that backward-looking considerations are among the most important in a reasonably just society, then it would seem that we must adopt a differentialist policy of affirmative action according to which those groups that have experienced the greatest amounts and kinds of harmful wrongdoings ought to receive the greatest kinds and amounts of benefits either directly or indirectly from those who have harmed them wrongfully, whereas those groups that have experienced lesser amounts and kinds of harmful wrongdoings ought to receive lesser amounts and kinds of benefits from those who have harmed them wrongfully. I use the locution "indirectly" in that governmental policies sometimes for the sake of expediency employ notions of collective or vicarious responsibility (with or without fault) in order to effect such programs.[17] This implies that the current policy of affirmative action, while well-intentioned, is in violation of crucial considerations of justice and fairness. It implies, moreover, that the forward-looking underpinning of the current program that ignores backward-looking considerations of differentialist historic evils experienced by various groups must be replaced by a more complex policy that does not place such a high premium on forward-looking considerations of social harmony while failing to take compensatory rights seriously.[18] After all, how can genuine social harmony accrue if affirmative action programs ignore the his-

---

15. For philosophical analyses of rights, see Corlett, *Justice and Rights* (forthcoming); Ronald Dworkin, *Taking Rights Seriously* (Cambridge: Harvard University Press, 1978); Joel Feinberg, *Rights, Justice, and the Bounds of Liberty* (Princeton: Princeton University Press, 1980), and *Freedom and Fulfillment;* Wesley Hohfeld, *Fundamental Legal Conceptions* (New Haven: Yale University Press, 1921).

16. Corlett, *Justice and Rights,* forthcoming.

17. See Corlett, *Responsibility and Punishment,* 3rd ed. (Dordrecht: Springer, 2006), chap. 7; Joel Feinberg, *Doing and Deserving* (Princeton: Princeton University Press, 1970), chap. 8, and Howard McGary, *Race and Social Justice* (London: Blackwell, 1999), chap. 5, for philosophical analyses of collective liability responsibility for past harmful wrongdoings.

18. For philosophical analysis of the concept of evil, see Joel Feinberg, *Problems at the Roots of Law* (Oxford: Oxford University Press, 2003), chap. 6; Corlett, "Evil," *Analysis* 64 (2004): 81–84.

toric oppression that presumably motivate the concern for affirmative action in the first place?

Implied in my revision of affirmative action policies is a restructuring of beneficiaries according to principles of compensatory justice currently at work in U.S. law. As noted, one such principle is that one ought, on balance, never be permitted to profit from one's own wrongdoing. Another is that those who have experienced wrongful harms ought to be compensated in rough proportion to the harms they have experienced from others. If we take these two principles as necessary conditions of any plausible public policy's implementation, then any violation of them is indicative of a public policy gone wrong and in need of revision. These principles imply that current programs of affirmative action must be revised in favor of a differentialist awarding of benefits. Going beyond what I have argued elsewhere concerning reparations,[19] I refer to the amount of resources that would and should comprise an appropriate affirmative action policy administration budget. Using a fair-minded and commonsense reading of U.S. history as our guide, it is unquestionable that Native and African American women and men should be placed at the top of the list of beneficiaries in terms of both the amounts of affirmative action benefits received and the kinds of such benefits received. Given the horrendous evils and levels of double-oppression experienced by these groups, it would be reasonable to think that all available kinds and the very highest levels of benefits should be reserved for members of these groups, taking sexist oppression and discrimination into account as well as racist oppression and discrimination. By taking sexist experiences of harmful wrongdoing into account, I mean to suggest that Native and African American women ought to receive qualitatively and quantitatively more affirmative action benefits than even their male counterparts. Following this, if there is adequate funding remaining, then certain Latino and Asian women and men, and perhaps some other ethnic groups ought to be included, though to far lesser degrees than Native and African Americans. A fair-minded and commonsense reading of U.S. history justifies this differentialist strategy in light of the moral and legal principles noted. My aim here is to make meaningful progress in the discourse concerning racist oppression and affirmative action programs: to repeat, "we need to think clearly about oppression" and "not

19. Corlett, *Race, Racism, and Reparations,* chaps. 8–9. For further discussions of reparations to African Americans, see Bernard Boxill, "The Morality of Reparations," *Social Theory and Practice* 2 (1972): 113–32; "A Lockean Argument for Black Reparations," *The Journal of Ethics* 7 (2003): 63–91; Howard McGary, "Achieving Democratic Equality: Forgiveness, Reconciliation, and Reparations," *The Journal of Ethics* 7 (2003): 93–113; *Race and Social Justice,* chaps. 6–7; Howard McGary, ed., *Reparations to African Americans* (Lanham, MD: Rowman and Littlefield, forthcoming); Rodney C. Roberts, "The Morality of a Moral Statute of Limitations on Injustice," *The Journal of Ethics* 7 (2003): 115–38; Naomi Zack, "Reparations and the Rectification of Race," *The Journal of Ethics* 7 (2003): 139–51.

all oppressive structures are equally harmful, and they should not all be regarded with the same degree of concern."[20]

But just as it is obviously appropriate to exclude Anglos from this list, it is also clear that Anglas ought to be excluded from it as well. The whitewashing of current affirmative action programs has led to an unfortunate result, namely, that Anglas (and many Anglos) have benefited by way of affirmative action more than all colored folk combined.[21] Yet they are the ones who previously benefited from their oppression of various folk of color in either their own ways or in their aiding and abetting their Anglo counterparts. As Gloria Watkins makes painfully plain regarding the racism of Anglas and their experiences of injustice, "the hierarchical pattern of race and sex relationships already established in American society merely took a different form under 'feminism': the form of women being classed as an oppressed group under affirmative action programs further perpetuating the myth that the social status of all women in America is the same?"[22] The truth of these words from Watkins serves to underscore the racist oppression perpetrated by Anglas on others from the very start of U.S. society, and which continues perhaps in different forms and manifestations, until today. It would take more conniving gall than that of Meletus to insist that Anglas are on average, on balance, and as a group anything less than oppressors of colored folk. And it would take more nerve to continue to insist, in light of my argument, that Anglas ought to be granted continuance as beneficiaries of affirmative action programs—especially at the same levels of benefits as Native and African Americans. After all, to continue to refuse reparations to Native and African Americans in light of the plausibility of the evidence for such reparations counts as a stark refusal to pay what is owed, a denial of compensatory rights that is a form of continued oppression. As Gerda Lerner argues, "Historians of women have long ago come to see that 'women' cannot be treated as a unified category any more than 'men-as-a-group' can. Women differ by class, race, ethnic and regional affiliation, religion, and any number of other categories. . . . If one ignores 'differences' one distorts reality. If one ignores the power relations built on differences one reinforces them in the interest of those holding power."[23]

History and affirmative action have proven to be the greatest bedmates of

---

20. See note 6.

21. By this I mean that those Anglos whose significant others are Anglas and who thereby benefit economically from the affirmative action employment of Anglas indeed benefit from the whitewashing of affirmative action. Also, insofar as Anglas benefit from affirmative action in education, Anglos close to them benefit also, etc.

22. bell hooks, *Ain't I a Woman* (Boston: South End Press, 1981), 121.

23. Gerda Lerner, "Reconceptualizing Differences among Women," in *Feminist Frameworks,* ed. Alison M. Jaggar and Paula S. Rothenberg (New York: McGraw-Hill, 1993), 237–38.

most Anglas in the U.S., for these women have oppressed various folk of color and yet have benefited from affirmative action programs from the start. And where are most of these Anglas today? Millions of them insist on their own rights being respected prior to, and often instead of, those others who deserve them more, such as Native and African Americans. Angla racism against Native and African American men is joined to their racism against women from those groups.[24] The very inclusion of Anglas in the group of affirmative action beneficiaries today is a form of injustice that they perpetrate on those more deserving colored folk.

Still one may wish to argue that Anglas on average, on balance, and as a class were and are themselves oppressed and that this entitles them to affirmative action benefits as the others. But it hardly follows from the supposition that Anglas are oppressed that they deserve affirmative action benefits. Remember the legal and moral principle that "no one ought to be permitted to benefit from her own wrongdoing." Even if Anglas were and are oppressed, their experience of oppression would hardly compare,[25] qualitatively or quantitatively, to the harsh experiences that accompanied genocide, slavery, and the massive land theft that were experienced by Native and African Americans. Moreover, even if it were true that somehow Anglas do rightly qualify as being on the list of genuine affirmative action beneficiaries because they are themselves oppressed, it would hardly follow that what they ought to receive is much more than the bare minimum of kinds and amounts of affirmative action benefits.[26] The differentialist approach to affirmative action benefits does not permit any group to benefit more than it deserves, as it cannot plausibly violate the legal and moral principle of proportional compensation.

Did the injustices experienced by Anglas occur at the hands of Native or

---

24. "Despite the predominance of patriarchal rule in American society, America was colonized on a racially imperialistic base and not on a sexually imperialistic base. Racism took precedence over sexual alliances in both the white world's interaction with Native Americans and African Americans, just as racism overshadowed any bonding between black women and white women on the basis of sex" (hooks, *Ain't I a Woman*, 122). "In America, the social status of black and white women has never been the same. Although they were both subject to sexist victimization, as victims of racism black women were subject to oppressions no white woman was forced to endure. In fact, white racial imperialism granted all white women, however victimized by sexist oppression they might be, the right to assume the role of oppressor in relationship to black women and black men" (hooks, 122–23). "To black women the issue is not whether white women are more or less racist than white men, but that they are racist? That means confronting the reality of white female racism. Sexist discrimination has prevented white women from assuming the dominant role in the perpetuation of white racial imperialism, but it has not prevented white women from absorbing, supporting, and advocating racist ideology or acting individually as racist oppressors in various spheres of American life" (hooks, 124).

25. Recall the above-cited claims to the effect that not all oppressive structures are equally harmful and ought not to be treated with equal concern.

26. Corlett, *Race, Racism, and Reparations,* chap. 7.

African American women? No. Nor did they occur at the hands of Native or African American men. Were Anglas abused by other men of color? Perhaps to some extent and in relatively few cases. But in general these injustices are clearly outweighed by the oppression of colored folk by Anglas themselves. So even if it were true that Anglas as a class and on balance were and are oppressed,[27] they were oppressed mostly by Anglos. The correct picture of Anglas is as perhaps oppressed (definitely treated unjustly), but themselves highly oppressive of others. This makes them poor candidates, on balance, for any kind of affirmative action, assuming of course that the moral justification of affirmative action is largely if not wholly backward-looking. By and large, the case of Anglas is against Anglos, not in the main against men of color. But Anglas should not be allowed to benefit from their own oppression of others, and not to benefit out of proportion to the balance of harmful wrongdoing experienced by them.

Yet this is a far cry from what Anglas have and continue to receive from affirmative action programs today. So even if the principle that no one ought to be permitted to benefit from their own wrongdoing is disregarded, certainly the principle of proportional compensation and benefits applies. The very best that Anglas could possibly deserve in affirmative action benefits are the very lowest levels of support. It is not only Anglos who are co-responsible for the greatest forms of racist evil in the history of the U. S., but also Anglas, though perhaps they are so to a lesser degree in light of their own oppression at the hands of Anglos. And there might well be very good reason to think that on balance the experience of injustice by Anglas is outweighed by the oppression they have wrought on others. And if this were true, then surely Anglas deserve nothing at all by way of compensation and ought to be excluded from affirmative action programs.

Still, it might be objected that only privileged Anglas oppressed colored folk and that Anglas of lower socioeconomic classes were not in positions to oppress them. Hence unprivileged Anglas ought to be included among legitimate affir-

---

27. "Every women's movement in America from its earliest origin to the present day has been built on a racist foundation: The first white women's rights advocates were never seeking social equality for all women; they were seeking social equality for white women. In contemporary times there is a general tendency to equate abolitionism with a repudiation of racism. In actuality, most white abolitionists, male and female, though vehement in their anti-slavery protest, were totally opposed to granting social equality to black people" (hooks, *Ain't I a Woman,* 124). "While they strongly advocated an end to slavery, they never advocated a change in the racial hierarchy that allowed their caste status to be higher than that of black women or men" (hooks, 125). "And it was in the context of endless comparisons of the plight of 'women' and 'blacks' that they revealed their racism. In most cases, this racism was an unconscious, unacknowledged aspect of their thought, suppressed by their narcissism—a narcissism which so blinded them that they would not admit two obvious facts: one, that in a capitalist, racist, imperialist state there is no one social status women share as a collective group; and second, that the social status of white women in America has never been like that of black women or men" (hooks, 136).

mative action beneficiaries.[28] This objection tries to undermine my differentialist strategy by pointing out that it is insufficiently sensitive to the many ways in which Anglas have suffered socioeconomic, class-based injustices and in which they deserve affirmative action benefits.

In reply, let me concur that socioeconomic status is relevant to this discussion of oppression. But I would remind those unfamiliar with U.S. history that it is false that even unprivileged Anglas experienced anything akin to the kinds and degrees of oppression that were wrought on colored folk (especially Native and African Americans). Anglas, privileged or not, were not enslaved, no matter how much some (certainly not Black feminists or other Black progressives, for instance) would have us think to the contrary. Anglas, privileged or not, were not victims of genocide. Nor were they victims of perhaps the largest land theft in history, an evil act from which most all Anglas benefited and to which they contributed by their support of Anglos. Injecting socioeconomic class into the discussion of racism and affirmative action simply obfuscates matters and ignores the fact that there are degrees of oppression, just as there as degrees of racist harmful wrongdoing. No appeal to "unprivileged" Anglas can obscure the fact that Anglas on average, on balance, and as a class participated in and greatly benefited from, for instance, the westward expansion that led to "Indian removal." Let us also remain mindful of the evil acts of many Anglas who helped direct the Indian Boarding Schools, which effectively deprogrammed Indian children taken from their families and reprogrammed them with some version of Christianity. Furthermore, were Anglas victims of the dangers and indignities of slave patrols and fugitive slave laws? No, but it is a fact that many Anglas enjoyed various of the economic benefits of that peculiar institution. Nor can one dissuade reasonable people of the historical fact that so many "unprivileged" (relative to Anglos, but certainly not relative to Native and African Americans) Anglas did also serve in the racist oppression of African Americans, especially during Reconstruction and under Jim (and Jane) Crow. Recall that the KKK was formed in large part to make sure that unprivileged Anglos and Anglas would not fall below the socioeconomic status of then newly freed slaves. Thousands of Anglas throughout the U.S. were members of the KKK, even though thousands were not. Yet implying that even the Anglas who were not KKK members did not share responsibility for the racist oppression of African Americans by the KKK is like arguing that the spouses of terrorist mobsters are not coresponsible in some significant measure for the harmful wrongdoings of the mobsters themselves when they very well not only knew basically what their mobster spouses did for a living, but themselves knowingly benefited from the injustices

---

28. I owe this point to Linda Alcoff.

of their spouse mobsters.[29] It is to take a rather simplistic stance on moral responsibility for acts of racist oppression.[30] It is, moreover, to assume that very bad Samaritanism is an excuse for not doing the right things by working to stamp out the racist oppression from which they as Anglas surely benefited. It is also to ignore how racist Angla feminists have attempted to divert the issues of their own racist oppression of others by adopting the language of their own oppression.[31]

It may be true that privileged (more than underprivileged) Anglas benefited from the racist oppression of Native and African Americans, historically speaking. But it would be implausible to hold that even the poorest Anglas of Appalachia did not both support and benefit significantly from the outright genocide and land theft and enslavement of the peoples in question. After all, those poorest of Anglas surely would not even be in the U.S. if it were not for the violent theft of those very hills in which they reside. And it is all Anglas today in the U. S. who continue to benefit unjustly from the past racist evils in question, that is, unless and until adequate reparations are paid to Native and African Americans.[32] Let us become ever mindful, Anglas as a group demanded (and being backed by laws that they themselves supported and never as a class protested) that African Americans step off the sidewalks as they walked by, sit at the back of the buses while Anglas sat in the front, and never be seated and served in "white" sections of restaurants and had to enter from the kitchens. Yet how many Anglas cried out for reform of Jim (and Jane) Crow?

Certainly, as some Angla feminists remind us, many women (read: Anglas) were and are raped (in most cases, by Anglos). But so many more women of

29. For accounts of collective responsibility, see Corlett, *Responsibility and Punishment,* chap. 7; Feinberg, *Doing and Deserving,* chap. 8; McGary, *Race and Social Justice,* chap. 5.

30. For a recent analysis of moral responsibility, see John Martin Fischer and Mark Ravizza, *Responsibility and Control* (Cambridge: Cambridge University Press, 1999); John Martin Fischer, *My Way* (Oxford: Oxford University Press, 2006). Also see the several articles in *The Journal of Ethics: An International Philosophical Review* for discussions of moral responsibility.

31. "Feminists did not challenge the racist-sexist tendency to use the term 'woman' to refer solely to white women; they supported it. For them it served two purposes. First, it allowed them to proclaim white men world oppressors while making it appear linguistically that no alliance existed between white women and white men based on shared racial imperialism. Second, it made it possible for white women to act as if alliances did exist between themselves and non-white women in our society, and by doing so they could deflect attention away from their classism and racism. Had feminists chosen to make explicit comparisons between the status of white women and that of black people, or more specifically the status of black women and white women, it would have been more than obvious that the two groups do not share an identical oppression" (hooks, 140–41). "This constant comparison of the plight of 'women' and 'blacks' deflected attention away from the fact that black women were extremely victimized by both racism and sexism—a fact which, had it been emphasized, might have diverted public attention away from the complaints of middle and upper class white feminists" (hooks, 141).

32. For a comprehensive philosophical defense of such reparations, see Corlett, *Race, Racism, and Reparations,* chaps. 8–9.

color have been and are raped, though with far less public sympathy, media attention, or legal recourse. And when was the last time an Angla was lynched simply because an Angla accused her of looking at an Angla, much less raping her? Yet thousands of African American men have been lynched in such manner, mostly with no legal repercussions for either the members of the lynch mobs or the Angla accusers themselves for, in many cases, obstructing justice. Indeed, the Mann Act was enacted precisely to protect Anglas. So while sexual crimes of Black men against Anglas were punished (or "telished," as John Rawls would describe it)[33] by death and excused in the name of protecting Angla womanhood, sexual crimes of Anglos against African American women were not only not considered crimes but were considered Anglo rights, or at least liberties.[34] And as Crenshaw astutely observes, "Rape statutes generally do not reflect male control over female sexuality, but white male regulation of white female sexuality. Historically, there has been absolutely no institutional effort to regulate Black female chastity."[35] The "erasure" by many of the African American woman's experience of rape at the hands of Anglos is further articulated by Crenshaw in no uncertain terms: The singular focus on rape as a manifestation of male power over female sexuality tends to eclipse the use of rape as a weapon of racial terror. When Black women were raped by white males, they were being raped not as women generally, but as Black women specifically: their femaleness made them sexually vulnerable to racist domination, while their Blackness effectively denied them any protection. This white power was reinforced by a judicial system in which the successful conviction of a white man for raping a Black women was virtually unthinkable.[36]

More generally, when was the last time any law was passed to explicitly and uniquely protect folk of color, especially from the Anglos and Anglas who oppressed and continue to oppress them? Consider the words of Lerner on the attempt by many to conflate the experiences of oppression of Anglas in the Old South by Anglos with the oppression of African American women by Anglos and Anglas, among others:

33. John Rawls, *Collected Papers,* ed. S. Freeman (Cambridge: Harvard University Press, 1999), chap. 2.

34. Lerner, "Reconceptualizing Differences among Women," 242. Also see Crenshaw, "Demarginalizing the Intersection of Race and Sex," 69.

35. Crenshaw, "Demarginalizing the Intersection of Race and Sex," 68.

36. Ibid., 68–69. The Angla feminist refusal to take seriously the rights of African American women is illustrated well by a women's studies major in my ethics course who, in emotive response to my pointing out how Anglas were not oppressed in nearly the same ways and degrees of enslaved women of the U.S. South and how it was part and parcel of the enslaved women's life to be raped often by her Anglo master, replied: "Well, think of how the poor wife of the master felt, having her husband cheat on her like that!" This sort of narcissistic attitude tends to distort U.S. history, conveniently in favor of Anglas' experience.

Although neither group controlled their sexuality or their reproduction, the differences between them were substantial. White women, regardless of class, owed sexual and reproductive services to the men to whom they were married. Black women, in addition to the labor extracted from them, owed sexual and reproductive services to their white masters and to the Black men their white masters had selected for them. Since the white master of Black women could as well be a white woman, it is clear that racism was for Black women and men the decisive factor which structured them into society and controlled their lives. Conversely, white women could offset whatever economic and social disadvantages they suffered by sexism by the racist advantages they had over both Black men and women. Practically speaking, this meant that white women benefited from racism economically, insofar as they owned slaves; that they could relieve themselves of child-rearing (and at times even childbearing) responsibilities by using the enforced services of their female slaves; that they were relieved of doing unpaid domestic labor by using slave labor.[37]

Nor will it close the tremendous gap between the levels and degrees of oppression between Native and African Americans on the one hand, and Anglas on the other, to note the unfortunate reality of domestic violence against women. For what this really does is remind us of how much more often it occurs in households of color than against Anglas, though some will surely want us to believe otherwise.

The reason for this excursion into some of the basics of racism in the U.S. is that it is believed that only a proper understanding and appreciation of such history can correct the confused rhetoric of many who conflate the oppression of Anglas with that of, say, Native and African Americans. Yet these historical facts of racism in the U.S. ground the differentialist approach to affirmative action. No one who has a proper grasp of the horrors of the oppression of Native and African Americans can hold that Anglas are oppressed in any way akin to the ways in which Native and African Americans were (and still are, as many would argue). Once we begin to see that history reveals that this is so, then the way is paved for the infusion of moral principles to be brought to bear on the matter concerning affirmative action.

There is no significant mode of harmful wrongdoing that Anglas experienced that Native and African American women have not experienced. But there are several kinds and degrees of harmful wrongdoings that Native and African American women and men experienced (sometimes at the hands of Anglas) that Anglas never experienced. Thus to say without careful qualification that Anglas were oppressed is quite misleading as it makes it seem as though Anglas op-

---

37. Lerner, "Reconceptualizing Differences among Women," 242.

pression is comparable to the oppression of Native and African Americans' oppression.

There is a real sense, furthermore, in which it might well constitute a fallacy of equivocation to say that Anglas were/are oppressed if "oppressed" is also supposed to describe the evil horrors of the Native and African American experiences partly at the hands of Anglas. To accept without careful qualification the claim that Anglas are oppressed on balance in anything akin to the ways in which those they helped to oppress were and are oppressed is to ignore the past and the manners in which the past effect significantly the present state of affairs in the U.S., ethnically and socioeconomically speaking. It is to accept by implication the claim that Anglas on average, on balance, and as a class are not co-responsible for the very evils that made it possible to found and sustain the U.S.[38] As Lerner concludes of Anglas, "It is their class privilege which helps them offset any disadvantages arising from their subordinate status as women."[39] To ignore the vast differences in the extent of the oppression between Anglas and folk of color in the U.S. (especially Native and African American women and men) tends to erase the significance of the worse forms of oppression, and conveniently much that was wrought on them by Anglas themselves![40] It is this that Lerner and Watkins argue amounts to a form of continued racist oppression of folk of color by Anglas. Practically speaking, Anglas exemplify this racist oppression today by willingly accepting what is not theirs by moral right. Instead of removing themselves from the list of affirmative action beneficiaries based on my principled arguments herein, they continue to accept what they do not deserve, effectively robbing from Native and African American women and men valuable resources that are in general not only far more deserved but can be used to address socioeconomic problems that exist in these communities that are greater than any problems Anglas have experienced in North America.

Moreover, it might be objected that there exist mitigating factors concerning Angla racist oppression of colored folk in the U.S. Both historically and currently, to some extent Anglas in many cases would likely be threatened with physical violence or institutional threats of loss of employment and such if they did or do resist the oppression of colored folk in the U.S. In light of these fac-

---

38. When I refer to the U.S. as "evil," I am making an on balance moral judgment based on the fact that unrectified evil is evil still, along with other claims and arguments made in Corlett, *Race, Racism, and Reparations,* chaps. 8–9.

39. Lerner, "Reconceptualizing Differences among Women," 244.

40. The notion that African American women are theoretically "erased" from racist Angla-oriented feminist frameworks is argued most eloquently in Crenshaw, "Demarginalizing the Intersection of Race and Sex," 57–80.

tors, our judgments of Angla racist oppression ought to be mitigated.[41] However true it is that there existed and do exist today various and sometimes complicated mitigating factors that undergird Angla racism, certain other factors must be borne in mind. First, several Anglas of old and even today seem to have had little difficulty in risking their own freedom or security when it came (comes) to pressing for their own rights, suggesting that they were simply bad Samaritans pertaining to the drive toward freedom for colored folk. To argue that Anglas on average, on balance, and as a class were so oppressed that they feared violent reprisals from Anglos if Anglas stood up for what was right ignores the fact that so many Anglas were not that afraid of Anglos to stand up to them in burning some of their undergarments and walking openly in the streets to proudly and bravely demand their own freedoms.

Second, even if it were true that Anglas deserve only our mitigated moral condemnation, it hardly follows that they are deserving recipients of affirmative action benefits based on the fact that they ought not to be allowed to benefit from their own racist oppression of others and because they on balance do not deserve such benefits in light of the oppression they on average, on balance, and as a class have wrought on others that clearly outweigh the injustices they as Anglas experience(d). Given a commonsense and fair-minded reading of U.S. history, the burden of argument lies clearly on those who would think that Anglas deserve to benefit from affirmative action because their experienced injustice outweighs the oppression that they brought on others. In most cases, Anglas on average, on balance, and as a class could have at least raised some substantial form of resistance to the oppression of colored folk, but they rarely if ever did and even rarely do today. Even when Anglas had no alternative but to support the oppression of colored folk as indicated, it hardly follows that they did not have a higher-order volition to do so in order to enjoy the grand and varied benefits of being privileged more than colored folk, both yesteryear and today. Both individually and collectively, Anglas are surely guilty of racist oppression as they rarely, if ever, cared or care today about the true plight of racist oppression. Remember the above wisdom from Crenshaw, Lerner, and Watkins: U.S. feminism was and is racist and seems to demonstrate no tremendous signs of change.[42] And if the most progressive of all Anglas were racists, then on what grounds are we justified in believing that the rank-and-file Anglas (hardly progressives in the U.S.) were not racist? Of course, one way to signal a significant change would be to refuse to accept affirmative action benefits and work politically toward the revising of such programs in order to steer such programs and benefits toward

---

41. I owe this point to Howard McGary.
42. Also see Angela Y. Davis, *Women, Race, and Class* (New York: Random House, 1981).

those who most deserve and need them. History will show whether or not Anglas in the U.S. possess the level of moral character and integrity to decide that this is something they will support. Thus I have argued that based on a fair-minded and accurate reading of the facts of U.S. history, generally and as a class Anglas have not suffered oppression nearly to the extent that Native and African American women and men have. This is a comparative judgment, one that clarifies greatly the extent to which Anglas have committed fraud concerning the system of affirmative action. But I also made the noncomparative judgment that there is reason to think that, on balance, Anglas do not deserve affirmative action because of their own incessant acts of racist oppression against others that clearly outweigh the injustices they have experienced by Anglos. Anglas' sheer power has awarded white folk in general the de facto largest amount of affirmative action benefits; they whitewashed affirmative action from the standpoint of white privilege. And their oppressive political power enabled this to happen. Furthermore, many leftists affirm Anglas' role as "oppressed" persons who deserve affirmative action. Anglas have once again secured their own desires at the cost of others who are far more deserving and in need. And they have accomplished this by way of an equivocation on the word *oppressed* and its cognates.

Finally, it might be argued that, given past and current factors of supply and demand pertaining to the availability of sufficient numbers of Native and African Americans, Latinos, and other minority groups, that it is morally justified to hire Anglas in their places for purposes of affirmative action. There simply are not enough of such colored folk interested in or qualified for positions in philosophy and certain other academic areas to fill the increasing demands placed on colleges and universities in light of growing student enrollments. Thus Anglas assist along these lines in filling these positions that would otherwise lie vacant.

In reply to this concern, it must be stated that while it is certainly true that there has never been a time in U.S. educational history—including the present era—in which there were sufficient numbers of qualified (degreed) African and Native Americans, Latinos, or other minorities to "fill" affirmative action hiring demands at all U.S. colleges and universities, this is no good reason to substitute for such would-be deserving hires those who, as we have already seen, are hardly deserving of affirmative action benefits. Valuable and already shrinking affirmative action resources have been effectively transferred to nonaffirmative action resources by the hiring of Anglas who do not deserve affirmative action benefits (or, they do not deserve them nearly to the extent that they have received them over the years). And it lessens the import of my argument in no way to point out that administrators are to blame for hiring Anglas instead of those deserving of affirmative action, as that simply emphasizes the significance of my argument. Policies of affirmative action must be revised so that this sort of fraud cannot occur again, and if it does it would be punished severely. Moreover, leftist Anglas would have a meaningful opportunity to step aside from affirmative action self-benefits and support—not just talk the talk—programs that would prepare Native and African Americans, Latinos, and others for careers in philosophy and certain other academic areas where they are underrepresented.

Conclusion

Having clarified a plausible differentialist strategy for affirmative action programs, I argued that well-intentioned policies of the past were ruined in part by race categories that were so crude and imprecise that they did not allow the differentialist thinking that could have prevented the oppressive horror of allowing Anglas to wrongfully benefit from their own oppression of others more than the folk who should have been the primary beneficiaries of such programs in the first place. Will Anglas consider the principles that undergird my argument to be essential to the implementation of justice and fairness? If so, then they would have to relieve themselves from further benefits from affirmative action programs on grounds that they most assuredly do not deserve them. Or, will Anglas continue on with business as usual approaches with recantations of the racist mantra of "equal opportunity" as the primary goal of affirmative action, thus sustaining their own ill-gotten gains from such a wrongheaded policy? It is time to do the right thing by way of affirmative action. Doing the right thing often requires the relinquishing of wrongfully acquired power and wealth by those who have devastated others with their greed and avarice. The whitewashing of affirmative action must cease if we leftists want to retain an important sense of moral decency in their support of affirmative action.

If it is true that what distinguishes many as members of ethnic groups is, among other things, their disparate experiences of racist harms, then what differentiates—indeed, alienates—those colored folk from Anglas is that such classes of ethnic groups have experienced directly and indirectly Anglas' racist oppression of us, while they have been racist oppressors who on average, on balance, and as a class (even many of the leftists among them!) fail to realize or admit their racist oppression of others.

And if it is objected that affirmative action would never have become a reality in the first place without the support of Anglas, my reply to this political point is that if Anglas begin to as a class and on average develop a genuine sense of ethical sensitivity and justice as expressed above, then their relinquishing their benefits vis-à-vis affirmative action and supporting much more deserving colored folk would seem to constitute just as much support for affirmative action as has been shown in the current situation. So the difference in political terms is whether or not Anglas possess the moral integrity to admit that what is argued herein is plausible, and to step aside and support wholeheartedly the fact that only certain colored folk should receive affirmative action benefits based albeit on a differentialist programmatic structure. For where there is tremendous injustice, there can be no genuine peace. Nor should there be.[43]

43. An earlier version of this chapter was presented at the Samuel Capen Conference on Black Ethnicity/Latino Race, SUNY at Buffalo, 1 April 2005, organized and directed by Jorge J. E. Gracia. I am grateful to the participants of that conference for their helpful comments on this chapter, especially to Jorge J. E. Gracia. for his in-depth comments on a previous draft. This chapter is a more developed version of J. Angelo Corlett, "The Whitewashing of Affirmative Action," in *Race and Human Rights,* ed. Curtis Stokes (East Lansing: Michigan State University Press), forthcoming. Each paper is based on Corlett, *Race, Racism, and Reparations* (Ithaca: Cornell University Press, 2003), 133f., and is inspired by discussions with Howard McGary several years ago concerning racism and affirmative action. Also see Corlett, "Race, Racism, and Reparations," *Journal of Social Philosophy* 36 (2005): 568–85.

CHAPTER 12

Race and Political Theory:
Lessons from Latin America

DIEGO A. VON VACANO

On the fourth Sunday of Advent on the island of Hispaniola, in the year 1511, the Dominican friar Antonio de Montesino reflected on the condition of the indigenous peoples of the Americas who had been mistakenly labeled "Indians," and asked: "Are these not human beings?"[1] Thus he originated a way of thinking about the native peoples of the New World. This way of thinking, largely unknown outside of the Iberian Americas and perhaps even within large segments of societies in that part of the continent, is a cardinal component of the discourse on race in Latin America.

What does the Latin American perspective on race tell us about this elusive concept? In this chapter I examine one particular strain of reflections on race that has become dominant since the encounter of European and pre-Columbian civilizations in 1492. While the complexity of the issue has led to various conceptual models in understanding what is meant by "race" in Hispanic (i.e., rooted in the Iberian peninsula) American intellectual history, I focus on one specific lineage that I call the "synthetic paradigm" of race.

In this particular narrative, there are many storytellers and characters. From Simón Bolívar to Enrique Dussel, thinkers from Latin America have grappled hard with the notion of race, understanding its many facets and transformations over the course of more than four centuries. In what follows (partly for the sake of brevity) I trace the *problématique* of race in three seminal thinkers writing in Latin America: Bartolomé de Las Casas, José Martí, and José Vasconcelos. These *pensadores* have in common a conception of racial identity that underscores the

---

1. See Las Casas, *Obras completas,* ed. Paulino Castañeda Delgado (Madrid: Alianza Editorial, 1998), 1:394.

fundamental unity of all peoples. The belief that beneath apparently accidental and superficial dissimilarities lies a basic human sameness that although it may lie dormant must be made explicit is a particularly Latin American conception of race.[2]

This view is "synthetic" in that it holds that one should think of races not as reified, discrete, and immutable entities, but rather as social categories. Although rooted in biological differences, they are the product of mixing disparate elements, and they, moreover, constitute the elements whose mixing creates the overarching "human race." This is the key paradigm that emerges from the Latin American tradition of thinking about race.

This view of race is not entirely metaphysical, for it also contains a political dimension. The thinkers I examine here do not think about race from an abstract, philosophical "view from nowhere." Rather, they conceive racial identities as immanently political and as having political contexts and consequences. Thinking about race in Latin America is a political enterprise, both because race contains something political in it, and because writing about it has real political and social effects.

1. "All the Races of the World Are Men": Las Casas's Catholic Universalism

Let's begin with Las Casas, a priest born in Spain who, nevertheless, lived for decades in the New World and shaped debates about racial and ethnic identity in the Americas. Indeed, he can be considered a founder of Latin American political thought. From a quasi-anthropological vantage point established on principles derived from Aristotelian notions in the Thomist tradition, Las Casas is the first to seek to answer Montesino's question: Are these not human beings? A few centuries later, the Cuban hero of Independence, José Martí, would build on some ideas of Las Casas to address the problem of racial divisions in Cuba and beyond. Later still, the Mexican philosopher and politician José Vasconcelos developed his idea of a "cosmic race," which constitutes a statement about the progressive role of *mestizaje*, or miscegenation, understood as firmly rooted in the intellectual and social history of Latin America but having a world-historical mission.

All three thinkers elude simple categorization. Las Casas was a missionary, but

---

2. Since the very meaning of race is the subject of this essay, no a priori definition of the concept is given. Suffice it to say that common understandings of race point to biological differences among people (such as phenotypes) whereas ethnicity is often used to refer to culture or traditions.

also a historian and an active defender of indigenous peoples. He can also be seen as the founder of liberation theology, one of the original proponents of human rights and international law, a proto-anthropologist, and an acute chronicler of events he witnessed in the Americas. Martí was the leader of Cuba's struggle for independence from Spain, but he was also a great modernist literary figure, and an incisive, critical journalist. And Vasconcelos, apart from being a major figure in Latin American philosophy, was active in the politics of revolutionary Mexico and the educational reforms that were part of the long process of social transformation after the end of Porfirio Díaz's dictatorship.[3] From such rich and variegated experiences, these *pensadores* came to face the matter of race in Latin America.

A few years after the arrival of the Spanish *conquistadores* to the New World, debates about the nature of the inhabitants of the Americas began to develop in theological circles in European cities. In Paris, the Scot John Major presented a view based on Aristotle that would come to be widely accepted among many European philosophers, theologians, and political leaders:

> The first persons to occupy those lands may by right govern the tribes that inhabit them. In Books I, III, and IV of the *Politics,* the Philosopher states that there can be no doubt that some are by nature slaves and others free, that this is inescapably to the advantage of some, and that it is just that some should command and others obey.[4]

Philosophers such as Francisco de Vitoria would disagree, but for a good number of thinkers and leaders in Europe, this would come to be the orthodoxy in dealing with peoples in newly discovered lands who looked and acted differently from those in some European countries. In spite of Spain's exploitation of the New World, it was the only country in which serious debate about the justice of "war against the Indians" became a pressing matter. Spain was "obsessed with the task of governing [the New World] with justice."[5]

Las Casas arrived in the New World in 1502. At the onset, he was merely one of many Spanish men seeking to benefit from the power of the Crown during the Colonial period of Latin American history.[6] He was given land and slaves,

---

3. It is a characteristic of Latin American political theory that important authors also played important roles in political life.

4. Cited in Gustavo Gutiérrez, "Foreword: The Indian: Person and Poor," in *Witness: Writings of Bartolomé de Las Casas,* ed. George Sanderlin, (Maryknoll, NY: Orbis Press, 1992), xiii. See also Lewis Hanke, *Prejuicio racial en el Nuevo Mundo* (Santiago, Chile: Prensa Universitaria, 1958), 39 (my translation).

5. Hanke, *Prejuicio racial,* 176.

6. According to Alvaro Huerga, the most cogent explanation for Las Casas's original motivation to go to the Americas was to gain wealth (see *Obras completas,* 41).

and thus was but one member of the colonial enterprise that sought to subjugate the native population, take over their possessions, and indoctrinate them with "enlightened" ideas rooted in reason as understood in Europe and in the Catholic faith.

Gradually, however, Las Casas would come to be disenchanted by the way the natives were treated by the Iberians. Being an eyewitness to the brutal acts visited on the "Indians" by the Spanish, especially the massacre at Caonao, Las Casas would attempt to provide a defense of the indigenous peoples, rooted in compassion and commiseration.[7] When Las Casas arrived in Plasencia, Spain, in 1515 and met the bishop of Burgos, Juan Rodríguez de Fonseca, to tell him about the atrocities he had seen, he was met by the reply, "Behold what a witty fool! What is that to me, and what is that to the king?" Las Casas replied with a visceral reaction: "What is it to your lordship and to the king that those souls die? Oh, great and eternal God! Who is there to whom it is something?"[8] For Las Casas, the natives were indeed soul-possessing humans, an extraordinary idea at the time.

Nonetheless, Las Casas never denounced the imperial presence of Spain in the Americas. He did not agree with Major's claim that the rational inferiority of newly discovered peoples ipso facto placed them in a subordinate political position. Yet, he did concur that it was in the best interest of the Indians to submit themselves to the power of the Crown for the sake of their souls' salvation, since the Crown represented the Catholic (and true, according to Las Casas) faith. Still, the pope had no authority over non-Christians, in Las Casas' view, and he could neither use force to persuade them to accept the faith nor take away their property.

Las Casas was in some ways rooted in the "imperial paradigm" of thinking about race, according to which non-European conquered peoples are inferior and racial categories establish the natural, moral, and political inferiority of indigenous peoples. Nevertheless he rejected it once he saw firsthand the brutality of the conquest. But we may ask, how did Las Casas's account of the ravages in the Indies bear on a 'synthetic' understanding of race?

The Dominican friar believed that the indigenous peoples that Europeans had encountered in the Americas had souls and reason.[9] In their innocent approach to life and the deep suffering they experienced at the hands of the Spaniards, they evinced spirituality. Moreover, in their daily practices, they displayed a certain rationality. Based on examinations of the way they lived, Las

---

7. As Pagden notes, the arrival to the New World was a sort of "rebirth" for Las Casas. See introduction to *A Short Account of the Destruction of the Indies* (New York: Penguin, 2004), xviii.

8. Gutiérrez, "The Indian," 82.

9. Hanke, *Prejuicio racial,* 43; "Las Casas insisted that Indians were rational men" (my trans.).

Casas concluded that, in spite of apparently inscrutable actions, the natives not only showed the kind of rational thinking characteristic of all humans, but also displayed God's design in their pacific nature and childlike condition. They were children, yes, but children of God. The Catholic faith was applicable to all. As Las Casas noted, "Our Christian religion is equal and universal, and it can adapt itself to all of the world's nations, and it accepts all of them equally without taking their liberty."[10]

With one foot in the Old World and the other in the New, Las Casas stood in defense of the Spanish Crown's right to rule over the Americas, but also for the Indians' status as members of the human family. He recognized physical differences between Indians and Europeans, yet he argued that since the former showed fundamental rationality, the fact that they inhabited lands conquered by Spain should mean that they should be treated as new members of the Spanish Empire.[11] By virtue of their membership in the empire, they should be treated as subjects of the king and queen in the same way that a denizen of Málaga or Valencia would. Thus, while Spanish rule was oppressive in one sense, in another it brought into its political fold new members in a manner akin to the cosmopolitanism of the Roman Empire. Paradoxically, this led to a more general, universalized application of the criteria of what it is to be human.

The *political* reality of the conquest, thus, integrated peoples who had been conquered into the community governed by Spain. To be sure, there were evident physical and cultural differences between the natives of the Americas and the inhabitants of Europe, but the underlying rationality of both made them equal members of humanity. Here we see the essentially political nature of the inception of the synthetic paradigm. It is rooted in an Aristotelian conception of human beings as both rational and social, but it also points to Aristotle's *zoon politikon*: humans are human by virtue of the fact that they can only come to full development in community, not in isolation. The Indians, Las Casas argued, showed precisely this quality, even if on the surface it appeared different.

Witnessing the atrocities perpetrated by some of the Spanish *conquistadores* against defenseless Indians, such as the unleashing of rabid bulldogs in villages full of women and children, Las Casas posed the question, "Who are the real Christians here?" The indigenous peoples that he encountered seemed to possess a pacific nature that was close to what one would imagine to be God's original design or to what one would expect of a dweller of Paradise. The infernal brutality of sinners, *par contre*, seemed to reside in the barbaric, murderous acts

---

10. Ibid., my translation.

11. Far from being animalistic, the Indians were fully human, in Las Casas's eyes. When referring to Beltrán Nuño de Guzmán, a tyrannical Spaniard who "bartered one mare against eighty locals," Las Casas refers to the locals as "members of the human race" (*A Short Account*, 65).

of the greedy Spaniards. He believed that "everything done to the Indians . . .
was unjust and tyrannical."[12]

Las Casas thought that the Indians deserved a much higher place in the hierarchy of beings than was generally granted them by European thinkers and
philosophers. Las Casas abandoned his European roots insofar as he distanced
himself from the imperial paradigm of race that saw non-Europeans as by nature inferior and perhaps even inhuman. Physical attributes such as skin color
and appearance, far from establishing an Aristotelian distinction between natural
slaves and natural masters (or the barbarian/civilized dichotomy), are in fact
merely accidental characteristics shaped by contingencies in the environment
and the way different people do things in their own way. Las Casas's anthropology paved the way for the reaffirmation of the Aristotelian principle that rationality is what makes one human, but on the new grounds that this rationality
can take different forms in different circumstances.

To try to convince theologians steeped in the scholastic tradition that vener-
ated "The Philosopher" (Aristotle), the church fathers, and Roman and canon
law, Las Casas made use of these sources to show that, although the idea of natural slavery made sense, it did not apply to the natives of the Americas.[13] His
Apologetic History uses Aristotelian categories to show how Indians are rational,
and it is thought that he might have used this text as the basis for his famous debate on the status of the Indians with Juan Ginés de Sepúlveda in 1550–51.[14]

Not only did Indians have souls, but these souls were rational. The religious
and political life of Indians, Las Casas argued, evinced human rationality, even if
it appeared exotic to Western eyes. As he states: the "thesis [of this text] is that
the Indian is not a 'slave by nature,' but is eminently rational. . . . He is the equal,
or in some things the superior, of the ancient Greeks, Romans, Egyptians.
Spaniards, etc; therefore his human dignity should be respected."[15] Indians lived
in ways that for Las Casas accorded with Aristotle's definition of rational organization: their houses were well built, they had complex markets, and had a
"clean unspoiled, vivacious intellect."[16]

12. Las Casas, *Witness,* 74.

13. It appears that Las Casas did regard the Indians as "barbarians" in some sense, perhaps because they
were pagans. However, he argued against Sepúlveda, who based his view on Aristotle, they were not irrational, slavish subhumans. See Hanke, *All Mankind Is One: A Study of the Disputation Between Bartolomé
de Las Casas and Juan Ginés de Sepúlveda in 1550 on the Intellectual and Religious Capacity of the American Indians* (DeKalb: Northern Illinois University Press, 1974), 75.

14. Ibid., 73. According to Hanke, Francisco de Vitoria might have been appointed as a judge in this
disputation had he not died four years earlier (104).

15. Las Casas, *Witness,* 96.

16. Ibid., 145. Las Casas often refers to their "intelligence." See *History of the Indies,* trans. A. Collard
(New York: Harper and Row, 1971), 280.

Moreover, while he at a certain point advocated the importation of African slaves to replace Indians so that the latter could be emancipated, Las Casas eventually came to see that this was a mistake: all such slavery was unjust, regardless of the race of the enslaved. As he tells us in one of his autobiographical accounts: "Not long afterward the cleric found himself regretting this counsel he had given, and judged himself guilty through carelessness. For . . . he later observed and found out . . . that the Negroes' captivity was as unjust as the Indians.'"[17]

Writing from a Christian—specifically Catholic—scholastic tradition, Las Casas promoted the universalistic notion that, while pagan peoples may be deficient in some ways, they are nonetheless as human as Europeans. Through "love, gentleness, and kindness," Las Casas argued, savages could be integrated into the political community of Christendom and the moral community of Christianity, "the reason for this truth is—and Cicero set it down in *De legibus,* Book I—that all the races of the world are men, and of all men and of each individual there is but one definition, and this is that they are rational."[18]

With great rhetorical effect, Las Casas was thus able to proffer the strongest case possible for the humanity of so-called barbarians. While he was not able to fully persuade his interlocutors, his voice was to carry across centuries, and its deep humanism would echo in other thinkers in Latin America.

2. "An Essential Likeness": Martí and Cuban Particularism

Cuba, a land Las Casas had admired for its natural abundance, would produce an *éminence grise.* For José Martí, the task at hand was not one of responding to the mass cruelty suffered by indigenous peoples at the hands of Spanish soldiers. Spanish soldiers were to be opposed because they prevented the real autonomy of the inhabitants of Cuba, most of whom were not indigenous. It is in the context for the struggle for Cuban independence that Martí's thought on race developed.

Whereas Las Casas grounded his defense of the Indians on an universalist principle, proclaiming the humanity of anyone who displays rational behavior, Martí proposed a defense of republican freedom from the perspective of Cuba's particularism. A master rhetorician, Martí would use tropes such as that of the "Natural Man" as a lover of freedom, but his political theory, while republican, attempts to provide moral and rational grounds to buttress the call for Cuban independence. Far from the Catholic universalism of Las Casas and Vitoria, the

17. Las Casas, *Witness,* 86.
18. Ibid., 175.

great Cuban poet sought to do for Cuba what other Latin American leaders had done for other areas in the mainland decades earlier: to provide a sense of national identity in order to cement the bonds of republican citizenship.

Although Simón Bolívar had originally wanted to have a united *América* (the Spanish-speaking territory of the New World) without national borders, his utopian dream soon collapsed under the pressure of regionalism, geographic obstacles, ethnic divisions, and local political competition. But eventually he became more pragmatic, abandoning his initial dream of a single political unit over the vast Latin American continent and accepting that subregional confederations would emerge, such as Gran Colombia. Ultimately, the fragmentation of the Americas into nation states became inevitable, and countries such as Peru, Bolivia, and Argentina would develop, each with a relatively distinctive sense of identity and different local political forces at play.

Nevertheless, the "Bolivarian Dream" would persist, and its preeminent heir was Martí. It was a revised dream, one that no longer imagined a single Latin nation, but a confederation of nation states aligning themselves—in a cooperative community—to counterbalance the power of European civilization and the growing influence of the neighbor to the North, the United States of America. In a sense, Martí sought to emulate the work of Domingo Sarmiento in Argentina: to engage in nation-building both at the real, institutional level, and at the ideological, consciousness level. He aimed to set up institutions, such as schools, to tie the nation's regions together, and to develop a sense of belonging, a sense of attachment to a particular land, and to the symbols of a new republic.

The difference with Sarmiento lies in the treatment of the "race question." Whereas the Argentine thinker and statesman was a follower of the "racialist paradigm" that saw progress as the Europeanization or "whitening" of native populations and towns,[19] Martí argued for the radical (and revolutionary for its time) perspective that in fact the distinction between races is false.

In his most famous statement about racial differences, Martí states simply, "There are no races."[20] For Martí, writing at a time when the scientific study of racial variations was prevalent in Europe, the project of seeking to understand the distinctive characteristics of each race was futile: ultimately, we are all members of the human species, and racial differences are rooted in superficial accidents. Martí derided pseudoscientific attempts to divide the human race into subgroups. He decried "attempts made by anthropologists to classify racial ori-

19. A tradition prominent in what we may call the "Río de la Plata School" of political theory, which includes Domingo F. Sarmiento, José Enrique Rodó, and Juan Alberdi, argued uncritically for the Europeanization of the Americas.

20. Martí, "Our America," in *The José Martí Reader* (Hoboken, NJ: Ocean Press, 1999), 119.

gin and identity," for he "judged all such efforts to label the different racial classifications entirely artificial, and he haughtily called them 'razas de librería' [bookstore races]."[21]

The key text for our understanding of Martí's view is an essay, entitled "My Race."Written in 1893, the work is a rhetorical masterpiece, an attempt to convince the reader that racialized thinking ultimately deludes. The context of the text is the quest for Cuban independence, which allows Martí to see the notion of race writ large. In it he makes the statement that "an essential likeness" underlies all of humanity.[22]

Martí tells us that he wants to explain what race is. Quickly, he goes to the heart of the matter: "No man has any special rights because he belongs to one race or another."[23] Any attempt to establish color lines among humans is "a sin against humanity." But Martí is careful not to point fingers: he blames black racism as much as white racism in creating a culture of mistrust and fear. "Public happiness" depends on racial harmony, and this can only emerge if all races (and here Martí is particularly thinking of Cuba's large white and black populations, rather than the decimated Indian one) renounce the vocabulary of racialization.

Echoing Las Casas, Martí underscores the presence of the soul of nonwhite men. Slavery, for Martí, is a moral wrong regardless of the race being enslaved, since there is nothing inherently inferior about the peoples that happen to be in bondage. Martí thinks of white and black men as equal participants in the creation of racism but also in the potential elimination of it.

What motivated Martí to speak of races as ultimately insignificant at a time when Europeans, under the influence of social Darwinism, were trying to do the opposite by applying scientific methodologies to the study of racial distinctions? Passages in the work of Martí seem to point to grand, universalistic ideas going back to Enlightenment principles of Freedom and Equality, but his real motivation was the urgent political project of Cuba's emancipation from Spain. "The peace of the nation" is Martí's foremost concern: the dream of independence required that revolutionary forces should set aside racial differences and fight for Cuba in unity, not for a specific race.[24]

For Martí no "race war" could be possible in Cuba, because Cubans will come to think of themselves as first and foremost citizens of the republic. As Nancy Raquel Mirabal states,

21. John M. Kirk, *José Martí: Mentor of the Cuban Nation* (Tampa: University of South Florida Press, 1983), 111.

22. Martí, "Our America," 320.

23. Ibid., 318.

24. Ibid., 319.

Martí recognized the importance of incorporating Afro-Cubans into the nationalist movement and in his famous 'Liceo Cubano' speech directly confronted the racial tensions within the Cuban community by reminding the audience that "this would be a revolution in which all Cubans regardless of color had participated"[25]

This sanguine image is a rhetorical instrument that helped to galvanize the *independentistas*. White, negro, and mulatto will fight side by side. Yet this image is not purely imaginary. We must recall that Martí himself fought alongside Antonio Maceo, a mulatto hero of Cuban independence. What others see as essential racial differences, Martí sees as essential likeness; and he sees differences as "details." What matters in a man is his character: his strength or weakness.

This strength or weakness can make or break a political party. The desire to seek independence can live in the minds of men of any race, and this is what Martí wants to elicit in his readers. He envisions that, after the triumph against Spain, "each individual will be free within the sacred confines of his home. Merit, the clear and continual manifestation of culture and inexorable trade will end by uniting all men. There is much greatness in Cuba, in blacks and in whites."[26]

Is there a universalist, Enlightenment spirit in the words of Martí? "Natural Man" is a trope often used by Martí to propose that man, by nature, seeks freedom.[27] There is a hint of Rousseau in his use of the term, for Martí seems to idealize the premodern, uncivilized man as a repository of true freedom and the desire to escape all bondage. Alternatively, the term seems to point to the Enlightenment idea that all men are equal, that humanity shares basic properties and rights that are inalienable. However, one must remember that Martí was trained as a journalist and pamphleteer, not a philosopher. For Martí the use of the "Natural Man" trope is a device to convince the reader to support all causes that aim at the liberation of people from unjust rule. The power of words was never lost on Martí: as a master of modernism in Spanish literature, he conceived of language as something autonomous yet powerful enough to be performative: to have an impact on the world through widespread readership.

As someone who spent considerable time in the United States trying to organize support for the cause of Cuban independence, Martí was able to see the potential problems of a society bent on being established along "color lines." Martí's writings are always critical, and this is partly the result of his keen awareness of the central role played by race in modern societies. Unlike the simple,

25. In *José Martí in the United States: The Florida Experience,* ed. Louis A. Pérez (Tempe: Arizona State University Press, 1995), 57.

26. Martí, "Our America," 321.

27. Ibid., 290.

unidirectional racism of Juan Bautista Alberdi, for instance, who argued that Latin Americans are Europeans and that the Indians of Latin America must be driven into extinction, Martí saw in his own country the political potential of increased racial mixture. A society like the United States, where color barriers are drawn almost like battle lines would eventually block social progress for Martí.[28] In contrast, *Cubanidad* was to be "more than white, more than mulatto, more than black."[29]

In his essay, "The Truth about the United States" (1894), Martí goes to the heart of the matter in very few words. Having urged Latin Americans not to idealize or condemn the United States unjustly, he adds:

> There are no races: there is nothing more than mankind's various modifications of habit and form in response to the conditions of climate and history in which he lives, which do not affect that which is identical and essential.[30]

By referring to race as soon as he begins the discussion of the United States, Martí underscores the color line that has been erected between blacks and whites in this country and at the same time urges Latin Americans not to commit the same error. Race is a concept that is both biological (related to environment, and hence nature) and social (related to history). It also borders on the concept of a people or ethnicity: for Martí a race is not only defined by its phenomenal characteristics, but also by its cultural and historical life.[31] Still, the essence (what others might call the *noumenon*) is the same for all races. Martí does not elaborate, but it seems that a spiritual and moral desire to be free is what is common in all men.[32] This is closely aligned to his republicanism, a political theory that is at once alive to the universal desire to be free and the particular attachment to one's place of birth.

"Nuestra América" (Our America), as Martí referred to Latin America, was a term used in contrast to "North America," which he understood as the United States. For Martí, the lessons he learned about the political and moral benefits of racial miscegenation in Cuba could be applied to the rest of Latin America.

---

28. His article "A Town Sets a Black Man on Fire" is a terrifying account of the moral degeneration of a society built along color lines (Martí, "Our America," 313).

29. Nancy Raquel Mirabal, "Más que negro: José Martí and the Politics of Unity," in *José Martí in the United States*, 64.

30. Martí, "Our America," 329.

31. For Martí, North American Indians, show an attachment to their land and essential human traits such as courage and hospitality. If they are morally corrupt, it is because they were driven to that state by white oppression. See Martí, "The Indians in the United States," 159–61.

32. For Las Casas the rational soul is what defines "man," for Martí a love of country and of freedom seems more fundamental. See Kirk, *José Martí*, 99.

Thus he tells us that Latin Americans are mestizos with Catholic roots who yearn for liberty: "our feet upon a rosary, our heads white, and our bodies a motley of Indian and criollo we boldly enter the community of nations . . . to conquer our liberty."[33]

The politically useful notion of race as merely accidental also has a moral consequence: the extension of the Enlightenment idea of equality beyond the limits it faced in Europe after the French Revolution. Martí was to argue for a critical view of the United States and Latin America, particularly with regards to international trade, and we see his Bolivarian lineage in his effort to enlighten the rest of Latin America. He did not have much success in convincing Latin America's diplomats to develop a regional sense of self instead of purely national ones. Yet this effort reveals his attempt to build a more universal, general political theory and not one adequate only for the Cuban nation.

3. "The Fusion and the Mixing of All Peoples": Vasconcelos's Cosmic Vision

If Las Casas exemplifies the universalistic strain, and Martí the particularistic one within the synthetic paradigm of race, José Vasconcelos combines these approaches. Both Las Casas and Martí engaged in moral projects that were political through and through. It is impossible to separate the ethical from the political in either case, whether at the level of historical location or at the theoretical level. Their thoughts about the synthetic nature of race in the Latin American context were born in this context.

The picture that emerges in Vasconcelos is more complicated. His most famous work, *The Cosmic Race,* is a philosophical attempt to explain the place of man in his larger *Weltanschauung.* Vasconcelos was a holistic thinker: he wrote many books on diverse subjects with the systematicity of an Aristotle or Hegel. For him, everything has its place in the well-ordered cosmos created by Providence. With hermetic precision, Vasconcelos emulates the Hegelian project of explaining history as a reflection of spiritual forces. However, he seeks to place emphasis on the aesthetic facet of life, rather than the rational, moral, or political.[34]

What is the thrust of Vasconcelos's prophetic vision of a "cosmic race"? Vasconcelos argues that the path of history tends toward the mixing of the various

---

33. Martí, "Our America," 291.
34. We must recall that he wrote a book entitled *Todología,* which explains how all the elements of the world fit together. *Todo* means 'everything' in Spanish.

racial types on earth. This mixing is most pronounced and advanced in Latin America,[35] where the principal races intermarry and procreate in a manner that is generating a new sort of people. This *mestizaje,* or racial mixing, is for Vasconcelos a progressive rather than degenerate phenomenon. In his crude terminology, the four basic races, the Red (American Indian), the White (European), the Black (African) and the Yellow (Asian), become subsumed into the new race, which synthesizes (in something that recalls Hegelian *Aufhebung*) their qualities and absorbs their characteristics. As he states,

> The purpose of the new and ancient continent is much more important. Its predestination obeys the design of constituting the cradle of a fifth race into which all nations will fuse with each other to replace the four races that have been forging History apart from each other. . . . The so-called Latin peoples, because they have been more faithful to their divine mission in America, are the ones called upon to consummate this mission.[36]

For Vasconcelos, this observable fact of racial mixing hides a normative step forward for humanity. Why is this new race "better" than the foundational races? Because of a qualitative leap of progress. The benefits provided by the new race are a consequence of his benign view of the way *mestizaje* occurs: authentic love, rather than domination, guides people in Latin America to marry those they find pleasing. In Vasconcelos's vision, the Latin American person is driven by a sense of beauty; aesthetic appeal promotes the search for procreation, even if this search is not conscious.[37] The Latin peoples of the New World, for Vasconcelos, are motivated to engage with each other out of affect and sentiment, not the instrumental rationality which has stultified human beings in the modern era. Feelings, emotions, and impulses lead the Latin people to seek out aesthetic satisfaction in those around them. This is the proper engine of human history according to Vasconcelos.

Arguing along the lines used by the Uruguayan José Rodó, Vasconcelos believes that the Latin American peoples, the new "race," will be culturally superior to Europeans and North Americans because they are more in touch with life's aesthetic experience, and this leads them to cultivate a spiritual sensibility that disappeared long ago in the European and North American mind.[38]

---

35. Particularly in Mexico. See Rafael Moreno, "La cultura y la filosofía iberoamericana de José Vasconcelos," in *José Vasconcelos: su vida y su obra: textos selectos de las Jornadas Vasconcelianas,* ed. Alvaro Matute and Martha Donis (Mexico City: Universidad Autónoma de México, 1984), 107, 114.

36. Vasconcelos, *La raza cósmica / The Cosmic Race,* ed. and trans. Didier T. Jaén (Baltimore, MD: John Hopkins University Press, 1997), 18. I am indebted to Steve Tammelleo for various ideas in this section.

37. Taste is an important criterion for Vasconcelos. See Moreno, "La cultura y la filosofía," 105.

38. There are only a few exceptions to this, such as Renan in Europe and Emerson and Thoreau in the United States.

In Vasconcelos's philosophy of history, three stages characterize the evolution of humanity. The first, the material stage, is marked by the dominance of primeval passions such as crass force and material gain. The second is the intellectual stage, which is concomitant with the ascendancy of Anglo-Saxon culture, and is centered on reason, science, and ethics as norms ordering society. The third is the aesthetic stage, which for Vasconcelos is the culmination of human history. Here, appreciation of art and beauty guides human conduct:

> In the third period, the orientation of conduct will not be sought in pitiful reason that explains but does not discover. It will rather be sought in creative feeling and convincing beauty. Norms will be given by fantasy, the supreme faculty. That is to say, life will be without norms in a state in which everything that is born from feeling will be right: instead of rules, constant inspiration. . . . Beyond good and evil, in a world of aesthetic pathos, the only thing that will matter will be that the act, being beautiful, will produce joy.[39]

It is with the leadership of the Latin race as a "vanguard" class in the third stage that all of humanity benefits. The Latin race in a sense comes to the rescue of the human species by pointing to what really matters for us: the spiritual and the beautiful.[40] Thus the Latin American man, while particular in origin, has a universal mission.

This idea, influenced by the cultural radicalism of Rodó's *Ariel,* is fundamentally a matter of moral philosophy and psychology. Vasconcelos implicitly constructs a moral psychology for humans by denying that socioeconomic progress is the most important component of a contented human life. Railing indirectly against the positivism of the Porfiriato period in Mexico and the quasi-positivism of liberal figures such as Sarmiento, Vasconcelos shares with Nietzsche the idea that human life can only be truly justified aesthetically.[41] By pursuing beauty and the artistic, one cultivates one's soul, shapes it into a finer work, and comes to appreciate the very experience of living. As with Nietzsche, music links human beings to the world. Vasconcelos sees some basic aesthetic a priori qualities in humans, such as melody, harmony, and rhythm, which allow humans to become "coordinated" with the pace of the world.[42]

Unlike the anti-Christian, antisystemic perspectivism of Nietzsche, however, Vasconcelos finds that there is a Providential divinity, and that the cosmos has

39. Vasconcelos, *La raza cósmica,* 29.

40. Vasconcelos's aesthetics is based on fantasy or creativity, rather than representation, emotion, or form. He is closer to Collingwood than to either Plato or Tolstoy in terms of what is art.

41. As Moreno states, "Vasconcelos is an enlightened disciple of Nietzsche," in "La cultura y la filosofía," 106.

42. See Abelardo Villegas, "La cosmología vasconceliana," in *José Vasconcelos,* ed. Matute and Donís, 88. This explains Vasconcelos's anti-Platonic valuation of poetry.

an internal order of which we are a part. By recognizing our place in the cosmos as a single human race that is to be unified over a long historical process,
we as humans come to see that, as Hegel would have it, the real is rational, and
the rational is real. Yet this rationality is of God's design, not the rationality of
human practices or instrumentality.[43]

This worldview is not entirely apolitical, however. Beneath the moral psychology and philosophy of history that make up the backbone of Vasconcelos's
chief work, there are political overtones in two senses. The first is that, if we understand "political" to mean something related to power, Vasconcelos's account
is one whose metaphysics is agonistic: the struggles between the basic races ultimately leads to an ameliorated human race, but only after all manner of con-
testation between the values of each of the race takes place. Here it is unclear
how "love," according to Vasconcelos, would triumph over the deep-seated tensions among the races. This is especially the case when one reads carefully the
incipient racism that is palpable in some passages of Vasconcelos's text, which
tends to favor the white race over the others. For him, for instance, the yellow
race tends to "multiply like mice," whereas the "Nordic man" is a "master of action." In other passages he denigrates the black race as possessed by "unbridled
lust" and associates the red race with the bloodthirsty practice of cannibalism,
which was eliminated by the heroic *conquistadores,* according to Vasconcelos.[44]
It is perhaps one of Vasconcelos's great failings that he was unable to find a central position for the 'red' Aztecs and Mayas of Mexico in the formation of the
third stage of history.

The second and principal concern in Vasconcelos's work is evident when we
understand "political" as something related to a community of values (the *po-
lis*): to provide the norms that would properly order a well-functioning, healthy,
stable, and progressive community of individuals. Love, beauty, and feeling would
constitute the norms that would form the basis of the political / communal identity of the members of the cosmic race. For Vasconcelos, in Latin America, "we
have all the races and all their aptitudes. The only thing lacking is for true love
to organize and set in march the law of history"[45] through free marriages and
freely chosen sexual unions.

By using the term *cosmic,* Vasconcelos makes a rhetorical appeal to the notion
that a well-ordered society is possible, if it is grounded on the right kind of
norms. Just like a cosmopolitan order in which universal values are protected

43. Vasconcelos had a Catholic reawakening of sorts late in his life. His Catholicism is evident in his
view of a well-ordered cosmos, similar to the mathematical vision in the writings of another Mexican,
Sor Juana Inés de la Cruz.
44. Vasconcelos, *La raza cósmica,* 19, 22, 5.
45. Ibid., 39.

and enshrined as well as extended to more and more members, the cosmic race is a vision of an ever-inclusive social system. In *Indología,* written about a year after *The Cosmic Race,* Vasconcelos portrays the new race born from the fusion of the four basic groups as "a *total* race, a race whose blood itself is a *synthesis* of man in all of his various and deep aspects."[46]

However, Vasconcelos is, like Rodó (and unlike Martí), someone who seems to think that the basis of the Latin peoples is fundamentally European.[47] It is a (pre-Socratic) Greek civilization, understood along the lines of Nietzsche's admiration for Attic tragedy and the Apollonian-Dionysian nexus that did not privilege reason, which should be the foundation of the coming utopia:

> Greece laid the foundations of Western or European civilization; the white civilization that, upon expanding, reached the forgotten shores of the American continent in order to consummate the task of re-civilization and re-population.[48]

Faced with this phenomenon, the Indian, in Vasconcelos's eyes, must simply adapt to modern culture, something inaugurated by the European and Latin man.[49] The Spanish as well as the English are the people who, for Vasconcelos, have shown the greatest courage in shaping the modern world. They, in turn, are locked in a battle to establish the norms for the future. Here we see the political agon between the Anglo-Saxon world and the Latin world, which Vasconcelos characterizes as a battle between reason and morality on the one hand and beauty and sentiment on the other.

There is no doubt that Vasconcelos believes a new system based on the latter values will emerge. This system is rooted in benign values, those of love and beauty, rather than the noxious values of a racial vision grounded on extermination, concentration camps (like those that would later appear in Nazi Germany) or polarization and marginalization (like those forces present in U.S. society at the time). One can read *La raza cósmica,* as the Latin American response to European eugenics and North American segregationism. For Vasconcelos, philosophy has to be truly universal, and only the variegated social bases of Latin American culture can produce it. As he declares in *Etica,* "We want a Hispano-American philosophy because we cannot see any other way to come

46. Vasconcelos, *Indología: una interpretación de la cultura ibero-americana,* in *Obras completas* (Mexico City: Libreros Mexicanos Unidos, 1957–61), 1:1179, 1137.

47. See Luis A. Marentes, *José Vasconcelos and the Writing of the Mexican Revolution* (New York: Twayne, 2000), 79 and 87.

48. Vasconcelos, *La raza cósmica,* 9.

49. However, Vasconcelos argues that nonwhite peoples are superior to whites in a key respect: "The mestizo, the Indian, even [sic] the black, are superior to whites in an infinity of specifically *spiritual* capacities." In Marentes, *José Vasconcelos,* 95 (my emphasis).

to a universal philosophy, since almost all contemporary thought is colored by nationalism, if not by particularism."[50] Perhaps owing to the weakness of most Latin American states, culture there comes relatively unmediated out of social roots, unlike European or U.S. culture, which is filtered by political *programmes* and nationalist projects.

Racial stereotypes notwithstanding, this is a text that offers a positive and optimistic account of the way that human history can take a turn for the better. Amidst the pessimism of the interwar years, the concept that more racial mixing, rather than less, is a morally and politically progressive move is something that was ahead of its time. If we take this to be Latin America's stance on the race question, it serves as a political counterpoint to the cultural aims of Europe and North America.

4. Conclusion

As in topography and national and cultural traditions, diversity marks the thinking about race in Latin America. From extreme racism to optimistic miscegenation, from indigenous separatism to liberal pluralism, many perspectives touch on the concept of race as it has been examined—directly or indirectly—within Latin American nations. There are, however, some prominent tendencies, and the synthetic paradigm of race is one of them. Unlike simple racism or racialism (which advocates the whitening of indigenous populations), the synthetic paradigm is particular to Latin America. It is a product of autochthonous thinking about local conditions in an area of the world characterized by ethnic diversity.

Does the fact that the synthetic model comes from a particular historical tradition mean that it has no applicability to other cases, other scenarios? One of the virtues of the synthetic model is that it unites both universalistic and particularistic principles. If we follow Hegel's notion that this sort of synthesis is the mark of a modern society, then we can see that the synthetic paradigm of race may be useful in understanding the problems of modern society. This is especially apropos if we take into account the integrating forces that we have come to know as "globalization."

One of the trademarks of globalization is the dramatic increase of mass migration. This phenomenon involves the movement of large numbers of people from one cultural and geographic area of the world to another, usually for economic reasons. Just as Hegel predicted, increased commerce is part of the mod-

---

50. Vasconcelos, *Etica* (Mexico City: Ediciones Botas, 1939), 665.

ern world, and this has significant cultural consequences. One of them is the issue of how newcomer groups will adapt or assimilate (or not) to their host societies. In this process, racial identity plays an important role. How one sees
oneself as different or similar to dominant racial groups in host societies may
have important effects on the ease of adaptation or the integration of new
groups. Depending on the prevailing paradigms of race, this integration can be
hindered or promoted. What sort of model of race should we appropriate as we
move further into the twenty-first century?

The European model of thinking about race, at least within the canonical tradition of political theory, has not tended to see race as a central political problem or concern.[51] Certain references to "barbarians," "savages," and "aliens"
notwithstanding, this tradition has largely neglected the cardinal position of race   ·
in the political order and the path toward a 'modern' society. When references
to race are found in canonical European political philosophy, such as in the
works of Aristotle, Kant, Hegel, Marx, and Mill, images of subordinate, subhu-
man beings in need of tutelage come to the fore, something that exemplifies the
imperial paradigm of thinking about race in this tradition.

The North American (or specifically in the United States) model of thinking about race marks a significant step forward vis-à-vis the European model.
Rooted in the complex experience of slavery, monumental figures such as W. E. B.
Du Bois and Frederick Douglass wrote with eloquence about the need to pay
attention to the "color line." Further afield, and with a Christian-liberal ethos,
the words of Martin Luther King, Jr. echo a desire to eliminate race from the
minds of recent American citizens. The predominant schema used by these authors is that of a binary paradigm: a black-white approach to racial issues that is
understandable given the dramatic and stark history of the civil rights era and
the movement against segregation. More nuanced and humane, the North American model of race thinking was able to put racial issues at the center of some
debates in political theory.

With the added multiplicity of national origins, ethnic attachments, and racial
identifications characteristic of modern societies in an age of globalization, however, the binary paradigm seems to be lacking in conceptual breadth. It is here
that one must begin to question what sort of schema about race one must utilize for either positive or normative analysis in multiethnic societies. It seems
that the imperial model is normatively undesirable and in analytic terms is not
able to cope with the manifold racial formations that we now see before us. The
binary paradigm also appears to lack intellectual purchase, for it cannot be usefully applied in societies that have more than two large ethno-racial groups. Can

51. Perhaps the most important exception is some of the work of Hannah Arendt.

the Latin American schema, the synthetic paradigm, help us in this conceptual dilemma?

Just as speaking about the aestheticization of politics, speaking about theoretical concepts of race and politics immediately appears to approach dangerous grounds. To be sure, fascism was prone to do so in both cases, and with nefarious consequences. Yet we must not flinch at the fact that race does continue to be a problematic issue for societies that seek to be democratic and fair. For this reason we should continue to explore analytic and normative models that will shed light on this nebulous terrain.

The concept of *mestizaje,* which denotes racial mixing, is something that is very much at home in Latin America but has not had much exposure in North America or Europe. In a sense, the synthetic paradigm of race, which is built on this notion, translates it for other cultural traditions. Doubtless, *mestizaje* is not always free from negative origins, such as the forced pairing of Spanish men and indigenous women of the Americas. However, given that high rates of miscegenation have indeed occurred in large parts of Latin America, some key thinkers, such as Las Casas, Martí, and Vasconcelos, came to produce normative understandings of this process. Unlike the Eurocentric racism of Alberdi in Argentina for instance, or the *indigenismo* of Alcides Argüedas in Bolivia, the synthetic paradigm accepts the historical fact of the mixing of populations, and then sets out to propose a variety of political and ethical accounts for well-ordered states based on multiethnic social bases.

Modern, industrialized societies such as the United States, dogged for so long by "the race question," would do well to accept, both at the level of common sense and at the level of government policy, the possibility of understanding its population as being comprised to a great extent by people of no single, categorical racial identification. Census polls and public policy would be more nuanced and accurate if citizens could freely come to think of themselves as having multiple racial and ethnic origins. The synthetic paradigm seeks to remove the stigma associated with the presence of "color" in one's lineage; it also provides a positive vision of the future where a universalist humanism is combined with the particular needs of a polity. Complex as it is, the question of race can benefit from this more nuanced tradition that comes to us from Latin America.

Bibliography

Alcoff, Linda M. 2006. *Visible Identities: Race, Gender, and the Self.* New York: Oxford University Press.

———. 2004. "Against Post-Ethnic Futures." *Journal of Speculative Philosophy* 18: 99–117.

———. 2001. "Toward a Phenomenology of Racial Embodiment." In *Race,* edited by Robert Bernasconi, 267–83. Malden, MA: Blackwell.

———. 2000. "Who's Afraid of Identity Politics?" In *Reclaiming Identity,* edited by Paula Moya and Michael Hames-García, 312–44. Berkeley: University of California Press.

———. 2000. "Is Latina/o Identity a Racial Identity?" In *Hispanics/Latinos in the United States: Ethnicity, Race, and Rights,* edited by Jorge J. E. Gracia and Pablo De Greiff, 23–44. New York: Routledge.

———. 1995. "Mestizo Identity." In *American Mixed Race: The Culture of Microdiversity,* edited by Naomi Zack, 257–78. Lanham, MD: Rowman and Littlefield.

Allen, Danielle S. 2004. *Talking to Strangers: Anxieties of Citizenship since Brown v. Board of Education.* Chicago: University of Chicago Press.

Allen, Esther, ed. 2002. *José Martí: Selected Writings,* with an introduction by Roberto González Echevarría. New York: Penguin.

Allen, John S. 1989. "Franz Boas's Physical Anthropology." *Current Anthropology* 30: 79–84.

American Anthropological Association. 1998. "1998 AAA Statement on 'Race.'" *Anthropology Newsletter* 39, no. 9 (September).

Anderson, Benedict. 1983. *Imagined Communities: Reflections on the Origin and Spread of Nationalism.* London: Verso; rev. ed. 1990.

Andreasen, Robin O. 2005. "The Meaning of 'Race': Folk Conceptions and the New Biology of Race." *Journal of Philosophy* 102: 94–106.

———. 2000. "Race: Biological Reality or Social Construct?" *Philosophy of Science,* Supplementary Vol. 67: S653–66.

———. 1998. "A New Perspective on the Race Debate." *British Journal for the Philosophy of Science* 49: 199–225.

Appelbaum, Nancy, Anne S. Macpherson, and Karin Alejandra Rosemblatt, eds. 2003. *Race and Nation in Modern Latin America*. Chapel Hill: University of North Carolina Press.

Appiah, K. A. 2005. *The Ethics of Identity*. Princeton: Princeton University Press.

———. 1996. "Race, Culture, Identity: Misunderstood Connections." In *Color Conscious: The Political Morality of Race*, edited by K. A. Appiah and Amy Gutmann, 30–105. Princeton: Princeton University Press.

Appiah, K. A., and Amy Gutmann. 1996. *Color Conscious: The Political Morality of Race*. Princeton: Princeton University Press.

———. 1992. *In My Father's House: Africa in the Philosophy of Culture*. Oxford: Oxford University Press.

———. 1990. "'But Would That Still Be Me?' Notes on Gender, 'Race,' Ethnicity, as Sources of 'Identity.'" *Journal of Philosophy* 87: 493–99.

———. 1990. "Racisms." In *Anatomy of Racism*, edited by David Theo Goldberg, 3–17. Minneapolis: University of Minnesota Press.

———. 1985. "The Uncompleted Argument: Du Bois and the Illusion of Race." *Critical Inquiry* 12: 21–37; reprinted in *"Race," Writing, and Difference*, edited by Henry Louis Gates, Jr., 21–37. Chicago: University of Chicago Press, 1986.

Baier, Annette. 1986. "Trust and AntiTrust." *Ethics* 96: 231–60.

Barth, Fredrick, ed. 1969. *Ethnic Groups and Boundaries: The Social Organization of Culture Difference*. Oslo: Universitetsforlaget.

Bell, Derrick. 2004. *Silent Covenants:* Brown v. Board of Education *and the Unfulfilled Hopes for Racial Reform*. New York: Oxford University Press.

Benedict, Ruth. 1940. *Race, Science, and Politics*. New York: Modern Age Books.

Bergmann, Barbara. R. 1996. *In Defense of Affirmative Action*. New York: Basic Books.

Bernasconi, Robert. Forthcoming. "Can One Understand Race in Terms of Facticity?" In *Rethinking Facticity*, edited by François Ralfoul and Eric Sean Nelson. Albany: State University of New York Press.

———, ed. 2003. *Race and Anthropology*. 9 vols. Bristol: Thoemmes Press.

———, ed. 2001. *Race*. Malden, MA: Blackwell.

———. 2001. "Who Invented the Concept of Race?" In *Race*, edited by Robert Bernasconi, 11–36. Malden, MA: Blackwell.

Bernasconi, Robert, and Tommy L. Lott, eds. 2000. *The Idea of Race*. Indianapolis, IN: Hackett.

Bernstein, Richard. 2001. "Comment on *Hispanic/Latino Identity* by J. J. E. Gracia." *Philosophy and Social Criticism* 27: 44–50.

Bilgrami, A. 1995. "What Is a Muslim? Fundamental Commitment and Cultural Identity." In *Identities*, edited by K. A. Appiah and H. L. Gates, Jr., 198–219. Chicago: University of Chicago Press.

Blackburn, Daniel G. 2000. "Why Race Is Not a Biological Concept." In *Race and Racism in Theory and Practice*, edited by Berel Lang, 3–36. Lanham, MD: Rowman and Littlefield.

Blake, W. O. 1958. *The History of Slavery and the Slave Trade*. New York: Haskell House.

Blum, Lawrence. 1999. "Ethnicity, Identity, and Community." In *Justice and Caring: The Search for Common Ground in Education*, edited by Michael S. Katz, Nel Noddings, and Kenneth A. Strike, 127–45. New York: Teachers College Press.

Boas, Franz. 1940. *Race, Language and Culture*. Chicago: University of Chicago Press.

————. 1912. *Changes in Bodily Form of Descendants of Immigrants.* New York: Columbia University Press.

————. 1911. "Instability of Human Types." In *Inter-Racial Problems,* edited by G. Spiller, 99–108. London: P. S. King.

Boethius. 1968. *De Trinitate* I. In *Theological Tractates,* edited and translated by H. F. Stewart and E. R. Rand. Cambridge: Harvard University Press.

Boxill, Bernard R. 2003. "A Lockean Argument for Black Reparations." *The Journal of Ethics* 7: 63–91.

————, ed. 2001. *Race and Racism.* Oxford: Oxford University Press.

————, ed. 2001. "Introduction." In *Race and Racism,* edited by Bernard Boxill, 1–42. Oxford: Oxford University Press.

————. 1992. *Blacks and Social Justice.* Lanham, MD: Rowman and Littlefield.

————. 1992–93. "Two Traditions in African-American Political Philosophy." *The Philosophical Forum* 24: 125–31.

————. 1972. "The Morality of Reparations." *Social Theory and Practice* 2: 113–32.

Brace, C. Loring. 2005. *"Race" is a Four-Letter Word: The Genesis of the Concept.* New York: Oxford University Press.

————. 1964. "A Nonracial Approach towards Understanding of Human Diversity." In *The Concept of Race,* edited by A. Montagu. New York: Free Press.

Braudel, Fernand. 2002. *Las ambiciones de la historia.* Barcelona: Crítica.

Brown, Michael E. 1997. "Causes and Implications of Ethnic Conflict." In *The Ethnicity Reader: Nationalism, Multiculturalism, and Migration,* edited by M. Guibernau and J. Rex, 80–99. Cambridge: Polity.

Bryant, Joan. 2001. "Why African American Reformers Opposed the Concept of Race." Lecture presented at Boston University's Institute on Race and Social Division, November 2001.

Burge, Tyler. 1979. "Individualism and the Mental." *Midwest Studies in Philosophy* 4: 73–122.

Butterfield, Fox. 2003. "Study Finds 2.6% Increase in U.S. Prison Population." *New York Times,* July 28. Late Edition.

Callan, Eamonn. 1997. *Creating Citizens: Political Education and Liberal Democracy.* Oxford: Clarendon.

Carter, Bob. 2000. *Realism and Racism: Concepts of Race in Sociological Research.* London: Routledge.

Castañeda, Héctor-Neri. 1975. "Individuation and Non-Identity." *American Philosophical Quarterly* 12 : 131–40.

Cavalli-Sforza, Luigi Luca. 2000. *Genes, Peoples and Languages.* Translated by Mark Seielstaad. New York: Northpoint Press.

Cavalli-Sforza, Luigi Luca, Paolo Menozzi, and Alberto Piazza. 1994. *The History and Geography of Human Genes.* Princeton: Princeton University Press.

————. 1994. *The History and Geography of Human Genes.* Princeton: Princeton University Press, 1994, abridged paperback edition.

Cohen, G. A. 1980. "The Labor Theory of Value and the Concept of Exploitation." In *Marx, Justice, and History.* Edited by M. Cohen, T. Nagel, and T. Scanlon, 209–38. Princeton: Princeton University Press.

————. 1989. *History, Labour, and Freedom,* 209–38. New York: Oxford University Press.

Cone, James. 1992. *Martin and Malcolm in America.* Maryknoll: Orbis.

Corcos, Alain. 1997. *The Myth of Human Races.* East Lansing: Michigan State University Press.

Cordero-Guzmán, Héctor R., Robert C. Smith, and Ram Grosfoguel, eds. 2001. *Migration, Transnationalization, and Race in a Changing New York.* Philadelphia: Temple University Press.

Corlett, J. Angelo. Forthcoming. *Justice and Rights.*

——. 2005. "Race, Racism, and Reparations." *Journal of Social Philosophy* 36: 568–85.

——. 2005. *Responsibility and Punishment.* 3d ed. Dordrecht: Springer.

——. 2005. "The Whitewashing of Affirmative Action." In *Race and Human Rights,* edited by Curtis Stokes. East Lansing: Michigan State University Press.

——. 2004. "Evil." *Analysis* 64: 81–84.

——. 2003. *Race, Racism, and Reparations.* Ithaca: Cornell University Press.

——. 2001. "Analyzing Latino/a Identity." *American Philosophical Association Newsletter on Hispanic/Latino Issues in Philosophy* 1: 97–104.

——. 1999. "Latino Identity." *Public Affairs Quarterly* 13: 273–95.

——. 1995. "Political Separation and the African American Experience: Martin Luther King, Jr., and Malcolm X on Social Change." *Humboldt Journal of Social Relations* 21: 191–208.

Cottrol, Robert J., Raymond T. Diamond, and Leland B. Ware. 2003. *Brown v. Board of Education: Caste, Culture, and the Constitution.* Lawrence: University of Kansas Press.

Crenshaw, Kimberle. 1991. "Demarginalizing the Intersection of Race and Sex: A Black Feminist Critique of Antidiscrimination Doctrine, Feminist Theory, and Antiracist Politics." In *Feminist Legal Theory,* ed. Katharine T. Bartlett and Rosanne Kennedy. Boulder, CO: Westview Press.

Crummell, Alexander. 1966. "The Problem of Race in America." In *Negro Social and Political Thought 1850–1920,* edited by Howard Brotz, 180–90. New York: Basic Books.

——. 1966. "The Relations and Duties of Free Colored Men to Africa." In *Negro Social and Political Thought 1850–1920,* edited by Howard Brotz, 171–80. New York: Basic Books.

Daedalus: Journal of the American Academy of Arts and Sciences. 2005. (Special Issue on Race) 134, no. 1 (winter).

Darwall, Stephen. 1977. "Two Kinds of Respect." *Ethics* 88: 36–49.

Davis, Angela Y. 2005. *Abolition Democracy: Beyond Empire, Prisons, and Torture.* New York: Seven Stories Press.

——. 1981. *Women, Race, and Class.* New York: Random House.

Davis, David Brion. 1997. "Constructing Race: A Reflection." *William and Mary Quarterly* 54.

Delaney, Martin R. 1966. "The Condition, Elevation, Emigration, and Destiny of the Colored People of the United States." In *Negro Social and Political Thought 1850–1920,* edited by Howard Brotz, 37–111. New York: Basic Books.

Deniker, J. 1900. *The Races of Man.* London: Walter Scott.

——. 1900. *Les races et les peuples de la terre.* Paris: Scheicher Frères.

Derrida, Jacques. 1981. *Positions.* Translated by Alan Bass. Chicago: University of Chicago Press.

——. 1976. *Of Grammatology.* Translated by Gayatri Chakravorty Spivak. Baltimore: Johns Hopkins University Press.

——. 1972. *Positions.* Paris: Minuit.

——. 1967. *De la grammatologie.* Paris: Minuit.

Dixon, Roland B. 1923. *The Racial History of Man.* New York: Charles Scribner's Sons.

Douglass, Frederick. 1991. "The Color Question: An Address Delivered in Washington, D.C., on July 5, 1875." In *Frederick Douglass Papers,* edited by John W. Blassingame and John R. McKivigan, vol. 4. New Haven: Yale University Press.

———. 1982. "Love of God, Love of Man, Love of Country: An Address Delivered in Syracuse, N.Y., September 24, 1847." In *Frederick Douglass Papers,* edited by John W. Blassingame, vol. 2. New Haven: Yale University Press.

———. 1982. "Of Morals and Men: An Address Delivered in New York, N.Y., on May 8, 1849." In *Frederick Douglass Papers,* edited by John W. Blassingame, 2:170–74. New Haven: Yale University Press.

———. 1966. "An Address to the Colored People of the United States." In *Negro Social and Political Thought 1850–1920,* edited by Howard Brotz. New York: Basic Books.

———. 1966. "African Civilization Society." In *Negro Social and Political Thought 1850–1920,* edited by Howard Brotz, 262–66. New York: Basic Books.

———. 1966. "The Claims of the Negro Ethnologically Considered." In *Negro Social and Political Thought 1850–1920,* edited by Howard Brotz, 226–44. New York: Basic Books.

———. 1966. "The Future of the Colored People." In *Negro Social and Political Thought 1850–1920,* edited by Howard Brotz, 308–10. New York: Basic Books.

———. 1966. "Letter to Harriet Beecher Stowe." In *Negro Social and Political Thought 1850–1920,* edited by Howard Brotz, 220–26. New York: Basic Books.

———. 1966. "The Nation's Problem." In *Negro Social and Political Thought 1850–1920,* edited by Howard Brotz, 316–17. New York: Basic Books.

Du Bois, W. E. B. 1970. "The Conservation of Races." In *W. E. B. Du Bois Speaks: Speeches and Addresses, 1890–1919,* edited by Philip S. Foner, 73–85. New York: Pathfinders.

———. 1968. *The Health and Physique of the Negro American. Report of a Social Study Made under the Direction of Atlanta University; Together with the Proceedings of the Eleventh Conference for the Study of the Negro Problems, Held at Atlanta University, on May the 29th, 1906;* reprinted in *Atlanta University Publications (Numbers 7–11—1902–1906).* Vol. 2. New York: Octagon.

———. 1940. *Dusk of Dawn: An Essay Toward an Autobiography of a Race Concept.* New York: Harcourt, Brace.

———. 1897. *The Conservation of Races.* The American Negro Academy Occasional Papers, No. 2. Washington, DC: The American Negro Academy.

Dworkin, Ronald. 1978. *Taking Rights Seriously.* Cambridge: Harvard University Press.

Elshtain, Jean Bethke. 1995. *Democracy on Trial.* New York: Basic Books.

Elster, Jon. 1983. "Exploitation, Freedom, and Justice." In *Nomos XXVI: Marxism,* edited by Roland Pennock and John Chapman, 227–52. New York: New York University Press.

Eriksen, Thomas Hyland. 1993. *Ethnicity and Nationalism: Anthropological Perspectives.* London: Pluto.

Evans-Pritchard, E. E. 1937. *Witchcraft, Oracles, and Magic Among the Azande.* Oxford: Clarendon.

Fanon, Frantz. 2001. "The Lived Experience of the Black." In *Race,* edited by Robert Bernasconi, 184–202. Malden, MA: Blackwell.

———. 1967. *Black Skin, White Masks.* Translated by Charles Lam Markmann. New York: Grove Press.

Fausto-Sterling, Anne. 2000. *Sexing the Body: Gender Politics and the Construction of Sexuality.* New York: Basic Books.

Feinberg, Joel. 2003. *Problems at the Roots of Law.* Oxford: Oxford University Press.

———. 1992. *Freedom and Fulfillment.* Princeton: Princeton University Press.

———. 1984. "Noncoercive Exploitation." In *Paternalism,* edited by R. Satorious, 201–35. Minneapolis: University of Minnesota Press.

———. 1980. *Rights, Justice, and the Bounds of Liberty.* Princeton: Princeton University Press.

———. 1970. *Doing and Deserving.* Princeton: Princeton University Press.

Fischer, John Martin. 2006. *My Way.* Oxford: Oxford University Press.

Fischer, John Martin, and Mark Ravizza. 1999. *Responsibility and Control.* Ithaca: Cornell University Press.

Fiscus, Ronald J. 1992. *The Constitutional Logic of Affirmative Action: Making the Case for Quotas,* edited by Stephen L. Wasby. Durham, NC: Duke University Press.

Foner, Philip S., ed. 1975. *Life and Writings of Frederick Douglass.* Vol. 4. New York: International.

Fletcher, Bill, and Richard W. Hurd. 2000. "Is Organizing Enough? Race, Gender, and Union Culture." *New Labor Forum.* Ithaca: Cornell University Press.

Frege, Gottlob. 1980. "On Concept and Object." In *Philosophical Writings,* 3rd ed., edited by P. Geach and M. Black, 42–55. Oxford: Blackwell.

Frye, Marilyn. 1992. "Oppression." In *Race, Class, and Gender in the United States,* 2nd ed., edited by Paula S. Rothenberg, 146–49. New York: St. Martin's Press.

Fukuyama, Francis. 1992. *The End of History and the Last Man.* New York: Free Press.

García, J. L. A. 2001. "How Latina? More Latina?" *American Philosophical Association Newsletter on Hispanic / Latino Issues in Philosophy* 1: 93–97.

———. 2001. "Is Being Hispanic an Identity?" *Philosophy and Social Criticism* 27: 27–43.

———. 1999. "Philosophical Analysis and the Moral Concept of Racism." *Philosophy and Social Criticism* 25: 1–32.

———. 1997. "Current Conceptions of Racism." *Journal of Social Philosophy* 28: 5–42.

———. 1997. "Racism as a Model for Understanding Sexism." In *Race / Sex: Their Sameness, Difference, and Interplay,* edited by Naomi Zack, 45–49. New York: Routledge.

———. 1997. "Interpersonal Virtues: Whose Interest Do They Serve?" *American Catholic Philosophical Quarterly* 71: 31–60.

———. 1996. "The Heart of Racism." *Journal of Social Philosophy* 27: 5–45.

———. 1992. "African-American Perspectives, Cultural Relativism, and Normative Issues." In *African-American Perspectives on Biomedical Ethics,* edited by Harley Flack and Edmund Pellegrino, 11–66. Washington, DC: Georgetown University Press.

———. 1990. "Primacy of the Virtuous." *Philosophia* 20: 69–91.

Gardner, Howard. 1999. "The Enigma of Erik Erikson." *New York Review of Books* (June 24): 51–56.

Garn, Stanley M. 1993. "Modern Human Populations." In *The New Encyclopedia Britannica,* 844. Chicago, IL: Encyclopedia Britannica.

Garnet, Henry Highland. 1966. "The Past and the Present Condition, and the Destiny of the Colored Race." In *Negro Social and Political Thought 1850–1920,* edited by Howard Brotz, 199–202. New York: Basic Books.

Garrow, David J. 2004. "Why *Brown* Still Matters." *The Nation,* May 3.

Geertz, Clifford. 1963. "The Integrative Revolution." In *Old Societies and New States: The Quest for Modernity in Asia and Africa,* edited by Clifford Geertz, 105–57. New York: Free Press.

Gil-White, Francisco J. 2001. "Sorting Is Not Categorization: A Critique of the Claim that Brazilians Have Fuzzy Racial Categories." *Cognition and Culture* 1: 1–23.

———. 1999. "How Thick Is Blood? The Plot Thickens . . . : If Ethnic Actors Are Primordialists, What Remains of the Circumstantialist/Primordialist Controversy?" *Ethnic and Racial Studies* 22: 789–820.

Gilroy, Paul. 2000. *Against Race.* Cambridge: Harvard University Press.

———. 1993. *The Black Atlantic: Modernity and Double Consciousness.* Cambridge: Harvard University Press.

Glasgow, Joshua M. 2003. "On the New Biology of Race." *Journal of Philosophy* 100: 456–74.

Glazer, Nathan, and Daniel P. Moynihan, eds. 1975. *Ethnicity: Theory and Experience.* Cambridge: Harvard University Press.

Goldberg, David Theo. 1997. *Racist Subjects.* London: Routledge.

———. 1993. *Racist Culture.* Oxford: Blackwell.

Goldman, Alvin. 1999. *Knowledge in a Social World.* Oxford: Oxford University Press.

Goodin, Robert E. 1987. "Exploiting a Situation and Exploiting a Person." In *Modern Theories of Exploitation,* edited by Andrew Reeve, 166–200. London: Sage Publications.

———. 1984. *Protecting the Vulnerable.* Chicago: University of Chicago Press.

Gooding-Williams, Robert. 1998. "Race, Multiculturalism, and Democracy." *Constellations* 5: 18–41; reprinted in *Race,* edited by Robert Bernasconi, 237–59. Malden, MA: Blackwell, 2001.

Goodpaster, Kenneth. 1978. "On Being Morally Considerable." *Journal of Philosophy* 75: 303–25.

Gordon, Milton. 1988. *The Scope of Sociology.* New York: Oxford University Press.

———. 1964. *Assimilation in American Life.* New York: Oxford University Press.

Gould, Stephen J. 1996. *The Mismeasure of Man.* New York: Norton.

Gracia, Jorge J. E. 2005. *Surviving Race, Ethnicity, and Nationality: A Challenge for the Twenty-First Century.* Lanham, MD: Rowman and Littlefield.

———. 2000. *Hispanic/Latino Identity: A Philosophical Perspective.* Oxford: Blackwell.

———. 1988. *Individuality: An Essay on the Foundations of Metaphysics.* Albany, NY: State University of New York Press.

Gracia, Jorge J. E., and Pablo De Greiff, eds. 2000. *Hispanic/Latinos in the United States: Ethnicity, Race, and Rights.* New York: Routledge.

Gracia, Jorge J. E., and Elizabeth Millán-Zaibert, eds. 2004. *Latin American Philosophy for the 21st Century: The Human Condition, Values, and the Search for Identity.* Amherst, NY: Prometheus.

Graham, Richard, ed. 1990. *The Idea of Race in Latin America, 1870–1940.* Austin: University of Texas Press.

Grosfoguel, Ramón. 2003. *Colonial Subjects: Puerto Ricans in a Global Perspective.* Berkeley: University of California Press.

Grosfoguel, Ramón, and Ana Margarita Cervantes-Rodríguez, eds. 2002. *The Modern/Colonial/Capitalist World-System in the Twentieth Century: Global Processes, Antisystemic Movements, and the Geopolitics of Knowledge.* London: Praeger.

Grosfoguel, Ramón, and Chloé S. Georas. 1996. "The Racialization of Latino Caribbean Migrants in the New York Metropolitan Area." *CENTRO Journal of the Center for Puerto Rican Studies* 8 (no. 1–2): 191–201.

Guibernau, M. 1996. *Nationalisms: The Nation-State and Nationalism in the Twentieth Century.* Cambridge: Polity.

Haney López, Ian F. 2005. "Race on the 2010 Census: Hispanics and the Shrinking White Majority." *Daedalus: Journal of the American Academy of Arts and Sciences* 134, no. 1 (winter): 42–52.

———. 2003. *Racism on Trial: The Chicano Fight for Justice.* Cambridge: Belknap.

———. 1996. *White by Law: The Legal Construction of Race.* New York: New York University Press.

Hanke, Lewis. 1974. *All Mankind is One: A Study of the Disputation Between Bartolomé de Las Casas and Juan Ginés de Sepúlveda in 1550 on the Intellectual and Religious Capacity of the American Indians.* DeKalb: Northern Illinois University Press.

———. 1958. *Prejuicio racial en el Nuevo Mundo.* Santiago, Chile: Prensa Universitaria.

Hardimon, Michael O. 2003. "The Ordinary Concept of Race." *Journal of Philosophy* 100: 437–55.

Harding, Sandra, ed. 2003. *The Feminist Standpoint Theory Reader: Intellectual and Political.* New York: Routledge.

Haslanger, Sally. 2004. "Oppressions: Racial and Other." In *Racism in Mind,* edited by Michael P. Levine and Tamas Pataki, 97–123. Ithaca: Cornell University Press.

———. 2000. "Gender and Race: (What) Are They? (What) Do We Want Them To Be? *Nous:* 31–55.

Herder, Johann Gottfried. 1989. *Ideen zur Philosophie der Geschichte der Menschheit.* Edited by Martin Bollacher. Frankfurt: Deutscher Klassiker.

Hohfeld, Wesley. 1921. *Fundamental Legal Conceptions.* New Haven: Yale University Press.

Hollinger, David A. 2005. "The One Drop Rule and the One Hate Rule." *Daedalus: Journal of the American Academy of Arts and Sciences* 134, no. 1 (winter): 18–28.

hooks, bell. 1981. *Ain't I a Woman.* Boston: South End Press.

Horowitz, Donald L. 1975. "Ethnic Identity." In *Ethnicity: Theory and Experience,* edited by N. Glazer and D. P. Moynihan, 111–40. Cambridge: Harvard University Press.

Huntington, Samuel. 2004. *Who Are We? The Challenges to America's National Identity.* New York: Simon and Schuster.

Huxley, Julian S., A. C. Haddon, and A. M. Carr-Saunders. 1935. *We Europeans: A Survey of 'Racial' Problems.* London: Jonathan Cape.

Isaacs, Harold R. 1975. "Basic Group Identities." In *Ethnicity: Theory and Experience,* edited by N. Glazer and D. P. Moynihan, 29–52. Cambridge: Harvard University Press.

Jablonski, Nina G., and George Chaplin. 2000. "The Evolution of Human Skin Coloration." *Journal of Human Evolution* 39: 57–106.

Jackson, John P. 2005. *Science for Segregation: Race, Law, and the Case against Brown v. Board of Education.* New York: New York University Press.

Jenkins, Richard. 1999. "Ethnicity Etcetera: Social Anthropological Points of View." In *Ethnic and Racial Studies Today,* edited by Martin Bulmer and John Solomos, 85–97. London: Routledge.

John Paul II, Pope. 1987. *Sollicitudo Rei Socialis.* Encyclical Letter.

Jones, Karen. 1996. "Trust as an Affective Attitude." *Ethics* 107: 4–25.

Keal, P. 2003. *European Conquest and the Rights of Indigenous Peoples: The Moral Backwardness of International Society.* Cambridge: Cambridge University Press.

Keane, A. H. 1899. *Man Past and Present*. Cambridge: Cambridge University Press.

———. 1896. *Ethnology*. Cambridge: Cambridge University Press.

Keller, A. G. 1909. *Race Distinction*. New Haven: Department of Anthropology, Yale University.

Kennedy, Randall. 2004. "Schoolings in Equality." *New Republic*, July 5–12.

———. 2003. *Interracial Intimacies: Sex, Marriage, Identity, and Adoption*. New York: Pantheon.

———. 1997. "My Race Problem—And Ours." *Atlantic Monthly* (May): 55–65.

———. 1997. *Race, Crime, and the Law*. New York: Vintage Books.

Kiernan, Victor G. 2005. *America: The New Imperialism. From White Settlement to World Hegemony*. New York: Verso.

Kim, David Haekwon. 1999. "Contempt and Ordinary Inequality." In *Racism and Philosophy*, edited by Susan E. Babbitt and Sue Campbell, 108–23. Ithaca: Cornell University Press.

King, James C. 1981. *The Biology of Race*. Berkeley: University of California Press.

King, Paul. 1997. "A Matter of Pride." *Emerge* (October): 62, 64, 65.

Kirk, John M. 1983. *José Martí: Mentor of the Cuban Nation*. Tampa: University Presses of Florida.

Kitcher, Philip. 1999. "Race, Ethnicity, Biology, Culture." In *Racism*, edited by Leonard Harris, 87–120. Amherst, NY: Humanities Press.

———. 2003. *Science, Truth, and Democracy*. New York: Oxford University Press.

Klarman, Michael J. 2002. *From Jim Crow to Civil Rights: The Supreme Court and the Struggle for Racial Equality*. New York: Oxford University Press.

Kleinig, John, ed. 1996. *Handled with Discretion: Ethical Issues in Police Decision Making*. Lanham, MD: Rowman and Littlefield.

———. 1995. "Bad Samaritanism." In *Philosophy of Law*, 5th ed., edited by Joel Feinberg and Hyman Gross, 529–32. Belmont, CA: Wadsworth.

Kluger, Richard. 2004. *Simple Justice: The History of* Brown v. Board of Education *and Black America's Struggle for Equality*. New York: Knopf.

Kozol, Jonathan. 2005. *The Shame of the Nation: The Restoration of Apartheid Schooling in America*. New York: Crown.

———. 2005. "Still Separate, Still Unequal: America's Educational Apartheid." *Harper's*, 311.1864 (September): 41–54.

Kuper, Adam. 1999. *Culture: the Anthropologists' Account*. Cambridge: Harvard.

Las Casas, Bartolomé de. 1988–1998. *Obras completas*. Edited by Paulino Castañeda Delgado. Madrid: Alianza Editorial.

———. 1992. *A Short Account of the Destruction of the Indies*. Edited by Nigel Griffin, with an introduction by Anthony Pagden. London: Penguin.

———. 1992. *Witness: Writings of Bartolomé de Las Casas*. Edited by George Sanderlin, with foreword by Gustavo Gutiérrez. Maryknoll, NY: Orbis.

———. 1971. *History of the Indies*. Edited by Andrée Collard. New York: Harper and Row.

Lentz, C. 1995. "'Tribalism' and 'Ethnicity' in Africa: A Review of Four Decades of Anglophone Research." *Cahiers des Sciences Humanes* 31: 303–28.

Lerner, Gerda. 1993. "Reconceptualizing Differences Among Women." In *Feminist Frameworks*, edited by Alison M. Jaggar and Paula S. Rothenberg, 237–38. New York: McGraw-Hill.

Lewontin, R. C. 1989. "Race." In *Encyclopedia Americana,* Vol. 23: 116–22. Danbury, CN: Grolier.

Locke, Alain. 1992. *Race Contacts and Interracial Relations.* Edited by Jeffrey C. Stewart. Washington, DC: Howard University Press.

———. 1989. *The Philosophy of Alain Locke.* Edited by Leonard Harris. Philadelphia: Temple University Press.

———. 1983. *The Critical Temper of Alain Locke.* Edited by Jeffrey C. Stewart. New York: Garland.

———. 1924. "The Concept of Race as Applied to Social Culture." *The Howard Review* 1: 290–99.

———. 1923. "The Problem of Race Classification." *Opportunity* 1: 261–64.

Locke, John. 1983. *A Letter Concerning Toleration.* Edited by James H. Tully. Indianapolis, IN: Hackett.

Lorde, Audre, et al., eds. 2001. *Identity Politics and the Woman's Movement.* New York: New York University Press.

Loury, Glenn. 1995. "Individualism before Multiculturalism." *Public Interest* (fall): 92–106. Reprinted in *Reinventing the American People: Unity and Diversity Today,* edited by Robert Royal (Ethics and Public Policy Center/Eerdmans, 1995). A modified version was published under the same title in *Harvard Journal of Law and Public Policy* 19, no. 3 (1996).

Lowie, Robert. 1917. *Culture and Ethnology.* New York: Douglas C. McMurtrie.

MacIntyre, Alasdair. 1999. *Dependent Rational Animals.* Chicago: Open Court.

Marentes, Luis A. 2000. *José Vasconcelos and the Writing of the Mexican Revolution.* New York: Twayne.

Mason, Ernest D. 1988. "Deconstruction in the Philosophy of Alain Locke." *Transactions of the Charles S. Pierce Society* 24: 85–106.

———. 1982. "Alain Locke's Philosophy of Value." In *Alain Locke: Reflections on a Modern Renaissance Man,* edited by Russell J. Linnemann, 1–16. Baton Rouge: Louisiana State University.

Matute, Alvaro, and Martha Donís, eds. 1984. José *Vasconcelos, de su vida y su obra: textos selectos de las Jornadas Vasconcelianas de 1982.* Mexico City: Dirección General de Difusión Cultural.

McGary, Howard, ed. Forthcoming. *Reparations to African Americans.* Lanham, MD: Rowman and Littlefield.

———. 2003. "Achieving Democratic Equality: Forgiveness, Reconciliation, and Reparations." *The Journal of Ethics* 7: 93–113.

———. 1999. *Race and Social Justice.* London: Blackwell.

———. 1998. "Douglass on Racial Assimilation and Racial Institutions." In *Frederick Douglass: A Critical Reader,* edited by Bill E. Lawson and Frank Kirkland, 50–63. Malden, MA: Blackwell.

Mendieta, Eduardo. 2006. "The Erotics of Racial Power or the Technologies of the Racist Self." In *Passions of the Color Line,* edited by David Kim. Albany: State University of New York Press.

———. 2005. "La latinización de 'América': Los latinos en los Estados Unidos y la creación de un nuevo pueblo." In *Relatos de Nación: La construcción de las identidades nacionales en el mundo hispánico,* edited by Francisco Colom, 975–98. Madrid: Iberoamericana and Vervuert.

———. 2000. "The Making of New Peoples: Hispanizing Race." In *Hispanics/Latinos in the*

United States: Ethnicity, Race, and Rights, edited by Jorge J. E. Gracia and Pablo de Greiff, 45–59. New York: Routledge.

———. 2004. "Plantations, Ghettos, Prisons: U.S. Racial Geographies." *Philosophy and Geography* 7: 43–60.

———. 2001. "The 'Second Reconquista,' or Why Should a 'Hispanic' Become a Philosopher? On Jorge Gracia's *Hispanic/Latino Identity: A Philosophical Perspective.*" *Philosophy and Social Criticism* 27: 11–19.

Mignolo, Walter. 2000. "Hispanics/Latinos [and Latino Studies] in the Colonial Horizon of Modernity." In *Hispanics/Latinos in the United States: Ethnicity, Race, and Rights,* edited by Jorge J. E. Gracia and Pablo De Greiff, 99–124. New York: Routledge.

Mill, John Stuart. 1991. *On Liberty.* In *The Collected Works of John Stuart Mill,* edited by John M. Robson, Vol. 18. Toronto: University of Toronto Press.

Miller, David. 1995. *On Nationality.* Oxford: Clarendon.

Mills, Charles W. 1998. *Blackness Visible: Essays on Philosophy and Race.* Ithaca: Cornell University Press.

———. 1998. "But What Are You Really?" In *Blackness Visible: Essays on Philosophy and Race,* 41–66. Ithaca: Cornell University Press.

Mirabal, Nancy Raquel. 1995. "Más que negro: José Martí and the Politics of Unity." In *José Martí in the United States: The Florida Experience,* edited by Louis Pérez, 57–69. Tempe: Arizona State University Press.

Montagu, Ashley. 1964. *The Concept of Race.* London: Collier.

———. 1946. *Man's Most Dangerous Myth: The Fallacy of Race.* New York: Columbia University Press, 1942; revised, Cambridge: Cambridge University Press.

Moran, Rachel F. 2001. *Interracial Intimacy: The Regulation of Race and Romance.* Chicago: University of Chicago Press.

Moreno, Rafael. 1984. "La cultura y la filosofía iberoamericana de José Vasconcelos." In *José Vasconcelos, de su vida y su obra: textos selectos de las Jornadas Vasconcelianas de 1982,* edited by Alvaro Matute and Martha Donís, 102–15. Mexico City: Universidad Nacional Autónoma de México (UNAM).

Morris, Thomas. 1984. *Understanding Identity Statements.* New York: Humanities Press.

Moya, Paula. 2005. " 'Racism Is Not Intellectual': Interracial Friendship, Multicultural Literature, and Anti-Racist Moral Growth." Unpublished ms., 1–33.

———. 2001. "Why I Am Not Hispanic: An Argument with Jorge Gracia." *The American Philosophical Association Newsletter on Hispanic/Latino Issues in Philosophy* 2: 100–105.

Murphy, Robert F. 1972. *Robert H. Lowie.* New York: Columbia University Press.

Myrdal, Gunnar. 1944. *An American Dilemma.* New York: Harper and Brothers.

Nei, Masatoshi, and A. K. Roychoudhury. 1982. "Genetic Relationship and Evolution of Human Races." *Evolutionary Biology* 14: 1–59.

———. 1974. "Genetic Variation within and between the Three Major Races of Man: Caucasoids, Negroids, and Mongoloids." *American Journal of Human Genetics* 26: 421–43.

———. 1972. "Gene Differences Between Caucasian, Negro, and Japanese Populations." *Science* 177: 434–35.

Nuccetelli, Susana. 2004. "Reference and Ethnic-Group Terms." *Inquiry* 6: 528–44.

———. 2001. " 'Hispanics,' 'Latinos,' and 'Iberoamericans': Naming or Describing?" *Philosophical Forum* 32: 175–88.

Nussbaum, Martha. 2004. *Hiding from Humanity: Disgust, Shame, and the Law.* Princeton: Princeton University Press.

Oboler, Suzanne. 1995. *Ethnic Labels / Latino Lives: Identity and the Politics of (Re)presentation in the United States.* Minneapolis: University of Minnesota Press.

Ogletree, Jr., Charles J. 2004. *All Deliberate Speed: Reflections on the First Half Century of Brown v. Board of Education.* New York: W. W. Norton.

Omi, Michael, and Howard Winant. 1994. *Racial Formation in the United States: From the 1960s to the 1990s.* 2nd ed. New York: Routledge.

Orfield, Gary. 2001. *Schools More Separate: Consequences of a Decade of Resegregation.* Cambridge: The Civil Right Project, Harvard University.

Outlaw, Jr., Lucius T. 1996. *On Race and Philosophy.* New York: Routledge.

Parsons, Talcott. 1975. "Some Theoretical Considerations on the Nature and Trends of Change of Ethnicity." In *Ethnicity: Theory and Experience,* edited by N. Glazer and D. P. Moynihan, 53–83. Cambridge: Harvard University Press.

Pérez, Louis A. Jr., ed. 1995. *José Martí in the United States: the Florida Experience.* Tempe: Arizona State University, Center for Latin American Studies.

Peterson, William. 1982. "Concepts of Ethnicity." In *Concepts of Ethnicity,* edited by William Peterson, 1–26. Cambridge: Harvard University Press.

Pettit, Philip, and Michael Smith. 2004. "The Truth in Deontology." In *Reason and Value: Themes from the Moral Philosophy of Joseph Raz,* edited by Philip Pettit, Samuel Scheffler, et al., 153–75. New York: Oxford University Press.

Piper, Adrian. 1990. "Higher-Order Discrimination." In *Identity, Character, and Morality,* edited by Owen Flanagan and Amélie Rorty, 285–309. Cambridge: MIT Press.

Plato. 1997. *Complete Works.* Edited by John M. Cooper. Indianapolis, IN: Hackett.

Pollak, Louis H. 2005. "Race, Law, and History: The Supreme Court from 'Dred Scott' to 'Grutter v. Billinger.'" *Daedalus: Journal of the American Academy of Arts and Sciences* 134, no. 1 (winter): 29–41.

Putnam, Hilary. 1975. "The Meaning of 'Meaning.'" In *Mind, Language, and Reality: Philosophical Papers,* 2:215–72. Cambridge: Cambridge University Press.

Rawls, John. 1999. *Collected Papers.* Edited by S. Freeman. Cambridge: Harvard University Press.

Relethford, John H. 1999. "Models, Predictions, and the Fossil Record of Modern Human Origins." *Evolutionary Anthropology* 8: 7–10.

———. 1997. *The Human Species: An Introduction to Biological Anthropology.* Mountain View, CA: Mayfield.

Rimer, Sara, and Karen W. Arenson. 2004. "Top Colleges Take More Blacks, but Which Ones?" *New York Times,* June 24.

Ringer, Benjamin B. 1983. *'We the People' and Others: Duality and America's Treatment of its Racial Minorities.* New York: Tavistock.

Roberts, Rodney C. 2003. "The Morality of a Moral Statute of Limitations on Injustice." *The Journal of Ethics* 7: 115–38.

Robins, Ashley H. 1991. *Biological Perspectives on Human Pigmentation.* Cambridge: Cambridge University Press.

Rodríguez, Richard. 2002. *Brown: The Last Discovery of America.* New York: Viking Press.

Root, Maria P. P. 1997. *The Multiracial Experience: Racial Borders as the New Frontier.* Thousand Oaks, CA: Sage.

Sartre, Jean-Paul. 2001. "Black Orpheus." In *Race,* edited by Robert Bernasconi, 115–42. Malden, MA: Blackwell.

——. 1976. *Anti-Semite and Jew.* Translated by George J. Becker. New York: Schocken, 1976.

——. 1954. *Réfexions sur la question juive.* Paris: Gallimard.

Schmidt, P. 2003. "The Label 'Hispanic' Irks Some, but Also Unites." *The Chronicle of Higher Education* 1, no. 14 (November 28): A9.

Schutte, O. 2000. "Negotiating Latina Identities." In *Hispanics / Latinos in the United States: Ethnicity, Race, and Rights,* edited by Jorge J. E. Gracia and Pablo De Greiff, 61–75. New York: Routledge.

Schwartz, Justin. 1995. "What's Wrong with Exploitation." *Nous* 29: 158–88.

Searle, John. 1995. *The Social Construction of Reality.* New York: Free Press.

Senghor, Leopold. 1961. "What Is Negritude?" *West Africa* (November 4): 1211.

Shelby, Tommie. 2005. *We Who Are Dark.* Cambridge: Harvard University Press.

Shnookal, Deborah, and Mirta Muñiz, eds. 1999. *José Martí Reader: Writings on the Americas.* New York: Ocean.

Skjeie, Hege. 1998. "Credo on Difference: Women in Parliament in Norway." In *Handbook: Women in Parliament: Beyond Numbers,* edited by Azza Karam, 183–90. Stockholm: International IDEA. Web posting at www.idea.int (accessed May 2005).

Smedley, Audrey. 1993. *Race in North America: Origin and Evolution of a World View.* Boulder, CO: Westview.

Smith, Anthony. 1997. "Structure and Persistence in *Ethne.*" In *The Ethnicity Reader: Nationalism, Multiculturalism, and Migration,* edited by M. Guibernau and J. Rex, 27–33. Cambridge: Polity.

Smith, Rogers. 1999. *Civic Ideals: Conflicting Visions of Citizenship in U.S. History.* New Haven: Yale University Press.

Spencer, Ranier. 1999. *Spurious Issues: Race and Multiracial Identity Politics in the United States.* Boulder, CO: Westview.

Sollers, Werner, ed. 1996. *Theories of Ethnicity: A Classical Reader.* New York: New York University Press.

Steffensmeier, Darrell, and Stephen Demuth. 2000. "Ethnicity and Sentencing Outcomes in U.S. Federal Courts: Who is Punished More Harshly?" *American Sociological Review* 65: 705–29.

Stubblefield, Anna. 2005. *Ethics Along the Color Line.* Ithaca: Cornell University Press.

Stuckert, Robert P. 1958. "African Ancestry of the White American Population." *The Ohio Journal of Science* 58: 155 (May 1958).

Sundstrom, Ronald R. 2002. "Race as a Human Kind." *Philosophy and Social Criticism* 28: 91–115.

Talbot, Margaret. 2005. "Supreme Confidence: The Jurisprudence of Justice Antonin Scalia." *New Yorker* (March 28, 2005): 40–55.

Tattersfield, Nigel. 1991. *The Forgotten Trade.* London: Jonathan Cape.

Taylor, Paul C. 2004. *Race: A Philosophical Introduction.* Malden, MA: Blackwell.

——. 2000. "Appiah's Uncompleted Argument: W. E. B. Du Bois and the Relativity of Race." *Social Theory and Practice* 26: 103–28.

Templeton, Alan R. 1998. "Human Races: A Genetic and Evolutionary Perspective." *American Anthropologist* 100: 632–51.

Thernstrom, Stephen, ed. 1980. *Harvard Encyclopedia of American Ethnic Groups*. Cambridge: Belknap Press of Harvard.

Thomas, Laurence. 2005. "Moral Equality and Natural Inferiority." *Social Theory and Practice* 31: 379–404.

——. 1995. "Evil and the Concept of a Human Person." *Midwest Studies in Philosophy* 20: 36–58.

——. 1995. "Power, Trust, and Evil." In *Overcoming Racism and Sexism*, edited by Linda A. Bell and David Blumenfeld, 152–71. Lanham, MD: Rowman and Littlefield.

——. 1993. *Vessels of Evil*. Philadelphia: Temple University Press.

Thompson, E. P. 1963. *The Making of the English Working Class*. New York: Pantheon.

Topinard, Paul. 1876. *L'Anthropologie*. Paris: C. Reinwald.

——. 1878. "De la notion de race en anthropologie." *Revue d'anthropologie*, Series 2, no. 2: 589–660.

Trumpener, Katie. 1995. "The Time of the Gypsies: A 'People without History' in the Narratives of the West." In *Identities*, edited by K. A. Appiah and H. L. Gates, Jr., 338–79. Chicago: University of Chicago Press.

van den Berghe, Pierre L. 2001. "Does Race Matter?" In *Race and Racism*, edited by Bernard Boxill, 101–13. Oxford: Oxford University Press.

——. 1967. *Race and Racism: A Comparative Perspective*. New York: Wiley.

Vasconcelos, José. 1997. *La raza cósmica / The Cosmic Race*, edited and translated by Didier T. Jaén. Baltimore, MD: Johns Hopkins University Press.

——. 1957–61. *Indología: una interpretación de la cultura ibero-americana*, in *Obras completas*, Vol. 1. Mexico City: Libreros Mexicanos Unidos.

——. 1939. *Etica*. Mexico City: Ediciones Botas.

——. 1925. *Indología: una interpretación de la cultura ibero-americana*. Paris: Agencia Mundial de Librería.

Villegas, Abelardo. 1984. "La cosmología vasconceliana." In *José Vasconcelos, de su vida y su obra: textos selectos de las Jornadas Vasconcelianas de 1982*, edited by Alvaro Matute and Martha Donís, 83–93. Mexico City: Universidad Nacional Autónoma de México (UNAM).

Vincent, Joan. 1974. "The Structure of Ethnicity." *Human Organization* 33: 375–9.

Virchow, Rudolf. 1896. "Rassenbildung und Erblichkeit." In *Festschrift für Adolf Bastian*, 3–43. Berlin: Reimer.

Visweswaran, Kamala. 1968. "Race and the Culture of Anthropology." *American Anthropologist* 100: 70–83.

Wacker, F. Fred. 1983. *Ethnicity, Pluralism, and Race*. Westwood, CN: Greenwood.

Wade, Nicholas. 2005. "DNA Study Yields Clues on Early Humans' First Migration." *New York Times*, International (May 13): A7.

——. 2002. "The Human Family Tree: 10 Adams and 18 Eves." *New York Times*, May 2, F1.

Wade, Peter. 1997. *Race and Ethnicity in Latin America*. London: Pluto.

Walker, Margaret Urban. 1998. "Ineluctable Feelings and Moral Recognition." *Midwest Studies in Philosophy* 22: 62–81.

Walton, Kendal. 1990. *Mimesis as Make-Believe*. Cambridge: Harvard University Press.

Waters, Mary C. 1999. *Black Identities: West Indian Immigrant Dreams and American Realities.* Cambridge: Harvard University Press.

Weber, Max. 1997. "What Is an Ethnic Group." In *The Ethnicity Reader: Nationalism, Multiculturalism, and Migration,* edited by M. Guibernau and J. Rex, 15–26. Cambridge: Polity.

Weiner, Mark S. 2004. *Black Trails: Citizenship from the Beginnings of Slavery to the End of Caste.* New York: Knopf.

Wertheimer, Alan. 1996. *Exploitation.* Princeton: Princeton University Press.

Wilfred, John Noble. 2000. "Skulls in Caucasus Linked to Early Humans in Africa," *New York Times* (May 12): A1.

Wilkins, David B. 1993. "Two Paths to the Mountaintop? The Role of Legal Education in Shaping the Values of Black Corporate Lawyers." *Stanford Law Review* 45: 1981–2026.

Williams, Bernard. 1985. *Ethics and the Limits of Philosophy.* Cambridge: Harvard University Press.

——. 1981. *Moral Luck.* Cambridge: Cambridge University Press.

——. 1976. *Morality: An Introduction to Ethics.* Cambridge: Cambridge University Press.

Williams, Patricia J., ed. 1997. *Seeing a Color-Blind Future: The Paradox of Race.* New York: Farrar, Straus, and Giroux.

Wilson, J. R. S. 1978. "In One Another's Power." *Ethics* 88: 299–315.

Wilson, William Julius. 1978. *The Declining Significance of Race.* Chicago: University of Chicago Press.

Wittgenstein, Ludwig. 1981. *Philosophical Investigations.* Translated by G. E. M. Anscombe. New York: Macmillan.

Wolpoff, Milford H., John Hawks, and Rachel Caspari. 2000. "Multiregional, Not Multiple Origins," *American Journal of Physical Anthropology* 112: 129–36.

Wu, Frank. 2002. *Yellow: Race in America Beyond Black and White.* New York: Basic Books.

Yamamoto, Eric K. 1997. "Critical Race Praxis: Race Theory and Political Lawyering Practice in Post-Civil Rights America." *Michigan Law Review* 95: 821–900.

Young, Iris Marion. 2001. "Social Movements and the Politics of Difference." In *Race and Racism,* edited by Bernard Boxill, 383–421. Oxford: Oxford University Press.

——. 1995. "Together in Difference: Transforming the Logic of Group Political Conflict." In *The Rights of Minority Cultures,* edited by Will Kymlicka, 155–76. Oxford: Oxford University Press.

Zack, Naomi. 2005–6. *Thinking About Race.* 2nd ed. Belmont, CA: Thompson Wadsworth; 1st ed., 1998.

——. 2005. *Inclusive Feminism: A Third Wave Theory of Women's Commonality.* Lanham, MD: Rowman and Littlefield.

——. 2003. "Reparations and the Rectification of Race." *The Journal of Ethics* 7: 39–51.

——. 2002. *Philosophy of Science and Race.* New York: Routledge.

——. 2001. "American Mixed Race: Theoretical and Legal Issues." *Harvard Black Letter Law Journal* 17: 33–46.

——. 2001. "Philosophical Aspects of the 1998 AAA [American Anthropological Association] Statement on Race." *Anthropological Theory* 4: 445–65.

——. 2001. "Philosophical Racial Essentialism." Paper read to Boston University's Institute on Race and Social Division workshop, February.

———. 1996. *Bachelors of Science: Seventeenth-Century Identity Then and Now.* Philadelphia, PA: Temple University Press.

———. 1994. "Race and Philosophic Meaning." *American Philosophical Association Newsletter on Philosophy and the Black Experience* 94: 14–20; reprinted in *Race and Racism,* edited by Bernard Boxill, 43–58. Oxford: Oxford University Press, 2001.

———. 1993. *Race and Mixed Race.* Philadelphia: Temple University Press.

Zaibert, Leonardo, and Elizabeth Millán-Zaibert. 2000. "Universalism, Particularism, and Group Rights: The Case of Hispanics." In *Hispanics / Latinos in the United States: Ethnicity, Race, and Rights,* edited by Jorge J. E. Gracia and Pablo De Greiff, 167–79. New York: Routledge.

Zinn, Howard. 2003. *A People's History of the United States: 1492–Present.* New York: Harper Perennial Modern Classics.

Index